1295

The Selected Correspondence of

KENNETH BURKE

—— and ——

MALCOLM COWLEY

1915–1981

The Selected Correspondence of

KENNETH BURKE

— *and* —

MALCOLM COWLEY

1915–1981

Edited by Paul Jay

University of California Press

Berkeley and Los Angeles

University of California Press
Berkeley and Los Angeles

First Paperback Printing 1990

First published in 1988 by Viking Penguin Inc.
Reprinted by arrangement with Viking Penguin,
a division of Penguin Books USA Inc.

1 3 5 7 9 10 8 6 4 2

LIBRARY OF CONGRESS CATALOGING IN PUBLICATION DATA
Burke, Kenneth, 1897–
    The selected correspondence of Kenneth Burke and Malcolm Cowley.
    Includes index.
    1. Burke, Kenneth, 1897–   —Correspondence.
    2. Cowley, Malcolm, 1898–   —Correspondence.
    3. Authors, American—20th century—Correspondence.
    4. Critics—United States—Correspondence.   I. Cowley,
Malcolm, 1898–   II. Jay, Paul, 1946–
III. Title.
PS3503.U6134Z485 1988   818'.5209 [B]   87–40652
ISBN 0-520-06899-8

Printed in the United States of America
Set in Garamond No. 3
Designed by Mary A. Wirth

Preface

〜

This book had its inception on an October afternoon in 1982. By that time, Malcolm Cowley and Kenneth Burke had been corresponding with one another on a weekly basis for sixty-nine years. As Cowley was going through his files, reviewing what remained of his unpublished work, it occurred to him that their vast correspondence might make an interesting book:

> *I made a review of my literary remains or disiecta membra and decided that they included material for nine, count them, nine books. . . . One project we ought to think about is the Burke-Cowley correspondence. By this time there's nothing like it in the American twentieth century.*

One of our most astute literary historians, Cowley realized that afternoon that his correspondence with Burke had, if only through its sheer longevity, become an important historical document. Dating from the summer of 1915 (there were earlier letters, but they have not survived), they span all but the first fifteen years of twentieth-century American literary history. Burke and Cowley had become close friends while students together at Peabody High School, in Pittsburgh. Their friendship developed in the context of a shared passion for literature and the world of ideas. By the time they graduated from Peabody they were writing poetry and arguing about the relative merits of classical forms and free verse. They made no distinction between the literary life and everyday experience, since everyday experience consisted of reading Mallarmé or Turgenev, discussing aesthetics, and questioning intellectual conventions in whatever guise they appeared. Well before either man had established a career or published a single poem or essay, Burke and Cowley were engaged in spirited literary and philosophical debates, where the stakes seemed dramatically high. Without knowing it, they had begun to chronicle lives and events that would help give shape to modern literature and literary criticism.

Their early letters are documents of ambition. Both men graduated from high school vaguely attracted to a literary career, though that attraction—characteristically—manifested itself in very different ways. Cowley left Pittsburgh for Harvard in the fall of 1915, proceeding in a methodical fashion to give order and coherence to his disparate interests in poetry, philosophy, and the classics by joining literary clubs, editing magazines, and taking a range of courses in European and American literature. Meanwhile, unsure about college, Burke moved with his parents to Weehawken, New Jersey, and launched a kind of assault on literary New York City. Through his friendship with the British writer Louis Wilkinson he met a number of other writers and critics, including Theodore Dreiser. From his letters, Burke seemed willing to write whatever might help him score a success; one day he is writing poetry, the next a play, and by the weekend he has begun a novel. If Cowley's approach to the intellectual life had become ordered and methodical, Burke's had become fragmented and peripatetic. By January of 1919 Burke had gone off to college at Ohio State, returned to New York City to study philosophy at Columbia, and decided to quit college to become "a Flaubert" in New York City.

It turned out that both men were wonderfully and differently situated to write to one another about the rise of modernism, a much-discussed topic in their early letters. While Burke remained in America in the late teens and twenties, in close contact with an emerging New York avant-garde, Cowley was writing from Paris (first, as a member of the American Ambulance Service, and later, as a student) about his friendship with Dadaists like Tristan Tzara and Louis Aragon. While Cowley became engrossed with European modernism, Burke wrote with fervor about the need to found a specifically American literature (and criticism) on American soil, sometimes angrily denouncing Cowley for coming under the influence of the Dadaists. In their arguments about the nature of American literature and the place of a European tradition within it, Burke and Cowley were participating in an important cultural debate generated by books like Van Wyck Brooks' *America's Coming-of-Age* (1915). This debate had, of course, been an ongoing one since Emerson and Whitman called for the birth of a characteristically American literature nearly a century before.

Both Burke and Cowley soon became editors and contributors to polemical modernist magazines like *Broom* and *Secession,* where they worked with others to formulate ideas about art and criticism meant to inaugurate a clear break with the past. These early letters also record the impact of the first World War on their generation and, as with their exchanges about modern literature, gain their interest from each man's very different vantage point, with Burke in New York and Cowley on the French front. The letters go on in successive decades to chronicle life in Greenwhich Village in the twenties, the impact of the Depression and of Marxism on the politics,

literature, and criticism of the 1930s, Cowley's years as literary editor at
the *New Republic* and Burke's emergence as an important critic, World War
II, the rise of the New Criticism, the spread of McCarthyism, the affluent
Eisenhower years, the emergence of a new generation of "postmodern"
poets and novelists, the Vietnam war, the moon landing, and the complex
impact of Freud, structuralism, and deconstruction on literary criticism in
the 1970s and 1980s.

The time span of these letters, then, is extraordinary. They document
the literary life of twentieth-century America from two consistent and quite
different perspectives, perspectives that change in identifiable ways but
remain characteristic. While the historical and documentary status of the
Burke-Cowley correspondence is real, it is complemented, and in the end
perhaps transcended by, its dramatic and novelistic qualities. This is a literary
correspondence in two senses of the word. The letters are predominantly
about literary matters, but they also have the intellectual, aesthetic, and
stylistic qualities we usually associate with literature. In this correspondence
the same young men go off to college, out on dates, complain about pimples,
struggle to write, drink heavily, enjoy success, go broke, do hack work,
become editors, write poetry, essays, novels, and criticism, marry, have
children, become public figures, divorce, remarry, get caught up in left-
wing politics, suffer under McCarthyism, feel ignored, reap awards, lose
their hearing, brood about the past, and begin to get their affairs in order
during the early sixties only to live on with increasing public recognition
into the late eighties. The letters dramatize the lives of two compelling
individuals with an extraordinary degree of intimacy, frankness, and emotion, at the same time allowing us to trace the inception and development
of the work of two important (and very different) literary critics. Reading
their correspondence, we come to *live* the emotional and intellectual lives
they embody, and we get caught up in the evolution of an intricate and
profoundly moving friendship.

In fact, if these letters are "about" anything, they are about friendship.
They're tactless letters. When Burke wrote to Cowley in January of 1916
asking him to destroy all the letters he had sent him during the last few
months, Cowley wrote that "if I were a tactful friend, I would tell you that
I had destroyed your letters, and then file them away in some drawer. But
I am not tactful. If either you or I had ever shown too much tact in our
dealings with each other, we would have remained mere acquaintances."
Both men recognized the value to their friendship of being tactless with
one another, for tact represented not only falseness, but worse, a mannered,
careful, "appropriate" use of language each found insincere and therefore
abhorrent. A tactful letter would be an unfriendly one, and when they
appear in the correspondence it is during a time of stress in their relation-

ship. Burke's approach to the question of friendship and tact is, characteristically, even more paradoxical than Cowley's. Writing in June of 1928, he
recalls an earlier letter in which he presented "a rather passionate thesis to
the effect that friends are friends within certain limits, and that friendships
are broken by increasing either the adversity or good fortune under which
they originated." Now, he insists, he wants to alter this formulation, for he
is convinced that "a friend is none other than that person whom one treats
with all the shabbiness and dilatoriness that he scrupulously rules out of
his business relationships." Burke's theory explains why Cowley so often
suffers, in this correspondence, a veritable barrage of criticism, name-calling,
and goading hostility. Burke is a friend who gambles on strengthening a
friendship by testing the stress it can handle; the more stress it can sustain,
the stronger, and the more valuable, it is. Not only did the gamble work,
but it tended to work both ways.

It is worth emphasizing here that these letters do not simply *record* a
friendship, they provide the very context in which it develops and deepens.
Far from being the passive record of a relationship, they constitute the
active engagement of two developing personalities whose friendship is realized in and by the act of writing. Their letters dramatize the extent to
which each writer's life has been given a kind of shape and logic through
writing to one another. They share, analyze, hypothesize, sum up, respond,
and accuse, all the while constructing for their lives and for each other's
what becomes almost a thematic and narrative coherence. The correspondence contains a kind of unrelenting self-analysis and impassioned dialogue,
the kind that can remind us how writing both shapes and sustains the very
self who writes. As a composite exercise in self-analysis, the letters represent
a kind of hybrid, a *double* autobiography, one in which two lives are recorded
simultaneously. Burke and Cowley become so intertwined in this correspondence that the letters have the uncanny effect of recording a single life
in an autobiography written by two subjects.

The emotional and intellectual vigor that drives this correspondence has
its roots in fundamental and persistent differences between Burke and
Cowley. Theirs is a friendship that is nourished and thrives on opposition.
Burke succinctly captures their different intellectual and critical orientations
in a letter written in June of 1933 (while Cowley was writing *Exile's Return*
and Burke *Permanence and Change*) when he notes that "fundamentally our
differences in emphasis, classification, etc. seem to derive from the following
initial or informing distinction in purpose: You are trying to write an interpretation of certain cultural trends; I am trying to write on the process of
interpretation." While Cowley was in 1933 trying to write a history of the
"lost generation" Burke was developing in his book a scheme for analyzing
interpretive systems per se, be they historical, philosophical, political, or

psychological in nature. Cowley was attempting to interpret history while Burke wanted to interpret interpretations of history. Throughout the correspondence, Cowley writes to Burke as a literary and cultural historian wedded to narrative, while Burke writes to Cowley as a critical philosopher and theorist whose style is discursive and densely analytical.

These fundamental differences generate a continuous series of aesthetic, philosophical, methodological, and critical debates in the correspondence. The specific disagreements range from discussions of the relative virtues of Dada to Yeats' attraction to mysticism and why Burke felt himself "born" to "hate Hemingway." Each writer is alternately on the attack or rising to his own defense over specific issues, but each too regularly calls the very nature of the other's work into question. Remarking on Burke's propensity to move rather abruptly from one philosophical or theoretical topic to another, Cowley wrote in 1936 that Burke has an "old vice, which is that of the very keen-nosed but undertrained hound dog—he starts out a-helling after a rabbit, almost tracks it down, but gets turned aside by the strong scent of a fox, runs into a place where the fox scared up a partridge, hunts for the partridge, feels hungry and digs up a field mouse." Cowley's impatience with Burke's critical method is matched throughout by Burke's impatience with what he called in 1940 Cowley's propensity for "journalism and diarism, and not enough criticism."

These intellectual differences are often characterized by the kind of tactlessness I mentioned earlier, and they make the Burke-Cowley correspondence the same kind of document that Cowley called *Exile's Return*: a "narrative of ideas." But these intellectual differences are matched by differences in temperament, personality, values, and states of mind that would put severe stress on any friendship, but in this case, seem to cement it. The two men emerge in their letters as vividly human, clear and finely articulated personalities. The order, logic, restraint, and plain good sense that often mark Cowley's dealings are matched by a freewheeling, stubborn, often paradoxical state of mind in Burke that *seems* to lack any sense of order but finally emerges in the letters as having a logic all its own. The minds at work in this correspondence are every bit as complex and challenging as the ideas they debate. There is much that is important in this correspondence because the people and events they refer to have themselves become important, but what surprises is how the substance of individual lives struggling simply to be, and to suffice, takes upon itself a value and importance of its own.

The letters reproduced in this volume were chosen from among over 1,700 that survive. Some of these letters are very short, but most run two to three single-spaced pages, while others are as long as ten pages.

Early on in the process of editing, I questioned the wisdom of a volume of selected letters (the kind of volume I had been asked by the authors to edit), and wondered whether it might not make more sense to produce the complete extant correspondence. However, when I read the correspondence all the way through, I became convinced that it deserved a wider readership than it would get as a multivolume edition destined to be restricted to the shelves of university libraries. In the future it will be important to have a complete edition. But for now, I have tried to produce a readable selection of the correspondence representative of the whole. In doing so I've chosen sequences of letters that have either a narrative or thematic thread, the various topics of which are typical of the complete correspondence. This necessitated deleting portions of individual letters. Such deletions of course mean that the range of topics in individual letters seems more limited than in the originals, but it has allowed for the inclusion of many more letters than would have been possible without making deletions. All of the deletions were done with the limitations of space in mind, and for the sake of coherence and continuity. None were made in the conscious attempt to suppress material.

I have divided the correspondence into four parts, and have included introductions at the beginning of each. The introductions are meant to provide biographical and historical background for the letters that follow, to lend narrative continuity at limited points in the text while avoiding the proliferation of explanatory footnotes that would only detract from the letters themselves. In this same spirit I have tried to keep the number and length of the footnotes to a minimum. In the great majority of cases I have left the original spelling and punctuation as is. Where it was clear that a word had been inadvertently misspelled, I have made silent corrections. But in the many instances where one of the authors clearly intended a misspelling or a neologism I have left them as they appear in the original. Where in doubt, I've erred on the side of a possible pun, since one of the joys of this correspondence is its freewheeling play with language.

Most of Kenneth Burke's letters to Malcolm Cowley are in the Pennsylvania State University library, while most of Cowley's letters to Burke are in the Malcolm Cowley papers at the Newberry Library in Chicago. A few of Burke's letters to Cowley are in the Newberry Library collection, and some of Cowley's to Burke are in the Penn State collection. I have indicated where individual letters are collected with a "PS" (Penn State) or "NL" (Newberry Library) after the originating address and date of each letter. I wish to gratefully thank each library for permission to print the letters in their collections.

My work on this project could not have been carried out without the assistance of a number of insitutions and individuals. The Graduate Research

Foundation of the University of Connecticut helped to fund my work in its early stages, and an Exxon Education Foundation Fellowship at the New-berry Library provided me with the time I needed to go through its col-lection of the correspondence. The final stages of this project could not have been completed without a leave of absence from my teaching duties at Loyola University of Chicago. I want to thank each of these institutions for their generous support.

The list of people who have helped me with this project is a long one. To Kenneth Burke and Malcolm Cowley I obviously owe everything. It was an honor to be asked to edit their correspondence, it has been a great joy to get to know them, and they have each been extraordinarily gracious and helpful, while at the same time allowing me absolute freedom to select, edit, and annotate the letters that appear in this volume. Their confidence in me has been most gratifying; they have supported this project in countless ways, saved me from innumerable blunders, and provided me with impor-tant information and materials without which this volume would have been diminished. It is quite impossible to thank them enough for their support.

Carolyn Sheehy, who oversees Cowley's papers at the Newberry, is an editor's dream. She was extremely helpful in facilitating ease of access to the materials I needed at the Newberry, and contributed in countless ways to the production of this volume. She also made some very helpful editorial suggestions as well. I am very grateful for her assistance. Charlie Mann of the Pennsylvania State University Rare Books Library has also been of great assistance, providing me with the material I needed with great dispatch. I thank him as well. A number of individuals either listened to my ideas about the correspondence, read part of it, encouraged me, or helped edit my introductions and preface. They include my wife, Lynn Woodbury, Kate Engelberg, my brothers Gregory and Criss Jay, and former colleagues in-cluding John Naughton, Bill Van Pelt, Linda Simon, and Ross Miller.

PAUL JAY
Chicago

Contents

PART ONE

1915-1923

Although Kenneth Burke and Malcolm Cowley began writing letters to one another in 1913, those that survive begin in the summer of 1915. They had been classmates and close friends during their years together at Peabody High School, in Pittsburgh, and during that summer Cowley awaited word about a scholarship to Harvard, while Burke tried to make up his mind about enrolling at Columbia University, Ohio State, or simply going to work. During their years at Peabody High, the two forged a friendship built in good measure on their intellectual and literary interests. In *Exile's Return*, Cowley describes their crowd as would-be writers who prided themselves on being "different" from the "happy" boys who were "competent in every situation, who drove their fathers' cars and led the cheers at football games and never wrote poems or questioned themselves" (16). "At seventeen," he continues, "we were disillusioned and weary . . . we had come to question almost everything we were taught at home and in school" (18).

As Cowley recalls, that sense of disillusionment was matched by a sense of belatedness. "Literature, our profession, was living in the shadow of its own great past. The symbols that moved us, the great themes of love and death and parting, had been used and exhausted" (19). As their reading ranged over Stevenson, Meredith, Hardy, Gissing, Wilde, Strindberg, Schnitzler, and Shaw, they began to measure the modernity of recent writing by the amount of paradox it contained. "If they were paradoxical," Cowley writes, "if they turned platitudes upside down, showed the damage wrought by virtue, made heroes of their villains—then they were 'moderns' " (20). As Cowley prepared for Harvard, and Burke for Ohio State and Columbia (he briefly attended both schools), they did so with a feeling that their literary interests set them apart from others, and that they were moving out into a wider world that seemed both hostile and inviting. "We were like others, we were normal," Cowley concludes, "yet we clung to the feeling that as apprentice writers we were abnormal and secretly distinguished: we lived in the special world of art; we belonged to the freemasonry of those who had read modern authors and admired paradox" (22).

In their letters of 1915–1917, Cowley writes about his intellectual and social life at Harvard, about the young poets there, his work at the *Advocate*, about classicism and free verse, football games, Cambridge girls, and drinking. He seems, in the main, delighted with himself and with Harvard. Yet, in a recurring fashion, he misses his freewheeling intellectual exchanges with Burke, and envies him his being near New York (Burke's family had moved to Weehawken, New Jersey). In a letter written in December of 1915, he declares that

> *You have the whip hand on me, villain. I was always anxious to see you in New York . . . You know I'm dying for a good philosophical discussion. I'm getting to be a brute. All I do is study, eat, sleep, take a shower, go to classes, eat, and study. I know more about Friedrick Hohenstaufen and Hildebrand and the Cluny movement than I do about such interesting matters as imagist poets or Bohemia. I want to eat again in an artistic restaurant . . . drink wine moderately, and talk to my heart's content. But I doubt, man, if I can talk. Too much study dulls the wits.*

Burke had been visiting New York often, cultivating a friendship with the British writer Louis Wilkinson. Through Wilkinson, he was to meet Theodore Dreiser. But soon he too was off to college, entering Ohio State with his friend from Peabody, James Light (who would later become a director for the Provincetown Players). At Ohio State Burke plunged energetically into modern literature and philosophy, reading and writing to Cowley about Flaubert, Dostoevsky, Baudelaire, Mallarmé, Schnitzler, and Anatole France. He also assisted Light in publishing a literary magazine, *Sansculotte*, to which Cowley contributed. At Ohio State Burke was introduced to the novels of Thomas Mann, and began to read Freud. By the time he withdrew—after a single semester—to enroll at Columbia, his desire to live in and through writing had become a passion. "If I write what I think," he wrote to Cowley in the summer of 1917, "I shall come much nearer to doing what I wanted to do than if I live what I think." Part of this passion was a passion to be known, and to make a difference: "The thought that I should die without having imposed my personality upon the world is the only form my fear of death takes. In other words, I don't fear death—I fear an uncompleted life."

While Burke was at Columbia studying philosophy, Cowley joined the war effort in France as a volunteer in the American Ambulance Service. He took advantage of his stay in France by immersing himself in French literature, especially poetry, and his letters to Burke are full of reports about his reading, as well as about life at the front, and the impact on their generation of fighting a war. He thanks "God constantly that I have crossed the water . . . that I have been drawn out of my fixed orbit":

> At present . . . everyone should serve his time on the western front. That is the great common experience of the young manhood of today, an experience that will mold the thought of the next generation, and without which one will be somewhat of a stranger to the world of the present and the future.

Burke's letters keep Cowley abreast of reactions to the war at home, and about the course of his work at Columbia, where he becomes increasingly frustrated. Attracted to the idea of being either a writer of fiction or a critic—and sensing the need eventually to choose between them—Burke finds his academic education too rigid and regimented. In January of 1918 he writes to Cowley that he is quitting Columbia to become a "Flaubert" in Greenwich Village:

> I am quitting Columbia . . . Suddenly becoming horrified at the realization of what college can do to a man of promise . . . I shall get a room in New York and begin my existence as a Flaubert . . . I don't want to be a virtuoso; I want to be a—a—oh hell, why not? I want to be a— yes—a genius. I want to learn to work, to work like a Sisyphus—that is my only chance. I am afraid, I confess it, but I am going to try hard . . . School is killing us . . .

Burke withdrew from Columbia in the spring, and never returned to college.

After the war, Cowley returned to Harvard, where he met Conrad Aiken and other Cambridge poets. However, he soon grew discontented. Withdrawing from Harvard later in the year, he joined Burke in New York City. Here, he became friends with Matthew Josephson, Gorham Munson, Hart Crane, and Allen Tate. Burke and Cowley exchanged relatively few letters during this period, since they lived so near one another. In May of 1919 Burke married Lily Batterham, and in August of that year Cowley married Peggy Baird. After his marriage, Cowley returned once again to Harvard, graduating Phi Beta Kappa in the winter of 1920. After graduation he and his wife returned to the Village, where Cowley took a job writing advertising copy for *Sweet's Architectural Catalogue*. During this period he published his first important essay, "This Youngest Generation," a piece about the literature and ideas that attracted his generation. It was, of course, an indication of what would become a lifelong interest. The essay caught Gorham Munson's eye, and led to Cowley's association with two important avant-garde magazines *Broom*, and *Secession* (both of which Burke also wrote for and helped to edit).

After leaving Columbia, Burke embarked on a mammoth scheme of self-education, reading systematically through the classics, modern French, German, and English fiction and poetry, and philosophy. He began to earn enough to live in poverty by freelancing in New York, reviewing for the *New York Times, Export Trade*, and the *New York Evening Post*. Later, he would begin to supplement this income by translating stories from the German for *The Dial*. By 1921 he was writing short fiction and developing an interest in literary form and philosophical approaches to art. Writing in June of 1921 about his friend, the painter Carl Sprinchorn, Burke writes that Sprinchorn "*feels* things; but my joy does not really begin until I *formulate* them." Burke spent that summer with his wife and child in Monson, Maine, and it proved to be an important time for him. In Maine, he wrote and revised many of the stories that would appear in his first book, *White Oxen and Other Stories*, and in so doing formulated more precisely his ideas about literary form. By the end of that summer he came to realize, as he wrote to Cowley in October, that in him the "critical outweighs the creative." Upon his return to New York, Burke soon became an editorial assistant at *The Dial*. (While at *The Dial*, Burke helped prepare T. S. Eliot's *The Waste Land* for publication.) In the spring of 1922 Burke and his wife bought a house in the New Jersey countryside (in Andover), where he still lives.

Meanwhile, Cowley had returned to France in the summer of 1921 to take up postgraduate work at the University of Montpellier (with a fellowship from the American Field Service). Here Cowley was able to continue his earlier work in French literature. He also saw friends from America who had come to Paris, and made the acquaintance of others in the expatriate community centered at the Rotonde Café. While in France, he became friends with André Salmon (who literally mapped out the history of modern French literature for him), and with Tristan Tzara and the Paris Dadaists, who met at the Dôme Café. Of Paris, Cowley writes that "it is Greenwich Village, only much more so than the village." And again, "Paris is like cocaine; either it leaves you tremendously elated or sunk in a brown fit of depression . . . Paris has rarely or never produced great literature. There are rare exceptions: Baudelaire, Verlaine, but the rule is pretty safe. However, Paris has been the condition of great literature. Occasionally a man tears himself away from it and writes like—George Moore, James Joyce."

Their letters during this period broaden out over a range of subjects, as Burke and Cowley argue about the relative merits of Dada in particular and modern literature in general, about philosophy and æsthetics, classicism, the essays they were helping to publish in *Broom* and *Secession*, and the question of how to go about developing a specifically "American" literature and criticism. While Burke continued work on his stories, and on the essays on literary form and aesthetics that would comprise his second book, *Counter-Statement*, Cowley wrote his first essay on bohemia, "A Brief History of Bohemia," (which compared the Paris art colony of 1850 with that of 1920) and a number of essays on French writers including Proust, Racine, and Rabelais. By the time Cowley and his wife returned to New York late in 1923, both he and Burke had begun to establish the range of interests that would see them through two remarkable careers.

989 Boulevard East,
Weehawken, N.J.
Nov. 6, 1915
[PS]

Dear Malcolm,

Last night I had the fullest hours of my life; I was at Dreiser's. I am not going to write you about all I experienced. It would seem almost like sacrilege to me. You see, to me the evening was an epoch. For all the time I was making my debut, I was wondering if my debut was to be my end. Dreiser was so cold to me, so perfunctory, that I was frightened. It was not until late in the evening that he would even let me talk, to say nothing of paying attention to me. But happily, I was not in bad form, and once or twice I managed to say something noticeable even under these difficulties. One fellow, for example, said that when Mark Twain wanted to think he would lie with his head near the fire. I made the unfair but effective reply that often he did not get close enough. I made the horrible blunder of picking out what Dreiser evidently considers his best book technically as an illustration of a fault. I brought the house down, but I had the good sense to immediately acknowledge myself beaten, although I am still quite certain that I am right. As we neared the end of our stay I managed to worm myself shyly into conversation with Dreiser, but not until I had suffered the painful humiliation of finding myself addressing the air. As he talked I made a very gratifying discovery; you and I could give him kindergarten lessons in convolutions.[1] He calls things subtle which are plainer as Hell—he talks about religion as though it were bread—he admits that the Easterners are in possession of greater brains, greater intellectual development, than the Westerners, and then adds that he cannot understand the more Eastern type, without seeming to be aware of the conclusion that was implied. He says he cannot explain the psychology of a weak temperament, a temperament which is not aggressive. There is my chance, eh? I am planning a novelette called the "Minotaur," in which I shall try to exploit the ways of weakness, and at the same time shall depict one of those creatures of my megalomania. I am very wise. To witness, I intend putting myself in a minor part. I am going to write this thing with a view to publication, although since it ends with either a ravishment or an attempt at one (the plot is another version of the one I told you about in the summer), I don't have much hope of seeing it in a magazine. I shall be melodramatic if I can, and follow more the spirit of the short story than the novel.

But to get back to the evening at Dreiser's—I did obtain an offhand invitation to come again. From a very charming friend of his I received a cordial invitation to come again. Needless to say, I am brimming over with gratitude for her. She is perfectly able to set one at his ease. It was she, by the way, who read your poem to us—but more of that anon. One of the astounding paintings Dreiser has on his walls is of her. When I saw it I forthwith described her to Mrs. Wilkinson² as a cash girl who had read Nietzsche. You can imagine how embarrassed and repentant I was when she made things so comfy for me. She is tall, and judging from the way her clothes hang on her, her body must be exquisite. She is exactly the type of woman Dreiser bestows upon his most favored villains.

Mrs. Wilkinson defies my Cicero. I could not have had a more suitable woman made to order. She is a small, neurotic woman, and as she stood by the coal fire, and spoke in an effectedly low voice, and let her cigarette go out so prettily, I was horribly infatuated. Great God, Malcolm! henceforth deliver me from the non-intellectual woman! Our strongest bulwark has been smashed. Beauty and brains are not anomalies. Henceforth I cannot cite my ugly mouth any more as a proof of my genius . . .

The men were very funny. One group was dallying around with the pseudo-philosophic. They started an endless number of discussions about the cosmos, every one of which ended with the conclusion that discussion was useless. One man claimed that the sun was hot—another claimed that the sun was cold—a third, to be agreeable, said that he was sure it was lukewarm.

Your poem was received as I had prophesied. It was neither enthused over, nor was it condemned. Dreiser, who is a great admirer of Masters, said it was the usual waves that one could expect to follow in his wake. But please don't think I am exulting over you. I was very pleased to find myself up in arms to defend you. I am honestly sorry the poem did not make a stronger impression. As I was still being consistently ignored by Dreiser when the poem came up, I did not venture to commence a long harangue in your favor, but we must take the will for the deed. I really think though, that the fault is where I pointed out—you are not dramatic. Before an audience which had no intention of stirring itself you would have to be a little more exclamatory. As it was, Dreiser got the impression that you were doing nothing more than imitating Masters. It so happens, from the way you used to plague me with your discussions about trees and all that, that I was able to read you in the poem. But, you see, to them it looked perfunctory.

I thought I was going to meet Powys last night, but I didn't. I am rather glad now that I didn't. I prefer to divide up these little pleasures. Besides, I have not heard him lecture yet. I am going to hear him on Tuesday. After the lecture, of course, I shall have more to talk about to him . . .

I hope you can come here for a little while around Christmas. I have a very assertive little Bohemian restaurant to take you to, a couple, in fact. It is done in the futuristic way—its yellow, for instance, is as shameless as that on the seats of the El cars. After being there one must blush to think that he ever was moved by the Gonfarone.[3] Then too, I am dying to show you the city just as a work of art. I cannot express it, it is too sweeping—and thus I want to purchase the consolation which comes of merely showing it to someone who can rhapsodize with me. To be out on the river by the Cortlandt Street Dock about a quarter to six is simply agonizing. Then there is that nocturne I was telling you about by the Latrine of Endymion. Oh, oh! if I ever can express those things with words I shall be proud and impregnable. And the skies—I often wonder if the skies are especially gorgeous here, or if I had not awakened to them in Pittsburgh. In one place Jennie Gerhardt[4] cries because she cannot express such things. I hardly dare to be so confessedly sentimental as that, naturlich, but at times I permit myself to swear most abominably. But I am neglecting my studies.

Kenneth Burke

1. With their friends at Peabody High, Burke and Cowley developed a theory of convolutions in which each tried to outwit the other by anticipating the expected response in an argument. Cowley recalls how the theory worked in *Exile's Return*, page 25.

2. Wife of the British writer Louis Wilkinson.

3. A restaurant in New York City.

4. The protagonist in Dreiser's novel *Jennie Gerhardt* (1911).

Stillman Infirmary,
Harvard University,
Cambridge, Mass.
[November] 22, 1915
[NL]

Dear Burke:

You always knew that I was a damn fool, and I am beginning to suspect that fact myself. As you perhaps noticed we beat Yale 41 to 0. Cambridge was full all morning of Yale and Harvard graduates and undergraduates. Tickets for the game were selling for as high as $75 a pair—damn fool that I am for not selling mine. The stadium was packed.

When Harvard made the first touchdown, the enthusiasm was wonderful to see, but after a while the matter of making touchdowns grew monotonous. Along with 2,000 other Harvard men, I threw my hat over the goal post after the game—and lost it. So much for the day.

I don't want to tell you about the evening. It makes me sick to think of it. At the Woodcock I poured everything I could get my hands on down my throat. I drank cocktails, lacrimal Christi, Moselle, Burgundy, sherry, champagne, beer, and ginger ale. I kissed two or three girls I never saw before and was rebuffed by more. I was happy. Thank god I was lost to the world before I started puking. Well, I began that at about 2 Sunday morning and continued it for twenty-four hours. And here I am now.[1] I really am not at all proud of myself—for once.

So much for news. Now for a little dissertation. Man alive, there are only three Universities in the United States, and two of them aren't so awfully good. Harvard men can find an infinite number of faults with the University. But those faults, as any one of them would tell you, have little bearing on the one shining fact that Harvard is America's greatest university.

If I only had a little time for outside activities, I would enjoy life better here. There is a remarkable lot of good verse written here—principally in the shape of free verse and sonnets. There is even a Poet's Club. Just now I am competing in the dramatic club's publicity competition. It is an honor to belong to any of the clubs here. For example one must write a comic poem in German on special invitation before being eligible for membership in the Deutscher Verein. To belong to the Cercle Française, one must act in one of their French plays. Both these two organizations are infamous for booze and smutty stories. I must belong.

The "Advocate" is a remarkably poor magazine, publishing some good poetry. The "Monthly" has a lot of good stuff in it. The atmosphere of the "Crimson" office is invigorating. I would like to get on the staff of all these three papers. "Lampy" is independent in what it says, and is really one of America's best humorous publications, in or out of college. The "Illustrated" is not much account, but the "Musical Review" publishes original compositions, and articles on Scriabin and on Mussorgsky's songs.

But in expatiating on Harvard I am forgetting my main theme, which is that America's only real universities are Harvard, Yale, and Princeton, of which Harvard is the only one possible for me—or you. You know that the names of Harvard, Yale, and Princeton are closely connected. The reason for this, I have lately discovered, is that the three universities are in somewhat the same connection that Cambridge and Oxford are in. Athletically, they treat all other colleges as outsiders. They have three covered debating meets. They play chess together. The University Press is a combination of the Harvard Press, the Yale Press, and the Princeton Press. Any custom that is successful at Yale or Princeton is sure to be followed here. Salesmen go from one university to another. And all these relations, coupled with the fact that prep school boys like to go to a famous school, have made the three universities what they are.

I have run out of paper.

Mal

1. Cowley was writing from the Stillman Infirmary.

989 Boulevard East,
Weehawken, N.J.
Nov. 24, 1915
[PS]

Dear Malcolm,

Today I received your horrible letter. It meant to me, of course, the same old contrast—the fight which always makes me call you a Philistine and you call me a snob. As you rushed impressively through your list of boozes and your boastful confessions about enthusing over things so insignificant, I thought with a certain melancholy humor of my Tuesday evenings with Wilkinson, when at times I become so excited over a topic of literature that I gulp down in one breath two mouthfuls of Bass Ale and Stout half and half, chew viciously at a Butter Thin Biscuit, and almost succeed in eating one of those uncooked pickled fish (I forget what they are called) which he tells me are the sign of the true European epicure. Great Heavens, Malcolm, how you college fops do abuse the channels of healthy goodfellowship! Wouldn't that jolly group which gathered about the English Apollo bring down their mugs with a bang to think of such a boorish interpretation being set on liquor. And Dionysus? I shall say nothing about him; I admit, Bass Ale and Stout half and half are no closer to him than you were.

The idea of losing one's hat over a football game is beyond me. Couldn't you remember, just about the time you were acting like the sturdiest flunker in the school, that Jim, and Joe, and Farrell, and Henry,[1] and I and millions of others didn't give a damn if Harvard scored every minute? . . .

I have asked you if you are coming home. While waiting for you to reply I answer the question myself. You are not coming home for Christmas. I asked you if you would temporarily exchange with me your Artzybashev[2] for my Dreiser. I dare not answer that myself. I am now going to ask you something else. What do you think of my poem "Revolt"? I have a special reason for wanting to know.

I have been thinking over a remark you once made to me, that you are a good critic. I am very cynical. I believe you are even more unstable than I am. Remember that frightful incident of the sonnet of Wordsworth's, where you objected in the classroom to his writing about soaring up to Heaven on the wings of a skylark. You complained that you didn't like the idea of stout old men flitting about that way. Noyes[3] was very angry with you that day. Then recall the other time when I slapped your face for speaking as you did of Elizabeth Browning's poetry. I admit, I had read none of it, and have not to this day, and yet my retort to your charge of sentimentality pleased Noyes. I said that we are very liable to accuse them of sentimentality into whose feelings we are unable to put ourselves . . .

You simply *must* read *The Idiot*, if only out of regard for me. I have always felt, when boasting to you of how much I found in common with the great novelists, that you said half-consciously to yourself, "Well, the poor devil is sincere enough, so why dispute him?" That, at least, is what *I* should have said if *you* told me about such things. But in *The Idiot* I have documentary evidence. The character of Ippolit Terentyev is exactly the fictionization of myself in my letters to you this summer. You will recognize the likeness . . . As a work of art the book is unspeakable. It was slung together. I suppose that if the Russians were to become architectural novelists all their virtues would vanish . . .

. . . . . .

. . . Kennerley,[4] I think I told you, now has Wilkinson's novel. Between Wilkinson and Dreiser I shall certainly have access to the publishers I want if I ever have a book. Dreiser is as you know connected with John Lane;[5] he is also a great friend of Mencken's. I am very anxious to meet Mencken, and am going to try my best to do it. He is a much better man than Nathan,[6] both in ability and in personality.

Send me some more of your stuff. I want to show it to Wilkinson. I think he will agree with me in liking it only moderately, but that doesn't matter. At present I am absolutely destitute of poetry. Of course, I could write some of those pretty things that I indulge in at times . . . but my Western mind gets little satisfaction out of them. I love to write around a grain of philosophy, rather than around a sensation; which proves, I guess, that I am no poet. But I make no secret of that. Surely I have boasted to you some time or other that I am no poet . . .

Meanly,

Kenneth duVa Burke

1. James Light, Joseph Monteverde, Russell Farrell, and Harry Saul were all high school friends from Pittsburgh. Light went on to become a director in New York with the Provincetown Players.

2. Mikhail Petrovich Artzybashev (1878–1927), Russian novelist, playwright, and essayist.

3. Noyes was an instructor at Peabody High School.

4. Mitchell Kennerly (1906–1938), a publisher.

5. John Lane, a London publisher with a strong American list.

6. George Jean Nathan (1882–1958). Nathan helped edit *Smart Set* with Mencken and Willard Huntington. He later co-edited *American Mercury* with Mencken.

[Harvard]
[December, 1915]
[NL]

Dear Burke:

I have an idea. I'm going in to see George Washington Cram—the Recorder. I'll tell him that through you (notice how important you're getting, little mouse turd) I have a chance to meet Louis Wilkinson, but that Louis is going to leave New York the 21st about 12 P.M. Wilkinson, I'll tell him, can get me perhaps an interview with Theodore Dreiser who is my favorite novelist. I'll lay the bull on thick, and try to get off the 20th. Now perhaps you could write me a letter telling me of my splendid opportunity to meet Wilkinson, and I could show it to Cram. And then, if all went well, I could see you on the morning of Tuesday the 21st, and probably travel with you as far as Philadelphia on the road home. This all depends on whether I can get to Washington for Christmas, but I have good hopes of that.

You have the whip hand on me, villain. I was always anxious to see you in New York, but now I am doubly so. You know, I'm dying for a good philosophical discussion. I'm getting to be a brute. All I do is study, eat, sleep, take a shower, go to classes, eat, and study. I know more about Friedrick Hohenstaufen[1] and Hildebrand[2] and the Cluny movement than

I do about such interesting matters as imagist poets or Bohemia. I want to eat again in an artistic restaurant—not Gonfarone's—drink wine moderately, and talk to my heart's content. But I doubt, man, if I can talk. Too much study dulls the wits . . .

If you think you can do any good, enclose that glowing description of Wilkinson on a separate sheet in your next letter. Tell me that my only chance to see him is the morning of Tuesday before Christmas, or on Monday evening. And if I can go, I will go in and bull the head off Cram and see you and get super civilized again.

> Hopefully,
> Malcolm

1. Friedrick Hohenstaufen, eleventh-century German (then Swabia) count.
2. Hildebrand was Saint Gregory the VII, Pope from 1271 to 1276.

> 989 Boulevard East,
> Weehawken, N.J.
> Dec. 10, 1915
> [PS]

Dear Malcolm,

Your disappointing letter reached here this morning, and from the depths of my resentment I am answering it immediately. You simply *must* contrive to get here on the evening of the Monday before Christmas, or Tuesday morning at the very latest. I beseech you, move heaven and earth to make it. For once in my life it is entirely of you that I am thinking.

Wilkinson leaves for his lectures in the West on Tuesday evening, and I don't know when you will get an opportunity like this again. Consider! it is not only the free verse people that you are to meet, but also Powys, and even Dreiser. I cannot understand how one who admires Dreiser's work so strenuously as you do could throw such a chance to the winds. Everything depends upon Wilkinson. For *me* to introduce you to Dreiser is quite out of the question. I hardly know him. Wilkinson, on the contrary, knows everybody literary, be he English or American. Wilkinson is your only hope. Even Monday night is too late for you to meet but one or two . . . I never was very proficient in social matters, you know, and I don't have the audacity to make appointments with anybody but a couple of obscure newspapermen. Brr! I am afraid of Dreiser . . .

Let me end as I began—with a plea that you do your best to get here early. I can talk of nothing else. I am wrapped up in it. And that is natural, after the lonesome time I made you pass with me the last time you were here. I want to redeem myself.

I am sincerely,

Kenneth Burke

E 13 Gore Hall
[Harvard University]
December 15, 1915
[NL]

Dear Ken:

Your letter worked like a charm. It worked better than I expected too. I came in to Dean Yeomans today. (I showed him the letter yesterday.) "I am letting you go," he said. "This is a very unusual thing to do, and we are permitting it only on account of your remarkable record."

"When do I get off, Mr. Yeomans?" I asked.

"Didn't the letter say that you were to be in New York by Monday? I am giving you Monday, Tuesday and Wednesday."

That means, Burke, that I can leave here Saturday night by either the Colonial or the Fall River Steamship lines. But first I must get money and permission from home. I just wired for both.

When I get to New York, and I will if all goes safely, I want to take a little rest. I want chiefly to walk, and if my tongue unties itself, talk. I don't want to meet Dreiser even if I can. Such a colossus could have no interest in a Harvard man. I would like awfully much to meet Wilkinson, though; not that I could impress him, but just out of desire to hear a great man talk.

I will write you particulars as soon as I hear further . . .

Malcolm

[Harvard University]
Jan. 5, [1916]
[NL]

Dear Burke:

After I left New York, I had a great feeling of intellectual superiority and intellectual degradation. I knew so much more than everybody else, and so much less than everybody worth while. I wrote two reams of bad verse expressing my contempt for everybody I saw—and tore it up. Then I got to work again and forgot everything except German and French. I decided, though, to drop a course at midyear and to devote a little time to literature. Also I made myself agreeable to my second cousin in Washington—the family of Mr. Alexander McKenna. That man is transcendentally good and remarkably generous. He is a thoroughgoing atheist. He gave me a hundred dollars. I am going to embrace atheism. Think of it, Burke. A hundred dollars. Damn.

But you are in more of a crisis than I. What is happening about that affair of Ohio State, Columbia, and work? I hope you get a newspaper job for this half year. If you want to go to college, you might as well start in the fall, after you know what it is to work. If your people are going to move west later, I don't see why you shouldn't go to Columbia. After all, Ohio State is a provincial university—poor Jim—.[1] But drop me a letter some time. As soon as I know where you are, I'll mail your Dreiser. And if you get it, you might mail my Spoon River Anthology. You know I forgot it.

Sincerely,
Mal

1. James Light, who had left Pittsburgh to study at Ohio State.

989 Boulevard East,
Weehawken, N.J.
Jan. 28, 1916
[PS]

Dear Malcolm,

I must ponder on the twist which makes a man glorify a life of whirlpools and cringe before a four-dollar-a-week doorkeeper, or wallow in a confused mass of squirming sensations while loving inordinately the existence of a flabby pet dog who, loading up his belly, flops down with a contented grunt to snooze before the fire. I talk of hasheesh and I talk of absinthe; invariably I will scorn the one that brings oblivion, and deify a quickening of pulse-beats—and yet I love a dreamless sleep. What is it that makes such a gutless fellow as myself long to write a book of shocks? Is it the mental indigestion which Meredith thinks produced Byron's "Manfred"? Is it the natural reaction against myself?

In any case, I am sick of it. I am tired thinking of Don't Spit On The Sidewalk signs, and want to vibrate to some mountains. I often think of those idyllic days when we took our walks around the Pittsburgh country. I recall with a heedless, daring tenderness the time we ate by a T of roads, and you cooled your butter in a creek I was sure had bugs in it. I called you a damned fool for preferring rye bread to wheat, that day, and in desultory literariness we lolled away the most delightful hour of pure bestiality I can remember. How I swore! I damned you for everything, ridiculed you for everything—and you called me indecent and little. Great God, Malcolm—that was the most affectionate time I ever passed with you. Indecent! Mean! You are so simple in your deductions. That you should have called me little at such a time! I could not have been little—for I was natural. I was a part of that hot, lazy afternoon.

. . . What anomalies we are! You used to tell me the names of trees, or more often, how much they sold for as lumber. And you were the defender of the country. But I boredly interrupted your hobby, and talked uninterestedly of the superiority of urbanity and convolutions. To think that it is *I* who must feel the pastoral, and *I* who must renounce the pettiness of society and complexity. I have always doubted art; now I understand why. It is because art to me meant the city, and I unconsciously hated the city. I laughed at back-to-nature schemes, because they were usually some damned bosh like Wordsworth's . . . Art must die, because art can explain nothing. It is art which is leading us into triviality—into society. It is art which produces wit and humor, and the super-refinement in arbitrary things which mean nothing. Or is it the novel? Is it the study of manners? But whatever it is, it is that thing I was striving for. It is in the end myself I am turning against, not the world. All revolutionists revolt against only themselves. And when I denounce art, I call art the difficulty because I thought myself an artist. I don't really know what it is.

· · ·

For some time I have been taking inventory of myself, and as a result of it, I ask you to destroy all my letters. Either they are not true, or, what is worse, they are all too true. They are the writings of a coward, with a mania for explaining himself, and a fear of being seen as he is. They are neither interesting, nor inspired. They are often urbane. They are chatty. They are everything but mountainous. They are not the expression of a personality, but the concealment of one. They have no more claim to permanence than a newspaper. Please do as I say; for this is not a sudden whim. It is the result of much thinking, much weighing in the balance. I see that they are the city, and I realize that they must continue to be the city. For this love of nature I have does not speak. To see a sky is to see a sky. There is an element there—the essential element—which, Whistler or no Whistler, cannot be reproduced. We are all isolated entities, and must learn to sink into ourselves. We must learn to bear up under the most terrible torture of life, silence. Those who think they can speak are fatuous. Those who find universal traits to write of are superficial. To go to the depths of one's own soul is to find that nothing has been expressed. Think, then, what pain it causes to go there only to find that you have been glibly expressing things for years!

You can understand now why I want my letters destroyed; they are not me. If from now on I were to begin writing in this new fashion, I should want the letters preserved as an example of revolt. But I cannot. I am filled too full of the love of expression to be silent, even though I know that silence is the only great truth, the only mode of expression. No, there is no mode of expression. It is not possible for me to retire into myself. I quake before the thought of such a restless isolation. I must reserve it only for certain daring moments when I can venture to stand the fright of feeling myself alone. But rather than resign myself to a continual burden of egoism, I would play with the lesser things—and indulge in the triviality of speech. For was I not renouncing this lonely tongueless ego, this restless intelligence, even when I stopped to tell you of discovering it? You have not understood me. I should have resigned myself to the burden of being unintelligible, and gone my way. No, instead I have subjected my secret to the very thing I am reacting against—expression.

But the pastoral is in me, and the country is alluring me. I long for more of those walks. But what is this? Companionship! What a mighty strength of asceticism it would take to follow up my ideal! The most elemental tendency in me is my desire for the sympathy of intelligence—and the great truth of this burden of silence is its denial of the possibility of sympathy. But that is it—since I positively cannot accept the burden of passivity, I must have someone who can talk with me this superficial subtlizing which is urbanity. My letters, then, must go—because they are inconsequential. I have not the courage to continue even in this way. I do not dare to express to you in endless letters how unexpressible I am. I am still frightened by urbanity's demand for novelty . . .

Burke

The Harvard Union
[January, 1916]
[NL]

Dear Burke:

I remember when I used to have stages—the vulgar stage, for example, the bored stage, the stage of love for the country, the stage of new theories of poetry, U.S.W. Now dammit I'd usually contrive to get a whim which you had already experienced. And I would, of course, feel a little humiliated, as much as a mountain can be humiliated before a squirrel. (Remember the poem in the Third Reader?) Now I have revenge. You have been brazenly passing into my states of mind. You began to be vulgar—I exulted. You show a love for the country. I exult more. Finally you realize the inexpressibility of everything. I have been realizing that poignantly for the last month, and have had times in the past when the general inexpressibility of what I felt made me as desperate as some Latin Quarter Impressionist.

You want me to destroy your letters. We will compromise. I don't want to destroy them. Some day you might be famous. Your letters might be worth anything from $100 to $1.75 apiece. I might be damnably poor and want to sell them. Take another instance. You might fall out of literature and want to console yourself with the thought of your former ability. You will probably change your mind sometime in any case and want to read them again. Now if I were a tactful friend, I would tell you that I had destroyed your letters, and then file them away in some drawer. But I am not tactful. If either you or I had ever shown too much tact in our dealings with each other, we would have remained mere acquaintances. So I am telling you the truth. I am going to bundle your letters and file them away in a drawer—perhaps two or three drawers.

You have been insulting me up and down lately. If I had more time, we might begin a contest in vilification. But such a contest would be against my dignity as a mountain . . . If you come here—I should say, when you come here, I will manage, I think, to keep you from that damnable loneliness which is the greatest danger here. I should think that you would do better to get a job in New York than to go to Ohio State. Columbus is an unthinkable town and lacks a good library.

Mal

989 Boulevard East,
Weehawken, N.J.
Jan. 31, 1916
[PS]

Dear Mal,

You win. I wouldn't dare enter a compact of vilification with you . . .

It is unpardonable conceit of you to claim precedence in my whims. Your vulgarity is different, because it has no element of protest in it, connotes no love of prudery, and wears no philosophic braid. It is innate, and not cultivated by endless castigation. Your love of the country? Shoosh! . . . You talk of a city apartment and a country villa, with a library in each, and an auto to transport you conveniently from one to the other. I dream of abandoned lyrics, pulsing liaisons, sacred lust, ferocious city life, and then a sudden rushing off into the hills, to live alone, to renounce, to torture oneself with a realization of solitude, and then to fail—to flee from the hills because they are too heavy, and to hate the flowers because they are so inexpressible in their loveliness, and to flee in fear of silence back to the common truths of society. You with *my* love of the country. Why, Great Christ! you know the market price of lumber! As to your sharing my inability of expression—it was when scorning the thought that I came to understand what 'egoist' means. I made the startling discovery that I was never really an egoist until a month ago, when this longing for the country began to take some tangible nature.

Why, damn it, I begin to feel some of that bias which I have been searching to help me write my first novel. A character who acts as fanatically as I think! A man who believes something strongly. A character who is happily freed from that dreadful burden of creators, the "skeptical hedonism with a philosophy of negation." Neither you nor I are gifted with that lucky failing which makes a Tolstoi. And it is a failing. I am sure that *Anna Karenina* and "What Is Art?" are from the same womb . . .

If only I could convince myself that I am what Symons[1] says of Tolstoi, abnormal only in my normality. Is there not more of Levin than Nastasya in me? But hold—I wonder now if I should rather be Levin than Nastasya. Perhaps my weak heart puts me on the side of Nastasya. Yes, my weak heart is another obsession. Look! my dear mountain, is not the philosophy of negation falling away! Weak-heart-good-health-creation-Slavism—I am filled with aberrations! I shall plan my new novel. Let's see—this will be my third novel. And lo! there will be no woman and pig! Not a single sensation . . . The theme will be quite Russian—the resolutions and counter-resolutions of a man of great artistic abilities, his doubting of himself and art, his Byronicism (occasionally cynical) and the utter unexpectedness of his actions. To keep myself from falling into autobiography in a minute way, I shall allow myself as I am to fill the secondary roll [sic] . . . I was pleased to have you not acquiesce readily to my desire that you destroy my letters. Let me explain my attitude toward them entirely, and then you can do as you like. It was my original intention to have the letters record my evolution into genius. In case I should die before completing a work of art, they were to be my one pitiful plea for immortality. Next I came to realize that the letters had no intrinsic value, and would only be worth keeping in case I should produce great art. When in this stage, I was somewhat disappointed, but continued them, hoping that they would assume the shape of a duty, an adventure. I wanted to drive myself so deeply into your disrespect, that I would positively *have* to make my letters valid. But now, I have come to realize a terrible truth. If I were to become a great writer, these letters would take away my greatness. At first I intended them to prove me great; now I want to have the evidence of my ordinariness, my inspiredlessness, destroyed. The letters are not up to the standard of what I am striving for. They do not even adequately express my failure to reach this standard. I am ashamed of their cowardice. I am ashamed that I feared to write page after page of myself, but I tried to appease you with criticism of books, little descriptions of yourself, flippancy. But I do not have the bravado to tell you again to destroy the letters. I have hopes—you are responsible for them—that there may really be something in them. Perhaps I have reflected the color of this age—its longing for tragedy, and its fear of it—its flaunted selfishness—its reversal of standards. They say that Whitman, in trying to sing of himself, sang of the world. Surely I have not reached this? But I warn you that I couldn't sit down and read my own letters all day. What right do I have to expect others to do it? In the end, a person's own judgment of himself is the right one; recall that Virgil asked to have his *Aeneid* burned.

·   ·   ·

This evening when my father comes home, it will be settled once for all about college. If he wants to send me to Ohio, with the definite intention of Harvard next October, I shall go. But I shall not go to Ohio without prospects of Harvard. Rather, I shall get a job here.

Burke

1. Arthur Symons, the English poet and critic who is perhaps best known for his book *The Symbolist Movement in Literature* (1899).

Gore E13
[Harvard University]
March 9, [1916]
[NL]

Dear Burke:

I haven't the least wish to write you—but I want you to write me. I find existence unbearable without plenty of letters. In a short time, you will too. At first, it doesn't make much difference. But after a few months, the novelty wears off, and you must hear from your fellows. Although you have no wish to write, you must receive letters. And so you write very dull and very dutiful epistles of three pages. Will it work out that way with you? It has with me.

I am out for the *Advocate*. None of my stuff has been published yet, but some will be soon, I hope. It is no good. I am rehashing every bit of hackwork I ever did. I have not had a single plot this whole year. I feel like underlining that sentence. It means a lot to me. No, Burke, I won't be the great one of the crowd. I repeat it, the burden rests on you. I am too willing to become a hack and—I don't have plots.

I think I have settled on a room for next year . . . I'd like to see you here next year. The first year you would be in the Freshman dormitories, but after that we could move together. If you came, you wouldn't be troubled with idle time. Harvard is certainly not a loafer's school, and graduating in three years and picking scholarships as you go, is a job for a full-grown man.

I want to see you next summer. I will have to be on the farm again.[1] Perhaps you could drop off in Pittsburgh and come up with me. We could walk up (your mother and the weather being agreeable) and once up there could have some talks until we were both deucedly tired out. Also I could promise you work. And if you want to see ordinary people, there is Doc Altemus.[2] You would have to become average with the two of us, and run around the country. In turn, Doc would furnish you with an agreeable insight into the life of a dashing young buck. He is an interesting fellow. He drinks, fucks, swears, works like hell, is popular with girls, makes a good fraternity at Bucknell, and is sure of an average of 92 in his studies. His philosophy is the unconscious acme of the double standard, and he always plays a fellow square, and is honorable to a decent girl.

This isn't a letter, though. I can't write one. You say you have leisure. If so, write me. But this much I want to say—I have an inordinate desire to talk. I haven't talked absolutely frankly with anyone since I saw you last. I am developing into a disagreeable prig and a good deal of a snob. I need someone to balance me. I try to express myself in letters, but I never can, and as you know, never could.

Sincerely,
Mal

1. The Cowley family owned a farm near Belsano, Pennsylvania.
2. Leaird Altemus, a boyhood friend, later a doctor in Johnstown, Pennsylvania.

[Ohio State]
[Columbus, Ohio]
May 1, 1916
[PS]

Dear Malcolm,

. . . Do you know?—fed on pretty German romances as I have been lately, I have contracted a consuming love for prettiness in women. And this love has resulted in my being taken with the cutest little thing in Columbus. Ma petite jolie, or mein lübsches Mädel. Oh god, it is all so refreshing. I want to talk baby talk every time I think of her, and I watch for signs of pretty immaturity in her ways. Of course, I don't know her, although I am sure that for better or worse she is aware of my interest. She is not a Jewess, and it is quite a relief to transfer my allegiance to a gentile again. I am quite sure that she is very dumb, of course, but I am greatly indebted to her. For although she gives me no good poetry, she gives me a feeling of good health. I feel so human for liking so normal a girl. And I specialize now in humanity. My isolation in New York has given me a passion for the boorish and the healthy and the trivial which will never leave me. And my English prof here, who knows what a pretty thing it is to contemplate a woman's ankle, has strengthened me. He, too, loves the trivial things of life, sees in them, as I do, the lifelong impressions.

Yes, I too have at times those morbid views of life and death which you speak of, but I no longer call them morbid. I fear death at nineteen, but at the same time I am sure I should not fear death at ninety. I trust to the provisions of nature. I believe that when our time is up, we are willing. Oh yes, I am an optimist—almost maudlin in my optimism, almost Methodist.

I thought a long while: which is greater, the Slavic view of life or the Anglo-Saxon one? In my letters of last year, the Slavic element was beautifully alluring. I loved to tell myself—I must know the truth, even if I am mangled by it; I want not happiness, but truth. I dare to examine into the very rottenest spots of the human soul. Then I wrote you a lot of ambitiously self-detesting letters. My character became tragic in its very detest of the tragedian . . .

Recently I decided that the Slavic view was all bosh. I saw that the very things that Slavs raged against, pettiness, spite, and all that, were laughed at by the Anglo-Saxon temperament. Since then I have gradually evolved into what Wilkinson would call a buffoon; that is, a self-satisfied soul who sets about to enjoy the foibles of the world. I cast my lot with urbanity, and I have become as healthy as I once was sick.

· · ·

Listen—and tell the King to guffaw. I am going for certain to take up exclusively the study of music. I have not only permission, but even co-operation from home. My father is actually pleased. I have been oppressed too long with the limited range of expression one has when he can do nothing but write; I want to master another, and a far greater, medium. I shall hop up my French and German, and read the select magazines in English—but beyond that I shall do nothing but work unifiedly at music for at least three years, at piano and harmony. This means that I shall learn music in just the same way as if I were going to work. I shall do my eight hours a day. It is not too late yet.

This means, of course, that I cannot come to Harvard with you. Indeed, I fear another dreadful period of isolation. But after a time I shall dare to meet musical people, and although I am sure that they are not so interesting as literary people, still I am sure I shall like them.

Think of it, Mal, to have two mediums! Perhaps I shall be able to set free verse to music? Hein? That would be fine. And the music is so much more satisfactory than literature, anyway. It is an exquisite enjoyment just to play chords, just to tantalize oneself with dissonances, and then resolve them. Music awakens more reactions in us, and reactions which are of a more organic nature . . .

Burke

Gore E13
[Harvard University]
May 3, [1916]
[NL]

Dear Ken:

Three things I want to talk about that you mentioned in your letter—the question of health, the question of becoming a "university man," and the question of your devotion to music. About health—Ken, I have gone before you. The passion for health struck me about the fourth of this January. And I am now a healthier animal than I ever was before. It is in the Harvard atmosphere. You know that I never used to care what hour I went to bed. Remember our poker games. Remember our walks and our nocturnal, almost matutinal, conferences at the corner table of the Mandarin. I was always the last to leave. Even this last Christmas you saw the change in me. I now go to bed at ten. For an hour each day I take strenuous exercise, rise at seven, and eat regularly. I have only one pimple. And I despise all men who are flabby, all men who don't love health.

And in this connection I too have fallen in love; rather, you would say, got a case. She is nineteen and not beautiful, but lithe and laughing. She and her side kicker—as she calls her—claim to be the worst roughnecks in Cambridge. She tells how drunk she has been. She is a delirious dancer, and has a pleasing habit of pressing her breasts close to you. And yet, I have heard that she is technically pure. What a woman to have as a mistress! But I can never have her. She would expect me to bring her wine suppers and take her out riding before she would be so rash as to lose her technical purity. I will have to satisfy myself with kissing her. Hell.

But we wanted to talk about this business of becoming a university man. It is dangerous and pleasing. Harvard has made me healthy. It has made me respect myself, and yet at the same time made me snobbish. It has ruined me as an author, and made me a much better citizen. It has taught me to kiss girls without blushing. The old views I had are dropping off one by one. Perversity I now adopt only as a pose to amuse people, and even then I soon drop it. I have come to believe that the Allies are right. If all goes well, I shall join the Harvard Regiment and later go to Platts-burgh. I even entertain ideas of becoming a professor. You see I have changed.

Now how does all this apply to you? In this way—you need it all. I was never very much of a literary man. I always, like Jake,[1] nourished conserv-atism in my heart. When I came here, most of my perversity dropped off. Now you, if you allow me to say it, are original from the core. It was Carlyle who said that originality was only a kind of individuality, and you have always claimed to be an individual. You need Harvard to balance you. You wouldn't come out of it a professor like I shall. You would only come out of it a little broader, much healthier, and much more sound . . . You would have something to write about. As it is all you know, all you can express yourself about is Self, sex, and the business of writing. You need other subjects. But I can't express all this in a letter.

What I can express, is a protest against your devoting yourself to music for those years. What I remember is Jim. He gave up literature. He wanted another medium. And what happened? He found that he was only the third best artist in his class, and went back to literature. When you find that you are only the third best musician in your class, when you find that almost everybody can play the piano better than you, and that someone whose father has been a concert player can compose better than you, you too will go back to literature! And if you go to a school where you are the best composer—god save you. You might as well study by yourself as go to such a school.

For, and here is the point, you are not primarily a musician. If you were plumped down in some backwoods settlement without a piano, you would sing no more than a few fugues to the moon, and still be quite happy. But even in such a backwoods settlement, you would still be literary. As long as there was one person near you, you would be acting out literature. And if you were alone, you would act out literature for your own benefit. It is in your blood.

And yet, I would not advise against specializing in music. But the music ought to be taken in connection with something else. The piano by all means, but the pen too. A little broadness as well as a little concentration. Remember that I thought of taking the musical course at Tech. Remember, thank god, that I didn't. A good compromise would be to specialize in music while up here. They give some very good music courses here. At the same time you could become a little more capable of pedantry in other lines.

Mal

P.S. I know some musical people, and god knows, they are *not* interesting.

1. Jacob Davis, a classmate at Peabody High.

151 W. Tenth Ave.,
Columbus, Ohio
May 27, 1916
[PS]

Dear Malcolm,

"I can stand off now and see life swallowing us up, one after another." "After a woman kisses you a few hundred times, it bores you." I quote from your letter to Jim. Sugared piffle . . . I am beginning to think that you have the intellectual equipment of de Maupassant. I am surprised that even Harvardian priggishness can give you the audacity to be bored, but I am even more surprised to hear you dealing in such tommyrot as "I can stand off now and see life swallowing us up." I will admit, you may be right in saying that I was almost swallowed up by life in New York, all those months when I was writing, watching, praying to be swallowed up. But why the [indecipherable] Matthew Arnold attitude? Are you, too, fooled by that stupid phrase of his about the Greek tragedians? . . .

Why do you go on so about *vers libre*? Have you forgotten that *vers libre* is an accepted fact—that Berrymann puts Rene Schickele[1] and Liliencron[2] in the same volume? And have you no sympathy with us moodish dilettantes, who have things that we *must* say? What would you do—have us lie, or stop writing altogether? And I, personally, would be lying grossly; for I hardly ever get a theme in terms of beats and rhymes. I will admit to you readily enough, that the man who could write stanza after stanza of "Mary had a little lamb" rhythm without setting us insane, like Coleridge in his "Ancient Mariner," has something better than the free versists. But that doesn't prove to me that Arensberg's[3] "Voyage à l'Infine" isn't a beautiful bit of music, as soft and well-cut as anything in conventional verse. To object to free verse because it is free verse is stupid and superficial, just as stupid and artificial as it would be to object to the other form (I almost made the mistake of saying the *old* form) for a similar reason . . .

Last night there was a carnival out here on our campus. I thought of Rome, and riot, and I became most stupidly sad. I stood watching the street-dancing, and thought how much it would mean to me to prostrate myself and kiss a girl's fingertips. And then I thought of ma petite jolie, and felt that I would be content if only I could catch sight of her in the crowd. But I didn't see her, and I came home unable to cry. There are no tears for wistfulness. How unkind the atoms may be at times. It seems so cryingly unfair that I, who am filled with so much willingness to love, must go on and on in this cruel preparation. Will the girl ever come, I wonder, who will love me, and whom I am not ashamed to love? And if she does, how grateful I shall be to her. That is it—my primary attitude toward a girl who will love me will be one of gratitude.

Before coming to the carnival I was downtown. I had been in a saloon and had had some excellent beer. I was smoking a Philip Morris. As I stepped out on Broad Street, you may imagine, I felt competent. Across the street were a group of Salvation Army people. I insisted that we watch them. There was one little girl, of about sixteen years, with a pale clear face, a neat-cut mouth, a straight, fine nose, and a slender body. Poor girl, I thought, what reactions she must have against the convulsions of her awakening sex! For she believes in the evil of pleasure, and the month and her age were begging ceaselessly for pleasure. And then I became more competent, and I blew out my cigarette smoke with ostentatious calm, and observed the girl, and smiled now and then. I noticed with peculiar delight that she looked at me frequently, and hoped that the way I carried my cigarette would make her think I was a sinner. Finally our car came, and I had to leave, observing to myself how wonderful it would be to be able to awake such a girl, to remold her whole character—or just merely to be able to imagine all her brain states, and write them down. And as I left, I felt so competent . . . And then I came out to the carnival, and saw the many many competent girls with their silk-stockinged ankles who were absolutely indifferent to me, and I became very sad. And now I can't feel competent about the Salvation Army girl, either.

. . .

Please write me soon. Every day I have been looking for a letter from you, although I knew you wouldn't write me until I answered your letter. And when will you be home? We have our last examination on the thirteenth, and shall come to Pittsburgh that day or the next. I want to be with you very much. And I hope we will be able to listen to each other.

Sincerely,
K.

1. Rene Schickele (1883–1940), German poet and novelist.
2. Detler Von Liliencron (1844–1909), German poet and novelist.
3. Walter Conrad Arensberg (1878–1954), American author and poet.

[Harvard University]
[Undated. May or June, 1916]
[NL]

Dear Ken:

No one but an animal wants the mere flow of semen. Everyone wants affection. And even when you are not in love yourself, it is very pleasant to feel that someone loves you. It is so flattering to the vanity.

And you, I can picture you. Striding out of a saloon, smoking a Philip Morris daintily (why not a Richmond Straight Cut?), and feeling competent. God, man, you ought to be in Boston. Girls are so easy to pick up here. You see, men are rather scarce here, and morals are scarcer. Two friends of mine picked up eight couples in one hour on Huntington Avenue. Even if you despise them, they satisfy that eternal need for female companionship.

. . .

You're on into me for attacking free verse. I don't like it, true, as a rule. Something like those three famous nuns, or like the voyaging swan of Mr. Arensberg, I do like. But after reading ream after ream of broken prose, I decided that a law ought to be passed prohibiting all poets excepting you and me and Arensberg and Fletcher[1] and Amy Lowell and one or two others from forsaking meter. God, the crap some of these young Columbia students can turn out and call it poetry. Do you really wonder that I have come to despise free verse and despise myself for writing nothing else?

But back to important personal matters. I am not afraid of feeling any longer. That is why I was going to write a page of near-sentimentality about getting back to the old town. Just now, I am having some infinitely sweet longing for it. But the ragtime player across the quad, who, by the way, plays awfully, tantalizingly well, prevents me from expressing myself! Anyway, I want to see you and travel the dusty road and swim in the little creeks and crawl down Chestnut Ridge just as the sun is setting, and all that.

. . .

And as for "standing off and watching life swallow us up," that was an unfortunate phrase. I can certainly see life swallow us up, but I can't stand off and see it. No one can. We're all getting in the same mess.

Mal

1. John Gould Fletcher (1886–1950), Harvard-educated poet who was a leader of the Imagist School in England.

> [Weehawken,
> New Jersey]
> Sept. 11, 1916
> [PS]

Mon cher M,[1]

J'ai déjà envoye *La Rebelle* à Belsano. *The Buffoon* restera chez moi, parce que je suis tout à fait sans argent. Tu peux l'obtenir quand tu seras à New York.

Of course, you are going to stop here for a few days on your way to Harvard. There is nothing to do—I have no money to entertain with, and no character to bore you with—except walk, play tennis, and read. Nothing hindering, I should love to take a couple of real venturesome walks with you; you know, start out for god knows where and get home in time for dinner. You could bring your sneaks along, and perhaps we could play some tennis. Your playing would be distressingly bad, ça se voit, but what of that? As to reading, I can lend you books written after your heart, for I have become somewhat of an authority on unpresentable French novels.

Did you know, by the way, that my going to France is no longer a mere Eintägsfliege? It has become not only a certainty, but even an actual propelling force, an aim which is already affecting my conduct. I have begun hunting a job now. Some of my wages I shall save, some I shall spend for books and beer, and some I shall invest in Berlitz French. J'ai une idée fixe. Dame! Mais oui!

I am not going to France to stay, as I first intended. That is much too drastic. If I went to France to stay, and my money ran out, and I had no job, I should have to starve, or come home in disgrace. And besides, I shouldn't like to leave my father and mother so definitely. I like them both quite a lot, you know. And Pa, since I have lost my temperament, seems really clever to me. No, I shall not live in France. I shall go to France on a *visit*. I shall have so much money saved up with which to pay for this visit. Then if I have a chance in France to get a job and thus prolong my visit, I shall take it. If, when that job fails, I get a chance for another job, I shall take it and prolong my visit a little more. As long as I can get money, I shall prolong my visit, and when money ceases, my visit is over. By this arrangement I run no chance of defeat. I gamble with loaded dice. I bet against doped horses. I take a decisive step without suffering the usual vacillation. Nom d'un chien, comme je suis habile!

I shall stop now, mon cher M; it is a glorious afternoon for tennis. But tonight, perhaps I shall write you again; for I shall probably be all alone, and there is an awfully tempting moon, "une âme toute nue," that haunts the boulevard these nights. A lavish donor of delicious sadness, she is, M.,and I should love to watch her with you over the chilly somnolent farms. I love the moon, and the memory of ma petite jolie, and the lesser Chopin, and the cross-eyed girl next door. All that doesn't fit me for literature, Malcolm, but oh Christ, it makes it hard to renounce.

K. B.

1. Part of this letter was quoted by Cowley in *Exile's Return* (pages 23–26).

[Harvard University]
Russell 19
Oct. 24, [1916]
[NL]

Dear Ken(ny):

If Lewisohn[1] hadn't written, I should hardly have thought of saying anything, but now I want to add my word to his. When you are feeling extremely competent, I naturally feel like toning you down a little, but here you are in a position where you distinctly don't need toning down. So the truth—you are a genius. Not that it means so awfully much to be a genius these days, but then you are one if the fact comforts you at all. Your poetry doesn't show it—or rather, I might say, shows more genius than good workmanship. Your stories don't show it—but how long is it since you have written a story? But there are your letters—yes, you can always point to your letters. You can't point to all of them, though.

This is all apropos of an interesting evening. You know I had been heeling for Crime—with more effort than success. Well, I was dropped and dropped flat. That same evening there was a meeting of Poetry Society, and I looked your letters over before going—object, to choose a few poems for reading to the society. First the members read their own work—and it was good. *The Advocate* and *Monthly*, Burke, are cowardly, castrated sheets, but nevertheless there has been poetry at Harvard in the past, and there is poetry there now. Norris, Paulding, Snow, Raisbeck, Cutler[2]—lord, you'll hear of them all some day. Cutler in particular has an uncanny skill with rhymes and meters, and Snow, a freshman, pleased me by his wonderful collection of rejection slips from *Smart Set*, and his occasional checks from Scribner's and God knows where.

Then there was beer—beer dark and light; Schlitz, Piehl, Budweiser. And after the beer, the poetry became all wonderfully inspired. Then later I read your work—il n'est allé pas. Not that they didn't like it, but then I had to explain some of it, and apologize for some of it, and at the end, they came to the conclusion that you were a most interesting fellow who wrote most interesting, amusing poetry. And that isn't the right attitude to hold toward you, is it? Then I went home and read your letters again, and even under the genial influence of the Piehl, I felt that I could never do such work. I came to the conclusion for the first time that you were a genius . . .

Mal

1. Ludwig Lewisohn (1882–1955), Berlin-born writer who taught at Ohio State. Lewisohn introduced Burke to the novels of Thomas Mann.

2. William A. Norris, Gouverneur Paulding, Royall Snow, Kenneth Raisbeck, and Cutler were young poets at Harvard.

[Harvard University]
Russell 19
November 1, [1916]
[NL]

Dear Burke:

. . . There isn't much hope for a fellow who doesn't wipe his mouth out. Gad, I've been going through a kissing epidemic lately, and I feel that you ought to send some of that antiseptic up for me. But anyway I have the girls for you whenever it suits you to come here and get them. Irish, you know, and the Irish don't have much social standing in Cambridge. Their male relatives are awful, true muckers. But then the girls themselves are so obliging; so affectionate. They kiss you readily at first, but my especial flame won't kiss me any longer. You see, I gave her a lecture on the dangers of indiscriminate kissing. I was out there last night till twelve o'clock; therefore the many mistakes and erasures today . . .

I am a snob—hurrah, a true snob. What pleasure it gives me to think that I can cut absolutely anybody I want to. What a feeling of superiority it gives me to have my boots blacked by the janitor of my Gold Coast dormitory instead of by an ordinary Dago. And just think—I hope to be invited to join a fraternity, and I am going to refuse—not because I don't want to join a fraternity, but because this one isn't good enough for me. Could anything be farther from the boy who used to associate with the social outcasts of a socially outcast high school[?] . . .

Mal

[Weehawken,
New Jersey]
November 7, 1916
[PS]

Mon cher M,

Your last letter was very distasteful to me. When you become competent you are unbearably common. As a masterful man you are nothing but a little snotty-nosed smarty. You disclose common ambitions, common standards, and common vices. You resemble my idea of what a Harvard kike ought to be. In all seriousness. Pray, go back to your usual letter-apology. What you are not doing, pessimism, swear words, and apology. I may rail at it, but it at least has the virtue of leaving me undisturbed.

If I were a Harvard man with money, I should be disgusted with the colossal cheapness of you. God, man, you are almost ripe for toadyism. You are a typical subordinate, the kind I meet every day in my life now. Subordinates can always be distinguished by their tendency to lord it over someone. That is you to perfection—with your ridiculous hatred of Jews and your parvenu notion that a gentleman always pays too much for his clothes. If I were in a better humor these days, I should make it a point to be highly amused at you (you are still somewhat of a kid yet, you know, and entitled to be a little fresh). But it really is a shame, you know, to see Harvard going to your head. You say you are no longer one of the outs. I am sure that I could spot your kind every time.

. . .

Is it that I am fortunate in my choice of books now, or is [it] that my working has added salt to my meager leisure for reading? At any rate, I am also being thoroughly delighted by *Le Lys Rouge*.[1] True, every once in a while old Anatole thumps his fist down on the table and shouts "Damn you all, I'm going to be poetic or bust," but that doesn't matter a whole lot. There is promise of the scene being carried to Italy, and an English poetess who is by no means pretty (perhaps even ugly?) is still to figure. All the characters so far are quite *du monde* and have the proper weariness. Often I am reminded of *La Maison du Péché*,[2] and a book which reminds me of that is a book after my heart.

. . .

Some day, when you are feeling particularly well disposed, you must tell me more explicitly why I am a genius. Cela m'intrigue. I am a little piqued. So far, all I know is that I am a genius because I have written letters which you, when you were drunk, decided you couldn't write. I can point to my letters, you say. And then you add, "some, not all" without telling me which ones. This letter, I know, is one. The letters I wrote about ma petite jolie ought to be my best. Or was I best during my poetry spree last fall, when I met the people of the Quarter? . . .

B

1. *Le Lys Rouge*, a novel by Anatole France, was published in 1894.
2. *La Maison du Péché*, a novel by Marcelle Tinayre, was published in 1902.

The Harvard Union,
Cambridge
Nov. 11, [1916]
[NL]

Dear Burke:

You gave me an undeserved bawling-out. With what I am beginning to believe is your usual power of misinterpreting some of my remarks, you said I proclaimed myself one of the ins. No, my god, no. You don't know what it is to be an in here. It is a matter of birth, clothes, speech, training, and money. The bitter outs here think that money is the only requisite for inness. Yet I could point them out millionaires' sons who are decidedly not in the running. No, to be an in at Harvard is an awesome thing beyond my ambition. I was just proclaiming my lessening outishness.

All this doesn't interest you. It interests me very much because I am here, and because Harvard has a soul. I remember Peter somebody-or-other, a hero of Compton Mackenzie's, who was trying to find the soul of Oxford. And at the time I thought to myself that no American university has a soul. But I was mistaken. The fraternity-ridden state universities have each a share in the spirit of state education. The little schools like Wesleyan have each a share in the spirit of secular education. Harvard, though, has a spirit of its own, a peculiar attitude that I am learning but can never express. With hearty honesty I wish you were here. I think if you once tried to get the idea, the pursuit of it would become fascinating to you . . .

Mal

[Harvard University]
[April, 1917]
[NL]

Dear Burke:

What in hell does your silence mean? Now look what it has resulted in. Instead of spending a vacation peacefully in New York, I shall be taking examinations here preparatory to entering the American Ambulance, headquarters Paris in Neuilly. I shall leave for France in about three weeks or a month. Before that time, New York. Now seeing the result of a two weeks' silence of yours, write immediately before a longer break between letters drives me to absolute suicide.

[Malcolm]

[Harvard University]
[April, 1917]
[NL]

Dear Burke:

Just now I should be writing you a sentimental letter, because I am in just the mood to write a good one. But mood does not supply effort. I'm packing. Did you ever do anything more sad than pack? Old letters, old poems, old faces. I read your Weehawken Lyric again, and found it excellent. As you said, I could have written it myself, if I had the inspiration. But I shan't let that detract from my judgment of it, for I find I can write some decent poetry at times.

I received one most flattering commission. When one is leaving, one is always roundly flattered. Try it and see. To return to the subject, Freddie Schenk[1] gave me a soft-soaping to the head of the ambulance in America, and he asked me to write him letters about my experiences, the understanding being that if they are good enough, he will publish them. He has done that for several already.

Kirk[2] wrote me a letter of recommendation. In the note which accompanied it, he seemed very near to self-pity. Listen: "I wish to God I were about twenty. I feel the blood and sauerkraut lust and would let some if I could do so."

That "God" there has a peculiar force coming from a professor. It seems to confess the full absurdity of having a man of Kirk's brains teaching stupid children in a stupid high school. A little more conceit and another university than Ohio State, and he could have been a Copeland.[3] Now dislike Copey if you care to, but Copey is almost a parent of present day American literature. Our writing today is done by Harvard men, and Harvard men of prominence in literature always take Copey's course. Yet he has no different mind, and only a little better rounded personality than the tyrant of the "Peabody."

A little business. If I am to sail May 5 and not April 27, I shall probably be able to spend a week in New York. Now would your parents be able to stand me for that long? I hope they will, for I shall not have opportunity to bother them again for a long time. Please break your recent custom and write immediately. You shall be called upon to write me often when I am in the field. Oh shucks, don't I talk about it seriously? Perhaps I have a right to.

Mal

1. Frederic Schenk was a friend of Cowley's from Harvard.

2. Kirkpatrick, an instructor at Peabody High.

3. Charles Townsend Copeland, a popular and influential professor of English and American Literature at Harvard.

[Weehawken,
New Jersey]
May 27, 1917
[PS]

Dear Malcolm—

Absolutely nothing at all to write to you, or I should have sent you something before this. With the exception of slightly blacker headlines the war has dropped out of existence over here, and if I don't go up to your farm I shall probably spend a very very moderate summer in New York reading up on philosophy. Jim[1] may be conscripted—he has gone to Pittsburgh to see what his being a British subject may have to do with it—and if he is I shall stay at home. I should not dare a summer in the country without masculine companionship; here in New York, with the library handy, I become pretty savage toward the end of August. God only knows what Belsano would do to me.

That little spurt of jingoism I had when you were leaving has completely died out in me, leaving me a calm champion of the aurea mediocritas, and with a quantity of self-contentment that I am still puzzled about. The feeling that I simply *must* write my novel this year—it has to be done by my twenty-first birthday, you know—has strengthened my confidence, and even if I don't do much the change in attitude is quite satisfying. The worse my poetry became, the more my belief in myself as a prose writer grew, until now the only thing I have to worry about is this very feeling of confidence. I have looked over my prose, and find a certain vividness to it, not the vividness of rich colors, but the vividness rather of a sharp black triangle on a white glazed paper. I am coming to recognize that I don't have the true "lyric cry"—or better, I always recognized it and wouldn't admit it to myself—and now that I see myself as a professor instead of a poet perhaps I can turn out a scholarly commentary or two on life. I want to write a book called "Fallow Ground," for I have grown weary of calling myself intellectually amorphous, and have decided that everybody is always intellectually amorphous, and that even the Cromwells and the Napoleons and the Luthers didn't live in the environment which could offer them their full quota of spiritual development—ce qui est bien académique, n'est-ce pas?

Of course, you are seeing Paris at the wrong time, which is some compensation to me for your seeing it before me. I trust it will be thoroughly sane again when I get to the Sorbonne. (For I am really going there. Even my mother talks about it now. My dreadful destitution after you left must have impressed her with what a trip to Europe means to me.) Bourget,[2] in his "Outre-Mer," says that New York, and not Paris, is the true cosmopolis, because in New York they *have* to speak different languages, whereas in Paris languages other than French are spoken simply as a sort of high-grade snobbism; but that makes Paris the *intellectual* cosmopolis, it seems to me, and that is all we care about. However, the more I watch the progress of things over there, the more I question my faith in Europe. For after all, *has* Europe shown itself to possess a cosmopolis anywhere? The German intellectuals, whom we all thought dominated from the time of Louis XIV by a consistent policy of franzoselei, have become hopeless flag wavers and singers of "Die Wacht am Rhein," while Rolland[3] and Russell[4] are undergoing a most unheard-of martyrdom, persecution for plain good sense. Is that the stuff of which a cosmopolis is made? We in America are showing better spirit, for although the determination is silently growing to act very immoderately, we are constantly exhorting one another to think moderately. Doesn't that thrill you, M? We are internationalists over here, internationalists who are overbearingly proud of our nationality. Thank God it is Wilson, and not Roosevelt, who is president. Roosevelt could send us raging to the front; Wilson is too big a man for that. Roosevelt is merely a very characteristic Harvard man.

. . .

. . . I am becoming a philosopher. At present I am reading "Uber den Willen in der Natur" by Schopenhauer, and Bergson's "L'évolution créatrice." Bergson is hard as hell, but I think it must be easier for me, who am still unformed, to follow him than it would be for some hardened metaphysician of the old school, since he is so opposed to the traditional systems. I am very much pleased to find myself interested in such an aloof subject, although my disaffection for mathematics makes me feel sure there is something wrong somewhere. But I find that reading philosophy is a much better preparation for writing novels than reading novels is. And it lends more dignity to my beer.

. . .

As the fifth of June approaches—the day of registration for the draft, you know—rumors of disturbances are increasing. The Sangers are busy, and it seems that no small number of people have taken a vow to be shot rather than cede to the "Prussianizing of America." The movement is especially strong among the students, of course. Even the capitalistic press is printing news now of anti-conscription meetings and formal resolves not to register. And although they are trying their best to make it out as a German plot, I believe that the rebels are perfectly sincere. Many things are pointing that the aims of the Allies are not quite so much to "make the world safe for democracy" as the Ally leaders were talking about, things, I mean, which the general run of the people would take notice of—for of course, those who thought much about the war were pretty thoroughly disillusioned already. The refusal of the government to allow American socialists to take part in the Stockholm Congress got farther than the Völkszeitung by a damned sight, and the silence of England and France to Russia's insistence upon "peace without annexation and retribution" shows that neither England nor France is thinking of overthrowing their traditional policy on the land-grabbing question. I hope to God this war is over soon—else I may become quite rabid on these matters and all my pride of my nationality may avail me not at all.

May 31.

Damn me for a piker if I don't finish this letter today. I have been so slow that the war situation has been developing even while I was writing to you. Three Columbia students were arrested today, and the evening papers announce it in three-inch type. This may be of big importance, as you can see, for the most impregnable of all platitudes is that one about how movements thrive on persecution. Heretofore the masses weren't downtrodden enough. But now things are all pregnant. The legislature of practically every state has "temporarily" removed all the labor laws, there is talk of importing three million Chinks in the West—with you know what kind of acclaim on the part of the American worker—the mayor of Chicago refused to invite the French and English legations to his city, has denied municipal buildings to the federal conscription clerks, and created other stirs of a similar nature. The *Times* this morning printed a copy of an entire anti-conscription pamphlet, and this on the front page; it seems to me that if the papers were completely out of sympathy with the movement they would not do this sort of thing. And of course they are still aroused about the attempts Wilson has made to get a press-censorship bill through Congress. Even the *World* is kicking. But I doubt very much if anything will come of it. Anglo-Saxons have been on the whole so satisfactorily governed for so long that they have lost the tradition of rebellion. And Wilson talks so earnestly about our fight for democracy that people here will probably soon forget that to force a nation, nine-tenths of which does not want war, into a war which does not seem to it to be fought by people who want war is not the most logical kind of democracy. And then again, there are lots of people here who have decided that between the Allies and the Germans the Allies are the lesser of the two evils. So I suppose that two days after registration some murder will be in the headlines, and the latest Allied victory over three hundred miles of Von Hindenburg's line will be used for filler.

But the censor might object to this sort of thing. I shouldn't write you about it at all—except that I must find something in the way of information to give you . . .

K.

1. James Light.

2. Paul Bourget (1852–1935), French novelist.

3. Romaine Rolland (1866–1944), French writer and pacifist.

4. George Russell (AE) (1867–1935), the Irish poet and nationalist, had denounced the war.

T.M. C3
[Paris]
June 7, 1917
[NL]

Dear Ken:

After some five weeks over here, a letter from you is still not forthcoming. I shall just write to tell you am arrived very much in health.

I, as you know, am engaged in driving a five-ton truck instead of a Ford ambulance. I can't say I'm a blowing success at it. In fact, along with Cunningham,[1] I was held over for another section. But I will léarn eventually.

I had quite an unhappy time the first two weeks. You see, my section was largely composed of Andover boys just at the conceited age. In addition they were gossipy, malicious, and quarrelsome. My present section is made up mostly of Harvard and Yale men, and I think justifies Harvard and Yale. There is another section here made up of men from California, and a Yále man explained to me:

"I hate to say it because I come from California myself, but really those California University men are impossible. They just don't know anything."

A very funny thing to put in a letter when you are no doubt much more interested—or are you—in the war and the people here. I tell you one thing—the poilus here are remarkably jolly, and companionable. Also that it is mostly bullshit about the intellectuality of the average Frenchman. Also that in America we don't realize exactly what it means to be at war for three years. On the surface the French act as if they also were careless, but God, they are tired of fighting. No militarists over here. Everyone, of course, is determined to beat Germany first, but after that they want to end war for good. These wars of today are no longer the toy wars of the Middle Ages.

If you ever get to feeling really generous, send me over a magazine to read—*Poetry*, *The Little Review*, if it is still running, *The Seven Arts*, or something of the kind. Also the last issue of the *Sans Breeches*[2] if there was one.

And Göttes Willen, tell me how Jim is taking the war.

Mal

---

1. Robert Alexander Cunningham, a friend from Harvard who served with Cowley in the American Field Service.

2. Cowley is referring to *Sansculotte*, a literary magazine published by James Light, with the help of Burke, at Ohio State.

[Weehawken,
New Jersey]
June 11, [1917]
[PS]

Dear M.

The novel is actually begun, and it seems so incredible that I am afraid to say it to anyone. My whole life now is filled with it, while I eat, while I sleep, even while I read. And the plot, once I began to tend to it, now seems to be moving along by its own inertia, and is adjusting itself satisfactorily to my needs of autobiography. Remember once when I used to afflict you with my endless analyzings, how you told me to go on with them, and write, write, write, until I had sucked myself dry, and then begin writing civilized stuff? That is what I am going to do. I am going to use this first novel as Keats is said to have used his "Endymion," as a sort of purgative to clear his system for different things. I am going to allow myself wild freedom of self-expression, since one cannot be too exacting about his first child. And first children are always the most erratic anyhow. They seem to lay claim to all the faults of the parents, their only possible virtue being the very marked possession of those faults. And thanks to some radical change that has come over me in the last year, I no longer hate revision, but on the contrary take a certain fastidious delight in it. And really, I even have hope of publication, although I am trying resolutely to write simply for the satisfaction of writing. Also, your honest disapproval of those ceremoniously despairing letters I used to send to Belsano has had a wholesome effect on me, so that your common sense—you *do* show good common sense in your judgments of others, you know, in spite of your ridiculous way of managing yourself—coupled with my determination to be a Horace has taken the quiver out of me. I shall try to write with cruel precision, which will be thoroughly needed, since although the theme of the novel is not sex, I know that sex will manage somehow to color every page. Beyond the bare announcement that the name is to be "Fallow Ground" I dare not go, since I have too many instances of how I have taken the zest out of my plans by outlining them in letters. And in treating my characters' personalities as fallow ground I feel that I shall come nearer my conviction that character is kinetic rather than potential, possibility rather than manifestation, and at the same time I shall run a better chance of producing what I admire most, a study of development. It is a great problem to make a man change and yet keep him identified with the original man, and since it can be accomplished only by intuition I stake much on the outcome. For genius is intuition, whereas talent is calculation, and I have always said that I had no intuition. I feel that my success or failure in this case will be fatal, by which I mean, of course, success or failure not according to the standards of publicity but according to the standards which I think will indicate my own intellectual capacities. My failure at poetry has thrown me heart and soul over to a reliance on prose; if I fail to satisfy myself in prose, then it is poison for me, or worse, a job in my dad's office . . .

• • •

June 16, [1917]

. . . I develop a different personality when I write, and I like to say things caustically which I actually sympathize with in reality. And on the other hand, when writing one learns to take sides on certain questions which were formerly disagreeable dilemmas. But at any rate, a few sheets of white paper are dirtied, and the very fact that they *are* dirtied gives me the almost mysterious ability of sitting down with my mind a weary blank and gradually becoming excited and voluble. And my style has become so personal as to have the appearance of being done by a foreigner. Can you imagine a man who knows nothing of the traditional set phrases of a language and yet possesses the language? That is what I strike myself as being. My almost exclusive reading in French and German, coupled with an incurable loquacity in English, has produced a queer sort of honest euphuism; I am anxious to have you read a chapter or two and pass judgment on it, although I feel beforehand that you will not approve of the style.

• • •

June 20, [1917]

. . . Nearly everybody has left Weehawken, and consequently I am almost wild for some exercise. Indeed, this living alone, with nothing but books and an irritating plot for a novel, is getting on my nerves already, although I have had only a couple of weeks of it. For the last year I have been a model of sweetness around the house, but now I am becoming grouchy again, and things bother me which ought to amuse me. That will be very disastrous to my career as a Horace, and might even take the present good nature out of my novel, although one's writing personality is more consistent than one's actual personality, I guess. Also, the weather here is hot and sultry, the kind of weather which makes some people commit suicide, but which simply makes me sleepy . . .

• • •

June 28, [1917]

Thanks to the delay in receiving a letter from you, and thanks to my ruthless silence in answering that delay, the same letter that heralds the beginning of my novel can also serve to herald its spectacular collapse . . . What pleases me most about my failure is that for all the youthfulness of my style there is a certain—I know you will be surprised by the virtue I claim—a certain good taste about my conceptions. This is brought out best by a comparison with Dreiser, who is the undisputed master of bad taste. For instance, when Dreiser wants to make a liaison, it is the simplest thing in the world. A man and woman meet, forthwith feel a great physical need of each other, and if there isn't a bed handy use the bathroom . . . The thought that my conceptions are so much truer than those of even big novelists makes me not the least bit humiliated by my failure . . .

I wanted to write a book about what happens when we come to a show-down. My egotist, the Carter who appears in the fragments I quoted, sick of the assiduous cultivation of himself, helpless, hopeless, at the very height of his self-disgust meets the idealist, grandiose, with a record of imprisonments. It is the egotist, of course, who rises to self-sacrifice when it comes to the showdown, and dies for the principles which the disillusioned idealist has abandoned. I have a love of such mild paradox, as for example, the little tale I wrote not long ago of the hopeless man who is too futile even to kill himself, whose life is on one dead level, but who finally does kill himself in a moment of elation and promise. It is essential to my existence, you see, that I believe in such paradoxes, for otherwise how could I stand this boxed-up professorial life I am dragging. It is my organic faith in things like that place in Bleibtreu[1] I used to quote you, the "Was du verlorst, nur das ist ewig dein," which makes me almost contented with my "continentia," my "sòphrosyne," to use academic words thoroughly in keeping with my present mode of living. To write novels, one must be careful not to live them; for it is the ruthless denial of action which fosters that feeling of incompleteness in us which makes us turn to art. People who do things blunt their sense of the need for expression; people who don't do things are invariably thrown into a state of agitation which is not healthy, but is productive. Art, of course, increases rather than lulls this dissatisfaction, but who, after all, would prefer satisfaction to art? Allow me to arraign alongside of little Kenney Nietzsche's statement that he lived not for happiness, but for his work. I, too, can assume as much genius as that bond of sympathy between him and me is good for.

· · ·

. . . You ask for some magazines. How in the name of God you have the audacity to make such a request when there are so many French novels within striking distance I can't imagine, but anyhow I shall send you some. Get Prévost's collections of short stories if you don't care to concentrate for long; they are easy French and very French. And eat lots of lettuce, for in my wanderings among classic lore I have discovered that lettuce is an aphrodisiac. But, in an aside, I hope it works more effectively on you than it did on me.

K. B.

1. Karl Bleibtrau (1859–1928), German novelist.

T.M.V. 527,
Convois Automobiles
par B.C.M. Paris
June 26, [1917]

Dear Ken:

Me voici still in camp and destined to stay here for some months more. I read by the official communiqués that there is pretty violent fighting just north of us—German counterattacks, etc. And so, although we are loafing just now, there is work in store.

Bob [Cunningham] is to be chauffeur for one of the staff cars at the training camp. I could not be with him, and so I have no excuse to quit this service. And anyway I am almost satisfied. Man, I was in for it at first. I was perhaps the poorest driver in camp, and everybody came to regard me as a general nincompoop. But a little judicious profanity and a great *deal* of silence, and above all [indecipherable] have worked very well together.

As for cultivation of the region above the eyes, I have a splendid anthology of French verse from 1866 to 1888. There are Rimbaud, Verlaine, bawdy Baudelaire, all of whom I accept at the current estimate and don't think much about. There is also a certain Leon Valode whom I like very well indeed. Catulle Mendès,[1] the same.

Apart from the French, I have read about half of that well known bastard piece of Dostoevsky's. I thought it quite insane at first, but after three hundred pages I begin to discern the chaos becoming vertebrate. A novel by W. L. George—*The Strangers Wedding*, I liked, and also Bennett's *These Twain*. In addition I was flattered to find that I could not swallow the author's potboiler, *Buried Alive*.[2] I think the difference between us two crystallizes about Dostoevsky, however. In the quarrel between the latter and Turgenev we should have taken different sides. But don't forget. Our differences, great as they are, are really insignificant compared with our similarities. I never realized that poignantly until I was left alone with fifteen jeering puppies from Andover. I think in a way we sometimes came as near to perfect frankness as one can get. You rather spoiled me for making friends. Since I left Pittsburgh, Bob [Cunningham] is the nearest to a real friend I have had. Before that I could point to Ally Crawford, Doss Paul, Ed Glenn, Jake, Jim, and at one time Joe Monteverde. I was best friend to all those people—not at once, but at various tangent points in our respective orbits.

I wonder if this is the kind of letter you always tear up. I should too, except that I am quite light-hearted this afternoon, and willing to humiliate myself a little by confession, and satisfy myself later with a boast as to the past.

You wonder no doubt how near we get to action. Twenty-seven hundred yards. In other words, our farthest north is the third-line trenches. But considering that shells carry some twenty-four miles the third-line trenches are quite far enough. We take to dugouts occasionally, but Lord! there's not a chance of anyone's getting killed. Of course we all hope to get slightly wounded so that we can receive the Croix de Guerre, but no one has the slightest hopes of the Croix de Bois which is the weed of damned fools in any other arm of the service.

We have a wonderful opportunity here to learn the language (which sounds like a prospectus). Some of us are even trying to learn it. Even the dullest soak in a little, and one can hear ribald Chicagoans wandering about camp shouting at every opportunity.

"C'est beau ça. N'importe. C'est la guerre."

Moi aussi have studied a little. I am now perhaps as fluent as you were last summer. The lack of further progress is due to ignorance of Esperanto, Greek, and applied perversion, I am quite sure. Otherwise I should have to lay it to my own stupidity. But tiens! nous verrons. Now at last I know merdre, cocu, con, ordure, foutu, grand morceau de cul de cheval, and a few such expressions which your nasty mind had acquired il y a une année. I talked crops, forest fires, and express trains with a camion driver this afternoon for two hours.

For God's sake, write oftener.

Mal

1. Catulle Mendès (1842–1909), French playwright, novelist, and poet. He was associated with Les Parnassiens, a group of poets whose positivist and scientific inclinations were a response to Romanticism.

2. *Buried Alive: A Tale of These Days*, by Arnold Bennett, was published in 1908.

American Field Service in France,
Section-Groupe Américaine,
TM526, Peleton B,
Par BLM, Paris
July 4, [1917]
[NL]

Dear Ken:

I received a second letter from you today, and will reply to it—one can take reply in its argumentative meaning—immediately.

Since it suits you and Jim to take my trip merely as a holiday, please do so. (This is the sentence indicating great defiance.) And (this is the hissed *aside*) you won't be more than a hundred miles from the truth. Of course when I started I was in the midst of a little throe of militarism. But since I'm over here, I find that as a camioniste I'm just as much of a slacker as Jim. The only difference is that I'm in a country new to me, doing work not very uncongenial—you know I always did like big lumbering things like camions, having my daily routine very faintly spiced with adventure, and above all seeing the events that are going to dominate the history of the world for the next century . . .

All this, I suppose, is pretty catty, and I hope Jim takes it the right way. I should like to see him come over here. I think he would agree that truck driving behind the lines has munition making beaten to a low pair. And you—I think you could write your novel about the world as it was very well indeed under the roar of the cannon that are destroying all the old order of things. For all we Americans realize too little that at the end of the war every nation—yes, even the Unites States—will be too exhausted in men and money, too much in need of quick recuperation, to go on with the old happy-go-lucky state of affairs. We Americans are fighting for personal liberty, and yet after the fighting is over, out of sheer need of efficiency, we shall have to forego it. And if the Germans win—oh gawd. In the captured portions of France, they are making even the little children work in the fields from five in the morning until seven at night. Imagine a regime like that for the world.

You asked for poetry about Paris. I gather that you are more anxious for dope on Paris. Well, in the first place, although whores are thick on the rue de Montmartre, they are much thicker around the place de l'Opera, Café de la Paix, boulevard des Italiens, etc. The great street for sporting houses is the rue St. Augustine.

The secondhand book shops along the Seine are there just as described. But the Seine itself is in size something like the Youghiogheny.[1] Yet there is a great charm about all French rivers. They are all so swift, silent, and deep.

As for French women, as a rule they are much less pretty than American girls. But there is a certain class in Paris—the midinettes—who can dress according to the advertisements. You would be disappointed, however, in their shoes, which are horrible.

· · ·

Today is July Fourth, and we have twenty-four hours' leave. The amusements are of all sorts—tilting at a water bucket, egg and spoon races, Arab dances by some Tunisians stationed nearby, Arab music—unearthly stuff—fencing, baseball, a banquet, and champagne—beaucoup, beaucoup. Champagne, by the way, has gone up in price since the war and is now from three francs to eight francs fifty the bottle at our canteen. We drink a great deal of it. Of pinard we get a daily ration—a demi-litre. All this talk about temperance at the front—balls. Aviators are drunk half the time, and troops on repos make it a point to consume as much pinard as they can the first throw—all very far from talk about our fourth of July.

· · ·

Since we pay no postage, I shall write you another letter instead of finishing this one. About books, I have discovered a splendid anthology of contemporary French poetry in three volumes (Librairie Delagrave). I intend to buy one set for you and one for myself. The Rosny I shall try to get on my leave, which occurs some time in August.

Yes, I am staying with the camion service. I could not get with Bob. Perhaps it is just as well.

Another mélange in a couple of days.

M.

1. The Youghiogheny is a river in Pennsylvania.

[Weehawken,
New Jersey]
July 20, 1917
[PS]

Dear M.,

Your letter of the twenty-sixth. It was opened by the censor, but evidently owing to the lack of French Anthony Comstocks[1] was allowed to come through unharmed. However, perhaps the censorship explains why you complain to me that I don't write often enough. God's peety, man, I thought I had glutted you with letters, and here you are yammering. Hereafter I shall take no chances with the censor—assuming that it is the censor who is ruining my reputation—but shall confine myself to things completely non-political. But in a way that will be hard to do, for there are some very vexing things going on over here, judged with the standards of a half-socialist like myself, and I should like very much to tell you about them. God knows, I never made much of a fetich of the Constitution, but it is rather disconcerting between beers to watch how the Constitution is allowed to go hang. Common sense is at a great premium over here, and the newspapers are conspiring to eradicate it completely. The trouble is not with the people; the people are acting admirably, and one can spread out a German newspaper before him in the subway without even being stared at. But a paper like the *Sun* is simply unbearable, and one cannot glance at its editorial page without becoming apoplectic. I think that the press has about reached the height of its influence, so that even now the only way it can really move people is by manipulation of its news items. But it has long ago ceased to be the mouthpiece of the people; and has gone too far in its attempt to guide them.

From the account of your reading you have been doing much more than I . . . I am going through no phases, I am having no spiritual upheavals—unless you consider the threat of more pimples—I am writing nothing. Good God, I shall be damned glad when we both get out of college; perhaps you and Jim and I can find ways to combat such dull periods, and renew the triumvirate . . . And often while I am sitting out here in my hideous room, patiently digging some smut out of Agathias Scholasticus[2] with the aid of a lexicon, two grammars, and an imagination, I begin to believe that we really can do something together. The apartment house behind us is full of artists, and I have been studying them to see if they are happy. They evidently are, since they have developed a society, a circle. They are all mediocre, as we are, and they have annihilated the pain by social intercourse. Maybe after we are out of school we can strike up the old note, and be something like the same joyous little fools we used to be. Jim says he is tired of salvation by faith alone; but I am sure that it is the only possible kind of salvation there is.

Your remarks about Dostoevsky and Turgenev got me to thinking. You said that we should take different sides, by which you naturally meant that you would have been for Turgenev, I for Dostoevsky. Undoubtedly, if I had to settle the matter by a "yes" or "no" I should say you are right, but my preference for Dostoevsky needs qualification. After all, if I condemn Turgenev, it is because he had one dominating quality which he evidently hated in himself, and which has disgusted me in mine. That quality is the quality of artist. But you are surprised, n'est-ce pas? to find me calling myself an artist; perhaps I had better use the phrase "artistic attitude." What I mean is that Turgenev, like me, was unable to forget himself; he lacked that magnificent capacity of striving to move the world, the social sense.

Nowhere, perhaps, is this more evident than in *Virgin Soil*, where the hero becomes bitter and ashamed because he cannot really enter into revolution, and lose his identity as a mere atom in the mass. He is in spite of himself a spectator, an ego. But Dostoevsky, with all his mania for being insulted, with all his Strindberg-like paranoia, was honestly one of the people. Dostoevsky writes from a feeling of vivid poignancy, Turgenev from that horrid subdued curiosity of the ego, of the plot hunter. After all, as I see it now, every chapter of my own still-born "Fallow Ground" is a chapter out of *Virgin Soil*, while but one slight episode is after the manner of "Letters from the Underworld,"[3] my first glimpse at great literature. Turgenev, it seems to me, is only so much bigger than I as a man who has produced is bigger than a sterile man, whereas if I wrote everything I want to write, everything that I have imagined, I should still be prostrate before that seething-brained madman, Dostoevsky. It is simply inconceivable to me how I could even write after his manner, although I find that he touches me at almost every point. And yet, look how the two have affected me: Although I always read Dostoevsky with as near an approach to reverence as my stenchy temperament is capable of, and although I read *Virgin Soil* at a time when I was very little interested in the hero, yet I have only an indefinite impression of touch after touch when I think of Dostoevsky, whereas *Virgin Soil* dominates me. Dostoevsky has paid for the richness of his inspiration by the fact that he overwhelms his readers and leaves them with nothing but the rumbling echoes of the book they have read. But Turgenev, being an artist, has only begun the effect of his book when he writes the last word. You remember, it is what Wilkinson said in justification of his preference for de Maupassant.

·   ·   ·

July 23, [1917]

Tonight I am very sleepy, and therefore am entitled to continue in the abominable fashion this letter was begun. Last night being Sunday, I went out with Josephson,[4] and we argued novels until one o'clock. This conversation, by the way, was held under the auspices of Washington Square, which may explain why we were so pleased with it. Or perhaps it was the copious imbibing of Knickerbocker, and the sweet contentment of our pipes. But poor Josephson is beyond a doubt honestly wrapped up in his letters, and the remark he applied to me, that my aesthetic theories are not mere theses, but part of my flesh and blood, could apply as thoroughly to him. Josephson is very naive, frightfully naive, at times even as naive as you, and yet like you he exhibits the paradox of glorifying in subtleties. Now, as he explains it, these subtleties that we toy with in heated discussions until the wee hours are not in themselves admirable—we don't yearn in self-astonishment for a dictograph—but when dilly-dallied back and forth by two men who enjoy them they produce intellectual orgasms that are very delicious. If you haven't been isolated too long there among the Andover puppies you will appreciate the aptness of the figure, for there is a certain response between the cerebralizations of impersonal egotists which can only be compared to "coming," as the word goes in New York slang. We are really not self-intoxicated; there is an honest attempt to get at something; and often we do get at it, so that henceforth a word springs into usage between him and me which has connotations that other people do not suspect. You can doubtless remember how the same phenomenon occurred when you and I lived in Pittsburgh . . .

· · ·

When is your time up over there, and when do you intend to be back in America? And when it is up do you intend to reenlist? My fear of the censor forbids me to essay any opinions about these matters, since the thought that one of these massive volumes may be cruelly destroyed simply because of a few indiscreet lines is very unpleasant. I hope to Christ this silly war soon ends before all the world is dead or insane, for it seems inevitable that the final peace settlement will contain nothing more than the compromise that might be possible now. Of course, there is still much grandiose pother from Berlin about annexations, but the annexationists are a small party, and even the government is continually insisting that Germany is fighting a defensive war.

[K. B.]

1. Anthony Comstock (1844–1915), American moral crusader who advocated the suppression of obscene materials. He wrote the New York State statute outlawing immoral works (1868), and founded the New York Society for the Suppression of Vice.

2. Agathias Scholasticus was a scholar, lawyer, and poet in Constantinople. He compiled a seven-book edition of poetic epigrams entitled *Circle*, and an anthology of Greek poetry.

3. Dostoevsky's novel, usually published in translation as *Notes from the Underground*.

4. Matthew Josephson (1899–1978), who became a lifelong friend of both Burke and Cowley.

Section-Groupe Américaine,
TM 526 Peloton B
July 31, 1917
[NL]

Dear K.

The Section is drilling today, but thank God I have a bad cold and am lying in bed instead. Last night I had my first accident for a month. Imagine the convoy stopped on a hill. I draw up, slip the clutch, set the brakes. The car slows up; half decides to stop; changes its mind; slips . . . slips . . . I jerk harder on the emergency, with a strange feeling of helplessness . . . slip . . . slip . . . Crash![1] Of course I get the blame.

I should leave on permission tomorrow, but the last permissionaires are not back yet, and there is some doubt. This damned cold! Last night I lay awake thinking of pneumonia. There are so many brave dreams I have spun in the last few weeks, and so many chances of dying heroically, or at least seemingly, that the thought of pneumonia makes me tremble.

I thank God constantly that I have crossed the water. Not that my soul has been transformed with wonder, but just that I have been drawn out of my fixed orbit. Now I have the desire to wander, and think of Russia and Spain, and American lumber camps and wheat fields. There are so many sides of life which no one can afford to miss. Paris is one, and a dose of horrible, hectic Greenwich Village is another, and Chicago yet another.

At present, too, everyone should serve his time on the Western Front. That is the great common experience of the young manhood of today, an experience that will mold the thought of the next generation, and without which one will be somewhat of a stranger to the world of the present and the future. That is the real reason I should advise you to get over here.

No doubt you want to know the effect of the war on France. Downes—a very drunken aesthete who has been here often—says that the France of today is discouraging. There is not much intellectual life remaining. What there is seems to have accepted the war as the normal state of things, as you will gather from the stories I am sending you. All love stories are a result of permissions, or of letters from marraine to filleul. Plays take the war for granted. Everyone longs for peace, but it seems so distant a possibility that no one dares to make it the condition, the background, of any literature. The most successful art exhibit recently was "Les Humanistes et la guerre."

I thought of writing you once that France as an average is no more intellectual than the United States. "La Revue le Deux Mondes" costs *three francs*, and is not on sale everywhere. The other magazines are often childish; many of the people remind one strongly of our own familiar ditch-diggers, the Sicilians. But on the other hand, a little reading of French poetry reveals a difference. Just as a matter of statistics, the Librairie Delagrave compiled an anthology of poetry from 1866 to 1914. None of the contents were bad; some, of course, were unsurpassed in English. The collection amounted to 2,200 pages of fine print. As I said, just as a matter of statistics, could that be duplicated in England, or in America, or in both?

Again there is the matter of artistic innovation. As one reads from Baudelaire to Mallarmé, one gets the origin of all English verse movements, averaging ten to twenty years later. A lecture of Amy Lowell's on Vers

Libre and the strophe—I saw where she stole it; from an exercise for his own methods written by Gustave Kahn in 1897.

Of course art movements would show an even more startling sameness in their origins, but of these I know little.

Yet I ask you for American magazines. Somehow I am not French, for all my intellectual admiration. I should like to be French before I come home—temporarily, of course. I think of living in a garret in Montmartre and of enlisting in the French artillery. But that is not yet. Meanwhile, remember that I am writing you frequently even if you don't get all my letters; that I have received all your letters up to June 28 (3), and that I am anxious for more.

M.

1. Cowley's ellipses.

[Weehawken,
New Jersey]
September 17, [1917]
[PS]

[Dear M.]

I am writing you this page in high glee, for I have just finished another story, "A Man of Fore-thought." Saturday morning I wrote a sorry attempt at smart-setism called "When the Gods Laugh," and a tour de force in the style I should like to continue, called "The Laying Down of Lives" . . .

But I admit that I am indulging in theoretical considerations of the short story, although happily I can disregard them when I begin to write. But I am not satisfied that the American form is the better. The American method at its best is to tell a story which prepares for a certain solution. This logical solution is given, and then is followed by one sharp swift stroke which comes as a surprise, but is an integral part of the story, and throws a new light on the whole thing . . . On the other hand, the typical French type, I suppose, is that one of de Maupassant's of the man who had a little dog that he loved. But he would have to pay something like seven francs to legalize his possession of the dog, and though he had the money he didn't like to part with it, and consequently, sad as he was, he had to let the dog be taken to the pound. The American story gives you a jolt that you don't forget, but the French story buries itself in you imperceptibly, and then goes quietly on eating away. Of course, the American form seems a bigger technical triumph, but I imagine it would be very easy to reduce the pro-ducing of it to a mere formula, so that to get a thrill one could merely contrive each time to leave some important part of his story unsaid, and then drive it home at the last with one mighty twist . . . Eventually I think the French type will be accepted in America, since it is less journalistic and more expressive. It has a certain quiet insistence about it that makes our little final jingle seem vulgar. And it is because "The Laying Down of Lives" is of the French type that I like it best. But I must look through Poe again, since I am not sure whether the difference between him and de Maupassant is as great as that between Burt[1] and de Maupassant.

· · ·

September 18, [1917]

. . . Yesterday afternoon and evening were spent with Josephson. In our capacity of super-intellectuals we supped at Child's. We roamed about aimlessly enough from Columbia down to the German library in the bowels of Second Avenue, and then had a war argument that entertained the city for blocks around . . . We are both socialists more or less, and as such he could make me admit that every shot an obedient American soldier shot was a shot into his own heart. He could make me admit that a campaign of systematic kriegshetzerei carried on by the capitalistic press had done man vicious things. I had to admit that more than ever more American capital and American labor are aching to be at each others' throats. But yet I claimed that it was better for the American proletariat to win the war than to back down and sue for an undecisive peace. For the point of the American pacifists, I will say that for them, is not to create sedition in America. They simply claim that the present attitude of the Allies makes it impossible for Germany to suggest peace, and is forcing them into even more deliberate avowals of pan-Germanism, with the counter-result that the Allies themselves immediately screw up their own avowals. This method, of course, will mean that peace can be obtained only by a decisive victory. Now the method of decisive victory, Josephson claims along with all the socialists, is not the way that is best for the masses. I, on the other hand, claimed that the socialists who were complaining were shortsighted. They had heavy German minds. They knew that war was a weapon against the proletariat, and therefore they must object to war. But they failed to realize whereas American capital is their enemy, both they and American capital have a common enemy, Prussianism. They must unite, kill their common enemy, and then resume their contest to kill each other . . . The argument wafted off in a turmoil of tremendous shouting, and in conciliatory tranquility we finished up our last five minutes together with a gentle agreement that the war was going to change the color of the Socialist Party; that henceforth it would have more students like ourselves, men who before the war would shout over a poem, but who didn't know the president's first name; that he and I ought to work for its intellectualization.

This, by the way, is my last week of freedom. Next week I retire again to my cloister, and shall try to dismiss all current topics until next May, when I shall be twenty-one. By then, fortunately, the war will be over, so that I may never know whether I am a coward or not . . . I had intended to flourish into literature up at school this year, but I have been told that the Columbia publications are exclusively frat affairs—which explains, by the way, why they are so damned miserable. In that case I can continue on in the same disdainful obscurity that I lived in last year, with the one heaven-sent difference that I know now where the people are I want to meet, and can meet them if I want. Perhaps, had I cultivated Bob's friend, I should be circulating in more standard circles, but I have a peculiar passion for human beings that keeps me from approaching those walled-up cenotaphs. I leave that to you in your capacity of a greasy-nosed gentleman. But the page, praise God, is ended.

[K.]

1. Maxwell Struthers Burt (1882–1954), American writer best known for his poems and stories.

Section-Groupe Américaine,
TM526 Peloton B
October 9, 1917
[NL]

Dear K:

I shall try to write you a letter this evening; a hard job with a crowd at the end of the barracks . . .

. . . Section 133 went up to a little advanced park some 300 meters from the lines, and underwent a severe bombardment, during the course of which one man had his hand shot off, and another was wounded in the body and the leg. A French ambulance section refused to bring back the wounded on account of the shelling, so the section chief got them in his Torok. For this, the first deed approaching heroism in the service, there was a meeting. Also a couple of our French captains received the Legion of Honor . . .

Your letter of the 14–20 September reached me last night. You complained of my indifference to your mental states. It's just part of my indifference to everything. You can't imagine with what a feeling of absolute negation I play cards . . . But I have climbed a little out of the depths. For those weeks I read nothing, wrote not even letters, confined myself, in fact, exclusively to eating, sleeping, rolling, and seven and a half.

In your letter you also asked for local color. I can give you that, and plenty. Zum beispiel, we leave camp at four o'clock on a rainy, windy afternoon, and go to the immense park to have our camions loaded. The bearings are loose on the fan, and the steering gear doesn't work well, but then it is much too cold to leave the seat, so we smoke cigarettes and wonder what is going to happen in the night. The trip is for O—another of the depots avancés—some 1,500 meters from the lines.

That night we left the park at six. One of the other camions broke down after a two-kilometer ride, and that caused us a two-hour wait. When we finally climbed the hill above Veste, the night was so black that I was reminded of G. A. Henty[1] and the mythical nights through which his trappers and Indians used to crawl toward Fort George and Fort William. I rode on the dashboard and called out whenever Root ran too near the ditch. Once I didn't call out in time, but we crawled out on first.

After that I had a great poetic emotion and lines kept running through my head like

> "The jolly star shells rioted"

> and

> "And in the valley a river of mist"

> or

> "While a cold cynical moon looked down"

The cold cynical moon actually crept in at just that point, for in the battle of the cold wind and the cold rain, the cold wind proved the stronger.

How conventionalized the night seems now to me, after reading thousands of war diaries. At S occurred the conventional road shelling, during the course of which Root, who is scary, ran a zigzag down the road, and bumped into the next camion. At our destination we encountered the conventional Franco-American who knew Root's friends in Hartford, Connecticut. We drove home past the conventional mule convoys. The only fresh note about it all, I think, was the barracks when we got home. From the outside these are plain wooden buildings, but inside at night, their shadowy length makes them as mysterious as ancient caves. Side by side a dozen lives—individual lives—go on. Some sleep, some sing, some read, some play cards. After five months of such life, they all become at home in it, so that the requests to shut up or to shade a candle are merely perfunctory. In a way everyone has become a stoic, believing that no one else can harm him. And that night at two as we came in exhausted to drop into bed, one man was just getting up to go on guard while those others were still playing cards.

M.

1. George Alfred Henty (1832–1902), English author who wrote very popular boys' adventure stories.

Royal Palace Hotel
[Paris]
October 29, 1917
[NL]

Dear K.—

My letters to you for the past two months have been, as you realized, masterpieces of futility. Things will change, however. I have things to talk about.

There *was* the offensive for one thing. For two months we had been expecting it. Toward the last the Aisne Front was clogged with batteries—all sizes. Then finally they opened up. Fifteen days and nights we had our ears battered and our sleep disturbed . . . Then one evening the relics and the prisoners came drifting back. The latter had strange stories. They had spent five days without food under a barrage [of] fire. At first they were trading gold watches and field glasses for loaves of bread.

Right in the middle of all this my time of service closed, and with a dozen others I packed up and came to Paris. Here I am now in the University Union, where my chief complaint is that to ring the bell for my breakfast I have to get up out of bed. Also the very pretty waitress doesn't know enough to throw open the curtains when she serves the chocolate. I am afraid, too, that she is virtuous.

In a way the decision of the next week will be very important in my life. If I should go into aviation, I should really be making a sacrifice, for even if I came out alive I feel I should be out of place at the end of the war. If I should go to Italy, I think that would start me on a career of roving. Finally, though, if I return to college for a half year I may find the old life again—and the old life a little broadened. This, I think, is what I shall do.

There is no use writing me, at any rate, until you hear more from me.

Mal.

[Weehawken,
New Jersey]
January 6, 1918
[PS]

Dear M,

. . . I hope you come to New York soon, for I am quitting Columbia. A long story, and one which I can best tell with interruptions from you. But the essential fact is that I am going in a new direction. Suddenly becoming horrified at the realization of what college can do to a man of promise, I went to my father and told him I wanted to quit. He suggested that I get advice. I turned to Wilkinson as the only capable man I know. His answer is a solution that wouldn't go in a book: at my age he met the same problem as I am meeting, and he never regretted having done as I want to do. Damn! Huh?

I shall get a room in New York and begin my existence as a Flaubert. Flaubert is to be my Talmud, my Homer, my beacon, my terrible [ten?]. Already I have begun going through his letters. They range from his ninth year to his fifties; name of god, how they illustrate the growth of the human heart. I am going to nourish myself with *Madame Bovary*, learn how every character is brought in, tabulate every incident. I am sure there is a triumph in every sentence of Flaubert; and I am going to find it. Flaubert and Balzac—add a bit of bread and water and we have banquet enough to get gouty over. I am willing to admit, along with the Roosevelts and the John Dos, that France is a magnificent country, but that is only because Balzac and Flaubert were Frenchmen. I fear learning German; thank god there is Thoman Mann, and Huch,[1] and once in a while Liliencron.

. . . I don't want to be a virtuoso; I want to be a—a—oh hell, why not? I want to be a—yes—a genius. I want to learn to work, to work like a Sisyphus—that is my only chance. I am afraid, I confess it, but I am going to try hard. This is my final showdown. I am in it for life and death this time. Words, words—mountains of words—If I can do that I am saved. School is killing us, M.; I am astounded that *I* should be the one to give it up first. *You* are the usual pioneer in things of this sort; you know how I envied you your rushing off to France. (Almost as much, in fact, as I should despise you if you did it again.) It is in the air evidently, for now *I* am rushing off to France. You say that we here at home didn't feel the war; yet I in the last couple of days have felt like a Kaiser, a Kaiser in 1914.

I am planning another novel. This time it is to be an analysis of the gradual process of vulgarization which a girl goes through between, say, the ages of seventeen and twenty. No girl is vulgar at seventeen, M. There are so many problems just beginning then, so much *inexperience*, and inexperience is never vulgar. New religions are always marvelous things, just as newly-coveted arms must be. But if inexperience is the antithesis of vulgarity, habitude is vulgarity itself. One is delicate so long as he has problems, so long as he is weighing things that are of no value, so long as he is in danger of dying for an idea. I want to trace simply the metamorphozing of these problems, the sort of thing a girl thinks at seventeen, her gradual and terrible compromise with life, her final arrival at a level where there is nothing but flatness, flatness, and then flatness. At the end of the book, however, I shall relent. When the musician poisons her, and she knows she is poisoned, a look of inspired terror comes over her; for here is a new life, even if it be but death. She is fine again, and he recognizes it. "If I were a painter," he tells her bitterly, "this is the first time I should come to paint you." But more when you get here. And I promise you, if you are not interested in my plans, I shall have the sad satisfaction of being assured of what I suspect . . . But you—back you will go to professional Harvard shitasses, intellectual corsets, a squib a month in the "Advocate," and a spew a week in the "Woodcock." It is unwarrantedly audacious of you, the way you are bored . . . You are pretty near old enough now to realize with Donnay[2] that the least one can do is be too bored to be bored. "The will to homelessness," I put it on that postal card; didn't you blush to read that? It is such a démodé attitude, you know, without the romantic tenderness of antimacassars or wax flowers, and without their tender romance.

And then again, I am going to make a contest with you. It is that you *answer* my letters. So far I have been like a pipe flowing into the ocean; a good simile except in so far as it makes you the ocean. I pour out, pour out, and after that, pour out, but nothing comes back. It is not exciting enough that way; I might as well write letters to myself, like one of my heroes. The letters of Flaubert have made me livid with resentment at you people; he had so many friends to whom he could talk shop. But I—I wrote Farrell one modest little paragraph about *Pervigilium Veneris*[3] and I know he will smile at Burke the pedant. That from a Latin scholar. I feel all alone; Flaubert must have been so happy. From the age of nine until the day of his death he mustn't have written a dozen letters without a discussion of his work, and from the wording of his correspondence he was evidently answering answers, which must make life worth living. You say you are bored; looking back on my own remote past I suggest that the thing for you to do is what I did, quit school and take a solitary room in New York. If only we could get together again! Another dream of Flaubert, the only difference being that he writes his in a letter from Egypt, I from Weehawken, and that his group was to be in Paris, mine anywhere except Washington Square and environs.

I shall be comparatively free when you come, since I am not going to bother preparing for the final exams; indeed, I shall not take them. It will be one more bridge burned behind me; seven bridges, in fact, since two weeks' work now means four months' work. No, school is over; from now on begins my academic career, the time has come for study.

But I must go to bed. A bientôt, mon ami. Je t'embrasse sur les grosses songes jous. Le tien pour le génie.

K. B.

1. Ricarda Huch (1864–1947), German novelist, poet, and historian.

2. Maurice Donnay (1859–1945), French playwright.

3. *Pervigilium Veneris* is an anonymous poem of the second or third century that celebrates the power of Venus.

219 Wallace Building,
Pittsburgh, PA
January 13, [1918]
[NL]

Dear K:

If everything breaks right, I shall be in New York Monday evening about 7:30. I shall have to trouble your hospitality for one night. I should like to talk to your father about the job. I could live on two per, and I hate hunting positions. However if work is not hard to get I may not trouble him. I could take his advice.

．　　．　　．

If you really are going to get a room, I should like to go with you. "Two can live as cheaply as one" etc. etc. I think you quite an ass to flunk your midyears. Otherwise I admire you utterly. Aber woher kommt das geld? Il faut beaucoup d'argent quand on vit seul, n'est-ce pas? One of my chief ambitions, however, has always been to starve in a garret for my Art. I should if I had enough faith in it. If you actually carry out your plan, you will succeed in touching the imagination, something you have never done before.

You asked me for *answers* to your letters; some real discussion of what you tell me. I . . . I . . . I . . . I . . . I . . . you write and I . . . I . . . I . . . I . . . I . . . I write,[1] and you, being the first to declare your genius, are the first to berate the other for not being a disciple. What's the use? Our friendship has usually consisted in our interchangeability as audience and performer. Now you ask the boon of being sole performer, and of allowing me to play audience continually. As far as I am able, I shall grant the said request. For one reason, in granting it I assume to myself the superiority that every benefactor feels. For another, you happen to be the interesting one of the two just now. Personally I confess to being a bit drab and discouraged. Therefore by all means let us discuss you.

But if the spirit is willing the flesh is weak. Farrell and I exchanged your two letters and discussed them until now I feel a little tired.

There is one defect in your plans. The one profession people of your temperament usually assume—if there are any of them—is teaching. Your one sure income would be the result of a Ph.D. I often wonder if you are not more student than creator. I often wonder if I am not, and I confess to being less of a student than you. Therefore I should certainly never throw away the tangible proofs of a semester's hard work, even to read Flaubert's letters. Anyway Flaubert's letters aren't as, can't be as, interesting as the monologues of M. Lucien Bérgeret[2] or l'Abbé Jerome Coignard.[3] And someday you might want to go back to instructing graduate students as to where to find the point in the modern French novel and as to when Liliencron equals Thomas Mann.

To revert brazenly to the pronoun of the first person, I ran through my opus totum this afternoon. By reason of half a dozen war poems I have written here, the count has mounted to thirty-nine. The whole series shows a procession formatically toward and away from the sonnet. I am always form conscious. Even the last two or three things I have done in vers libre are as organic as a sestina. Yet always I am striving to be unorthodox. I think however that my tendency toward organization and regularity is more fundamental than my heterodoxy. And even this latter is only formatic, and hardly ever extends to the substance of what I write. But I am getting dull and involved as an editorial in the *Times*!

. . .[1]

I wrote a story in the *Gazette* for which I should receive $10 or so.[4] I tried to peddle others but failed. I made one French translation and sold it. (Ha ha, I told you so.) But how much I will get, I do not know.

I hope I see you, in the classic stage term, almost as soon as this letter.

M.

1. Cowley's ellipses.

2. Lucien Bérgeret is a character in Anatole France's *Histoire Contemporaine* (1896–1901).

3. L'Abbé Jerome Coignard is a character in Anatole France's *La Rôtisserie de la Reine Pédauque* (1893).

4. "U.S. Volunteer Tells of French Battle Front Visit—No Union Hours," Cowley's first paid publication, appeared in the January 6 issue of the *Pittsburgh Gazette Times*.

[Weehawken,
New Jersey]
February 18, 1918
[PS]

Dear M,

Very disconsolate, although for no utterable reason. My writing is going well enough. Already "The White Oxen" is as long as any complete story I have written up to date, whereas I am only closing up the first of its five parts. I am writing in a style that you would not like, very detailed and analytical, preferring rather than having things too sketchy and swiftly moving that I should as in the Peabody days err on the side of redundancy . . .

I write with the queerest of attitudes. It is that I feel no one will find my story interesting, certainly at least no one of the people I have now. I place some hope in Wilkinson, since he has always spoken of my stuff the way I wanted it spoken of. Oh, and I forget Matty.[1] Matty and I agree pretty well with each other; and I remember now that he listened to me very patiently and attentively last summer when I was toiling at the novel. But what I miss in him is your capacity for—and I confess I don't find it in you the way I used to—your capacity for adding something, for giving a man something more than intelligent appreciation (although the good god knows that that is invaluable enough). As I said to Sue[2] last night, a social sense is your predominant attitude at present; and although I have claimed that a social sense is a great aid to a writer, I think that it is so only when it is secondary to a creative sense. But I don't want to argue that with you; my pen has taken me where my intentions did not.

• • •

Your criticism of German is, of course, simply silly. Who in the hell is going to decide what is a clear logical word order? And I must say that I experience no difficulty whatsoever in accepting the German order. Furthermore, I don't see why a man who has so little in sympathy with German and things German as you do would take another course in it. Such half-hearted acquiring of the language as will result will mean only one more recruit to that large but indistinguished army who find it much more convenient to deplore German than to master it. My own problem in the matter is whether to let myself loose on German again, rereading Mann, looking into his brother, going through at least three books of Frenssen,[3] or to stop resolutely my reading of other languages for a while to soak myself in our own Lamb, Coleridge, Carlyle, De Quincey, and Pater. Who else? I must study the stylists. Already I have begun De Quincey's *Confessions* again. I find that in my admiration for the Anglo-Saxon side of our language I was overlooking the Latin element too assiduously. I was almost horrified at the sight of one sentence in my "White Oxen," a sentence of perhaps forty words, and one ceaseless pitty-pat of monosyllables. De Quincey is the proper remedy for this proclivity; he is a medicament at once prophylactic and therapeutic. Peruse a page of him, and your ear will reverberate with the tintinnabulations of his superabundant Latinity; you will sense the triumphant grandeur of the rostrum. But I find his declamatory phrases very beautiful to read aloud, just as I enjoy the most verbose of Cicero's vilifications and laudations.

Burke

1. Matthew Josephson.
2. Susan Jenkins, a friend from Pittsburgh.
3. Gustave Frenssen (1863–1945), German novelist and minister.

Randolph 20,
[Harvard University]
Cambridge, Mass.
February 25, 1918
[NL]

Dear K:

Since I last wrote you, I've been busy just like I was last year, only more so. I thought I was going to get out of all that this year and spend my time in study.

Last Thursday night, I dined with Conrad Aiken. I should have written you immediately afterward. In a last analysis, he scared me. He is a development, a successful development, of most of my present tendencies. Married and with two children, quiet, a bit shiftless, he devotes himself to the writing of remarkable poetry that doesn't sell. He agrees with me on a great number of points. In one, he surprised me. Without knowing a bloody thing about Wilkinson, he is an enthusiastic admirer of the latter's two novels. He said that after reading *The Buffoon*, he was possessed by a fear that W. was the sort of man who writes only one book. *A Chaste Man* he wanted to send to all his chaste friends.

Aiken's own "Jig of Forslin" is something I wish you would read. It is a study in form; its verse is infinitely modified with each of the hundred moods. Aiken strung it out on a Freudian basis, which accounts for the large number of rapes, suicides, whores, vampires, etc., etc.

. . . . .

. . . Tim Whittlesey[1] took me to lunch at the Signet, a Harvard literary club, where I met the sons of various millionaires, who talked about going horseback riding just before tea. I think he will nominate me and fail. But the whole thing shows that my snobbery, which I thought I had conquered, is powerful.

Nothing more. I just manage to be busy, and to go out evenings. Boston I am finding quite a tolerable town. There are saloons where Bass ale and Guinness stout are both on draught at a nickel a glass. There is a large Italian quarter and one Bolshevik joint. So I can get along. But I wish they'd ship the Millay[2] family up here.

I don't want to discuss the German language except to say that my cheap sneers at it are really justified. Just now I am studying French literature. As I go along, I see brought out clearly what a consciously developed medium is the French language. Germany never had a Rabelais in the XVI century to introduce all sorts of Latin words, Greek words, technical words, manufactured words, or a preciose school in the XVII century to purify it; or an eighteenth century Voltaire to make clarity a deity. The chauvinistic attempt to make German a "pure" language, and the retaining of the de-clensional forms are not the characteristics of a language of the highest development. Chaucer's English was structurally as advanced as modern German. And there was no imperially supported set of professors to forbid it to dip into the rich stores of other languages. Grillparzer[3] has been compared to Racine. My God, to read the two at once! Grillparzer is wildly beautiful at times, it is true, but his diction sprawls all over itself like an adolescent elephant.

M.

1. Tim Whittlesey, a friend and poet at Harvard.
2. Cowley is referring to Edna St. Vincent Millay and her two sisters.
3. Franz Grillparzer (1791–1872), Austrian dramatist.

Randolph 20
[Harvard University]
March 17, 1918
[NL]

Dear K:

When I wrote you my last letter, I was quite enchanted with myself. Of course the inevitable disenchantment has set in. Nothing special has happened, but as usual the little bubble of conceit has been pricked. One reason is that I am broke; another that I haven't written anything of late except a poem for the Lloyd McKim Garrison prize, which of course doesn't count.

Last Thursday night I went to dinner with Aiken again. We had a charming conversation afterward—all about How To Sell Poetry. Kennerley is a crook, although an altruistic crook. Macmillan doesn't accept anything unless he—she, rather—expects to sell two thousand the first year. Sherman French[1] are damned Jews, but they have gone out of business, and a young altruist has taken their place. And so on and so on. I was entranced.

Aiken himself is now criticizing poetry for the *Dial*. He rips everybody to pieces; you must read him. He is getting so unpopular that he can't get anything published in a magazine. He decided to let his fortunes rise or fall with those of Edmund Brown of the Four Seas.[2] The latter I went to see recently to get some books to review for the *Advocate*—a good graft, by the way. Young Brown has a head full of grand schemes: a popular literary weekly, a new Yellow Book for the Back Bay folk,[3] etc., etc. So at least there is some literary gossip in this town.

. . .

God damn it, I wish the *Sansculotte* would take down its breeches and get to work. There is a tremendous need for a magazine, not merely wild and Hebraic like the *Pagan*; not run by a temperamental woman, like the *Little Review*, and not inspired with nothing but love of the masses and other dirt, like the *Liberator*, but which would print decent stuff by (us) new men. Aiken would come in without hesitating. So, I think, would all the other contributors we need. And the money necessary is such a small sum.

The way Aiken puts it, there is a quiet conspiracy on now between Harriet Monroe and Braithwaite,[4] with the aid of almost all the critics, to stifle the new poetry at birth. For such rot as the cheap Semiticism of the *Pagan*, I don't blame them, but when it comes to passing Aiken and John Gould Fletcher and William Carlos Williams over in silence, it becomes too much. Gad, it sets me off toward writing criticism myself. But the best sort of critical encouragement is a magazine that publishes.

And oh gad, read "Al Que Quiere" (Williams). It is the framework and the suggestion of much good poetry, much excellent, superexcellent poetry. Only it is merely the framework.

Tell Sue to write, Goddamnher. Tell Ellis[5] to go nut himself on a briar bush. I'll buy him a bottle of absinthe if you think that will hasten the end.

M.

1. Sherman French was a Boston publisher.

2. Four Seas was a Boston publisher.

3. "Back Bay folk" was a term used to refer to Boston aristocrats.

4. William Stanley Beaumont Braithwaite (1878–1962), American poet and critic.

5. Charles Ellis, an artist who at the time was working in Greenwich Village. He married Norma Millay.

989 Boulevard East,
Weehawken, N.J.
March 21, 1918
[PS]

Dear M.

I have sent Wilkinson a copy of my "White Oxen," with the request that he forward it on to you. I ate with him one day last week, after which we went over to Mrs. Whitney's exhibit of sculptors, and then spent a couple of hours at 86, where I met Jim . . . I read Matty the last two parts of my story yesterday, after which he discussed the whole thing in such a damned decent way that it made us both very warm friends from half past two in the afternoon until half past twelve in the evening. Certainly a magnificent day, with much of Arthur Symons, Baudelaire, Flaubert, Mann, Shelley, Keats, Coleridge, Platonism, Elizabethanism and Burke-and-Josephson in the air. Indeed, I believe that no great writer failed to come in for something, including yourself. Also, a French lecture for a couple of hours in the evening—in French, natürlich—during which I was tremendously impressed much against my will by the veritable glut and fraught of intellectual fermentation that must characterize Paris art circles. While over here the best we can do is simply get down and write, in France they have room in addition for much weighing of general propositions, and actually carry out in long novels ideas which we would simply bring up in a conversation as something worth trying, it never occurring to us to go any farther with them.

I am afraid that I must capitulate for good and all, and recognize that it is hardly fair for a man like me, who reads five French books to one in German or English, to continue damning French influence. Rather, I must turn around and begin interpreting French influence, for our danger lies not in borrowing the French, but in borrowing fatuously and injudiciously. We must always bear in mind the distinction between French and Frenchy; Baudelaire, for instance, was French, magnificently and triumphantly French— but in revenge there is no better example of Frenchiness than Baudelairians . . . I believe now that Baudelaire was perhaps the most unadulterated poet that the world has known. His inspirations were all general conceptions; it was not of individual women, but of woman, that he wrote; courtesans to him were not a place to rub the mucous membrane—they were an attitude, a frame of mind. And then there is his almost mad ability to express a thing by a simile drawn from the opposite end of the universe. And think how significant it is that he detested violent passions, turned everything into half nonexistent contemplations. And knowing him at heart to be a poor incompetent little wretch, I see with something akin to cosmic wonder how this shrinking, excessively polite Baudelaire suddenly turned on himself to come out with something so insolent, so gloriously self-complacent as "Une nuit que j'etais près d'une affreuse Juive." Heavens, why aren't you around here? For two days I went about alone, resolutely damning up my enthusiasm, ready to perorate to street-car conductors or house dogs, over this man whom I, in my eighteen-year-old maturity, my adolescent sagedom, had deemed worthy of a parody and a dismissal. God d——n such shitasses.

· · ·

When are you, by the way, coming to New York? I advise you to begin sleeping o' nights now, so that you won't have that Damoclean somnolence of yours to interfere with things. I expect to move into 86 next week. In answer to your pleas about the *Sansculotte*, Jim says that if he makes any money in this afternoon job of his—did you know that he is to be publicity agent for the independent art exhibit?—he will use it to start up his paper again. Oh essays on Milton and Baudelaire! oh stories of suicides who never kill themselves! oh serial installments about white oxen! oh this! oh that! oh verses about ethyl alcohol turned down by the *Advocate*! oh poems about the weather! oh Schnitzler! oh! oh! N'est-ce pas?

But you are just as godless a correspondent as ever. I make no secret of it, I wait for your letters. It is very humiliating; kindly notice, when the story comes to you, the passage about letters—it is written with the blood of your heartlessness.

K. B.

Randolph 20
[Harvard University]
May 25, [1918]
[NL]

Dear Mike (since you must be called Mike),

. . . Somehow I feel that this isn't going to be a long letter even by my 700-word standards, to say nothing of your triple-deck monstrosities. But thank God you typewrite. I sing dithy-rambs of praise to your red-and-black typewriting. It charmed me with the letter so much, that I insisted on reading from the brilliant parts of it to everybody of intelligence I have met during the past week, insisting with Nan[1] that you are the only American genius. I'll make them believe it yet, damn them.

The (supply any superlative you like: queerest, best, most decadent, most adolescent, most intellectual) place I read it was at the house of a most intelligent young person of eighteen years, a pretty girl who paints, sings, plays the piano, writes a bit of verse, and is very, very decadent. The room was piled with old bric-a-brac; chests of drawers, old lamps, high-backed chairs, and much else of the kind. Foster[2] played the piano; modern French music, of course, or Russian; I don't know: Mary (our accomplished hostess) brought out an ouija board, and two perfectly ridiculous freshmen who dropped in discussed Huysmans. It was very romantic. Later the lights were turned down, and we discussed sadism a bit, and I read poetry. AND they call Greenwich Village dilettante! From there we went about half past twelve to see some other acquaintances of Foster. The girls were out and would shortly be back; meanwhile their mother, who was changing into negligee, stuck a tip of nose out of the bedroom door, and informed us that the Scotch was on the table in the living room, and that if the water wasn't cold enough, we should find ice in the kitchen. But the water was cold enough, and we stood there for five minutes, observing the paintings, and rugs, and miniatures, and cretonne curtains, and being a bit soothed by the comfort of it all. For they were decidedly persons of taste. The girls came back soon, and we left a trifle after one o'clock.

· · ·

If you can get money enough to come to Boston, I could entertain you next week. I have no examinations until June 7. On the other hand, I haven't money enough to go to New York. Headache grows worse.

Mal

1. Nan Apotheker, a friend of Susan Jenkins and an aspiring Village poet.
2. S. Foster Damon (1893–1971), American writer and critic.

Candor, New York
June 21, 1919
[PS]

Dear Mal,

Everything at Candor is very plentiful this year—birds, flowers, berries, snakes, frogs, fish, etc. etc. I have found a swimming hole which is up to my neck in one part, and the sunsets and storms are out-and-out Hearst editions. Not only are the strawberries and raspberries thick, but we have also found good blackberry patches, with some huckleberries and a few gooseberries. Indeed, even the poor old patriarchal orchard reacted somewhat to the mild winter, so that there are two or three trees with apples and about as many pears. Our garden has been doing so well that even the woodchucks were charmed with it, with the result that our proud little beans are much less proud, and our peas are razed to the earth. By some good luck, the kale, radishes, onions, beets, and carrots were spared. Five monster pink peonies are blooming in the yard, while our three rose bushes are just wilting.

The first week was one long Jobiad of trips to town, but by now we have everything going smoothly, and provide the village with a topic for conversation only twice a week . . . What a place for an American Flaubert! If one is only willing to be a martyr to his country's stupidity, and write an exhaustive analysis thereof. I spent one maddening evening in a social gathering at Kelsey's where every instant was a pearl—from the two giddy high school girls who whisper out on the porch with their arms wrapped around each other's waist, to Gen's suggestion that Bea-though-ven appealed to everybody, and was the Longfellow of music. Gen says she would never go to hear McCormack, because he drinks . . . I shall surely die of a bursted blood vessel in the head.

· · ·

So far, I have done very little reading here. I tried to get through *Sixtine*,[1] but for some reason or other, could not get into it, and gave it up after a time. The main value of the book was that it encouraged me in my own venture. Being at present in a virulent form-over-substance phase, I was irritated by de Gourmont's continual excursions; he has all the time in the world. An essay on Mann, on the other hand, I found quite exciting. The more I look back on Mann, the more I begin to disagree with his basis. I still do believe that he has added a great deal to the technique of letters, however. What a shame that literature is not more of a tradition that is picked up and carried on, as painting is, or philosophy. They can speak of painting before and after Cézanne, or philosophy before and after Kant, but the mechanism of literature has been too much neglected to have a pivot on which it swings. Of course, I am going on with my Latin. Every day I read up my saint in the Breviary, and occasionally I go through a bit more of the Confessor. I have found many of the hymns and cantica singled out by Huysmans and de Gourmont . . .

K.

1. *Sixtine: roman de la vie cérébrale* (1890), a novel by Rémy de Gourmont.

Belsano, Pa.
August 24, 1919
[NL]

Dear Kenneth:

. . . Today is my birthday, and having suffered everything else in the damned world, I must now suffer my majority. Up to date I have written letters, fished, and butchered young pine trees to transform them into the clipped semblance of what I believe a young pine tree should be. Peggy[1] writes me once a day, as regular [as] sex; I reply with the persistence of the little morning drop, and sleep ten hours a night.

Funny our last week together. I honestly was half sick for intelligent companionship—either yours or Aiken's or Long's,[2] as I told you, then you arrived and we discussed wives and sustenance, finding that our intellectual engines, for the time being, were running on different tracks. You are a strange, silent Kenneth, already a thousand years old in some ways; worried somewhat over the next few years and unbending only over the third beer. Family life has a tendency to make a man much more self-sufficent. Public opinion affects him less; he has always the probable approval of his wife to fall back on, and so he craves less the approbation of his friends. I talk like Guffey's Fifth Reader.

My poetic renaissance has not yet arrived; indeed it shows no special signs of arriving. They keep me too busy here to write much except the letters owing fifty people for a year or so.

Very anxious to hear about your job. I hope you like it. Call to see Peggy occasionally.

Mal

1. Marguerite Frances Baird, Cowley's first wife.
2. Haniel Long (1888–1956), American poet, and a teacher at Carnegie Tech.

Belsano, Pa.
August 30, 1919
[PS]

Dear Kenneth:

I received your Lines Written in Dejection near Weehawken on the Occasion of Receiving a Letter from a Friend. Ah! what a delightful Early Romantic title! What an interesting Neo-Romantic style! After a year of polite nothings, you reverted to form and spoke the sad, sad truth—which I never would have spoken. But you only spoke part of the truth. Here is the rest of us.

We have lost the faculty of talking to each other. If we had anything to say, we could still say it—anything such as we once mumbled for hours. We haven't got it; measured by our ideals of adolescence, we are failures. And it isn't so much that we have developed along different lines. Our goals differ slightly, our theories a little more, but I believe that our experiences have been so nearly identical that I could sit and repeat to you at length certain brain states that you must have passed through within the last two months. Or vice versa. And since these common experiences have not all been pleasant, we hate each other tacitly.

We are both failures. Not on the basis of the work we have done, which is Promising, as anyone would tell us; rather because we have been caught up in the machinery of life. For two years or so you will be in what Mr. Harold Bell Wright[1] would call the Valley of the Shadow. In the same mail that brought your letter, I had an almost parallel communication from Peggy. She is having her troubles and discouragements and depends on me to carry her through. Little Does She Know that she is leaning on a Hollow Reed. In the morning she, like you, added a cheerfully conversational postscript, but God, she is certainly in the dumps. Go to see her, and alone, if that is one of those great favors you can render me with little trouble to yourself. All this as an aside.

We are failures in each other's eyes, and that makes us uncomfortable. However we can still seek out some Sub-Matty, who won't see through us and who will admire us as accomplished litterateurs. And I believe that the literary companionship of our respective wives is just about on that order, which is a cruel thing to say and for God's sake don't repeat it. But such companionship—as far as writing and discussing the universe goes—won't satisfy us forever. Some day we are going to be able to talk again, and I think that the thing which now makes us uncomfortable is the high standards of past discussions. We haven't those things to say today; the platitudes stick in our throats.

But my solution of the matter isn't so drastic as yours. I don't know how much faith you have left in me, but I still believe that you are going to pull through. And if either of us becomes a success—even in his own eyes— our relationship can get back on a more comfortable basis. Meanwhile beer and poker and kaffeeklatsch; smuttitudes on married life, and discussion of salaries. I have a great feeling for institutions which you lack; our relationship had become institutional in my eyes, and even if I knew quite well it was hollow, I refused to speak. Now I suggest that we leave it on an institutional basis for a little while, counting on the chance—which is a good one—that it will swing around. Personally I don't feel capable of cutting apart from you. It would be too much of a blow at my self-respect. However if that is what you want, don't answer this, and we'll meet in a year with a little fresher outlook.

Mal

[Postscript] The fact that you can talk to a Greek bootblack better than to me is a damning indictment of your present self. The same holds good of me, when I find myself on more confortable ground with a farmer.

I've got some other troubles, too, that I never told you—isn't that a commentary on the past and the present?—but for God's sake let's brace up and get drunk.

1. Harold Bell Wright (1872–1944), popular American novelist and minister whose work praised traditional moral values.

24 Mt. Auburn St.,
Cambridge, Mass.
November 16, 1919
[NL]

Dear Ken:

I have about twenty minutes before the ten o'clock lights-out of our infirmary, in which time I shall try to write you . . .

Kenneth, I fear my affection for you is alas! greater than yours for me. A sad dose of salts, and something that you wouldn't offer me to swallow for the world or two pipes after breakfast (I borrow your own imagery) and nevertheless true. Perhaps I need a friend more than you, being much more opposed to oysters-Epicureanism. My own philosophy I shall dignify with the name of Ecstatics or Ecstatic Mysticism. The premises are the following. Your oyster philosophy is absolutely true, if one regards the physics-mental state of the body alone. We have retrograded from the contentment of the mollusks. But there are moments of ecstasy in which we feel the flesh drop away from us, and in which we feel united to something outside of us— the universe, the Eternal, God, a woman, whatever you want to call it. Those moments are the only thing that justifies our existence. Life is a rope bridge between them. Those moments are also the cause and the effect of poems, of other works of art . . . twelve minutes of my time are gone already.

All this does not explain why I need a friend more than you. But with such a belief, you can imagine me in a hectic search for ecstasies, reading through old poetry and plays, writing occasionally, sexing desperately (an act empty without symbolism!). Through all this, of course, I feel the need of someone to talk to, in fact I am even lonely here. Another factor: this mental instability leads me to desire that my worldly relations be things settled beyond the possibility of worry. No register.

The time is up . . . Did you ever have the belief, like me, that the world was really a dull place and that life wasn't half so important as novelists make it? This new philosophy of mine at least does away with that attitude, and lends some dignity to our rather stupid sufferings.

Mal

143 Waverly Place,
New York City
February 1, 1920
[PS]

Dear Mal,

. . . At present . . . I am frankly ill-disposed. For in "The Woman of Thornden"[1] I have discovered further intimations of mortality. Ecstaticism here has gone back to its fountain-head, a mere froth of lax adjectives. Along with the loss of your own self-consciousness, has gone the loss of it in your writing, with the result that you can do all the standard things without the least discomfiture. In this, of course, you are partaking of true greatness, as you have assured us, but you have also made your criticism exactly like the one preceding it, and the one following. I hope you made a lot of money from it, so that it will at least be justified on some basis.

But frankly, I am afraid of your recently acquired peevishness. Perhaps an adverse remark may strike you in just such a way as to make you through with me forever, so that I shall have nothing left to pick at but Matty and the stars. So that it is with great misgiving that I confess you are not the prototype of the Arrived Critic. Not you, but Floyd Dell.[2] In spots, that is, and in other places it is no one at all . . .

K. B.

1. "The Woman of Thornden" is the title of a review of two novels by Sheila Kaye-Smith that Cowley published in the February, 1920, issue of *The Dial.*
2. Floyd Dell (1887–1962), American novelist, critic, and editor.

24 Mt. Auburn St.,
Cambridge, Mass.
February 9, 1920
[NL]

Dear Kenneth:

You are safe when you attack "The Woman of Thornden." I justify it on one ground only; the pragmatical. I wrote it to get ten dollars and I got twenty. Could Shakespeare, Michel-Ange,[1] Goethe, Jesus Christ, Voltaire, and Edmund, Thomas, and Kenneth Burke say any more? In my class is only Coleridge, who wrote "The Rime of the Ancient Mariner" to get five pounds, and received thirty guineas therefore . . .

Remember Pittsburgh and the walks up Ellsworth Avenue? One scene comes to my mind especially clearly; it was on a long driveway in Highland Park; you had just developed another new Weltanschuung as all-embracive as Kant's and founded, I believe, on a sentence in *Diana of the Crossways*.[2] We fell from world generalizations to theories about us twain and decided that you progressed by revolutions, I by sane, steady development. And now by sane steady development you have reached the logical resolution of your attitudes; I have lost most of my pimples, grown a mustache, and had a revolution. I feel offended because you don't understand me but I don't know why. For both you and I realize that your discernment has always been brilliant and microscopic. You would sympathize with the biologist who builds a theory of the descent of man on the number of chromosomes in the male reproductive cell; everything depends on whether there are 23 or 24. Or to put it another way, you see one facet of every personality, and build a theory of every personality on that facet; your universe reminds me of a Jonsonian comedy of humors. But now I am building a theory of you on one facet of a very complex personality.

Every once in a while you shock me. I shall never for a moment forget the time I sent you some platitudes of Herbert Kaufman's[3] for a joke, and you took them seriously and questioned my mentality . . . I continue to write you because despite all our disagreements I never learned how to talk to anybody else, and I don't know why you continue to write me.

The exams are finished. One short thesis, and my connection with the college will be severed definitely. Peggy's teeth are keeping me in Cambridge more than anything else, but teeth or no teeth (no teeth at present) I shall be in New York about the end of this week.

Mal

1. Michelangelo.

2. *Diana of the Crossways*, a novel by George Meredith, was published in 1885.

3. Herbert Kaufman (1878–1947), American newspaperman and author. During the years 1916–1919 he wrote a syndicated editorial column.

88 West Third Street,
New York City
June 9, 1920
[NL]

Dear Kenneth:

In my pocket at present is a long letter which I am mailing you more for documentary purposes than for any other. To a certain extent it represents the history of an evening. I started it at eight o'clock; very bored and with nothing to say. People and booze drifted in; at intervals I returned to write a paragraph, each a little wilder than the last. And when it was finished, I could not even dare a signature.

And yet since that time there have been a great many things I have wanted to tell you. People go away like that; things happen and you want to put them into the current of your life and find that there are a thousand things to explain which one day together would do much better . . . The crowd that surrounds me is almost entirely different than the one that circulated when you left . . . there is Carl Kahler, an abstract painter. Do you know what it means to be an abstract painter? I don't, except that you make queer marks on canvas that don't represent anything except an emotion, and live on an allowance from your wife, who is in Paris . . . Charles Duncan is another abstract painter, only he supports himself by a membership in good standing of the signpainters' union.

I repeat that I have a great deal to tell you, but a certain inertia keeps me from hammering these recalcitrant keys. A proposition about Life; one about Art. Art first. I want to start a school with you. We might call it The Courve, as your manufactured word seems to express the school about as well as any. It exists in the fourth dimension; in other words in the time factor in measurement. Up to this time, practically all the motion expressed in art has been the motion of the object; the motion of the observer and its curious effects remain practically unwritten and unpainted. Also double motions and triple motions, as, for example, a subway express passing a local while the posts seem to stride backward at a terrific rate. Or the unrolling of a landscape like a reel of film . . .

But the school. We should have one or two poets, one or two prosateurs, a sculptor, a painter. And then hold an exhibit. The prose and poetry would be cast by the sculptor; for example a poem expressive of spiral motion would be engraved on a sort of circular staircase. Of course that part of it is freakish, but what sport . . . Man Ray's revolving doors should certainly be part of the exhibit . . . Comments and suggestions are respectfully solicited address all queries to.

The life idea is one that Peggy and I have worked out, and it should suit you as well as it does us. I decided against regular commuting, but around Haverstraw there is regular farming country and it is within thirty-five miles of 42nd Street. Why not rent a house for ten or fifteen a month—it can be done—and live there during the summer, or perhaps during the whole year and raise a large vegetable garden . . . The little money necessary for existence can be raised through a carefully cultivated typewriter and one or two trips a week to the city. Think it over. It combines all the best features of the plans we have talked over. Mountains, woods, groundhogs, trout, literature. If we are to undertake this vita nuova it will begin next spring very early . . .

Mal

Beech, Buncombe Co.,
North Carolina
June 12, 1920
[PS]

Dear Mal,

Received the two letters . . . As to the propositions of Art and Life, they please me immensely. The scheme of Living is excellent, so long as there are enough rooms in the house for everybody to get away from everybody else. A sort of communal boarding house, excellent; one big family, rotten. My experience with the many shades and nuances of Batterhams[1] has convinced me that it is absolutely impossible for two independent units to exist as one amalgamated unit; or, to make my point clearer, protracted spiritual copulation is impossible . . . Perhaps the scheme would be to alternate masters, the house being turned over to the Burkes for so long, and then being transferred to the Cowleys for so long. On one condition, that you and I pledged ourselves to drink at least three glasses of 2.75 together after the bust came, and that you promise not to skim the cream; this latter must be a hard and fast rule with anyone who is sheltered by the same roof as I, since I don't drink coffee. But the Rousseau-ism of the idea is magnificent, especially Rousseau-ism so near to Times Square. We should, of course, have to make ample arrangements about all practical details before trying it, but the idea appeals to me because I do not expect to be able to get away next summer, because I expected to have to move out of town and was damned worried about being lost out there, and because farming is the only work in the world which is not degrading. Roughly, I should suggest a joint pooling of all finances until we got the increment of our labors, an even split of this increment, and thereafter only a joint paying of expenses if we cared to continue the affair . . .

As to the Art, it is one way of many, and as good as any of them, I suppose. I shall speak with greater authority on the matter later on in the week, when I have attempted to embody Courvism . . .

I am sending you the carbon of "The Birth of a Philosophy." My plan is to write a trilogy, "The Birth of a Philosophy," "The Dungeon," and "Thebaide: An Anatomy of Sensation." Please do not read it until you can read it all, and then tell me inexorably, damnably, the truth. I think that at last I have the idea as to how to go about this thing: each story, while in a fashion continuing the ones before it, would be independent of the others.

If those bastards just publish "Kajn Tafha" in the next issue.[2]

K. B.

1. The Batterhams were Burke's wife's family. They lived in North Carolina.
2. Burke's story, "The Soul of Kajn Tafha," was published in the July issue of *The Dial*.

Beech, Buncombe Co.,
North Carolina
July 18, 1920
[PS]

Dear Mal,

To write you on a typewriter still warm from revising the last pages of "The White Oxen." Why no word of you? My last letter, if I remember rightly, was a touching plea for more correspondence. For Christ sake, write me something, so that I can write back and tell you how wrong you are.

Next week I go down to Asheville, to stay in town there for a month. So you may as well address me from now on 82 Church Street, Asheville, N.C. And a request: that you return me my Laforgue, and send along with it your Spoon River Anthology. I am thinking of hatching up some sort of a club-article on Eliot, Williams, and Masters. Also, if you don't soon write me that you have begun your essay on Laforgue, I am going to snatch it out from under you. Just now I am taking notes on a very rambling essay on sterility, in which a couple of half ideas are to be nearly captured . . .

. . . This is a family of undercurrents, which is particularly distressing to my love of overcurrents. Never go out to piss without whistling, for you are sure to hear plotting behind one of the bushes. Sometimes, down here, I get the impression of myself as a little round hard rock; it is rained on, snowed on, sunned on, thrown, kicked, and yet it retains its identity as a rock, little, hard, and round. With the bullets flying, and glances setting fire to the curtains, I march inexorably up the hill with Corona, and play upon her *ad orgasmum*. I come back to dinner; my feet falter in the undercurrents, my fingers are scorched with the glances, my ears are singed with bullets, and after the second pipe, I trot out Corona again, and climb the hill, and replay her *ad orgasmum*. There is the possibility that I go on writing through pure devilment, to taunt them silently with the plain evidence that they can't move me, for I have always been a master of such nasty tortures. In any case, their niceness and respectability has turned my brain into a House of Horrors, a Charnel House, a Slaughter House. A year among the old maids of Asheville, and I should eat the head raw off my own child . . .

K. B.

88 West Third Street,
New York City
August 25, 1920
[NL]

Dear Kenneth:

Probably one can attribute it to the fact that I had supper in Gallup's tonight—a bbbad supper—and the girl said—hello stranger I haven't seen you for a long time, and I said no I'm living way across the town, and the girl said—none of the old crowd are here, she said, and I walked out with Où sont les neiges d'antan, où sont, etc. etc. and then came home to reflect that I had just accepted another job thereby cutting into my free time still further and that yesterday was my birthday and that—

But let us phrase it another way. "In that moment the realization came to him that even in his twenties he was growing old, and that death was not an occurrence of the vague sixties but of the twenties. The words of a forgotten poem rang through his head:

We die at the top first; the toes
are the last members that turn towards the daisies."

But this fit of Viennese melancholy, this lavender-and-old-rose regret for other days, grows simply out of inability to adjust myself to my financial conditions. This week Peggy lost seven dollars, and as a result I had to hock four cameos and wrap the pawn ticket carefully around the fountain pen ticket and the ticket for my Phi Beta Kappa key. Contrast this situation ludicrously with yours. Soon my salary goes up to fifty; I am to get ten a week extra from the *Post* for handling their briefer stuff, and yet I bet I am still the width of a bank vault from the nearest savings account . . .

.　　.　　.

On the subject of finances: I hope you don't take a job when you get back. The freelance market is excellent if you don't wait till November or thereabouts. I can get you plenty to do for *Export Trade*, and unless something unforeseen happens, I can turn you over my ten-a-week job on the *Post*. After counting checks, I found that [I] actually earned between forty and fifty a week as a freelance, and it was only my inability to stick it out that dished me . . .

On the subject of poetry: I have written very little during the last months. The one I am sending you is the most important since "Four Horological Poems." It is intended as part of the Courve. I was thinking that perhaps we could preempt a number of the *Little Review* for our cute little movement, with your "Vomitory," my "Day Coach," the play,[1] a Manifesto against Manifestoes, and a few drawings by Charley. Think it over.

Yours, etc.

Mal

1. For a number of years Burke and Cowley were co-writing a play, which they called *Hamlet*. It was never completed, and the manuscript has not survived.

Beech, Buncombe Co.,
North Carolina
September 6, 1920
[PS]

Dear Mal,

A few rapidly scrawled words before the mail goes down. The buzzards are flying hungrily over Hawkbill, having taken it very literally that my brain is dead. Once I decide to move, I am no good until I have moved. I have decided to leave Asheville on September twentieth; so we can prophesy a petty renaissance on Tuesday the twenty-first, if all things turn out for the best. And you know, Malcolm, they always do, for a kindly Providence.

As to your poem, I must admit morosely that I like it a good deal[1] . . . The distinct appeal of its sections in varying keys and modes, coupled with a sentence I once read in William Carlos Williams and the nature of my own "Thebaide," has suddenly disclosed to me that we at last have a school, a school, my friend, which lives with the throbbing of our hearts. Our school is INTEGRALISM, the emphasis of the unit, the vision of art as a succession of units, or integers. A Scherzo I wrote while in Asheville exemplifies the far reaches of Integralism. Unfortunately, it is back there in my volume, so that I cannot send it to you. Willy-nilly, W. C. W. is the first of our Integralists, and we should write and tell him so. His illuminating sentence, published in the *Little Review* in one of his Notes to "Improvisations," runs something to the effect that "the poet, slashing about in his thin exaltation or despair, often realizes an acuteness of expression by which the contact is broken, rather than established." This is the very heart of Integralism. By striving for essences, by attempting to fix one entire facet of approach in a few sentences, we thus attain a unit, so distinct that it almost gains complete independence of the form as a whole. These units fall together exclusively by emotional laws. Between us, the one great difficulty to overcome in Integralism is the attainment of organism; and again between us, it is a difficulty which will never be overcome. But Integralism, by its very nature, by the very nature of present conditions, must attain its valor in spurts, or remain villainous. Integralists or Post–Late Victorians—we have our choice.

"Day Coach" is an excellent Integralist masterpiece. Section three is so precise, so immaculately exact, as to almost bring tears to my eyes . . . You have a habit, every now and then, of turning out something which seems flawless; "Day Coach" is clean and easy in a way that I shall never get a smell of. I detest messy things, but so far it has been my fate to write messily, as much as I try to avoid it.

Certainly, your program of attack on the *Little Review* is reasonable. Let us go ahead, produce an entire number, and then take it to M. A.[2] in toto. We could even suggest that plan of having alternate numbers of the *Little Review* as whole volumes to one man, if Integralism appealed to her strongly enough.

I have a lot more things to write, but the mail is going. I shall write later in the week.

K. B.

1. "Day Coach."
2. Margaret Anderson, editor of the *Little Review*.

50 Charles Street,
New York City
January 14, 1921
[PS]

Dear Mal,

Yours of December 23–January 2 to hand. Here are some hilarious developments: First, as to the *New York Times*. I think I told you that my short reviews met with such phenomenal success that I was given a long one. Of course, I was very careful, and wrote something which I thought was excellent *New York Times*, without a word of K. B. And I was right, for my article comes out, signed, on the second page, while Le Gallienne[1] does not come until the third, and Brander Matthews[2] has to wait until the seventh. Of course, this is rather unfortunate, although it has at last succeeded in winning me the respect of my father-in-law. But I had hoped for a lovely anonymous corner on the *Times*, where my whole concern would be with writing *New York Times*. But I simply refuse point blank to begin crapping on my signature. Modest as it is, it is all I have. And so I must hesitate, although my balance last month was $3.86, and the *Times* paid me two cents a word. But frankly, the thing is not quite so bad as it may seem.

For I received a mad Yiddish letter from Matty the other day, pulsing all over Paris, extremely left-wing; and after it was all over I just sat down and said Well I guess by God I'm closer to the *New York Times* than I had thought.

Development number 2 is that Paul Rosenfeld[3] came around the other day to ask me to contribute to a sort of pamphlet-magazine, to be my own editor, and to associate with Rosenfeld, Waldo Frank, and Sherwood Anderson. Now that, of course, is ridiculous. If I had attained a greater stature as a critic here, I should have decided immediately that they were trying to make an ally of a constitutional enemy. Christ, what a combination! I fully expect them to relent and finally publish the thing without me; but anyhow, I gave them the nearest approach to them I had: "Olympians." Now, I don't know how many times I have decided to write a wild condemnation of Paul Rosenfeld as a greasy Jew, and next to Waldo Frank the sloppiest critic in America.[4] As to Frank, I already took some shots at him in the *Post* a year ago. While everything I had ever written implied a dislike of Anderson, and once I even mentioned this dislike specifically in the Dial. (Although Anderson, I think, is primarily a victim of the Jew aesthetics . . .)

I finished my article on "Some Aspects of the Word," and took it around to the *Freeman*. It ends with a long plea for the un-musicality of literature, the use of the word to acquire definition rather than emotion. The metaphysics are very extensive, involving sociological, mythological, and philosophical matters—very ambitious—and being very patriotic. I emphasize, for instance, mathematics as a branch of literature, and re-discover Plato's distrust of music for his Republic. My patriotism enters when I maintain that a superior age will place literature as its highest art, and that only a muddled age will allow literature to be influenced by musical standards.

You have, I believe, received a letter from Gorham B. Munson, Esq.,[5] asking you to contribute to a magazine of his to be founded in New York next spring, and based in a general way on your formulation of "This Youngest Generation."[6] Ich auch. But I have my doubts. People are asses, to speak of getting out a magazine with Tristan Tzara and Malcolm Cowley, as though the two were quite synonymous. Indeed, I am coming to believe that the ordinary person is absolutely unable to draw the implications out of a thing at all; they take each poem or story individually, with no sense of its correlation into a general aesthetics. In any case, I shall send him something, as I may as well decide for good and all that my stories are doomed.

·   ·   ·

January 17

At present, by the way, I am meditating a grand series of articles, each dealing with some phase of our great classical revolution. The first was, of course, "Some Aspects of the Word." Now comes, "The Logic of a New Classicism"; I accept the usual theory, that is, that an intellectual movement goes with certain political and sociological conditions (not that it is *caused by them*, however; obviously, the Spenglerian principle is nearer the truth; I speak of the doctrine that all manifestations of a culture are modes of one Ursymbol, that social conditions do not cause intellectual conditions, but both social and intellectual conditions are manifestations of the same underlying tendency). Then my song is simply to develop analogies between today and the former great classical wave in Europe. Classicism, I maintain, comes at the time of a nation's definite formulation. This is due, perhaps, to the conformism which is so essential a part of the classic, making for an excellently aggressive nation. Seen in this way, classicism becomes ridiculously bound up with foreign trade, and marks that time in national development when external aggression becomes a necessity . . .

I revert to your interest in the drama. And in any case I believe that we must agree on the destruction of the novel. The main objection I have to the novel is that one simply cannot display form in it, unless by form you mean the gradual acceleration of tempo which is the best thing in a book, say, of W. H. Hudson.[7] To recall Aristotle, the work of art must be small enough to grasp as a whole. And as to my own personal interests, I am beginning to wonder whether my four- or five-thousand-word stories are not too long to bring out my effects. But here, of course, we get in quite a muddle, if the *Aeneid* is taken as a muster of classicism. But hell, I am too weary to straighten it out; this morning, certainly, I understand your psychology perfectly; the ease, that is, with which you tire of saying something (without a penny a word).

· · ·

January 19

. . . If I could afford it I should give up belles lettres entirely and go in for a few years of niggling with pure ideas. It seems to me, for instance, that the art-process is much more interesting than any work of art, and that art seen from a philosophic standpoint begins to have more appeal than when seen from merely artistic standpoints of excellence and interest. This, certainly, is a dire confession, and probably marks my destruction as a writer of prose fiction. (Unless, like Mallarmé, I continue to write simply because no one else happens to have written just as I should have ordered it; write, that is, to exemplify one's theories, although three-fourths of the creative process are probably used up in the statement of the theories.) There you have it; nobody has ever expressed Mallarmé's case so accurately as that before, because nobody was ever nearer to Mallarmé than I am. But indeed, so hopelessly am I enchained by my admiration of apriorism, that I would give all the Doc Williamses in the world for a chance to examine Mallarmé's posthumous notebooks . . .

K. B.

1. Richard Le Galliene. His review of a collection of Spanish poetry appeared in the January 9 edition of the *New York Times*.

2. James Brander Matthews (1852–1929), American author and professor of drama at Columbia University, 1920–24.

3. Paul Rosenfeld (1890–1946), American author and critic.

4. In a reprint of *White Oxen* (1968) Burke noted with embarrassment his early use of racial slurs, which surface in his correspondence as well:

> I grew up in an uncouth age and neighborhood in which it was taken for granted that minorities 'normally' referred to one another as Dagoes, Hunkies, Niggers, Micks, Kikes, and such, along with our sound suspicion that we were all minorities of one sort or another . . . Thus, some of my early stories show occasional pre-Reichstag Fire laxities. Since then Hitler and his noxious Ism have made it hard even to remember the climate in which such laxities were taken for granted . . . .I leave the bumpy passages as they were . . . I have the firm conviction that my subsequent work makes my position quite clear on the subject of ethnocentric bias . . . (xvii)

5. Gorham B. Munson (1896–1969), American editor and critic. Munson was involved in the editing and publishing of two important little magazines in the early '20s, *Secession* and *Broom*.

6. "This Youngest Generation" is the title of an essay Cowley was working on. It appeared in the *Literary Review of the New York Evening Post* on October 15, 1921.

7. William Henry Hudson (1841–1922), English novelist and naturalist.

Monson, Maine
April 18, 1921
[PS]

Dear Malcolm:

If, after a trip of nightmares, and after two days of sullen weather—and me without an overcoat and having forgotten my vest—further, the trunk not having arrived as yet, while there is a daily fourteen-hour fire for me to feed with hands still tender from a winter of knocking on the radiator—if, added to this and other lesser and greater disorders, I should claim that this country is lovely beyond your imagination. On most of the trees, the buds have not even begun yet. The mountains are a scattering of evergreens and silver bark birch. The big mountains are off on the horizon. Our lake is not more than a quarter of a mile from the house, and stretches off in a valley to the north and south. Also, over the hills in any direction there are other lakes, or ponds. The fish, according to reports, are mostly trout, salmon, and lakers; there is another name for lakers, but I do not remember it. The ice is still in the lake, but is expected to go out any day now, at which time anybody is supposed to be able to catch fish. And two evenings ago there waddled across our garden my first porcupine; I think they are called hedgehogs here. He was much larger than a bear cub, and will probably be back as we have a large apple orchard here, and they eat the bark of the apple trees.

· · ·

At present, as usual when returning to the country, my life is being lived in facts, healthy but without concatenation. Have you ever conquered a birch stump, for instance? I go at them armed to the teeth, with axe, wood saw, and wedge. And at the end of the pasture I can whistle six notes, stop, and hear the whole six repeated across the lake. The pumps here are all built in the kitchen, so that you can get your groceries, pile up your wood, and look through glass for hours. When my big shoes and heavy clothes get here, of course, I shall get out and tramp.

More later, when I can write two consecutive sentences. At present I chop wood, go to the village, eat five meals and sleep ten hours. The three books I have here have not been opened since arrival. I wish you could come up here this summer, instead of giving up New York bedbugs for bedbugs in France. France, bah! . . .

K. B.

Monson, Maine
May 1, 1921
[PS]

Dear Malcolm:

Shit, my friend. I am tired asking in the village for Burke's mail, and getting two letters for Lielie[1] and something from the gas company. Further, what sits up in a tree at night, black against the horizon, about the size of a woodchuck, in Maine? Are there possums here? We were within ten feet of it, but it was too dark to make out its features . . . The first flowers are here: wild oats, benjamins, white violets, Mayflowers, while the ferns are a stock with a twirl on the end, all wrapped in fuzz . . .

Last week I got started on my first story. It is probably to be called "The Death of Tragedy," and runs like this: Part I opens with a kind of informal essay on America, trusts, pool rooms, boys in a tent in the back yard sitting around with their peeties hanging out, laxatives, bonfires at night in the autumn out in a black field, etc., jumbled together quite brokenly. Then climbing upon the ruins of America, we come upon Clarence Turner, whose book has now reached its fifth edition and who has the reasonable prospects of a play on Broadway. Such a triumph is, of course, sufficient to end Part

I. Part II then takes up Clarence in somewhat the usual narrative fashion, a love scene of parting with a former mistress, a poetess. Here, I think, we have established his low-visionedness without being too banal ourselves. Clarence, of course, is quite up on the aesthetics of love, so that the scene ends with him stumbling down the stairs blindly; "reaching home, he hurried to his room and wrote feverishly for hours." The right touch, I believe, was added by having the poetess' phone ringing as the perfect scene comes to a close, while they both tacitly rule it out of consideration.

I am to begin Part III tomorrow. If it turns out as planned, it will go after this fashion: In the beginning the attempt is made to continue the plot. There are difficulties, however, in that agitated asides keep creeping in, until finally the narrative has been swamped completely in the qualifications. These qualifications then become a thoroughly morose batting of wings, done in twisted sentences, frequently unfinished, illogical grammar, generally choppy. Suddenly breaking free of it all, however, we sail off into a vision of lovely landscapes, until the exaltation becomes so intense that the author, feeling called upon to pray, prays. After the prayer there is one last vision of landscape, broad contours of snow—which I hope to get in one long spreading sentence. Then in an addenda, we learn that Turner has just received a note from a Bronx Jewess, saying, "I want you."

If this suggests anything to you, please write it, as I am going to try this year letting my stories lie around in manuscript for a while before definitively typing them. In the first place, I feel sure that you will condemn the ending as a bit patently clever; but I see nothing else. Part I was for the most part simply glib; Part II is there mainly because it is necessary; it is Part III which offers possibilities.

·   ·   ·

But it is already ten-thirty, so that the wheels are slowing down. We have a Moloch of a stove which eats up my wood shamelessly. I am plowing our garden with a trench shovel. It is hard hauling these heavy boots over the boggy roads. So that in the evening I get tired like a baby. Suddenly everything stops. Surely you can find time to write something—at the office, between loafs.

K. B.

1. Lielie is Burke's wife, Lily.

88 West Third Street,
New York City,
May 5, 1921
[NL]

Dear Kenneth:

The problem is to find a substitute for rhyme (which, I believe, is too difficult a device for English, and too patent a device for almost any tongue). The problem is also to find the equivalent of the old stanza forms; indeed to surpass them in musical structure. Thus the following:

POEM FOR TWO VOICES

We will go together out of this city: Come!

    It is too late now.

We will find once more a place where orchard grass
and blue grass and sour grass and white clover
grow under the apple trees; where juneberries
ripen and fall at the edge of the deep woods.

    But it is very late and I have grown into this city
    the city turns
    like awkward vast machinery in my head
    like vast wheels turning in a void.

Under the chestnut trees there are ferns knee-deep;
if we trample them we shall discover the spring
that issues miraculously from the chestnut roots.
And if we follow the stream among the thickets
and through the burned ground, where briars snatch at us,
under the hill we shall find—

    It is too late now for finding;
    I have lived here too long where no moons rise;
    the juneberries will be rotted; the chestnut trees are dead.
    It is too late now . . .

But again the problem may be to revert against everything which you have written and to rhyme shamelessly. I read you a sketch for this once:

FOR A METHODIST HYMNAL

The day begins at eight o'clock
    O my people;
The whistles blow at eight o'clock
    My people, O my people.

Set your feet in the proper way,
Set your hearts in the right direction
The heavens are counted with your pay.
Discontent is hell's affliction.

Lose yourself at eight o'clock
In the river of people flowing
Every day at eight o'clock
Towards the factory whistles, blowing

In the honor of the state
That made us, and that keeps us, free:
We are the members of Christ's great
Industrial community.

The day begins at eight o'clock
    O my people
The whistles blow at eight o'clock
    O my stricken people.

This stands for everything that I don't.

For two weeks I have led the life of a traveling salesman. April 23 I went to Boston to sell the piano; sold it; deposited $250 in a Boston bank; returned Wednesday night.

This Saturday my father was very sick; death prognosticated. I took a day train, weeping at intervals; arrived in Pittsburgh to find him with a temperature of 104; stayed till his temperature was fixed definitely at normal. I got back to work yesterday (Wednesday again). Peggy brought your letter to the train when she came to meet me.

This is an interval of leisure at the office.[1] The Boss is out to lunch.

The trees in Bryant Park are in full leaf; the great cottonwoods tremble in the wind; two robins bathe themselves in the vernal fountain. Yes, no doubt it is spring; I subscribe to your sentiments.

There is a certain chastity of outline about these office buildings. I miss you especially during the keen swoop of the elevator through space. Hobukken Bay (*Hoboken* Bay, that is; so named after the town) sparkles in the sunlight. I took a six-mile walk with Jack Wheelwright[2] through the leafy aisles of Stuyvesant Square. Now I am tired; ready to drop shamelessly into my chair.

I have to force this burlesque; I really envy you.

                                                            Malcolm

1. Cowley was working at *Sweet's Architectural Catalogue*.

2. John Brooks Wheelwright (1897–1940), American poet and former classmate of Cowley's at Harvard.

Monson, Maine
May 10, 1921
[PS]

Dear Mal,

"The Death of Tragedy" having been finished, and "The Book of the Twice Dead" having been begun, a cold spell came along, temporarily killing the bud of my art. I hope to have both of these stories definitively typed to show you before you leave for France, however, and receive your condolences darüber. Further, I warn you that in the third part of the latter story I was obliged to steal your religious service . . .

.   .   .

As to your "Poem for Two Voices," I feel that the grave complaint against it is that line twenty has got us no further than line two. After alpha and beta have alternated their parts for three stanzas, there should be some sort of resolution beyond. Perhaps this might be a song sung by alpha and beta in unison, moralizing on the situation; or gamma, the author, enters and tell[s] what he thinks of it all. Then again—what is certainly a mere mechanical invention—since the first two statements and replies grow concomitantly (that is, one line balanced against one line; four lines balanced against four lines) what is now your last stanza should call for six lines. Or do you scorn such easy symmetry? . . . But above and beyond all that, the poem is a protest without illumination. There is room somewhere, even yet, for an aggressive beauty. Perhaps because of our upbringing, we are both of the yammering sort, so that our first reaction is a critical one. Still, the aggressive beauty must be attained. I humbly suggest aesthetic unities. Gloria.

A letter from William Carlos Williams saying that another number of *Contact* is coming out in May. He asked me for that spring poem of mine which I sent you in a letter from Fifteenth Street. I answered, protesting, that he had taken an essay of mine—which I had written for money—and now a poem—which I had written in an off-moment—but that he had fought consistently shy of my fiction—which is what I am trying to write, and what I put most into. Similarly, if you have a story or a play about the house, I suggest that you send it to him. I asked him to take "My Dear Mrs. Wurtelbach," both because I should like to see it appear there and because I should like to slobber on that bastard buttock-licking *Dial*, so that they would be properly bullied into taking some of the stories I shall write this summer. And since they have gone in for bellyaching so about Williams; what! shall we be driven into the Church by the scurviness of our free-thinkers! Also—which means another six weeks' living—Farrar[1] wrote me a very sweet letter telling me how much he liked my "Chicago and our National Gesture" . . .

K. B.

1. John Farrar, American writer and a critic at *Bookman*. Burke's essay was later published in the July, 1923 issue of *The Bookman*.

88 West Third Street,
New York City
June 17, 1921
[NL]

Dear Kenneth:

I have been unhappy—alas. I *am* unhappy—alas, alas. I don't know what it is; it resembles more than anything else the *mal du siècle* of the Romantics. One gets up, putters around the house, putters around the office, putters around the house, and goes to bed. One wakes suddenly and wonders when the devil it is all going to end. One tells a client professionally about a boom in building that one doesn't believe in—and while waiting for his reply wonders when the devil it is going to end. Not having any thoughts, one is afraid to be alone with them, and reads Mr. Hearst's "Journal," and the *Saturday Evening Post*, and accounts of the coming fight at Jersey City (put your money on Dempsey), and any other scrap of paper. And wonders vaguely "when in Christ's name is it . . . ?"

As you can see, the reason I haven't written you is that I haven't had anything to write. Not even your outrageous theft of my religious ceremony moved me to speech. And it was outrageous, for you did it well enough to prevent me from doing the same thing. I have few ideas at present; for Christ's sake let them alone and don't steal from the poor man's pantry. I feel as if I were (was?) dying at the top; nothing can save me now short of a new life.

.　　.　　.

The advertising manager for Moon-glo silk wrote in to the *Dial* for a poet to do some work for them. I was recommended. I made him $35 as a submission price for a brief poem, and *$100* as acceptance price, the charge was ok'd, but as yet I have done no work on it. Only assets to date are: 1 lunch at Delmonico's; one supper (Peggy included) at Enrico & Paglieri's.

Djuna Barnes is going abroad.
Harold Stearns[1]   "   "   "
Ivan Opffer[2]   "   "   "
Bill Brown[3]   "   "   "
Estlin Cummings is already   "
Dos Passos   "   "   "
Dorothy Day   "   "   "
Mary Reynolds[4]   "   "   "   and oh God

I can't continue this list for weariness. I suppose Joe Gould[5] will drop in on us at Montpellier to borrow money.

Have you read about the *Dial* prize for $2,000 to be given next January to a *young* author who has contributed to their paper? I really think that you and Estlin Cummings have the best chances—if the prize really goes to a *young* writer.

You should contribute to Kreymborg's magazine, *The Broom*. He pays. I will find you the address if I can. He's another of next week's departures for Europe.

. . .

And even the recital of all this gossip leaves me empty and desolate. Maybe a sea voyage will be a tonic, but I doubt it.

Mal

1. Harold Stearns (1891–1943), American writer and critic, editor of *Civilization in the United States: An Inquiry by Thirty Americans* (1922). Cowley discusses his significance on pages 74–79 of *Exile's Return*.

2. Ivan Opffer was a Danish artist Cowley had met in the Village.

3. William Slater Brown, the American writer and critic who was imprisoned with e. e. cummings in an incident described in cummings' *The Enormous Room* (1922).

4. Mary Reynolds later married Marcel Duchamp.

5. Joe Gould was a Greenwich Village eccentric, an old friend of e. e. cummings, and a would-be writer who, according to Cowley and others, was composing a huge work called "A History of Our Time from Oral Sources."

Monson, Maine
June 25, 1921
[PS]

Dear Mal:

Received your letter, which made me go out and look at the stars, and your postcard, which made my nostrils quiver with the almost forgotten smell of lucre . . .

As to Kreymborg, I shall be damned glad to take up your offer, and shall look through my opera for something to submit. True, I do not know the *Broom*, but unless Kreymborg has changed a good deal from the time of *Others*, my "Rhapsody Under the Autumn Moon" (pinx. 1916–17) looks like the most promising thing . . .

* * *

June 26

Here is my L'Allegro and Il Penseroso for yesterday. Begin the day, perhaps, when one rises in the night, to find a mixture of full moon and 3:00 dawn, with the birds already highly individualized. At eight, however, I actually stay up, light the fire, get the milk, put baby at the table. Then go out in the garden, and kill potato bugs and the little striped bugs that get on the cucumbers. Then, while eating breakfast, exclaim from excessive elation; "My goodness, let us go for a long walk today!" It is agreed to; we decide to go around the lake, beyond the cemetery, eat our lunch there, see Mr. Wilkins about a stove for Matty,[1] and then examine the slate mills. Lielie starts preparing the lunch, while I return to potato bugs. Then I come in, and shave; and then manicure my nails. At which point Lielie discovers that she is doing all the work. Quarrel. Very well, we shall not go. Food is put back in the pantry; milk, butter, and salad dressing returned to the cellar. We place ourselves about. The burden of a disappointing day begins to depress us. Lielie cries; and I say, "Let's go down back of the house to the lake, eat lunch by the spring, and then after a while go in swimming." Immediate reconciliation; Jeanne Elsbeth Dutch Lumphead Piddle-Bum is put into her carriage; the food is packed in odd corners; we move as a body over an old road with the grass as high as in a meadow. Arrived at the spring, we reconnoiter, finding the thickest strawberries we have seen to date. We simply cannot resist it. I go back for the baby, put her in the shade, and we begin. So far we have scared up two partridges; hens and peeps can be heard off in other parts of the patch; Lielie thinks she saw a deer; but the baby crawls into thistle, and thereafter will not be comforted. Picking is over. We return to the spring, erect a canopy over the baby carriage, and she goes to sleep after much howling and much citronella. Mr. and Mrs. Burke eat; and then note that they are in the midst of the thickest mint patch in America. Simply cannot resist it, and add a pint of mint leaves to our quart of strawberries. Dutch awakes, and joins in the meal, shrieking at every ant which turns up for crumbs. After this is all over, and things are repacked, and tied, and put away, we move back to the lake. The baby plays half in the water and half out, shrieks at the leeches and the moose-flies, and beholds her parents swim with great awe and reverence. We build a causeway, out into the deep water, of rocks, so that we do not have to walk on the mucky lake bottom, where you sink in up to your knees. After an hour and a half of this, home . . .

Tomorrow I begin writing again, after a couple of weeks of sterility. I feel that I have learned a number of things in writing these three stories; in fact, I do believe that my work is based on a really sound aesthetics, that decent people should be able to see the shop in my work, and that occasionally I get little isolated forms which have a complete existence of their own, while at the same time fitting into the larger unit. Once in a while Sprinchorn[2] and I run across a productive vein of conversation for a half hour or so, but there is always the obstacle of the two mediums; and besides, he, like McAlmon[3] and Williams, does not enjoy our weakness for definitions and fixations. He *feels* things; but my joy does not really begin until I formulate them . . .

K. B.

1. The Josephsons were also spending the summer in Monson, Maine.

2. Carl Sprinchorn (1897–1971), Swedish-born painter who came to the United States in 1903.

3. Robert McAlmon (1896–1956), American writer and critic who lived and published in Paris. He helped edit *Contact*, and is best known for his autobiography, *Being Geniuses Together* (1938).

Monson, Maine
June 30, 1921
[PS]

Dear Malcolm,

Enclosed please find soul to date.[1] As to the three recent stories, it is my fervent desire that you do not read them until on the boat,[2] and do not read any of them then until you can go straight through from the beginning to end (of one, i.e.). In other words, I am much more anxious to have you note what I am doing than what I have done. The finished masterpiece, to bring up a type of metaphor which I have not been guilty of heretofore, and which may shock you, the finished masterpiece is like confetti thrown at a carnival, and looked at the day after. So let us, sir, rather discuss the throwing of the confetti.

In the last analysis, I fear that all I am doing is rediscovering tangents in all their possible variations. That is, a work of art is that which becomes something else, but natural, rather than logical, progression. (Vid. Davey Hume, if I remember rightly. There is nothing *logical*, for instance, in a pod following a blossom, or a fever following germs in the intestines. Yet the art processes should evolve in just this way.) This same principle of something becoming something else would be reproduced in both the broad outlines of the story, the layout of the subdivisions, the paragraph—and ideally, I suppose, even the sentence. (One way of looking at this, as I said, is that whereby it becomes simply variations of tangents.) In "The Death of Tragedy," where I did this at all, you will find it a little too blocklike. The close of "The Book of Yul" probably represents it at its best. In "An Odyssey" the problem is somewhat different from that of the preceding two stories and "My Dear Mrs. Wurtelbach." For whereas in the case of them the plot could be called static, in "An Odyssey" it is decidedly dynamic. That is, the first three evolve about a fixed point, but "An Odyssey," as is evident from the title, is a journey or a progression. I do not feel now, after finishing "An Odyssey," that the three-part arrangement quite gets the thing across; and on this basis, I am making "In Quest of Olympus" in five parts, the first three on one plane, the fourth in a second, and the last in a third . . .

As to the smaller incidental forms with which the perfect work should be strewn, the stories which I am sending you are by no means as proficient in this respect as I should like them to be. But I discover all parts of my method as I go along; *emphasize*, that is, for any paragraph by anybody contains the germs of all possible movements—it is simply a matter of emphasis which gives it some particular distinction. As illustrative of the sort of thing I intend trying more of in the future, let me transcribe this note, which, without the exhaustive exegesis given above, I admit, looks pointless enough:

> *Working among the briars, especially the insistent blackberries, insistent because they seemed to be actually reaching out to catch in the wool of our coats, we came upon an even thicker muddle of ferns and alders. As the country was rough, our feet would slip from the rocks, and lodging in some unnoticed cavity covered with dead leaves, they would be held there by a tangle of roots, while at the same time we were kept busy dodging beneath the low, crooked branches, making detours, or creeping through holes— And then of a sudden we broke through to the road, and went striding away like gods.*

In a similar rhythm is the punctuation of some specific scene by some natural phenomenon, like the burning of a city, and after it is over, a mass of low, sullen embers, a full moon rises calmly out of the water. It is in something after this fashion that Part Three of "In Quest of Olympus" ends, since the Blizzard God rapes Hyelva, and bits of her torn white garments fall out of heaven, making snow on earth (the point of view being instantly turned from heaven to earth, the snow is seen falling upon us rather than away from us).

Eh bien. I have exegetized sufficiently. Why, oh why, do you consistently refuse to back me up anymore in these things? Do they bore you? In any case, you have the three examples of what I have attained so far, with a rough statement of my intentions . . .

K. B.

1. Burke is referring here to the stories he has enclosed, as well as to the contents of the letter.
2. Cowley was returning to France on an American Field Service graduate fellowship to study at the University of Montpellier.

c/o American University Union,
1, rue de Fleurus,
Paris (VIᵉ), France
July 12, 1921
[NL]

Dear Kenneth:

"An Odyssey" is a failure. Considering which I shall return you the manuscript without further parley and without even decent care of the manuscript.

"An Odyssey" fails because you don't follow your own rules fairly. The growth from the first part to the second depends artificially on a footnote. The theme is not established before you strike off at a tangent. The first tangent is dogmatic. The second tangent is better in relation to the first but the original circle is too small . . . and only the third circle is perfect. Your construction should be . . . with the third circle tangent to both the others and closing the gap in the first.

So much for a theoretical discussion of "An Odyssey." To be specific, it should be in 4 parts, not 3 or 5. Or if in 3 parts, the first part should be at least as long as the other two together . . .

•   •   •

I think I could rewrite "An Odyssey" into something better than "The Death of Tragedy," which, if blocklike, is built at least on good blocks. I could not make it better than "Yul"; there you have done better than your theories. At any rate, your theories came very naturally in "Yul." "Yul" is the only proof to me that they are valid.

MC

                                      c/o American University Union,
                                      1, rue de Fleurus,
                                      Paris (VIᵉ), France
                                      July 13, 1921
                                      [NL]

Mr. Kenneth Burke,
Monson, Maine.

                    Re Manuscripts forwarded to our firm

My dear Mr. Burke:

We regret that "The Death of Tragedy" does not quite measure up to the high standard we have set for our publication.

In line 2, the word is guerilla, not gorilla. If you change the spelling we may reconsider the decision.

There is, however, something very satisfying about the construction of the story. Out of the general into the particular, out of the particular gradually into the general. Evidently you waver between two endings: one on the particular theme, one on the tangent. We prefer, as a rule the return to the theme. It depends on the length of the tangent. A long tangent demands a return, a short tangent is more apt to be satisfying by itself.

The weakness of the construction is the fact that America does not lead to Clarence Turner. Clarence Turner may be escaped by blocking out the contours of the Maine lakes, but he may not be introduced by the rolling on of the great bump of the country. At that point you almost suggest Rupert Hughes;[1] he has the same tendency to generalize about America and thus to lead ridiculously up to his hero. I think a discussion of American literature would lead more naturally to Turner.

You will build a literature on the ruins of Floyd Dell.[2]

Your method of associating thought is really that of dreams or the subconscious in general. Thus your method is much more successful in a dream story like "Yul." "Yul," as we said, justifies post-masturbationalism.

                                      Very truly yours,
                                      Malcolm Cowley, Inc.

---

1. Rupert Hughes (1872–1956), popular American novelist, short-story writer, and playwright.

2. Floyd Dell's novel *Moon-Calf* (1920) and its sequel *Briary Bush* (1921) were acclaimed as representative novels about the disillusioned postwar generation.

Monson, Maine
August 3, 1921
[PS]

Dear Mal,

Just returned from a three-day trip in the open forest, during which I ate portions of a fourteen-and-three-quarter-pound laker, caught on Long Pond, some twenty miles beyond the frontiers of civilization. No deer sighted—owing to the loquacity of the party—but plenty of hoof marks of both deer and moose, and whole stews full of the little black eggs. Mountain climbing, canoeing . . . One of the natives guided us, a member of the Maine fire-fighters, a distributor of spruce gum and a boiler of maple syrup.

· · ·

As to what you write of my stories, I am inclined to agree with you in a good number of your criticisms. The blocklike treatment which I almost invariably fall into is what I consider the greatest problem at present, although strangely enough I felt that in "An Odyssey" I had gone a long way toward obviating this . . .

· · ·

Still, I agree with you that "Yul" is a better product per se, perhaps as you suggest because it is a dream story. I did more in that story for no reason at all. As I believe I wrote you, I have found that that type of story is easier to write, in that the quality of a static idea is more apparently a unity than the quality of a dynamic idea. (Dream, static; journey, dynamic.) But the latter kind seems to offer more possibilities. In any case, I am writing another like it at present, between dirths [sic] of intense heat, when one is content to swim, and dive from his private raft, and reread *Buddenbrooks*. I hope to be able to send it to you by my next letter.

· · ·

In defense of "The Death of Tragedy," particularly the Rupert Hughes beginning—you have unfortunately turned the thing around on me. That is, I started out here to restore that very type of beginning, although I was thinking of Sir Walter Scott rather than Rupert Hughes. That is, Scott begins with his general background, followed by the emergence of the particular protagonist. But the Scott method—as exemplified by Hughes— had completely lost its significance as a form, a natural and contenting development. I, therefore, to emphasize the value of the process *per se*, began with America in general and then drew out Clarence Turner. Your suggestion to begin with American literature—if you will believe me—was the first thing I thought of, and the first thing I discarded. And it was discarded simply because in that case the break between the general and the particular, being completely logical, would hardly be recognized . . . The problem, as I said before, is to emphasize the natural rather than the logical.

And if you have ever looked for cucumbers among cucumber vines you will remember how startling the natural can be. I never find a cucumber without a positive jolt. So be it with Clarence Turner.

.   .   .

But for God's sake, send me something of yours. This letter happens to be concerned with my stuff. I assure you I should have been just as engrossed in it if it were about yours. If I could give you some advice, and with the best wishes in the world toward both Peggy and Lielie, I should suggest that you become less married. As I think of you playing pinochle with your wife in the evening, and Matty playing chess with his wife in the evening, while Sprinchorn spends his evenings walking, or reading, or drawing, I begin to realize what the old bunkum really means about the artist not marrying. You and Matty talk about writing; I talk about it and do a little; Sprinchorn finishes one painting and goes on with another . . .

.   .   .

I hope you are going to be half decent about writing. And in the meantime, I shall write you at least once every two weeks.

K. B.

c/o American University Union,
1, rue de Fleurus,
Paris (VIᵉ), France
August 10, 1921
[NL]

Dear Kenneth:

After the burst of confidence on the boat, during which I wrote you those (3) letters in those (3) successive days, I haven't had the courage to write you anything else. Nor to anybody else. Let us now (since you probably have some remaining interest in the five-feet-nine of me) recount my bodily adventures, which are:

> item—Safe landing at Havre.
> item—Arrival in Paris during the heat spell.
> item—Trip to Giverny to see Jim Butler.[1]
> item—Resumption of heat spell.
> item—(to be entered this Saturday) Departure for Dijon.

Paris, as you may imagine by putting two together with two, has an American colony. That colony centers at the Rotonde, and at times straggles over to Boudet's. Members of that colony, when asked the location of the Louvre and of Montmartre, said, "*Anybody* can tell you where the Louvre is and Nobody goes to Montmartre." They dine at Boudet's and sleep with one another, or, if they are not homosexual, with the tarts of the Quarter. It is Greenwich Village, only much more so than the village. But if you don't go to the Rotonde, Paris is quite as charming as the guidebooks. One has to look at it historically. After going through the Musée Carnavalet, where all the antiquities of Paris are stored, you begin to realize the datelessness of all the people you see. The large man with one arm lost the other at Malplaquet.[2] The little fille seduced Napoleon when he was a student. Voltaire plays chess at this table in the Café Blank; here he comes now. Voila l'aristo! His head will go through the faubourg St. Honoré on a pike—past the dressmaking establishment of Mr. Paul Poiret, whom I am to interview Thursday.

In 1914 and 1735 the English were very popular. 1918 (almost as much as 1779) was the year of Americans. We are still fairly popular; I should advise you to come over before the signs go up:

MAISONS FRANÇAISES
LES ALLEMANDS ET LES AMÈRICAINS
N'ENTRENT PAS ICI

You make a grand gesture of avoiding Paris (where the grapes hang too high) but really you should drop off for a week on your road to Munchen. If for no other reason because wine is 9 cents a quart and the beer not to be scoffed at.

Tell me when you are leaving Monson—and in your next letter.

Malcolm

1. James Butler was an American painter living in France.

2. Malplaquet, France, was the scene of a decisive battle during the war of the Spanish Succession, in which the French met the combined forces of England and the Holy Roman Empire. It took place on September 11, 1709.

Monson, Maine
August 20, 1921
[PS]

Dear Malcolm,

I'm up, you're down; I'm down, you're up. This has been, roughly, our programme for the last five years or so—the only important deviation being that brief session when we drank beer together in Weehawken and Tenth

Avenue. Then we were both decidedly down together. But if the seesaw still worketh, you are so Goddamned up at present that it is a shame.

To envisage the situation, first, financially: I have sold practically nothing all summer. En revanche, the garden has done well. The balance of the two countermovements, however, is highly distressing. To envisage the situation athletically: We have lived through the crowning ridiculous August. Under the general caption of dog days, there have been blows and fogs and cold snaps, so that I, not possessing the brute body of an M. Cowley, Esq., have spent considerable days without catching of frogs. So that while July was a prosperous month, we must pocket a loss for August . . .

My writing period seems once again to be behind me. I finally dragged my body across the last line of "In Quest of Olympus," and since then have been consistently drugged with the coke of no-register. Perhaps when the fall sets in in earnest I shall come out of it again; but at present there is nothing to do but go on reading *Buddenbrooks*. I should like to write one more story, and then aesthetic unities could go to hell forever if they cared to. Thus, the imaginary volume would contain: "Scherzando" (included for its value as a keynote), "David Wassermann," "Olympians" (perhaps), "Death of Tragedy," "Book of Yul," "An Odyssey," "In Quest of Olympus," and X. Still, my carbon copy public has been at best mediocre in its praise. (And oh yes, I neglected to include "My Dear Mrs. Wurtelbach" in the volume.) And that filters into me once in a while. But if I consider the broadside of this significant part of my Opus Totum, when I think of offering a man a completed volume of exactly those things, I feel a little less diffident. After all, to set into those things ought to be something like closing one door and opening another. And if I can really do that, it is all I should demand.

· · ·

I neglected in my last letter, by the way, to accredit your remarks on tangents. The long tangent, you should return to the theme from which it originated, while in the short tangent this is not necessary. I agree with you on that; but there is a difference between a tangent and a succession. A succession follows out some gradation of a super-plot, and in this way can simply ignore the adjoining part without being a tangent to it at all. To continue geometrically, the difference is that between the tangent and the plane. One plane, that is, while having its position in the figure as a whole, need not come in contact with another plane. The tangent, on the other hand, has an immediate contact with something else, and grows out of it . . .

Another thing which might offer possibilities, and which I want to try in my X-story, is a greater disintegration of the figure of speech. A writer says that something is like something else, for instance; but why not, instead of a mere simile, have the story actually become that other thing? To rise from a toothache to a tropical storm would be really quite invigorating, for instance. In any case, in one particular point a story might progress that way with great efficacy; as a variation of the tangent ending, for instance. But perhaps this is all more of that unwritten primer?

.　　.　　.

What more? I have heard from you only once, but am writing you as per schedule announced in my previous letter. We shall in all probability be here until the first of October. Mathjew Jewsephson and wife leave for Italy about that time. Sprinchorn tells me that a friend of his put some of his drawings on exhibition at Woodstock, and that Jack Wheelwright is in the market with $75. He wants seven drawings for that seventy-five, however, whereas Sprinchorn has offered him two for that amount . . . Our baby is eighteen months old now, and cries when we sex. So much for cullings from the Monson Bugle.

K. B.

Monson, Maine
August 28, 1921
[PS]

Dear Mal,

Yesterday morning, while stooping under one of my plumb trees and picking up plumbs—as no less than fifteen bluejays visit these trees at sunup every morning to knock off the ripest plumbs, I go out before breakfast to profit by their expert advice—so while picking up plumbs yesterday morning under one of my plumb trees, something went pop in my guts, the process seeming, as far as I could gather, to exactly parallel that of squeezing a ripe pimple. Now, Malcolm, this would all have been very good, except that one of my sisters-in-law is now in the hospital after a narrow escape with a ruptured appendix. I had never known before of a ruptured appendix, and fortunately I had learned just in time to be able to diagnose my predicament. By noontime, as you may imagine, I was very sick, and after supper I thought I was going to vomit, while my right side was torn asunder with pains. I went to bed early, tumbled to sleep, in fact, from the poison in my blood, and this morning I was much lower. Soon after this Sprinchorn came along, and as he happens to have lost his appendix, he knew something about it. And it so happened that I had misplaced the position of my appendix by exactly one foot and four inches, which is a good deal on a man of my stature. So I underwent a quick recovery—without an operation—and spent about two hours in the lake. Still, I am a bit uneasy even yet, all of which explains why I am writing you this evening. To try and take his mind off it.

Received your second letter, anent nine-cent wine, and have noted same. Likewise details on the Rotonde. I envy you a little less than I did in my preceding letter, as a warm spell seems to have set in again, making our squash fairly spin and giving an urgently needed push to corn and tomatoes. Also, the lake has warmed up again, after I had renounced it for the year, so that we picnic on the shore, have anchored the raft again, and live in and out of the water most gratifyingly. All things considered, I suppose we shall go back to New York about the first of October. Already I have begun getting my hack in shape, trying especially to lay out roughly a number of general essays which are to be filled in with research as soon as I get back to town . . .

Then again, *Dial* or no *Dial*, I must write on Our Flaubertian Inheritance,[1] the essential whine here being first a division of artists into the prophetic and the critical, Flaubert falling into the second lot. Then, taking Flaubert as a critical artist, show how the art-to-conceal-art aesthetics is so poorly fitted to his type of accomplishment. The reason for this is that the concern with processes is the most vital phase of the critical artist, whereas the art-to-conceal-art aesthetics demands a complete covering of the tracks of these processes. Another point here would be to stress the incompletion of either romanticism, realism, or a mixture of the two, Flaubert's own dissatisfaction being indicated by the way he vacillated among them . . .

·   ·   ·

Maintain something. I saw in your last letter evidences of a poetic renaissance, especially in that paragraph devoted to a general scrambling of time and history. I used to say of Jim Light that his genius lay in the conceit; who knows, perhaps we shall eventually hand that glory over to you . . .

. . . I have become bullied by the thought of New York. This has been caused principally by a discovery I made recently. The discovery, namely, that I know nothing of a life without a war. You could say that my eyes opened, that is, in high school, about the time of the advance through Belgium. Since then I have graduated from high school, been to two colleges, permanently renounced writing four or five times, married, labored, rested, bummed, ein Kind gekriegt, laid the cornerstone of my career, etc., ad inf., and all in a belligerent world. (For last year, although the war was over, we were still existing on the fat of the war; indeed, I shall be doing so until this fall.) Now, I was admirably fitted for belligerency. Selfish, unpatriotic, with poor eyes and defective hearing, treacherous to any employer, I could be depended upon in war times to attain complete florescence. Yet even in war times my florescence was markedly mediocre. And oh God, what shall I do in peace times! . . .

K. B.

1. This essay appeared as "The Correspondence of Flaubert" in *The Dial* (February, 1922). It was also the basis for part of a chapter in *Counter-Statement*, "Three Adepts of 'Pure' Literature."

> c/o American University Union,
> 1, rue de Fleurus,
> Paris (VIᵉ)
> September 10, 1921
> [NL]

Dear Kenneth:

Mrs. Wilkinson says, "I think *all* Frenchwomen are a little fast, *don't* you?"

Mrs. Wilkinson says, "I met an *American* in Lyons and he was *so* amusing." (With the air that there is something nice about some Americans—after all.)

Mrs. Wilkinson says, "I *don't* think you have any literary criticism in America. I *don't* understand why you dislike Conrad, Mr. Cowley." . . .

Wilkinson himself talks French correctly but with English intonations; one hears his voice at fifty yards and says, "Who is talking English in this town?" And one is surprised to find that the words are French . . .

I am writing in bed, against a pad propped up on my knees. It was the grape that brought me to this state—not drinking it but eating it. I arise solely to visit the W.C., where I have long conversations with my landlady, who is dusting outside the door . . .

. . .

I am sending the "Book of Yul" to Wilkinson, who will return it to you.

And I am affixing only half the necessary postage to this letter to remind you that 5 cents, not 2, is necessary for letters to France. Your two letters have cost me 60 centimes.

Malcolm

Monson, Maine
September 12, 1921
[PS]

Dear Mal,

Perhaps the last of my letters of bounty. It was very hot, that is, up until the tenth, and then a rain set in, and now that rain threatens to be cleared away by a wind from the northwest. All of which occurring in such a manner, we shall have a frost . . . I have been swimming with almost complete regularity from the beginning of July to the tenth of September. There is not a spot on my body that I can't make as hard as a skullbone. My wife and child are, so to speak, in the pink of perfection. I have made the first step of my career as an authentic writer. (I have, that is, seen my way clear of imitation, in mentality as well as form.) Glory, glory.

· · ·

This I claim, Malcolm, as irrefutably mine; this I have patented: An art dealing with subjects which undergo changes in dimensions. I, that is, retain exclusive rights to having the toothache mentioned in a previous letter become a tropical storm, by the identical process as described in same letter.

As to Dr. William Carlos Williams, I have just decided that:

1. His moi and my moi are irreconcilable.
2. Neither of us has gained by our contact, and certainly I have not gained by his *Contact*.
3. I should write a letter of protest about him to the *Little Review*.

The situation stands thus: In early April the Burkes were invited out to the Williamses for a Sunday dinner. After dinner, it being a warm day, we all sat out on the grass in the back yard, while I explained what pathetically little I then knew about the aesthetic unities. The doctor, having wearied of calling me cerebral, became suddenly charmed with my wares and talked rashly of a literary correspondence. I came here and started off quite bravely, maintaining quite a variety of things. Doc answered in the capacity of a vigorous young American, making much of certain things being beyond him, or beside him, or beneath him. Then at times I would get two irate letters, the second trampling the first one's heels, cursing, steaming, stamping about, and affirming generally that there was too much to be said, that it simply could not be harnessed, that he had gone up in smoke. For a whole summer, Malcolm, I patiently poured my most valuable discoveries into the sewer. Then recently I sent him some stories, and God bless me if he didn't begin at the beginning again, and complain that they were too cerebral. I was remarkably self-possessed, Malcolm. I counted ten, walked around the house, smoked a pipe, and then sent him a questionnaire. This questionnaire was introduced by rehearsing the above facts about a literary correspondence. Then I wrote down a list of topics to be answered by yes or no, so that in this way no one could accuse him of lacking opinions. Needless to say, the answer was rather sharp, although there was no mention made of the topics. I am now waiting for his issue of *Contact* to appear so that I can write and congratulate him that there is not a cerebral line in it . . .

K. B.

50 Charles Street,
New York City
October 30, 1921
[PS]

Dear Mal,

A bit sour, having piddled around all day with my "Modifying the Eighteenth Century," the book review on Schnitzler. It is as solid as a review by a professor of botany—which is doubly a shame, as I was especially anxious to make something of it. I have discovered, I fear, the technique of the well-made review: general orientation, substance of story, rating of same, discussion of treatment (this being a translation, comparisons with the original are inserted here), how similar theme has been treated by another, close. However, I stumble along in the dark, perfectly aware that it is just as likely as any other to be acclaimed the greatest book review ever written. But Christ, how solid!

The difficulty lies in this: in reading Pater, I get into Plato; in reading his introduction to Plato, I decide that I must read Hegel; now, Hegel may throw some more light on Spengler, since Spengler's cultural seasons must be simply one more twist to the Zeitgeist; at the same time, along comes a symposium of leading Critics of England and America in the *New Republic*; subject "The Function of Criticism." General rehashing of impressionism; absolutely not a word of aesthetics; not the least mention of what remains today as vital as when de Gourmont asked it: does art or aesthetics come first? General snotting around concerning the un-morality of all criticism, the only penetrating word on this subject being said by some theologian who claimed that it was impossible to escape the moral judgment (driven into the Church again by the scurviness of our freethinkers). Christ, it's one thing to ask critics to understand good work, and another to ask that they say something valuable on criticism; I at least demand the latter. At the same time, planning an inventory of literary currents, to take up such things as realism, romanticism, decadism one by one and maintain their bankruptcy; Gide has said that every once in a while we should reestablish our attitude toward Lessing's *Laocoön*, by which he meant that no aesthetic principle should be taken for granted; historic criticism of no value to literature, since by it a bad book is as illuminating as a good one; impressionistic criticism fails in that it betrays a complete lack of comprehension, of breadth, of underlying laws . . .

•　　•　　•

. . . I continue to meditate on the distinction between the relative and the absolute, in the meantime also feeling on the verge of some sort of article on a priori art, beginning perhaps with Wagner—who seems to have been the basis of some of Mallarmé's distinctions between the theater and the book; then going through Mallarmé himself, and ending with my dogma of "inherent properties." Which dogma is, simply, that any medium should attempt exclusively to exploit its own fundamentals, and which would lead, for instance, to the overthrow of vagueness in literature—a conclusion just the opposite, evidently, of Mallarmé's. My point is this: (on the matter of vagueness) the one property which literature possesses to the exclusion of all other arts is that of ideological clarity. If a man wants "atmosphere," let him turn to music; a literature which strives for such things will always be of secondary importance. Or better, and the qualification comes to me now for the first time, the *means* of literature is ideological clarity; the overtone, I suppose, the purpose, the effect, must remain something vague, something sentimental, as with *Marius the Epicurean*. Pater gets a more authentic "emotion" out of his fixed statements than Mallarmé gets out of his ellipses; and all simply because Pater was closer to the inherent properties of words.

•　　•　　•

As to the old ideal of the welding of form and matter, it is linked with the search for the Absolute. The search for the Relative involves the triumph of form over matter, for it is relations which always give matter a new complexion. Thus, we accept this much as axiomatic: Art in the deepest sense is always contemporaneous, that is, parallels the general complexion of the times; the basic white-and-black distinction between modern and ancient (omitting Heraclitus) is Absolutism and Relativism. Accepting that much as axiomatic, we must accept the triumph of form over matter as the channel of art.

Why not, then, a book on aesthetics? And aesthetics, based not on metaphysics, but on a philosophy of history. On Spengler, that is, through Hegel. As to those who object to pure theory in art, there is no such thing as pure theory in art. A man precedes himself out of his own emotions; which is a quack way of saying that a man makes principles of his desires, and then follows these principles instead of following the desires. But as for those who are content to follow their desires simply, I for one maintain that they are uni-cellular and inarticulate. The prime wonder, I suppose, is movement; but that is the prime wonder of nature. The prime wonder of man is disintegration. Which leads us a new way to Benda,[1] who is a humanist over against the immersed-in-lifers.

November 3, 1921

·   ·   ·

Very deliberately, I am coming to realize just why New York is distasteful, and why I must get free of it . . . [T]he edge of the commuting distance is perhaps the ideal summit of modern civilization, since one is within easy range of both magazines and hospitals, since the country has a certain freshness and cleanness—lacking, however, that sense of the frontier, of the pathless beyond, which is to be found in Maine—since, in other words, it combines all elements most harmoniously. As to New York, I, at least, will not be able to work here satisfactorily. Literature is something which must soak into me, like my white ox—these things are always significant— I cannot acquire things except by saturation. In other words, I cannot take a regular job and write; on the other hand, I cannot make a living in New York on writing what I want to write, whereas I could do so living outside of New York. (Of course, in time I could probably be making enough out of some hack channel, but that is as bad as, if not worse than, having a regular job.) . . .

K. B.

1. Julian Benda (1867–1956), French novelist and critic known especially for his attack on the romantic philosophy of his time, especially as embodied in Henri Bergson.

[November, 1921]
[Montpellier, France]
[Date and location torn off original]
[NL]

Dear Kenneth:

Your last letter was a panegyric of small successes. For which I envy you and congratulate you. But if you have the stuff, and have it written, there is no reason you should not be successful. Unrecognized genius is a commodity which does not exist in America. Our great problem is rather to be geniuses and to continue to be geniuses after forty. The rest comes. It does not come naturally or easily, it does not debouch necessarily into the *Saturday Evening Post*, but it comes. The critics have proclaimed— until they now believe it themselves—that we are in the midst of a renaissance. And having proclaimed the renaissance they look busily around—like you and me—for the other half of this youngest generation. You are one of the few young American writers who writes. You cannot long be overlooked.

Even I meditate on what you would do with the two thousand dollars of the *Dial*. You will of course come to Europe. (a) because you need Europe and (b) because two thousand dollars goes farther here . . .

You would find me vague. Vague about the aims of literature and the worth of modern literature. Vague about politics. Vague, more especially, about my own intentions in art and life. Vague about my reactions to your estival theories of form. When you say that you wish to write a story in which you proclaim definitely the formatic steps, such as *introduction, transition, theme, climax*, etc., I follow you perfectly. I follow your theory of planes also, in theory, although in practice I should tend to put a man with a toothache on board the storm-wracked vessel. As for overtones, I think you are still talking enthusiastic balderdash. I don't refuse to see the overtones which crowd "In Search of Olympus"; nevertheless I don't see them . . .

But after this lapse into didacticism I become vague again. Even I am vague about what I am going to study during the year, although classes have already commenced. The courses given to foreigners are a mixture of erudition and puerility. The courses given regularly require the writing of a great many reports, something which I still find difficult. Meanwhile I study Corneille as if I were in Peabody.

. . .

Walking to classes I make reflections on literature. Without the ambition of Aristotle, I try to arrive at a formula which will at least satisfy me. Vainly. I then think of inaugurating a new classicism (alas, without knowing much of the old). I feel the need of rules, especially to break. I meditate reading Boileau, and extracting from him the principles which still hold good. Or Pope: "The chief study of mankind is man." I was halted by my inability to decide whether this principle was still valid. I thought of drawing up a questionnaire which I should send to the literary men of my acquaintance. I thought of a questionnaire but not of the questions. I remained vague.

But this vagueness can last only till the end of my scholarship and no longer. When my boat steams into New York harbor, I must know definitely what to do. Like you I am living my adolescence over again. And long may it wave.

Malcolm

[50 Charles St.]
[New York City]
November 26, 1921
[PS]

[Dear Malcolm,]

Just received your letter on vagueness, and with some relief. It seems, then, that we can run along in the same channels no matter how many miles are between us. At present I am in as thorough a dispersion as a conscientious sinner. My article on Pater, for instance, has certain absolutely hideous aspects, as I recall it. I talked of dynamic form, musical form; but perhaps what we really want is mass form, architectural form, static form, since that is the most evident opposition to dispersion. However, this new element comes into the discussion, which I think is ridiculous, but inevitable: (i.e, the element) every whole thing contains its thesis and antithesis. In this way, we must reconcile both dynamic and static form in the one production. This could be done—and here I rediscover myself—by my method of last summer, with more such things as my change of dimension added; that is, in its larger aspects the plot is balanced by blocks, while these blocks themselves are disclosed as energies; which, halleluia! is something of the predicament of the electron itself, so I am no worse off than God . . .

. . . I did, however, read one book today which I came nearly sending to you . . . It is called *A Defence of Philosophic Doubt, Being an Essay on the Foundations of Belief*,[1] and is a real display of skill. On the whole, it must be admitted that I am not particularly concerned with the matter . . . but the processes here made me positively coo with delight . . . The really interesting point, however, comes up in a chapter at the close, laying the foundations for an ethics. You will recall that at school we were always taught that ethics was a byproduct of metaphysics; given a certain metaphysical assumption, from that one could deduce an ethics. The Right Honorable Balfour, however, claims that ethics begins with itself, which is a real revolution. I am going to look into Spinoza to see whether he really succeeds in arriving at ethics from a metaphysical beginning . . . We should learn from metaphysics, which is never valuable as a search for truth, but for the byproducts it produces on the way. Art, then, is the only certainty, since it is the only outlet which can utilize these byproducts legitimately. Metaphysics becomes one branch of fiction. Oh shit! . . .

K. B.

---

1. A book by Arthur James Balfour, English statesman and writer, published in 1900.

Villa Marcel, rue Marguerite,
Montpellier, Hérault
November 28, 1921
[NL]

Dear Kenneth:

Please send me Brooks'[1] article against us; I think I might be able to make something out of it.

You complain with utter justification about my letters which do not arrive. The University is open now, and most of my time is occupied with the mysteries of French pedagogy. In other words I have left only two or three hours a day in which to write you. And naturally when I have finished paring my nails, poking the fire, rolling a cigarette, and trying to bite Peggy on the left buttock, I have expressed myself; there is nothing left to write.

And however I have a great deal to tell you; it is only the idle chaos of my mind which has prevented me. In the first place I see very clearly that my eighteen months in New York were as effective as eighteen enemas. They cleaned me out; I left there like a sheet of paper with nothing on it except a few erasures and the marks of having been used in a toilet. The abortive gestures which I made during those months do not even exist now as memories. The six letters you sent me might as well have been written from Mars by Matthew Josephson.

A little review of this summer will show you how complete has been my forgetfulness. On shipboard I wrote nothing. For the first two weeks in Paris I wrote nothing . . .

Beginning with my second week at Dijon, I detected the rumors of a renaissance. They were false, for although I must have worked fully forty hours, I was only developing a few of the projects I had conceived in New York. Ordinarily this would have been a laudable undertaking, but I did not realize at that time that I was several thousand miles from New York and that my renaissance could be nothing but abortive. I came to Montpellier.

And there I reached down into the void and found that it was infinite. If you want to know why I replied to none of your basic conceptions, it was because I had none myself to measure against them. I spent five weeks of undelicious idleness and chaos.

I hope I tumbled all the way down to the bottom. At any rate I am trying at present to lay foundations, beginning with a statement of what I think I should write, and ending up by writing it. Probably I am going at the problem backward. But I have to contend not merely with a lack of ideas, but with a lack of impressions . . .

I think it is about time we instituted a New Classicism. I have thought of reading Boileau for this purpose, and of copying such of his maxims as still hold good. Then of sending them around as a sort of questionnaire to various literary men of our acquaintance . . .

December 1

• • •

I feel at home in the seventeenth century, as if I had just been introduced to a very pleasant company of very kindred minds. The two sides of it: the grand tragedies in which one could use only noble words, and the low comedies in which one could say anything; there are two waterproof compartments in my mind like that, and I have always felt ashamed of their existence. How regally I should have licked King Louis' ass, meanwhile composing the satire for publication after his death. In you also I seem to detect the ruin of an excellent satirist: if Floyd Dell had been Chapelain[2] or Shadwell, you should already be enjoying a pension from His Majesty the second Charles or the fourteenth Louis . . .

M.

1. Van Wyck Brooks, who had written an article critical of those writing for *Broom* and *Secession*.
2. Jean Chapelain (1595–1674), French poet and critic.

50 Charles Street,
New York City
December 23, 1921
[PS]

Dear Mal,
. . . I smile with my eyes shut in contemplation of that joyous retreat lying somewhere just beyond the commuting distance. Being a chronically bad poet, the Baudelairean formula n'importe où, hors du monde, becomes simply n'importe où, hors de New York. In fact, my plan of action is already completed; I have set to work; and it can be done without a cent, I do believe . . .

Perhaps you might be interested in my plan of campaign. It is to find a small farm which is at present unoccupied, but is still in fair living condition. (The house, that is.) Then I get in touch with the owner and offer to take it on a partial rent-partial payment basis. That is, supposing that it is to be sold for two thousand. I offer to rent it for six percent of that, and pay for all repairs myself. In addition to that, I may pay off as much of the two thousand as possible each year. If the first year I paid off five hundred, then the owner's invested capital would be valued at only fifteen hundred, so that my rent for the second year would be six percent of fifteen hundred. As soon as the holidays are over I am going to put an ad in the Poughkeepsie *Courier*.

．　　．　　．

Williams sent me his new book of poems, some of which are very good. True, I admire them the way a doctor would admire a diseased liver: the more diseased the better. They represent excellence in an angle of approach which does not interest me *per se*. But even so one cannot be blind to their excellence. I quote the closing poem of the volume,[1] because I believe it a perfect example of *Contact*. (And I take the word Contact to mean "man without the syllogism, without the parode, without Spinoza's Ethics, man with nothing but the noumenon and the eye to make that noumenon a phenomenon") . . . I see now just why I am interested in Williams: because he has frequently done to perfection just the sort of thing I do not want to do. In other words, in him I find a superb adversary, thus making one less likely to grow lax in his own productions . . .

K. B.

December 26

. . . As to Boileau, there is no reason why we should be made to begin with the damned fools of classicism. Further, I doubt whether we could build on past precepts; we can only build on OUR OWN NEW INTERPRETATIONS of past precepts. A sentence from Boileau is not worth a pfennig. A new classicism is not a mere rehashing. It must, obviously, begin with an element of its own.

1. "The Great Figure Five."

Villa Marcel, rue Marguerite,
Montpellier, Herault
January 23, 1922
[NL]

Dear Kenneth:

Whatever resolve you have taken about writing me you seem to have kept it. I have received no letter from you for over two weeks.

．　　．　　．

A few days ago we had a stroke of luck. Stewart Mitchell[1] commissioned Peggy to do his portrait in watercolor and paid her $60 for the work, bringing our grand total to nearly $300. There it rests. *Broom* has bought another poem, but it pays in lire. I have done a translation of a silly article on Georges Braque, for which I demanded $30 (s'il plait à Dieu que je sois paye). My problem seems rather to write the stuff than to sell it; bankruptcy is the event of four months; life has been costing us 370 francs a week. So much for finances.

Apropos of *Broom*. When I sent two poems lately, I addressed them with a personal letter to Kreymborg (who is a nice little chap and doesn't justify your polemics). Two weeks later I received a brief note from Loeb,[2] on paper which carried his name only as editor. Has Alfred been fired? (Just as I always blamed the *Dial*'s shortcomings on Thayer,[3] so I have been blaming those of *Broom* on the richer Jew. I should regret Kreymborg's demise.)

My thoughts have been taken up increasingly with the theories of classicism. One night I even began drawing up an aesthetic, but I walked too quickly, and I arrived home just before I should have succeeded in defining my subject. I had drawn up two principles: "Art is the creation of the beautiful," and "Beauty is the object of art." Since these two principles formed a circle, I had to abandon them both.

"To test whether a piece of prose is a work of art, it is only necessary to inquire whether it is disinterested." This proposition is a favorite one among amateur aestheticians; it applies to some cases but not to all. Machen's[4] theory of ecstasy is dangerous. When I arrived into my own gaslight I had not yet succeeded in stating the subject of my aesthetics, so that the laws themselves still remain in the air.

• • •

Do you know, I was always rather ashamed of myself because I wasn't sufficiently unintelligible. Now I see that the most ridiculous feature of modern writing is the fear of being understood. We wish to be the priests each of our own little sect, and each sect has its Rosicrucian secrets, only to be revealed to the proselyte who has passed through the seven stages of the novitiate. Meanwhile the proselytes are too busy founding little sects of their own. And literature remains the art of conveying ideas and shows no disposition to adopt either Dada or Rosicrucianism.

I want instead to reduce everything to its simplest terms, and to build up subtlety by the opposition of simple statements.

I never had your passion for filling each page I began.

M.

1. Stewart Mitchell (1892–1957), an American writer and poet, was a friend of Cowley's at Harvard and a managing editor of *The Dial*.

2. Harold Loeb, co-editor of *Broom*.

3. Scofield Thayer, publisher, with J. Sibley Watson, of *The Dial*.

4. Arthur Machen (1863–1947) was an English novelist who wrote semiautobiographical fantasies and supernatural tales.

989 Boulevard East,
Weehawken, N.J.
February 6, 1922
[PS]

Dear Mal,

Rejoicings and lamentations. Rejoicings that M. Cowley Esq. came out of his greatness long enough to surprise me with a letter three weeks before it was expected. Lamentations that the same party has some more piffle about being misunderstood . . . If a metaphysic is not expressed in a paragraph as lucid as one of Anatole France's narratives, one surely cannot damn the metaphysic categorically. On the other hand, if one says How d'ye do with obscurity, one need not rate him higher in the scale of poesy than Mina Lois.[1] But there really are, by heavens, such things as intricacies of thought; if one's position is cogent, there will be no confusion, but there will be intricacy. Such intricacy has nothing whatsoever to do with your hypothetical desire to be misunderstood. Anyone who has a desire to be misunderstood is an ass. Even Mallarmé, the patron saint of obscurity, had no such desire. Further, there is always the problem of where one situates his obscurity. If, for instance, I write "Eternally the however possesses the ratio of a but to an indicative," we will grant that it is obscure. But if I am giving this sentence as the speech of a maniac or a mountebank, the reader finds no obscurity, in that he understands the sentence's *application*, and therefore realizes that it would be idle to look for a coherent meaning. Thus, in the same way, places in my stories may seem obscure if taken *per se*, but not if taken through an understanding of their purposes. When this is the case, I have tried to make these purposes plain; and when I have failed to make them plain, I have been dissatisfied.

In any case, that is my defense if you were really including me in the professional obscurists. I do still claim, however, that I am an *obscurantist*, even though I have renounced being an *obscurist*. That is, I believe that art is the possession of the initiated, that there are some who understand through creative taste, and some who can be taught, while the great bulk of the world remains as unsensitive to aesthetic values as an ape does to a Cézanne. I further believe that the creative artist also creates an aesthetic, and that those who must be taught will not grasp this new art until the aesthetic has sunk into them to a degree. At one time the whole world flowed toward the building of Gothic cathedrals; at such times a vanguard of aesthetics was unnecessary, since there was nothing which needed to be fought for. At the present time, if there is anything which could be called a concerted European movement, this movement is the development of individual talents. Thus, Mallarmé's cosmogeny idea is quite reasonable as a statement of the necessities of the times. Further, I maintain that a marked critical tendency will be found in any of our significant writers, and that this critical tendency must necessarily manifest itself in a more or less carefully elaborated aesthetic programme. As I said of Mallarmé in a previous letter, the formulation of the aesthetic is part of the man's sum of expression. Now, if writing done under one aesthetic is tested by the standards of another, in this way also it may look obscure . . .

· · ·

Why don't you, by the way, adopt my system of propaganda? That is, hitching one's theses to the name of accepted past writers. People who will turn aside from a general article will read something on a specific man, especially if it has a few dates thrown in, and the name of his mistress. I find the thing working out very satisfactorily, and believe that after four or five more essays I shall have rounded out a pretty definite statement, covering the nature of technique, form, ideology, beauty, subject matter, dogma. Which reminds me that, judging from little things here and there, I believe my Flaubert article has more than served its purpose. In its essentials, it is this: I took Flaubert away from the realists, by establishing very definitely— mostly by his own statements in his letters—his detest of realism as it would be understood by the present American realists. Now, Flaubert is the modern password; so it is no mean triumph to have dragged him into our camp . . .

K. B.

1. Minna Loy (1882–1966), American poet.

989 Boulevard East,
Weehawken, N.J.
February 20, 1922
[PS]

Dear Mal,
 . . . Do you know, Malcolm, that criticism is a subdivision, not of dialectics, but of rhetoric? By which I mean that we must all vituperate and deify, and the one with the cleverest tricks wins. For there is no ultimate element on which a critical system can be based. We place the intellect

above the emotions, but this is a matter of choice. Pursued, we can move on; we can say, for instance, that the intellect sees the object from without while the emotions strive to become in sympathy with the object. Thus, that the emotions imply subjection, while the intellect implies freedom . . . One prepares his set of oaths, his reductions to absurdity, his calumniatory analogies, and then one takes a topic . . .

· · ·

February 22, 1922

Today, on the birthday of the father of our country, I began the great work which is to be the father of American art. Twenty dollars' worth of "The Priority of Forms" has been written.[1] The remaining eighty dollars' worth already exists in notes. I begin by stating three possible attitudes on the relation of form and matter: (a) that form is prior to matter, and simply utilizes matter to bring forms within the range of our organic experience; (b) that matter is prior to form, and uses form to bring out the best possibilities of matter; (c) that the perfect art involves the marriage of form and matter. This third being the current piffle, I first disposed of it in this wise: obviously, when we speak of striving for the perfect marriage of form and matter, we have not made a sufficient statement. For what is the purpose of this marriage? Is it to bring out the best in matter; or is it to bring out the best in form? The marriage has no meaning in itself; it is heralded as a great thing because it accomplishes something. And this something must be either that we have found the exact form in which to bring out the best of our subject, or the exact subject which will best exemplify our form. Thus, the great modern tenet disappears, and we are left with the choice between a and b. Then I take up b, the greatness of matter, the use of form as ancillary to matter. This involves, first, a long harangue on the modern notion that art should be a substitute for life, whereas as a matter of fact, art is the crowning of a life. It is this supreme emphasis on realism, on a vicarious existence in art, which is leading to art's loss of dignity . . .

An art forced to fit itself to the requirements of life must of necessity be dwarfed out of dignity, just as the philosophy of the schoolmen was dwarfed by being forced to fit itself to the requirements of the Church . . . [I]f art is a question of subject matter, what is it that distinguishes art from a scientific treatise? Obviously, it is the striving after an organic form; the denial that subject matter has any intrinsic value. If subject matter has value of itself, let someone conceive of a play in which some character read for half an hour a travel sketch of India. A travel sketch of India could be very interesting. One has read many such things for the bare facts involved. But we could not stand such a thing for two minutes in a play, unless every word of this sketch *had some bearing on the plot*, unless we saw people being put in a new light . . .

After my explanation of ratios, I take up a new attack, this time to defend my theory from the incrimination of universals. For if I speak of ideal forms and pure movement, I shall give the philosopher the impression that I have reverted to the old conception of archetype ideas existing in heaven. I emphasize that my aesthetics is not metaphysical, but psychological. (And when I say psychological I am very careful to add: "This does not lead to the Dostoevsky type of analysis. For I situate the psychology in the forms, Dostoevsky situated the psychology in the subject matter". . .) . . .

We must, perhaps, assign to criticism a two-fold purpose. Technically, it is a guardian of the forms; and also, it fights the old battles of subject matter. It worries over the possibility of categorical judgments, of whether philosophical subject matter for instance, is categorically superior to farce, so that the acme of philosopher-poet would be superior to the acme of farce-writer. Indeed, even as I write I see a possible way out. "Pure" forms are at the reach only of intelligence; ideas are the same; thus, can not philosophy and art be reunited, as they were with Plato? Hurrah! a category!

K. B.

1. Although Burke did not publish an essay by this title, the material described in what follows appears in a number of the essays on literary form he wrote in the next few years, and in his book *Counter-Statement*.

Villa Marcel, rue Marguerite,
Montpellier, Hérault
February 27, 1922
[NL]

Dear Kenneth:

I am writing you briefly, to let you know that my silence has not been caused by pique.

I just passed an unnecessary examination for an unnecessary Diploma of French Studies. I worked hard, tried to think in French, worried a little, and finally received a *Mention très honorable*. I am now trying to write some articles to keep the wolf from my open French windows; the *Dial* aided me by sending me four books.

My delights have been purely physical. Spring, coming north over the Mediterranean, arrived here about February 15. The almond trees are now in flower. The buttercups are fading, except in the shade, but there are fields white with narcissi and the jonquils are beginning to bloom. The sun shines down brazenly and my feet are beginning to perspire, by which signs I know that summer is coming.

Food is another of my physical delights. Fresh salads all the winter. Fresh peas. New potatoes since New Year's. Artichokes and brussels sprouts at the price of American cabbages. Fresh lamb chops; eating the cold storage product I never realized the savor of lamb. Roquefort is only a hundred miles away, and the cheeses arrive fresh and biting.

Wherefore your two last letters aroused in me a sort of full-bellied tolerance, which of all emotions is the most hateful to you. I mean your indignant attacks on my *Ridicules of Current Aesthetics*. As a matter of fact I was proceeding on a confusion of thought, or a confusion of objects. I was mingling you—and me—and our opponents in the word "contemporary." You do not partake, except at rare moments, of the Desire to Be Misunderstood. You do partake, however, of the substitution of art for religion, which, in spite of your indignant protest, I still consider to be touched with ridicule. But my treatise wasn't in the least aimed at you; it was more an examination of my own mind and a denigration of my own ideas, inasmuch as I had accepted them from other people. Some other evening I am going to explain myself at greater length; just now I have fallen back into Futilism: the futility of life, art, and explanations . . .

M.

989 Boulevard East,
Weehawken, N.J.
March 13, 1922
[PS]

Dear Mal,

I sit down to answer your letter now for a peculiarly avengeful reason. It is, namely, that I have been walking, and standing, one or the other, for a number of hours. As a consequence, if you were to offer me a brand new theory of the universe, I could answer. But what in the hell does that matter? And, if you undertook to prove to me why a certain line of somebody was a little better than a certain line of somebody else . . . In other words, I hasten to write you now, since I feel myself your dialectic equal. With Socrates before me, I could turn my face to the wall.

How unfortunate, then, that your last letter contained no elaborately thought-out statements for me to be bored with. Or no, not exactly that. But, to make a new start, by Jesus, you have reverted to that art-religion business. Now, let us see. To begin by making the broadest possible distinction, we could speak of two religions: there is the religion of the early Father, the monastic, the religious discoverer, that is; then there is the religion of the inheritor, the contemporary Methodist deacon, the ordinary churchgoer. Now, when we say that art should not take the place of religion, we obviously mean that art should not mean to the lover of beauty what the Church meant to the early Father. At least, I assume that this is the attitude you find ridiculous, for you, like me to a lesser degree, react against the elite rather than against the stupid. The stupid, that is, do not count; but the elite can be exposed as stupid; it is no accomplishment to do as the representative progressive sheets (*New Republic, Freeman, Nation*, etc.) and prove that the stupid are stupid; the trick is to prove that the elite are stupid; wherefore, you shall attack the elite. (In the same way, Benda attacks Bergson, although compared with the run of Europe Bergson is elite.) But note: in attacking the elite, one must not be tricked into taking sides with the stupid . . .

So, for the life of me, I still fail to see where you are getting off at. It is simply one of the first principles of being a human being that if one is vitally interested in something, he follows up the bent of his interest. Edison perfects his inventions, Spinoza works out his ethics, Flaubert goes to the depths of his aesthetics; these three are parallels of the early Father, and over against them is the casual churchgoer, who sits down in a more or less morally regulated world, to read *Madame Bovary*, by electric light. Problem: find the ridiculous. Answer: situated in the brain of M. C. . . . .

. . .

I am sorry we are so scattered. If we were all in America now, I believe that we could really put this damned magazine on the map.[1] For I believe that we could really be formidable. Christ, give me five good issues in which to pamphleteer to my heart's content. But it means nothing to me to pamphleteer in Vienna. I dream of a paper which will prey upon the progressives. Although this, of course, is dangerous; for so far as I can see it would involve the attacking of our sole organs of publicity. Still, I should be willing to undertake the damned thing somehow. If everyone got a job on a trade paper, and really were capable of following up literature in addition. But that, of course, is a pipe dream. For when you return to America you will return to drinking red ink with Dave Sullivan,[2] and to worrying for a week over Djuna's getting mad because you deliberately walked up to her and said something or other, and being a proud young blood because Greaser Bill drinks with you; all this is inevitable, a return to type, and at this very moment is to be found carefully preserved and nourished in your thesis that it is ridiculous to find letters of any vital interest. Oh shit, oh shit, sometimes I wonder if you are not simply a hangover from Chekhov, one of those architects of his who put up a building somewhere with some damned fine qualities, and then spent the rest of his life playing cards. Which, if I understand you rightly, is the road to dignity . . .

K. B.

1. *The Gargoyle*, an English-language magazine edited in Paris.
2. Dave Sullivan was a New York acquaintance of Cowley's.

> Villa Marcel, rue Marguerite,
> Montpellier, Hérault
> March 30 (Ste. Amedee),
> 1922
> [NL]

Dear Kenneth:

I have come to the point where I have to ask you for help again. Money, of course—not from you, but from other people. North published a story of mine back in January, a little story for which he owes me $11.50. A little later I sent him a story on Marseilles which I have not as yet seen in print ($25 when published). Next time you get a chance can you ask him about the two stories skillfully?

. . . I am going to write an article on the centenary of Murger[1] for the *Freeman*. I have it all doped out. A Brief History of Bohemia. Murger was the founder of the romantic Bohemia. Nothing has changed since his time, except that the artists and writers have gradually withdrawn from it, leaving it to people who paint on pottery, romantic fairies, and vendors of peanut novelties. Plea for classical life as a basis for classical art. Evidently the article will skim the edges of banality, but it is a case where my theory of "big subjects" applies; if I skim successfully it will be a very authoritative article. I want you to peddle it, and *definitely* to take out enough to pay for your trouble.

Cussy Wright[2] has taught me the new trick. Don't criticize current literature; write about Molière and Petronius. It's just as easy—or easier, because Cussy cribs most of his material—and it gives you a great deal more standing. If Murger goes I shall continue with Racine and Wycherley.

You and Jack Wheelwright, when you assigned me my precise niche in literature, were more kind than just to my poetry and more just than kind to the excellent tool which is my brain. It is perhaps true that by taking thought I shall add never a cubit to my stature, but by thinking I shall at least develop what I have. My brain is a practical brain, a brain that likes to work on definite lines, a brain that thinks about means rather than ends and that can make at least A— on any subject set for it. No one ever does justice to this type of brain. It is the classical brain which builds a perfectly proportioned edifice, which writes prose that is simple and clear, and poetry studiously incorrect. It does not question enough; it respects ability and authority. It is the brain of Boileau and Pope and Congreve; that is the real reason of my classical campaign.

62 days to starvation.

Mal

1. Henry Murger (1822–1861), French poet and novelist famous for his *Scènes de la vie de Bohème* (1845–49). Cowley refers to the book in *Exile's Return*, pages 56–57.

2. Cuthbert Wright, a friend of Cowley's from Harvard.

R.D. #1,
Andover, N.J.
May 5, 1922

Dear Mal,

Hooray, old soak! Let me quote you from the letter I received from Brooks this morning; "Thank you so much for sending us the two articles by Malcolm Cowley. We are delighted with them and are happy to have them both." Once more, therefore, I must sweetly retire from the field; your articles so plainly sold themselves. I did, however, follow your blurb suggestions, I raved about your rare anti-romanticism in these days of the professionally hectic, said that the articles had been suggested by your line of study in Montpellier; also, I invented the subterfuge of saying that you had sent the articles to be disposed of according to my lights, and that to my lights they seemed very appropriate for the *Freeman*.

In any case, you are very plainly all set. I have at best been able only to make Brooks lukewarm to my stuff. You have evidently touched Nock,[1] which is divine. Between us, now that the articles are sold, I think I can voice my open dissatisfaction with them. Your virtue of clarity, I felt, was a bit overrated, (1) because your subject matter was not very complicated at most, so that there is no reason why it should not be clear, and (2) because it was not clear. An article, to be clear, can be reduced to an inevitable syllogism, a statement of premises and a cogent conclusion from them. Clarity, then, is nothing other than a broad grasp of the issues involved. And most of all it is opposed to latent assumptions. Clarity means simply that implicit dogma is made explicit . . .

Today is my birthday; twenty-five. For a present, I received a letter from Waldo Frank, praising my review in the last *Dial*[2] . . . Frankly, I don't know what in the name of hell I shall do. First Rosenfeld, than whom I have detested no other greater; then *Vanity Fair*, which I had always used as a symbol of smart nonsense; and now Waldo Frank, whose books I have openly clamored against. Add to the complications the fact that, for the article which I am preparing for *Vanity Fair*, Brooks' "Ordeal of Mark Twain" is the ideal text, the perfect anathema.[3] And this morning from Brooks I receive, "I am so glad you find the Croce book to your taste. That is an interesting point you suggest in regard to Croce and Bergson." Is it any wonder that I have been niggling with the *Vanity Fair* article for two weeks without results.

Just what one should do I do not know. One must not toady; and on the other hand one must not cut off his revenues with an unnecessary vandalism. My solution is to attempt a more constructive type of criticism, not merely to attack the existing, but to build up a counter-structure. Of course, we have always done this to a degree. My method now would be to minimize the attack and emphasize the counter-structure. Thus, I do not modify my attitude, but modify my method. Tell me, is this a lousy opportunizing? I do not think so. The important thing is to round out one's own conception of intellectual excellence, to develop a consistent and synthetic system of approach. This can be done without growling.

News on the *Dial*: They are a bit huffed about the first number of *Secession*. And as I prophesied, they ruffled somewhat about your sponsorship. Indeed, I had made no mention of *Secession*, was talking about you and me (gently blurbing), when Seldes[4] suddenly says, "Cowley seems to be pretty much the sponsor for *Secession*." The discussion then fell upon the anti-*Dial* stuff. I assured him that you had had nothing to do with that phase of the magazine. I told him that Munson's idea was eventually to make a board of editors, of which he was director, but that up to now his editorial policy was independent of the other contributors. Then Seldes, "Well, we are not going to do anything to our youngsters. In fact, I believe magazines like that are a good thing." . . . We are, you must never forget too long, "their youngsters." At times we become bad, and they do not know whether or not to spank us, and then they decide that they won't this time . . .

And oh! there is the possibility that I shall work for the *Dial* from July to November, filling Sophie Wittenberg's[5] place. In fact, it has already been definitely settled between Watson, Seldes and me, but the thing seems too good. Christ, what a chance! I should get thirty-five dollars and pay for all contributions. Not a great pile, perhaps, but with my present low expenses it would leave me in positive affluence. I shall get my secondhand Ford to ride to the station, and commute from Andover . . .

K. B.

1. Albert J. Nock (?–1945), author, educator, and editor of *The Freeman*.

2. Burke's review was of Paul Elmer More's *The Religion of Plato*, published in the May issue of *The Dial*.

3. Burke's review article on Brooks' *The Ordeal of Mark Twain* appeared in the December, 1922, issue of *Vanity Fair*.

4. Gilbert Seldes (1893–1970), author, critic, and associate—later managing—editor of *The Dial* from 1920 to 1923.

5. Sophie Wittenberg was an assistant editor at *The Dial*. She later married the critic Lewis Mumford.

Villa Marcel, rue Marguerite,
Montpellier (Hérault), France
May 20, 1922
[NL]

Dear Kenneth:

Your letter arrived yesterday in the same mail as the announcement of the renewal of my fellowship. . . . My sentiments about it are mixed. Latterly I have been frightfully homesick for a country where No Trespass signs can be disregarded, and where there are trout streams. Also at times my head becomes frightfully empty, and I lie around the house in a frenzy of idleness. My talent is not cosmopolitan, and I have no desire to spend my life in France. On the other hand this existence in the French provinces—like that in the Argentine or a Chinese river town—gives an excellent perspective on America, and under its influence my ideas seem to be clarifying slowly.

Another mention of clarity. I should not be so proud of it if it came without effort. For example this Murger article. It was unjust for you to say that my subject matter was not very complicated at most; it took me ten days to de-complicate my subject matter. Even at that I did not fully succeed, so that you were perfectly just when you said that the essay could not be reduced to one syllogism. What I succeeded in doing was to give such an illusion of clarity that Brooks was taken in; he mentioned this quality in a conversation about me with Jack Wheelwright—which was exactly what I wanted Brooks to do . . . One quality I like about my prose is the fact that it connects. It is a prose that doesn't quote easily. One cannot, without some violence, wrench a sentence out of it, or even a paragraph; everything hangs together. But all this is only a praise of my tools; it is as if I said: I have the finest set of chisels in the world. It would be more logical to praise the work I can do with those chisels, and that I cannot do.

•　　•　　•

God, we laughed over the letter from Waldo Frank and the dilemma it aroused. Really, you are crawfishing, and Frank's letter of praise remains just as ridiculous a document; if more justified than his blurbs on Anderson and Rosenfeld.

I am just as much interested in your success as in my own; I make that transference of egoisms which is required in a friendship, and I see danger sometimes of transferring my egoism too much, which would be suicidal. At present I am a little afraid that your success, like all American successes, is coming too fast; it would be safer in ten years after your habits are more firmly molded. See whether you can't ride it into a trip to Europe instead of a Ford; several people would see that you didn't starve to death, and Europe is tremendously stimulating, either to the ideas—as it has proved in my case, or the sentiments, as it has proved in Matty's . . .

Malcolm

R.D. #1,
Andover, N.J.
June 1, 1922
[PS]

Dear Mal,

Yours of May 20th to hand. I, like you, receive the news of your scholarship renewal with a mixed interest. It had seemed to me that this winter could have marked the beginning of a drive here in America. We might possibly have gotten the illusion of a national ferment. We could in any case have organized a little group of serious thinkers. Or, taking it down to a minimum, to the ideal of Flaubert's letters, we could have smoked and spat together. On the other hand, you are assured of another year's squat, and it is, after all, better for the soul to loaf in hell than to so much as turn a hand in Paradise . . .

We are, perhaps, the back-to-the-soil movement in American letters, although we are involved in a search for root rather than for sentiment; not for purification à la Rousseau, but for good sturdy Sitzfleisch. Strangely enough, you have been much farther from the hearth than I, and yet you are greatly more locally minded. You, going to the Argentine or a Chinese river town, would go there precisely to get a better perspective on America. That is as it should be. Our future, for better or worse, is inevitably associated with this country. Nothing has brought this fact so strongly to my mind as Jewsn's[1] avid swallowing of the French. You have certainly been a more consistent apologist of France than he, and yet the influence has always been translated into our terms.

America I am coming to look upon as a responsibility. Like Mr. Sumstine,[2] I must point out that the country is what we make of it. We cannot move out magnificently, like Stearns; for such a gesture leaves us with nothing but yammering. Stearns will never see an inch farther. He has made a yammer out of the very transplanting of his body; he is henceforth yammering incarnate. As to the Americans in Paris, they have simply made France the whorehouse and barroom to America; I hope that French chauvinism is appeased thereby.

· · ·

Concerning Waldo Frank, and my too early success . . . [I]f by some chance I should be successful (my present unusual fame is netting me about thirty dollars a week) I think it would do me very little harm. For I am too religiously grounded in my belief that the public is stupid, and that if one is successful there is something wrong. Why the Stieglitz group has paid attention to me, I shall never understand. But to set things right I am making an out and out anti-Stieglitzian declaration in my article for *Vanity Fair*. But my first ideal of culture is to have three meals a day; and my second to sleep in the hammock after luncheon; and my third—not yet attained—is to smoke two cigars per diem . . .

K. B.

1. Matthew Josephson.
2. David R. Sumstine, the principal of Peabody High School.

c/o American University Union,
1, rue de Fleurus, Paris (VIe)
July 2, 1922
[NL]

Dear Kenneth:

I haven't written you, and god knows how I'm able to write you now. Paris is like cocaine; either it leaves you tremendously elated or sunk in a brown fit of depression. I begin now to understand its fascination, and I subscribe to the opinion of the ten thousand Matty Josephsons: you must come to Paris. Only, you mustn't stay here.

Paris has rarely or never produced great literature. There are rare exceptions: Baudelaire, Verlaine, but the rule is pretty safe. However, Paris has been the condition of great literature. Occasionally a man tears himself away from it and writes like—George Moore, James Joyce. He never writes till he goes, or if he does it is *genre boulevardier*; *pour épater les etc.* So witness Aragon, Cocteau, all the rest.

We have been doing the Dôme as usual. The crowd: Art Moss,[1] Percy Winner,[2] several nice boys, several Jewish girls, Ivan Opffer. This time, however, I was luckier. Ivan has a commission for the *Bookman*, to draw great European Men of Letters. Under cover of his commission, and to do the accompanying interviews, I have met Barbusse,[3] Paul Fort[4]—nice but no good to me—finally André Salmon,[5] who was just what I was looking for.

Salmon is nice. He is forty, and belongs to the generation of Apollinaire, Picasso, Max Jacob[6]—which means that he was very closely associated with them, and that his work bears the strong influence of Apollinaire, the great man of that group. More particularly he is interested in literary history, and he gave me wonderful dope on the last twenty years, which I will pepper-and-salt through a dozen articles. He even drew up for my benefit a chart: Thus,

1902 Soirées de la *Plume*; appearance of Apollinaire and Salmon·
1903 Appearance of Max Jacob
1905 *Vers et Prose*, founded by Paul Fort, unites the younger writers
1906 Period when Apollinaire and his group frequented the little English bars around the Gare St. Lazare. They meet with Pierre MacOrlan[7]
1903–7 Everything new in literature and art is centered in the atelier of Picasso in Montmartre
1908 Salmon and Apollinaire originate the new art criticism

And so on. Salmon has almost a superstitious reverence for Apollinaire, who, he says, originated all the tendencies which are occupying French literature today.

There was a dance Friday at the Bal Bullier which was very Webster Hall, except for one nude lady. I got drunk and enjoyed myself. Met Vina Hamnett, an English portrait painter, who knows more dirty songs than Lionel Moise.[8] The rest is a dull catalogue of [bocks?] and bridges . . .

When I think over your last letter, I shall be able to answer. Your last trinity: life, style, art, is very satisfactory to me, more so than the *Freeman*'s check for $20 . . .

Mal.

1. Arthur Moss was an American writer who edited *The Gargoyle* in Paris.
2. Percy Winner was a friend of Burke and Josephson from Columbia.
3. Henri Barbusse (1873–1935), French novelist.
4. Paul Fort (1872–1960), French poet.
5. André Salmon (1881–1969), French poet who befriended Cowley and taught him much about modern French literature and art.

6. Max Jacob (1876–1944), French poet.

7. Pierre MacOrlan (1883–1970), French novelist.

8. Lionel Moise was a newspaperman.

R.D. #1
Andover, N.J.
September 2, 1922
[PS]

Dear Mal,

Nothing has as yet turned up from you for Number 4.[1] I hope to God something is on the way, as we must soon be sending our material across the water. In case, by the way, you have anything at the last minute, send it direct to Matty, address Post Lagend, Reutte (Tirol), Austria. We continue to get nice letters from odd corners concerning *Secession*, and an occasional write-up in some remote sheet. Wheelwright sent a poem which we had to reject; Grant Code[2] sent in a number, of which we accepted the least weak; Wallace Stevens survived one rejection and came back with a poem which we have taken. A man by the name of Allen Tate, a poitrinaire in North Carolina, has been sending us stuff, strongly Laforguian, and we have taken one thing in which the adolescent disillusion was at a minimum. Also, a poem by Hart Crane, faintly experimental, good but not overwhelming . . .

I have not seen Brown[3] for a while, but I have a sneaking idea that Cummings has been scared off by Munson's editorials. Between us, I think that this is less of a calamity than some might suppose. Cummings is verbosity plus sentimentality, tears behind laughter; his poetry is a continual stepping around banalities; occasionally the stepping is very neat, neat to the point of genius, but if one translates him, as you translated Bodenheim,[4] one discovers many a distressing flatness. Cummings reminds me of a very skillful boxer doing his steps before a babe in arms.

Your protracted silence at this time is especially dissatisfying as I should like to know just how radically you intend backing up *Secession*. I wish to Christ you had in your character just one slight modicum of a capacity for answering my letters. Points, point-blank points: How far do you care to participate in the policies of the magazine? What do you think of my fond hope of making the magazine a nucleus for a self-hypnotizing group of fifteen or so men interested in literature? What do you think of a pamphleteering drive on the various New York critical diseases, a dogging of the liberals? Or, over against this, are you for a magazine of pure letters, without polemic, a magazine which will be respectfully and willingly lost, each issue appearing with weight and dignity, and being weightily and dignifiedly dumped into the ocean, until, ten years from now, some press-agenting ass whom we despise comes along and admires us, and puts us across? As to myself, I was long and stubborn about going into *Secession*, because for some reason or other I felt it as a responsibility. I refuse to be connected with just one more piddling paper. So far, as I am not writing now, I have given Munson the best back stuff that I have—you have done the same. But I have no intention of unloading . . .

●   ●   ●

Anent *Ulysses*, perhaps it has freed us of a great bondage. We can take it as the culmination of an era, take it as exemplifying many things we might have wanted to exemplify, but which were really hang-over things so far as we are concerned. *Ulysses* is the last word in romanticism, the flowering of the abnormal vision, the perfect exploitation of the individual province. *Ulysses* is the book Matthew Arnold was talking about all his life; but Arnold was at the start of the current which produced *Ulysses*. Incidentally, I think that *Ulysses* is a boring book; it is not an organism, but a compendium. It is amazing and formidable by reason of its sheer bulk; it has even done Joe Gould out of a job. It enlightened thereby. When I think of it, I think of Virgil's monstrum horrendum informe ingens cui lumen ademptum. Surely, the book was made to order for Djuna Barnes.

All of which is rather hasty, and dismaying principally by reason of its bluntness. Which means, I suppose, that it must continue to be dismaying until next December, at least. But I am sleepy; and this is all dumped into the ocean anyhow.

K. B.

1. Burke was helping prepare and edit the fourth number of *Secession*.

2. Grant Code was a former classmate at Peabody High.

3. William Slater Brown.

4. A reference to Cowley's forthcoming review of Maxwell Bodenheim's *Introducing Irony*, which appeared in the October 1922 issue of *The Dial*.

c/o American University Union,
1, rue de Fleurus, Paris (VIᵉ)
September 25, 1922
[NL]

Dear Kenneth:

I just blew in from Vienna, where I corrected the proof-sheets of *Secession* 3. I swore lustily as I corrected. Kenneth, that number stinks of bad writing, Dada, and the ghetto. The story by Waldo Frank is abominable. The story by Matty is abominable. The comment is the abomination of abominations.

In this same issue is printed a solidly perfect piece of architecture, a romanesque church by Kenneth Burke.[1] It rises out of a huddle of wooden tenements. Possibly they may burn, destroying the church also.

Possibly the whole number may be suppressed. Certainly it will be if the postal authorities happen to read that story by Waldo Frank. Let us hope they do.

• • •

The whole weakness of *Secession* is the fact that it is supposed to be a group organ and that the group falls apart in the middle. I often contradict myself, but if there's one thing I believe in, it is good writing. With you I have been trying to work toward solidity and elegance, toward a to-some-extent classical reaction against the muds and fogs of contemporary literature. And then I stand sponsor for the Austrian child which is of high import psychologically. I repeat that the third number of *Secession* has got to be suppressed and that Matty alone cannot edit another number. Otherwise to save our self-respect we have got to secede from *Secession*.

You asked me for my opinion of *Secession*, and it has changed considerably since I saw the last issue. It changed considerably from the first issue to the second, and I hope it will change again after the fourth. Nevertheless here is my opinion. *Secession* should be a group organ, but I doubt whether it can be the organ of a group of fifteen, because I doubt whether there are fifteen young and intelligent writers in the United States. Talent is cheap but intelligence is rare, and *Secession* has more need of intelligence than talent. However it may, if it is successful, form a group of five or six, which is quite enough.

Secession should not be a dignified medium for perfect stories and elegant poems which will be discovered ten years from now. What's the use? All those stories and poems could be published today—in *Broom*, if nowhere else. The purpose of *Secession* is not really to be the organ of a group but to form a group which as yet does not exist. The purpose of a group is to be an audience for poetic drama and to make intelligent literature possible. The way *Secession* can form a group is by publishing both literature and polemic.

• • •

You mentioned jealousy, speaking of Matty. At present any jealousy between you and me would be suicidal, because as things have worked out I think our fortunes are rather intertwined. For our own times, which are the only times that matter, we go up or down together.

M.

---

1. A short story, "First Pastoral."

R.D. #1,
Andover, N.J.
October 14, 1922
[PS]

Dear Mal,

Yours anent mine anent seriousness . . .

. . .

In a sense, I have become serious. I do, that is, stop at one particular spot on my bicycle trip each morning, and survey the valley gravely. I do get a bit wild, not at the superficiality, but at the *complacent* superficiality, of our contemporary journalists. I do feel that I have a soul to be saved, and that this involves more or less the formulation of a programme. I do feel that if certain of my friends would take my advice, not only I, but also they, would be happier (evangelism). And I do look at my little girls with contentment, and think vaguely of dangers. But is not all that, after all, simply the growth of *decency*? I was once appallingly indecent. I am trying to be less so, and I suppose that is seriousness. At times, I almost feel called upon to inform you that I still drink and swear; but I fear you would accuse me of doing it out of parti pris.

As to our standing back to back, our rising or falling together—why, by God, I fear the time is approaching for our great drive. Look! two columns in *The New Age* by Edith Sitwell, on *Secession*: two columns on Matthew Josephson. It is as though I were suddenly asked to become the king of England. I simply cannot understand it. The same day that your letter on the abomination of abominations arrived, this enormous clipping reached Munson from England. No one else is even mentioned. Similarly, in the *Double Dealer* some imbecile, some slop-gullet, some committed nuisance, howls against the two issues of our magazine, and finds Josephson the only hope. Again, in the latest number of *Littérature* Aragon in his Depuis Dada paragraph lists (1) JOSEPHSON (2) Brown (3) Cummings. Finis. All of this I read yesterday. It was, decidedly, Matty's day; and by a peculiar quirk it all fell on the very day following the receipt of your abominations letter.

. . .

You say, Art is the function not of the individual but of a civilization. Have you read Pierre Lasserre's *Romantisme Français*? Do so, and you will observe that your definition is exactly contrary to the definition which he finds for romanticism: judging the world from the standpoint of the individual, and finding the world wanting. But what do you mean by "function"? Art, it seems to me, is exactly like morality: it is the building up of a superstructure to encompass and provide for contemporary material facts. It formulates the facts, and formulates the requisite spiritual latencies or anti-bodies. That much is Hegelian, or Spenglerian. There must be more in the definition, to save art from the perishability of the contemporary. The added element, I feel, should be sought along these lines: the encompassing superstructure is erected according to principles inherent to humanity as a whole. That is, I feel that we must place both the contemporary and the absolute; one can ignore Hegelianism if he chooses, but that simply means a willful disregard of half the facts. Flux and station; both of these elements are in the work of art . . .

K. B.

Chez Tellier,
Giverny par Vernon,
Eure
November 27, 1922
[NL]

Dear Kenneth:

I came to regard my letters to you as a sort of record not of my life but of my intellectual life, which tacitly we regard as life. Therefore during those relatively long periods when my brain ceases to function, I have written you little. And sometimes even when I was thinking, I wrote you little, because I had come to regard only certain departments of the intellect as being of interest to you. Whereas you write me not more conscientiously but with a different sort of conscience; you are capable of making literature out of your household chores; mine I have never succeeded in intellectualizing. It is like the French and German armies during the war; the French, even after four years, never succeeded in regarding the war as something permanent; they lived in makeshift hovels and complained because the roof leaked; the Germans built concrete palaces. I have always regarded chores as being something which in a perfect but attainable state could be avoided entirely; you, like the Germans, have made the best of them and even elevated them into the intellectual life; chores persist and your course is so much the wiser that I try to imitate it.

Having decided that the intellectual life was the only real life, I drew such restrictions about it that I entered it seldom, thus only living at moments.

The class will now read the above paragraphs aloud. What comments do you make? Kenneth, I see you raising your hand; what is it? Yes, you are right. The author has been reading Marcel Proust.

Proust bathes everything in some luminous mental fluid which does not alter the facts but makes them stand out in unfamiliar relief, as if seen by moonlight. He is jealous. His brain is incapable of altering his jealousy, but it can make his jealousy effective. He loves. His brain cannot destroy his love, but it can define the exact nature of his passion. The brain of Proust is a tool which he has fashioned to serve his egoism. It is the sharpest of tools; nevertheless Proust belongs to an inferior category of artists; whatever type he belongs to, he is its foremost specimen.

●　　●　　●

Giverny is hardly a winter resort. The north winds are cold and wet, the south and west winds warm and wet; only the east winds are cold and dry, and the east wind seldom blows. Fogs and mud. However our apartment is warm and comfortable; the country is genuine, and life costs considerably less than at Montpellier.

A long hill running east and west, with little copses and wheat fields. A huddle of stone cottages. A little river bordered with poplars, damp green fields, then finally the Seine. Giverny should be familiar to everybody; it has been painted for the Luxembourg, the Metropolitan, the Autumn Salon, and the Independents; by Cézanne, Monet, T.E. and J. Butler and Robert W. Chambers . . .

Here in Giverny we shall spend the winter and the spring. I shall make fortnightly trips to Paris, one visit to London, perhaps a trip to Montpellier in the spring. I want to write a thesis, prepare a book of poems, write some more portraits for *Broom* and criticisms for the *Dial*, make enough money to go home. I want to do too much. If I had come here to write a novel or a thesis, I should write it. Under the circumstances, with divided aims, I shall probably accomplish little. But more, by God, than I did last year. By God.

M.

Chez Tellier,
Giverny par Vernon,
Eure
January 6, 1923
[NL]

Dear Kenneth:

Loeb sails tomorrow for New York to try to arrange for the financing of *Broom*, and he will have landed already by the time you receive this letter. He says he will visit you at the *Dial* office. He will expect you to tell him what you think of *Broom*, and to give him advice as to his future policy . . .

What is the "modern" note that distinguishes authors of the present "advance guard"? Those terms are so distasteful to me that I can't repeat them without quotes, and yet I possess the current weakness for modernity. And the modern note at present is the substitution of associational for logical thought. Carried to its extremity among the Dadas, the modern note is the substitution of absurdity for logic. You were most "modern" at the time you wrote "My Dear Mrs. Wurtelbach," and boasted of your calculated errors. "First Pastoral" and "Prince Llan" are both individual and traditional. But my dear Mrs. W. was more completely successful than the three stories you wrote the summer afterward, and I doubt whether you, at the present time, realize how successful it was. The transposition from the speech to THE WORLD IS WITHOUT A TOY had an absolute emotional rightness. I still think that the speech should have mentioned Wurtelbach, or that Wurtelbach should have delivered the speech. But Gawd, it's a fine story. Critically, the thing that surprises me about it is the way in which you anticipated several literary developments of the next two years. You have a knack for doing that, a knack which you first discovered when your Peabody play turned out to be almost the same as Wilkinson was writing. Is "Prince Llan" equally prophetic, or have you at last found the path where nobody will follow you?

· · ·

Personally I have done little work since I sent the Proust to the *Dial*.[1] Nearly a month has passed, and I begin to wonder what they are doing with it. Here in Giverny we have had a succession of visitors, each of whom has done his or her little to prevent me from working, and all with the best intentions. Bob Coates and Elsa Petersen[2] were here for a week. Coates has been improved by his year in France. He writes stories without punctuation, but he is beginning not to need this camouflage of modernism; he begins to have ideas . . .

· · ·

Since writing "Two American Poets"[3] I have evidently right about faced on the question of the importance of American material. The change is largely psychological. America in the distance begins to loom up as a land of promise, something barbaric and decorative and rich. The form-matter pendulum has taken another stroke, and I begin to believe strongly in the importance of using contemporary material. To tell the truth I am not at a point where I can define my attitude clearly, especially not to myself—I might succeed with a stranger, but personally I am more in the air than ever. I don't know (a) when I shall land in New York (b) what I shall do when I land in New York (c) what I want to do when I land in New York. Till those questions are settled, everything—even my ideas on literature—remains in the air.

·

It is certain, however, that I want to live in the country and to work out the plans for a pleasant grove-walking Academy with you.

Mal

1. "A Monument to Proust," published in the March, 1923, issue of *The Dial*.

2. Robert Coates (1897–1973), American novelist and art critic. He later married Elsa Petersen.

3. "Two American Poets" was a review of volumes by Conrad Aiken and Carl Sandburg. It appeared in the November, 1922, issue of *The Dial*. In his review Cowley concludes that "there is no poetry so deeply rooted in our soil and and our tradition that a foreigner can never fully understand it . . . America remains a thing seen and not a manner of seeing."

> *The Dial,*
> 152 West Thirteenth Street,
> New York City
> Telephone: Chelsea 6540
> January 18, 1923
> [PS]

Dear Mal,

Your letter of January 6th . . .

Yes, you are right in looking to America as "a land of promise, something barbaric, and rich." But alas! I feel that in your admiration (theoretical, gained from Harold Stearns and faugh! strengthened by Matthew Josephson) you have neglected to distinguish between a qualitative and a quantitative richness. Broadway is qualitatively rich; not a single light on it is worth a damn, but the aggregate of so many million lights demands attention. The same is true of our buildings downtown. It is the old fight against mass, a fight which you used to combat along with me: the fight for quality. There is, for instance, a great emotional richness, no doubt, in our lynching bees; but quite obvious[ly] this demands that we consider as valuable not emotional richness per se, but the richness in certain specific emotions. There is, for instance, not a trace of that really dignified richness, the richness which makes for peasants, household gods, traditions. America has become the wonder of the world simply because America is the purest concentration point for the vices and vulgarities of the world. America, in other words, is what Prussia used to be. That is, when imperialism was in the unquestioned ascendent, then Prussia being most thoroughly so was the most admired country. And in the same way, since the whole world has come to put an actual premium on superficiality, then it is bound to worship the nation in which the population roves the most, in which there is no dignity whatsoever, in which the only admirable quality is its "very"-ness.

I can only say to you what I said to Matty months ago: We *will* build a literature out of advertising, we *will* build a literature out of economy, directness, psychological salesmanship, and the like. But in the refined artist the use of this material will be so subtilized, so deepened, that the ad writer would not even suspect that this artist is thinking in the ad writer's set of terms. That is the thing you do not take into account. And to me it is the only important thing.

God knows, I am grateful to you for your kind words on "My Dear Mrs. Wurtelbach." And I think you have spoken very accurately when you speak of the substitution of association for logic. In the same manner, our ethical and aesthetic systems will no longer have a metaphysical basis, but a psychological one. The difference between association and logic I had encompassed less accurately in my distinction between plot and super-plot, and said that the incidents of my stories were meant to bear on the super-plot. But I insist that if psychology is the basis of our concatenations, the associated ideas cannot be put down in the Dada manner. For what is the purpose of such an association? It is, quite evidently, to produce a unity of effect. As for instance, in "The Waste Land," Eliot assembles the various associated ideas which all focus on the idea of sterility. Sprinchorn paints in exactly the same manner: in trying to give the lightness of snow, for instance, he paints two delicate horses with a flowing, graceful position to their legs, makes his trees with branches outstretching like planes or wings, and then throws a shadow over the base of the picture, a shadow which points upward like a finger. Thus, all these objects contribute to the idea of levitation, and when he finally adds a lot of blue to his snow, the result is something so light and fluffy that you could blow the picture away. None of this is beyond Blake. It is all contained in Blake. It explains why Blake is all the rage. And if Foster does not have it in his book, then Foster has missed the whole reason for writing his book.[1]

But the Dadaist association chains are simply idle. One cannot reduplicate their experience—which is absurd. The trouble with Dada is that there are no first-rate Dadaists. They are swine lying in a whole pen of pearls. I refuse to hear more of them. YET AT THE SAME TIME I ADMIT THAT IF ANY OF US DOES ANYTHING OF LASTING IMPORT, IT WILL BE DONE WITH THE SAME EQUIPMENT WHICH THE DADAISTS ARE USING.

· · ·

Oh hell, come along home, Malcolm. Or the first thing you know we won't be talking the same language any more. Come back here and put in a field of rye, say, and then watch a storm coming after it has been cut, and then wonder where in the hell Dada stands. This is meant as a logical point, not an emotional plea. I mean simply that the world has not changed until water runs uphill and the sun shines at night. I mean that the arrant and sterile modernity which we get out of Dadaism is founded entirely on a complete obliviscence to about nine-tenths of the facts. It is all city products. We detest those people who lay aside two hours a week for God. And we should detest similarly those people who lay aside two hours a week for bodily exercise. The body should be in the texture of one's living: and when one follows through this idea of the body, one gets to the whole matter of nature over against cities. But all this, I believe, I spilled to you in a previous letter.

You write that you are completely unsettled. And strangely enough, after all this dogmatizing, I believe that I am as unsettled as you. How, for instance, can I reconcile my extreme technical interest in letters with my extreme detest for the modern trait of specialization? (As per my review on Gentile,[2] in the *Dial*.) Specialization is technique; and technique is the opposite of humanism. The basis of humanism is not form, but subject matter, as Brooks very rightly pointed out in his two-column article on *Secession* in the *Freeman*.

And Brooks, by the way, is an awfully likable man. I have been with him several times lately; we have, as a basis of mutual respect, the fact that each of us has two children. And also, he, like me, is a dreadfully serious cuss, so that we really can weep over things. The other night he, Loving,[3] Munson, and I had dinner together; Munson had to leave immediately afterward, but I stayed on with them until nearly eleven. Loving, to the great astonishment of Munson and me, was at the best quite accurate in his objections to *Secession*, and at the worst neutral. Brooks was quite simply anxious to find out just how much of a programme we had; and for the very simple reason that he wanted to know.

I felt here the justification for any "promise" there may be in America. I do not find it in advertising, or penny slot machines, or confidence men, or city atrocities. I find it in a man like Brooks, who would get more pleasure out of being right than out of carrying an issue. I find it, in other words, in a man who exemplifies to me the very opposite of what Matty exemplifies. When we were leaving, Brooks asked me if all my time was taken up by the *Dial* at present. I told him that it was, but that within a few months I should be back on my farm. Whereupon, he answered divinely that I must let him know when that time came, as he wanted me to do work for him. This is the man whom I attacked in *Vanity Fair*! And Frank,[4] the other man I attacked, has offered to blurb my book of stories to a publisher. That, it seems to me, is answer enough to the dissatisfaction you express in your objection that it "was too sane, too right to be exciting." I have felt the solidest elation of my life when I think that I could go at the very basis of these men's work, could muster every argument against it that I could invent, could convince them that my objections were of validity, and could retain their respect. I could have been more exciting, as you suggest—and that would have been the end of it. On the other hand, I have gotten closer to two people who share my new religion, the desire to be decent.

· · ·

No more paeans, except to add that we received a cheque for five dollars from Ezra Pound. For *Secession*, that is. He signs himself "Your affectionate grandfather" . . . You would be astonished to see the range of our scrapbook. No little review, or even big review, has received so much editorial comment as our dirty little sheet. I tell you, except for the finances of the thing, it is better business to put an article in *Secession* than in *Broom*. . . .

K. B.

1. S. Foster Damon. His book *William Blake: His Philosophy and Symbols* was published in 1924.

2. Giovanni Gentile (1875–1944), Italian philosopher and educator. Burke reviewed his book *The Reform of Education* in *The Dial*, vol. LXXIV (1923).

3. Pierre Loving, a Greenwich Village poet.

4. Waldo Frank.

Giverny par Vernon,
Eure, France
January 28, 1923
[NL]

Dear Kenneth:

Yours of January [18] to hand this morning, to which mine of January 28 is only the briefest of answers.

· · ·

I want to quote a sentence from your paragraph on quality and quantity in America: "There is, for example, not a trace of that really dignified richness which makes for peasants, household gods, traditions. America has become the wonder of the world simply because America is the purest concentration point for the vices and vulgarities of the world."

That really dignified richness—shit, Kenneth, since when have you become a furniture salesman. You seem to have the disease of the American lady I met in Giverny. "You know, in America the wallpaper hardly seems to last a minute, it fades or peels off so quickly, but heah the good European papuh dyed with European dyes and put on with *that good European glue* . . . it just seems to last forevuh." Let me assure you that the chiefest benefit of my two years in Europe was the fact that it freed me from the prejudices of that lady—whose European flour paste was so much better than the American product—and of Harold Stearns. America is just as Goddamned good as Europe—worse in some ways, better in others, just as appreciative, fresher material, inclined to stay at peace instead of marching into the Ruhr. I'm not ashamed to take off my coat anywhere and tell these cunt-lapping Europeans that I'm an American citizen. Wave old Glory! Peace! Normalcy!

America shares an inferiority complex with Germany. Not about machinery or living standards, but about Art. *Secession* is less important than *Littérateur* because it is published in New York. Marin,[1] being American, is a minor figure beside even such a minor French watercolorist as Dunoyer de Segonzac. The only excuse for living two years in France is to remove this complex, and to discover, for example, that Tzara, who resembles you like two drops of water, talks a shade less intelligently than you. To discover that the Dada crowd has more fun than the *Secession* crowd because the former, strangely, has more American pep. That people who read both Suares[2] and Waldo Frank from a sense of duty bracket them together but think Frank is superior. THE ONLY SALVATION FOR AMERICAN LITERATURE IS TO BORROW A LITTLE PUNCH AND CONFIDENCE FROM AMERICAN BUSINESS. American literature—I mean Frank, Anderson, Oppenheim,[3] et al.—is morally weak, and before it learns the niceties of form its morale has to be doctored, or all the niceties in the world will do it no good at all.

Doubtless you have observed that this whole incoherent paragraph is no answer to yours. I say nothing to your theory of quality and quantity because I have nothing to say. It's only a theory. A single electric light on Broadway has the same value as a single lower-case "e" in *Hamlet*. As for America being the concentration point for all the vices and vulgarities of the world—shit. New York is refinement itself beside Berlin. French taste in most details is unbearable. London is a huge Gopher Prairie. You give me a pain in the ass. Mr. Burke, meet Mr. Stearns. You'll be crazy about each other. You have *so* much in common.

I get carried away. I intended to write only a short note. Honestly, I hate to see you falling for this American Civilization by Thirty Prominent Americans.[4] Let us repeat in chorus that if I were in New York or if you were here in Giverny the disagreement would hardly exist. We are both showing ourselves the rebellious slaves of environment, even our rebellion being determined by our slavery.

· · ·

. . . As for the Dadaists, Aragon has done some obviously fine work, and Tzara, if he carries out his present ideas, may do some. One of Matty's poems—"In Back of the Wind"—I admire immensely. That is about the limit of my admiration, except that they have found some interesting formulas and seem to be having a good time when they write—which I envy them. I am infected with the desire to write excitingly. Otherwise I am in a stage which lacks clarity. . . .

Mal

1. John Marin (1870–1953), a landscape painter.

2. André Suares (1866–1948), French poet and critic.

3. James Oppenheim (1882–1932), American novelist and poet whose work embodied a popularized version of psychoanalysis. He was the founder and editor of *Seven Arts* magazine.

4. Cowley is referring to *Civilization in the United States: An Inquiry by Thirty Americans*, edited by Harold Stearns and published in 1922. It contained essays critical of American culture.

Giverny par Vernon,
Eure
February 8, 1923
[NL]

Dear Kenneth:

Paris is a town I enter with joy and leave without regret: I repeat that experience weekly and have repeated it since November 1917. I can't imagine people living in Paris. It is a town where one spends weekends which occasionally last a lifetime.

My last voyage was spent chiefly with Dadas. The crowd is trying to re-create itself. Tzara, Rigaud,[1] Breton, Ribemont-Dessaignes,[2] Aragon, Picabia were assembled together for the first time in eighteen months. They fought but finally decided to stage a joint manifestation. About twenty of us signed a paper. I suppose I am now officially a Dada, although none of them greet me with great warmth except Aragon and Tzara. A poem of mine is to be engraved in the program of the Russian Ball, along with Tzara, Ribemont-Dessaignes, and thirty others. Tzara is translating *Valuta*[3] for *les feuilles libres*. At the same time I lunch with the hated enemies of the Dada group: Salmon and MacOrlan, and interview in the most fraternal manner the enemies of Salmon, MacOrlan, and the Dada group, like Vildrac[4] and Duhamel.[5] Like Matty last year I am being received into the complex life of Paris. To become a true citizen of that fantastic and unlivable city, I should only have to steal the mistress of, let us say, Vitrac,[6] and to hand on Peggy to, let us say, Tzara. I have no wish to be a citizen of Paris.

Dada c'est le jemenfoutisme absolu. It is negation of all motives for writing, such as the Desire for Expression, the Will to Create, the Wish to Aid. A Dada has only one legitimate excuse for writing: because he wants to, because it amuses him. Therefore the movement becomes a series of practical jokes. Dada c'est le seul état d'esprit vraiment logique.

But not entirely logical. A writer who was truly dada would disdain collective action as he would disdain any other attempt to influence the mind of the public. The actual Dadas, on the contrary, try to accomplish things which are sometimes serious. They try to work together.

Their love of literature is surprisingly disinterested. At their memorable meeting it was proposed that none of them should write for any except dada publications during the next three months. No dada publication is widely read or pays. The proposal would have been carried except for the objection of one man out of twenty.

Their commerce is tiring and stimulating. I left Paris with fifty new ideas and hating the groupe dada. They are a form of cocaine and personally take no stimulants except their own company. Last Wednesday all the Americans I knew went to a tea and got divinely drunk. The French had a three-hour meeting at which not even water was served. And much more excitement than at the tea where gin only was poured from the pot.

They take their wives and mistresses everywhere but in the sole quality of wives or mistresses. This, perhaps, is a valuable suggestion for the *Secession* group. Our anti-feminism went the wrong way to achieve its ends.

Talent. We have as much as they, perhaps more, but less vitality, less courage. Because we write for other aims we achieve less fun out of our writing, which is often equally true of our readers.

They live in Paris. That is my final criticism. They are over-stimulated, living in a perpetual weekend. I like to meet them on weekends.

I have grown very fond of Tzara.

Will any of them ever accomplish anything? Yes, but not while they remain in the group. As they grow more powerful they will break away, as Soupault[7] has done already. Aragon is immensely talented but follows the stronger and less talented Breton with a sort of canine devotion. Till he breaks away he will write interesting sketches. Tzara speaks well of Eluard[8] and Ribemont-Dessaignes, but I am unfamiliar with their work.

Whatever my judgment they have affected not my thinking but my writing profoundly. I wish you could meet them because I think you would react in somewhat the same way to the stimulus.

．　　．　　．

Loeb came back from New York with the impression that Matty had made himself vastly unpopular. The fate of *Broom* is in the balance; it may end with the next issue and may go on with more money.

[Written in margin] Letter from Loeb this morning: *Broom* ends with

March issue short of a miracle, thus depriving me of the second magazine which would publish anything I wrote, and the first which would pay me for it. *Tell nobody yet and especially not Munson.*

M.

1. Jacques Rigaud, a poet who committed suicide in 1929.

2. George Ribemont-Dessaignes (1884–1974), dramatist and novelist.

3. *Valuta*, a play by the German writer Ernst Didring, was published in 1909.

4. Charles Vildrac (1882–1971), essayist, critic, poet, and dramatist.

5. George Duhamel (1884–1966), novelist, poet, playwright, and critic.

6. Roger Vitrac (1889–1952), playwright, poet, and essayist.

7. Phillipe Soupault (1897–), playwright, poet, and essayist.

8. The poet Paul Éluard (1895–1952).

The Dial,
152 West Thirteenth Street,
New York City
Telephone: Chelsea 6540
February 8, 1923
[PS]

Dear Mal,

No, no, I will not get into one of these Burke-Josephson name calling contests with you. You call me Stearns, and I call you Stearns—which probably still means that we consider the same thing anathema.

But you did misread me egregiously. I said nothing about the superiority of Europe. And if I talked about the peasants, I did so with a perfect realization that if there are still peasants left in Europe it is simply because they don't have character enough to become Fordized. America *is* what Europe *wants* to be; to that extent we are privileged to want to be something else. And I believe that you were perfectly aware how completely unfair you were in all your indignations; you knew, that is, that your were ridiculing what I hadn't said.

My thesis is simply this: that when eight or ten people with a vital interest in the humanities get together they produce (a) a renaissance or (b) the illusion of same. The thirty yammering Americans are yammering simply because they don't have sufficient vitality to arrange interesting lives for themselves. One can arrange an interesting life for himself in America. I assure you I see the matter in just those terms, and am under no inferiority complex. Indeed, I have kept yelling all along that if anything happens it will happen in America, and come from America; and that is why I object so strenuously to your pious acceptance of Europe's angle of vision. That is, you are always trying to talk America to me in terms of Tzara and Aragon. You are praising the hilarious crudeness of the country. While I am not dogmatically set against this, I am continually trying to ask myself and you whether this does not involve a latent acceptance of democracy, and whether we really do have to accept democracy. You are accepting America as a proposition; which seems to me like accepting the air as a proposition. It lays too much emphasis on subject matter. There is society, and there are the tides, and I want to see them both from the standpoint of art forms. It has simply been impossible to chew up this country, so that, consequently, there is nothing to complain about.

That is, I object that it is the Europeans who insist on your seeing America as a proposition. I insist that America is, for our less idealistic purposes, simply the sum of Mrs. Bosney and Howard Slothwell,[1] et all . . .

K. B.

1. Both of these names are fictitious.

Giverny par Vernon,
Eure
March 17, 1923
[NL]

Dear Kenneth:

Written in the *Café de la Ville d'Argentan*, Peggy having missed the Giverny train, thereby causing a delay of two hours 44.

Notwithstanding and in spite of everything we are going home this evening, after four days in Paris which could have been more hectic but hardly more tiring.

I saw Tzara, Aragon, John Bishop,[1] Pasin,[2] Dos Passos, the last of whom arrived two days ago. He spoke well of you. Tzara has arranged an exhibit for Peggy at the Galerie Six (Mme. Soupault). Her new watercolors are extremely interesting. She is drawing everybody's portrait.

. . .

I saw the *Dial* for a moment at Bitch Sylvia's (Shakespeare & Co.), long enough to discover that you had run the Proust as an essay. Was it what I wanted to do? No, it was insufferably pompous, full of fine writing (only partly excused by the deliberate imitation of Proust), and generally too gushy-blah. But I don't admit *your* charge that it was too informative. Take knowledge for granted. Whose? I must be one of ten Americans, or perhaps five, who have read the collected works. I made a certain number of remarks which were a personal contribution to Proustiana. Thus: life conceived as a series of situations coexisting, whose connection is more logical than temporal. The rest of the essay was a deliberate vulgarization which the circumstances justified.

You believe that a critic should judge a book, according to aesthetic laws which he formulates. In effect, you believe in using the book as a text for an essay on Form. More modest, I believe in defining a book. I believe that there is no distinction, except of degree, between a book criticism and a book review, and that your essays in aesthetics parade under a false name. They are good essays but bad reviews.

Book reviewing is a distinctly minor medium which, for material reasons, has attracted a number of the best intelligences in America. Following their instincts they are attempting to elevate book reviewing. They are succeeding, not in elevating reviews, but in writing essays which perhaps would be more successful if they marched under their own colors. Our critics are at most invariably more intelligent, more creative, than our artists . . .

Mal

1. John Peale Bishop, who was then editor of *Vanity Fair*.
2. Jules Pasin, an artist.

The Dial,
152 West Thirteenth Street,
New York City
Telephone: Chelsea 6540
March 27, 1923
[PS]

Dear Mal,

Yours from Paris (March 17) and Giverny (March 18). The Paris one contains, most pimply of all, that old saw about book reviewing, carried over from such ultra-modern minds as Richard Aldington[1] and H. L. Mencken. Book reviewing is exactly as good or as bad as the equipment one brings to it. It is, categorically, neither superior nor inferior. Which also applies to the carving of cameos (are cameos carved?) and the writing of tragedies. Like Gide, my ideal review is a "pretext," a tremplin [sic]. And I believe that I *am* talking on the subject. The judgment of a book involves formulating the principles by which the book should be judged. In a critical age, the emphasis switches from these formulations as means to these formulations as ends. In either case, however, the ideal result should be the same. For the principles should dig back in every case to the book under discussion, like that seaweed one finds at South Beach, with a chain of mussels linked to it, and a shoot of the seaweed planted in the belly of each mussel. Of course, just now we are brutally at odds; and there is nothing more discouraging than to think that if I wrote a review exactly as I wanted it, it would thereby appeal to you least. And the less perfect it was after my conception, the more you might like it. All I say is that if reviewing is a distinctly minor medium, that is all the more reason to write criticisms under the guise of reviews. I suppose garbage could be hoisted into a wagon aesthetically. At least I operate on that assumption . . .

K. B.

1. Richard Aldington (1892–1962), English poet and novelist, was an acquaintance of Ezra Pound and a member of the Imagist school.

[Giverny]
April 28, 1923
[NL]

Dear Kenneth:

Book Review—Essay—Criticism

For purposes of discussion let us accept your division. We both understand what it means, though certainly by any strict definition a Criticism is at the same time an Essay, the latter term being of the most uncompromising generality.

Very well.

Our difference at present is this: I believe that it is not fair to good contemporary books to write criticism about them, since your sort of criticism takes a foreknowledge of the book for granted, and since this sort of foreknowledge rarely exists. In the case of contemporaries, one has to tell what they are writing about.

A pure criticism of judgment can be fairly applied only to the classics, or to the complete works of a moderately familiar modern author. One can write a criticism of *Hamlet*, *Tom Jones*, *Phèdre*, Yeats, Hudson.[1] It is difficult and unfair to write a criticism of a new book. You really should apply your method to a revaluation of the great figures of French and English literature. Practically, the *Dial* and the *Freeman* would be glad to publish these criticisms.

When you restrict criticism to judgment you are falling into a fallacy which you named yourself; the Fallacy of Subtraction. Once you wrote me in about these words: "Any man who devotes his whole life to literature or any man who devotes his whole life to a study of beetles is a moron." I think you were right, and should be willing to apply the term to Flaubert, with restrictions.

. . .

For one week I have been walking with Loeb in central France—southern Burgundy—eating a great deal, exercising, and thinking not at all. We return to Paris tomorrow. Louis Aragon is now living in Giverny. Peggy's exposition came off nicely but tired me out, especially since our house was full of people for two weeks before the event. That is the reason I seized the opportunity to go walking with Loeb. The trip has rested me, fattened me, otherwise has accomplished nothing . . .

Malcolm

1. William Henry Hudson.

R.D. #1,
Andover, N.J.
May 26, 1923
[PS]

Dear Mal,

The event of the day: going into Netcong to get my bicycle repaired, I stopped in an ice cream parlor and got to discussing prohibition with a Wop. He turned out to be a bootlegger, took me to his home, and let me sample his wares; with the result that I rode home a-flying, with a quart bottle in my knapsack. He will deliver wine to the farm for a dollar a quart; it is good and effective. The current price in New York is two dollars, although Brown has ferreted out good wine for one-fifty. So from now on I shall have my steady bootlegger. Every gentleman should have a bootlegger, and speak of him as "my" bootlegger. I feel much more established than ever . . .

Please do not think, Malcolm, that I forgot to take a pencil and paper with me when I started out this morning on my bicycle. Two pieces of paper, in fact, so that by writing small I could have jotted down quite a good deal. And one piece did come in handy when I pulled in among the bushes for a short spell. Its fellow is still with me, wrinkled but virgin . . .

With us, the justification for writing is negative. We write because we cannot be fully happy without writing. And while I have not been desolate (vid. supra) I will admit that I have not looked at the cucumbers with a full to overflowing heart. Could the job, by lasting until next October, be lasting just a little too long? Too long, that is, for me ever to write stories again? The financial urge can be depended upon to keep my reviewing and criticism organs from atrophying. Stories are almost an outworn convention with me, something carried over from another set of circumstances and not spontaneously suited for the present circumstances. Perhaps farming and reading would be the most logical pair. I look upon any future with a certain grim equanimity, provided only that it does not involve either material starvation or the loss of one's former connections. One's former *geistliche* connections.

K. B.

Giverny par Vernon,
Eure
June 29, 1923
[NL]

Dear Kenneth:

. . . Yesterday, Kenneth, it struck me with the force of revelation that the time has come for us to write some political manifestos. We are not critics or short-story writers; we are poets; in other words we are interested in every form of human activity. To be ticketed and dismissed as such-and-such sort of a writer makes my ass tired. Also I am eaten with the desire to do something significant and indiscreet. An Open Letter to President Harding. An Open Letter to the Postmaster General on the Censorship, in which I admit the right to censor, point out how dangerous my opinions are, and demand why I am not suppressed. And other manifestations: for example a call to voters to cease voting, an attack on the liberals, an attack on the socialists and communists. Imagine all these documents appearing together in a political number of *Broom*. What a stink. But the stink would mean something. In a country as hypocritical as the United States, merely to enumerate the number of laws one has broken would be a significant gesture. And if all the literary forces of law and order rose up against us, we could always retire to farming or reading proofs. And, Kenneth, I have the feeling that some such courageous and indiscreet step is required of us, if we are not going to resign ourselves to petty literary wars with Ezra Pound, Robert McAlmon, Floyd Dell . . .

Yrs
Malcolm

Giverny par Vernon,
Eure
July 5, 1923
[NL]

Dear Kenneth:

. . . Tomorrow morning I go to Paris to arrange for passage. Probably it will be three weeks before we can get a boat. Anyhow you can expect us the first week in August. I get stage fright every time I think of New York. How in hell's name are we going to live? But there is a more immediate problem which I mentioned to you once before: when we dock in New York harbor where are we going to send our trunks? Do you know of a place where we can spend two weeks? S[ue] Jenkins might be able to help if you ever see her; she often answers such problems. Write immediately if you know of any answer.

Only to mention such matters takes my mind away from anything else I might write you. The famous two years is ending with little accomplished and much learned. It seems to me that their great value was not so much what I learned about literature as the aid they gave me in developing a personal philosophy. I haven't defined that philosophy, and I am even uncertain as to what manner of life it demands me to lead. I am considerably less anxious to be a hack writer. My ideal would be to find somebody to pay my expenses for five years on condition that I published nothing during that time. The only important matters are friends, books, sex, the cultivation of the mind, but not especially in the order named. I can't write anything more tonight.

M.

The Dial
152 West Thirteenth Street,
New York City
Telephone: Chelsea 6540
July 12, 1923
[PS]

Dear Mal,

Yours of June 29. The political number strikes me as an excellent idea. Discussing, for instance, exactly how one should go about it to evade the laws, or to beat the system within its own terms, etc. I should make as the first postulate that we accept as our lawful sovereign the Standard Oil Company, we work on the unquestioned assumption that this is the government and that it will continue to be the government. We discuss in what ways our sovereign is a good sovereign, and in what ways he is an unwise one. We point out that he has endangered his own system by enacting unnecessary prohibitory legislation. For by forcing disrespect for such laws, he gives incentive to a "sympathetic" disrespect for all laws . . .

Discussing the sudden influx of lustful emotion in art, we point out that modern life has made this inevitable, owing to the fact that one must see so many thousands of people per diem who simply cannot exist for one except as bodies. Not knowing of their personal habits, one cannot differentiate them spiritually; one can take them only as corporeal objects, one like another. Thus, the simplification in outlook comes about, and we have, as with everything else in modern life, the development of "pure" lust, lust, that is, which is not centered in one object, but is generalized, and takes one object for its vicarious expression. We decide that this cannot be combatted, it can only be modified; one can, accepting it, make it as refined as possible. For this purpose we advance wicked books written by men of subtle and refined intellects, by poets and stylists . . .

We could, similarly, discuss economics, centralization, the possible remedy for centralization; here our main point would be that the situation is gradually tightening, the submerged classes are gradually crystallizing into submerged classes and the upper classes into upper classes; we point out, that is, that the talk of flux is an illusion, that in reality there is simply enough flux to confuse the issues and make crystallization possible. We point out, for instance, the growing feudal relation between employer and stenographer—the situation, creeping in, whereby the employer can own his stenographer. She can move from one employer to another, but she cannot move out of the whole situation. We discuss the matter of intelligence, and admit that democracy has narrowed down to this (which is no different from any other society, no matter how aristocratic) that a very keen man, no matter how low in the scale he may have been at the start, can beat the system and rise to prominence. The less keen, from now on, will tend more and more to die in the same station into which they were born. (Which, God knows, is not altogether a bad thing, as it will tend to eliminate the lesser parvenus.) At the present time, however, it is still possible for the individual, without sacrificing his life forces to the task, to beat the system. This he can do by decentralization (read, Andover). But he must recognize that this is only an individualistic solution. A great decentralization movement would soon be met with the rigorous law of supply and demand, and it would become as expensive to decentralize as it now is to live in the big center.

· · ·

Yahoo, yahooo—I suppose I should go mad if I began writing for your damned political number. In any case, if you and Loeb do decide to run it, please do not lose this letter, but return it to me and let me follow one of them through. I should think it would be great sport. We might also let a fart at the *New Republic* and *The Freeman* in passing . . .

K. B.

R.D. #1,
Andover, N.J.
October 3, 1923
[PS]

Dear Mal,

Back at the old poison, bringing down wood, hauling water, taking the last fruits from the garden. I have written you too many sales letters on this matter of functioning with the weather to venture another one. Further, I am by no means a full man. I feel as though I were recovering from some long period of aphasia, of which I retain simply a vague sense of discomfiture. My life begins each morning, and ends each evening—but the cycle is no more positively contenting than respiration, it simply *is*.

All this, however, is very misleading. For before I decided to write you a letter I had not even thought of such things . . . I had not even noticed it before sitting down to this public inventory. So that this is misleading, through the placing of emphasis where none is due, like going up to a stranger and explaining that you don't hate him.

If you are going to have a vacation in about three or four weeks, and if you cared to come out here, let me know definitely when it is going to be. Doc Williams is coming out for a while, and I thought that the three of us might have a princely time together. Friday night I got semi-piffed with Williams and Waldo Frank, and we talked five hours on fornication. As we were walking to our trains, Williams said that the only indiscretion is names; and we had not divulged them, except our own—which was bad enough. The two men took so halely to each other that I felt rather like Pierre Loving when he introduced Goethe to Schiller: delighted with my accomplishment, but a bit to one side.

The night is crisp and clear. I am going out for a walk.

Remember me to the family.

K. B.

———

16 Dominick Street,
New York City
November 8, 1923
[NL]

Dear Kenneth:

My head being empty, a letter becomes a catalogue of events. Eugene O'Neill, Mr. O'Neill the playwright, Gene, came to New York. We drank at Jim's. Peggy went back to Ridgefield with Gene and Agnes.[1] There was a Hallowe'en party at our office, much dancing, pretty girls; my head still buzzes with jazz. (Rings with rag?) I went to Ridgefield, stayed till Sunday, went to Woodstock, stayed till Tuesday. We played hide and go seek. I wrote a jazz poem in jazzy prose and swore I should write no more verse. Matty is publishing "The Poet Assassinated" to clear off some of *Broom*'s deficit or pile it on—one becomes so confused. Munson seems to have Broken Off Relations with me. Mr. O'Neill speaks a language so different from ours that I seemed to converse with him from different worlds. Cummings' book appeared.[2] The beer is getting poorer. New York has enveloped itself for me in a haze of ragtime tunes, a sort of poetry which leads me to a melancholic happiness. To work in an office is a refuge. Are the trees indeed bare? Who is this man Burke?

I dashed out of the subway and down 42nd Street. She was standing on the corner. So there are prostitutes in New York. I shall never speak to one, but the knowledge of them makes the city more livable. Behind swinging doors. Draw two. Did you hear about the new show? Matty has gone to Woodstock. The rumble of trucks is doom approaching. When the skyscrapers tumble, when cornices fall to crush the people in the street. Speed.

Speed. See people. Gossip. Drink. Smoke. There is a quieter land. Some day surely, and not too far in the future, we shall buy a farm. I am counting a great deal on your being here this winter. Violent physical exertion when drunk is the solution of every moral problem.

M

1. Agnes Boulton, Eugene O'Neill's second wife.
2. *Tulips and Chimneys.*

PART TWO

1924–1942

In its own way, Cowley's disjointed description of New York City in his letter of November 8, 1923, recalls the "Unreal City" of T. S. Eliot's *The Waste Land*. New York registers in a series of fragmented images careening toward some "doom approaching." An elegant, intelligent "Shakespeherian Rag" buzzes, but "one becomes so confused." In his letter, Cowley seems to glimpse, amidst the "melancholic happiness" of a speeding city enveloped in the "haze of ragtime tunes," the coming crash. It is as if he senses that, having returned to New York, he has come back to a city that is breaking apart.

The "refuge" he refers to in this letter is his office at *Sweet's Architectural Catalogue*, where he had been rehired upon his return from France. For the next few years Cowley will spend his time freelancing in New York, writing essays and reviews, and doing translations, struggling with his wife to stay afloat as the depression approaches. In the beginning he was working nine- and ten-hour days at *Sweet's* while trying to write and publish his own work, a routine that became so exhausting that in a few months he resigned, moving with his wife to a small house on Staten Island. Until the fall of 1929, when he was hired at the *New Republic*, Cowley lived solely on his income from reviews and essays in the *Herald Tribune Books* and *Charm*, a magazine edited by a friend of his wife.

Burke, meanwhile, had settled in at Andover, putting in a rather elaborate garden, working on the essays on aesthetics that would later appear in his first book of criticism, *Counter-Statement*, and commuting by train to New York to work at *The Dial*. In 1924 his book of stories, *The White Oxen*, was published, but in writing the stories his interest in literary form had deepened, and his desire to write about aesthetics began to pull him away from his earlier aspirations to become a successful novelist. In March of 1925 he wrote to Cowley that while his original "program" was to write a saleable novel and retire, he was now "going in madly for criticism." He would continue to write fiction and criticism simultaneously until 1932, when the emotional and psychological pain of completing his novel, and its failure with both the critics and the public, led him to turn resolutely to criticism.

Burke was able to supplement his income from reviews, essays, and translations between 1926 and 1929 by working as a researcher at the Laura Spelman Rockefeller Memorial Foundation, and later, as an editorial assistant for Colonel Arthur Woods, who was doing research on drugs at the Bureau of Social Hygiene. Burke later drew on this research in writing about the role of opium in Coleridge's poetry. During this period he was also the music critic for *The Dial*. In 1929 he received *The Dial* Award for distinguished services to American letters, and used the money ($2,000) to build a small dam on the creek running through his property, thus creating a pond for swimming.

While Burke remained at Andover and commuted to New York, the Cowleys were often on the move. In the spring of 1926, after a short stay on Staten Island, they moved to Sherman, Connecticut, living in the same neighborhood with Allen and Caroline Tate, Matthew and Hannah Josephson, Robert Coates, Hart Crane, and the artist Peter Blume. In 1928 they moved again, this time across the state line to a farm in upstate New York. When Cowley was offered a job at the *New Republic* he and his wife again settled in New York City. In 1936 they bought and remodeled an old barn in Sherman, where they still live.

The letters Burke and Cowley wrote to one another between 1925 and 1929 register a series of rifts in their friendship. Their personal and professional conflicts were exacerbated by economic hardship, and by a recurrent aimlessness and ennui that plagued both men as they sought to carve out careers as writers at the worst possible time. In January of 1925 Burke complains that Cowley is not the man he was in high school, that he suffers from "a persecutional mania" and must therefore "be treated with tact." The need for tact, he continues, is a "discredit" to their relationship. Cowley, in response, rejects the suggestion of tact ("it would only make us very uncomfortable"), writing that "each of us, till his end of days, will defend his own manner of life." As his letters to Cowley make clear, Burke always felt like an outsider, and had a kind of "persecutional mania" of his own: "I sometimes feel that people unconsciously sense that I am in retreat," he writes in 1925, "and spontaneously pile after me like hounds after a fox." While Burke was in retreat, Cowley regularly suffered during this period from a lack of direction or purpose. He writes in July of 1926 that

I've spent most of the summer on my back, mapping the rivers and mountains on the ceiling . . . nothing accomplished. Or seemingly noth-

ing accomplished. What frightens me is that I have no margin. Having finished one poem or one essay, I have no plans for another; I am a perfect vacuum . . .

By February of 1927 Burke writes that his own "aesthetic paralysis" is so acute that it has "definitely spread to my letters, and silence seems even gradually to be encroaching upon my speech": "But I do not write you because I have to say such things. I say such things because I have to write you." Cowley writes back that theirs is a "vague dissatisfaction that is worse than hostility," and that instead of "not writing and not talking," they may simply have to fight it out.

In the main, these rifts simply took care of themselves. Burke, however, went through a very difficult time as he completed *Counter-Statement* (1931) and *Towards a Better Life* (1932). His marriage was breaking up, and this, combined with the economic pressure of the depression and the stress of writing a novel full of oblique but painful self-analysis, left him on the edge of a nervous breakdown by the end of 1932. But by 1933 he and his wife, Lily, had divorced, and he married Elizabeth Batterham. Completing his novel and placing his book of criticism gave him a lift. By the time the books were published he had made a commitment to the writing of criticism, and his economic situation had stabilized. Likewise, though Cowley and his wife Peggy divorced in 1931 (he married Muriel Maurer in 1932), his steady position at the *New Republic* brought a welcome period of stability to his life. By 1931 the differences between Burke and Cowley began again to center around literary, intellectual, and political matters.

In their correspondence during the 1930s there are a number of specific exchanges about the books and essays they are writing, exchanges that demonstrate how both served as critic and editor for one another. Here, fundamental differences between their critical projects began to emerge. When Cowley was well into writing *Exile's Return* in the summer of 1933, and Burke was at work on *Permanence and Change*, a complex book about interpretation which applies concepts derived from literary criticism and philosophy to an analysis of social and political change, Burke wrote to Cowley that they have an "initial or informing distinction in purpose: You are trying to write an interpretation of certain cultural trends; I am trying to write on the process of interpretation." Burke's observation can of course be extended over the course of both their careers. By 1933 Burke's interest was less in criticism than in the *criticism* of criticism and critical systems, and with *Exile's Return* Cowley began to establish his career as a historian of modern American literature and culture.

The letters they exchanged during this period also reflect—and reflect on—their interest in Marxian criticism, specifically as an antidote to their aestheticism and art-as-self-expression orientation of the 1920s. In October of 1931 Cowley writes trying to explain why he feels "driven toward what is known as Marxian criticism." While it "doesn't attempt to reduce all art to its economic, or rather its social, causes," he insists, "it does consider art as organically related with its social background, and functionally affecting it." Moreover, he has begun, he says, to judge Burke's own work by "the Marxian elements in it." Frankly acknowledging those elements, Burke writes to Cowley that while he shares many of the objectives of communism, he is "not a joiner." "I am a literary man," he continues, "I can only welcome Communism by converting it into my own vocabulary . . . My book [*Permanence and Change*] will have the communist objectives, and the communist tenor, but the approach will be the approach that seems significant to me." "I am," he concludes, "in the deepest sense, a translator. I go on translating, even if I must but translate English into English." One of the significant differences between the two that emerges during this period is Burke's decision to resist becoming involved in People's Front groups. It saved him from the kind of public criticism Cowley's involvement in these groups brought him, though in the 1950s both men found themselves losing teaching positions for their political sentiments and affiliations in the 1930s.

While during this period Burke wrote essays on literature that appeared in a number of journals, and which in 1941 were collected in his book *The Philosophy of Literary Form*, Cowley's writings (aside from *Exile's Return*) appeared almost exclusively in the *New Republic* (some of the most important of these were collected in 1967 in his book *Think Back on Us: A Contemporary Chronicle of the 1930's*). After finishing *Permanence and Change*, Burke turned immediately to his next book *Attitudes Toward History*, a study of historical change that relied on concepts from literary criticism. "I have simply extended a criticism of art," he wrote Cowley in June of 1934, "until it included areas of production which do not happen, in the language of common sense, to be called art." By the late '30s he had begun to teach part-time, first at the New School of Social Research, and later at the University of Chicago.

Cowley, of course, had become increasingly active in a number of People's Front organizations, and in the late '30s and early '40s those activities began to bear bitter fruit. His inability to recognize the true nature of the Moscow Trials, as he later admitted, turned out to be a huge mistake. With the collapse of People's Front groups in the wake of both the Moscow Trials and the Hitler-Stalin Pact in August of 1939, Cowley had come under increasing criticism, and by January of 1941 he was writing to Burke with the clear sense that an era was at an end. In December of 1940 there was something of a purge at the *New Republic*; Cowley took a salary cut, was kept out of the office, and asked to send in a weekly review from Sherman. Though he continued to contribute essays and reviews to the *New Republic*, this effectively marked the end of his job there.

At this time he began to outline to Burke a book on the 1930s. It was to be about "the writers' crusade," a crusade he saw as essentially a "morality play." His book on the '30s was not in fact written until 1980, when he revised portions of essays written in the '60s and '70s, and combined them with new material in *The Dream of the Golden Mountains*. These letters thus represent a contemporary record of his thoughts about the 1930s, and Burke's spirited reaction to them. After the attack on Pearl Harbor, Cowley set aside the book, taking a position in Washington at the government's Office of Facts and Figures (headed by the poet Archibald MacLeish). However, he quickly came under attack in the press and in Congress for his People's Front affiliations. Resigning under fire in the early spring of 1942, he returned to Sherman to tend his garden, vowing to avoid the world of politics and turn his attention to literary matters.

16 Dominick Street,
New York City
February 1, 1924
[PS]

Dear Kenneth:

I live by clocks which deceive me. I rise at 8:45 and reach the office at 8:45. I rise at 9:05 and reach the office at 9:20. I rise at 8:00 and reach the office at 9:30. I never keep engagements, but on no principle. I have time for nothing. What I lay down is never picked up again. Suddenly I had a hysterical desire to read Plato, and rushed to the library to consume *Phaedrus* and the *Banquet*, out of which latter I remember that Alcibiades compared Socrates to a flute player, which I thought an obscene remark. As soon as I put off writing you so long that it became a duty, I did not write. Why is it that this fragmentary life puts me in extreme sympathy with you, so that my ambitions now are to read Plato and Goethe, and to write an aesthetic in 96 theses to be nailed to some church door, perhaps the *Dial*'s, out of a sense of the necessary disproportion between end and means. But since a letter should accomplish something, let us enunciate a few of the 96, pell mell, for you to arrange and comment on:

1. Art is disinterested creation.
2. Art is the expression of a sensibility. (N.B. Instead of Art read Poetry.

"And all creation or passage of non-being into being is poetry or making, and the processes of all art are creative; and the masters of arts are all poets." And our volume, instead of an Aesthetic should be called Poetics, for the very project of writing it is Aristotelian.)

3. The function of poetry is to make the world inhabitable, a process which must be repeated for every generation . . .

4. From 3 it follows that Eternity or Immortality is a false aim for poetry.

5. And also follows that Abstract Beauty is a false aim. (Pragmatic proof:— People who pursue Beauty only fall into fantaisisme, and the pursuit of Immortality leads to dullness.)

6. From 1 and 2 it follows that the two faces of the coin to which Poetry is compared are not Form and Matter but Creation and Expression. (N.B. This solves the difficulty of the antinomy, for if only a Neo-Platonist could imagine the wedding of Form and Matter, a more direct mind can see that, on a higher plane, creation is expression and expression creation.)

7. Definition: Expression is communication. Robinson Crusoe singing on a desert island is not, in our sense, expressing himself, nor is the unintelligible writer a poet.

For tonight I shall not continue. On these seven maxims one should meditate a year, or perhaps one could be satisfied with having stated them and die like the Greek philosopher who is known by his two tropes.

Out of Paul Elmer More[1] I derived a statement of the great truth that the basis of philosophy is to attain ataraxy (free security, or more vulgarly [Oxford], stoical indifference, from *a*, not, and *tarasso*, disturb). Philosophy is the power of not being disturbed. After six months of New York, one takes refuge in such preoccupations, and the atmosphere of New York is mysticism or a (hysterical) classicism, to be distinguished from the classicism of the Mediterranean, which results from sympathy with one's environment instead of rebellion against it. Let us repeat, however, I AM NOT DISTURBED I AM NOT DISTURBED I AM NOT DISTURBED I AM NOT DISTURBED DISTURBED NOT AM I NOT DISTURBED NOT I AM NOT. NOT.

NOT.   neti   not . . .

MC

1. Paul Elmer More (1864–1937), American critic who was associated with the New Humanist Movement. He is best known for his *Shelburne Essays*, fourteen volumes of which were published between 1904 and 1936.

82 Church Street,
Asheville, North Carolina
February 5, 1924
[PS]

Dear Malcolm,

. . . As to Paul Elmer More, I have been reading a couple of volumes of his Shelburne essays. And the main reason I see for reading him is that he is more our contemporary than, say, Mencken or Macy[1] or Van Doren.[2] When he talks of such things as ataraxia, I will admit, I get a bit discomforted. For too often he asks for things which are too much a denial of one's natural self—and we all have a bit of Rousseau in our blood, especially during those years when we have virility in our members. The basis of his attack, however, this advocating of dualisms over against the usual romantic tendency toward monisms, I feel much drawn towards. And his definition of skepticism is a truly ingenious thing, and something which—if people were intelligent enough—would result in his dismissal from any university. For it completely undermines the tacit conception of discipline which is ruling the modern world: it would not, that is, allow us to consider as a worthy example of discipline some man who applies himself to his goal, works night and day with his eyes focused upon it, and rises from canal boy to president. Skepticism demands a much higher degree of complexity than this, and will not allow a man this easy certainty of action. Also, a man like D. H. Lawrence is the phenomenon of a slight complexity. While even some died-in-the-wool hundred-percent skeptic would, I suppose, fall by More's definition. More's skeptic would, I suppose, fall by More's definition. More's skeptic clings to religion because he is too skeptical to do without it: he sees that the omission of religion is an unjustified simplification.

To turn to your own formulas:

Art is disinterested creation. But, art is also interested creation. You yourself farther on say that the function of poetry is to make the world inhabitable. (Habitable for whom, the artist or the reader?)

Art is the expression of a sensibility. This I do not quite get the gist of. Is it a parallel to the much quoted statement of de Gourmont's that the honest critic attempts to erect his sensibilities into laws? In any case, it is not enough to say that one man feels sad and writes sad; another feels happy and writes happy—for this, I imagine, would be what it means for art to be the expression of a sensibility. But one's expression is often very much determined by one's gifts as well as one's attitudes. Mark Twain being the classic example . . .

.   .   .

It follows that abstract beauty is a false aim. At this point I beg your leave to recall my essays on Gustave Flaubert and Carl Sprinchorn.[3] There

I plead that the artist, immersed in his subject matter, finally shoots out over the top—that of a sudden things which had been tools suddenly become aims. The artist, in other words, goes beyond his message into the glorification of the gesture per se. The objection to abstract beauty is that it is usually aimed at without this initial purging through the hells of subject matter.

There. I have objected to all your formulas, and you will turn aside with disgust and observe that the cock is crowing again. But as I have found before this, our objections usually arise when we have not driven each other to ultimate definitions. The point is, will you finally consent to write five and ninety with me, and write them without the jazz tinsel? Will you be willing to place more emphasis on being right than on being new, even preferring good Aristotle to poor Burke or Cowley? . . .

K. B.

1. John A. Macy (1877–1932), a critic who wrote often for *The Nation*. His book, *The Spirit of American Literature* (1913), called for the use of specifically American material in American literature.

2. Either Carl Van Doren, who was a literary critic, professor of literature at Columbia University, and editor at *The Nation* from 1919 to 1922, or his brother Mark Van Doren, who also taught at Columbia and was editor at *The Nation* 1924–1928.

3. "The Correspondence of Flaubert," published in the February, 1922, issue of *The Dial*, and "The Art of Carl Sprinchorn," which appeared in *The Arts* in December of 1921.

16 Dominick Street,
New York City
February 19, 1924
[NL]

Dear Kenneth:

Today I called on Miss Gregory.[1] She has the air of always being embarrassed, or was it assumed for the occasion? I took away two books for briefers, refusing others. It frightens me how my life is episodic. To find any personality for myself, I have to reread my own letters. Let us estimate that I can think a maximum of 2 hrs. per day. Every day the topic changes, my interests change, I am more or less downhearted. I plan different futures. To read Plato. To construct an aesthetic. To write a novel. To be independent. One aim conflicts with another, and our lives are held together only by the calendar, by the daily paper, by the chain of Saturdays. Mr. Cowley, you write, don't you? No, Mrs. Smith, I can take it or leave it alone. Period. The function of poetry is to make the world inhabitable. Period. Period.

NOTES—ADDENDA

Matty says that Wall Street is an "Experience." "I will recover from it." "Nothing is possible except fatalism."

Hart Crane—lost job—losing room—disgusted with New York and thinks of returning to Cleveland, O. It is disquieting to find a man more episodic than myself.

Munson—Went to visit him, being lonely, thought to be excited, I was sweet, bored, got drunk, went home. Period.

Sue—has tonsilitis.

Cowley—Is busy denying everything he did before Xmas, with the belief that everything he did was right. Simply, the standard was higher than he could maintain alone, when most of his time was taken by an office. He writes amiable reviews, and for the first time has the sensation of walking backward.

Messiah—Wanted badly.

Reread "Llan," also your review of Waldo Frank, and found them excellent, in their different categories.

Broom—Last night we went through the Accepted files and found little Acceptable. A second story by Durbarow[2] is good, not so amusing as the first. But the necessary at present is to write a number of *Broom*, say things that will put an end to the gesture, make the period, project the following paragraph. We must (1) Write a letter to the subscribers; (2) to the Postmaster General; (3) Write on the situation of literary New York (a general survey), and (5) Leaving all this behind, talk about the major problems as if *Broom* would always be or had never existed. Which do you wish to write? Will you?

Unless things change, I leave for Woodstock Thursday morning, but will be back late Sunday night. And, hopefully, see you Monday?

M

1. Alyse Gregory, managing editor of *The Dial.*
2. Charles L. Durbarow, a writer from Chicago.

82 Church Street,
Asheville, N.C.
February 21, 1924
[PS]

Dear Mal,

Your card yesterday afternoon, your letter this morning. After your card I went right upstairs and sat down and began writing, and I shall not tear it up, I shall bring the four pages along to show you that I really wrote them, and I shall let you tear them up. The material, however, is sound; perhaps you—or you and I together—might patch it up. It should be called probably "The Young Men, As Young Men" . . . I swear by God that I shall write something. Perhaps this very article, which in its roughness is an appeal for the catacombs, a proclamation that the young men as young men hereby vanish, that H. L. Mencken, Floyd Dell, and F. Scott Fitzgerald are hereafter to be known by the definite and undisputed title of The Younger Generation, that Munson's formula of the skyscraper primitive could have easily been capitalized except for the failure of the young men to get behind this slogan, a failure caused by the spirit of qualification among themselves. "At a time when certainty (genuine or assumed) is the most essential requirement not merely of success but even of production, at a time when it is much more important to be assertive than to be right, they still clawed at one another, and attempted to destroy whatever meager bits of certainty any of their members threatened to acquire." Or further, "The abortive movement represents men who would allow themselves neither of two opposing certainties: they could not accept the sheer determined optimism of being skyscraper primitives, nor the fixed plaintive attitude of the Seven Arts tradition. Either type is a brand, a soap label, and has its future if adequately backed" . . . Let the young men, as young men, vanish.

"The only reason I see for championing the young men as young men is that they happen to have an older aesthetic vision; that they are shaping a reaction against a new movement; that they, the young men, are turning away from precisely those sickly aesthetic standards which made the admiration of youth *per se* fashionable." Wherefore, we plot our future, a future without polemics, for one cannot martyrize himself to an evil which can be remedied so easily by mere disinterest. Since we can write and read as we please, there is not sufficient hatred to make polemics profitable to ourselves; while further, the press is in the hands of a group of cretins whose preoccupations are so trivial that it would be disastrous even to take the trouble to refute them. Polemics, to be passionately pursued, must be rooted in economics, whereas we have no economic quarrel with the diarists and colyumists and pleasant personalities. For if we produce what we desired to produce, the readers of this commodity would not stomach our productions. Let each man, therefore, see to his private still and his private printing press, that he may live like a gentleman in the midst of prohibition and journalism. If we have to live by our typewriters, let us consider this an unavoidable evil placed upon us by the bent of our talents. In America today there is but one magazine where the study of letters may occasionally be pursued in public; I refer to a few scattered articles in the *Dial* . . .

K. B.

33 Bank Street,
New York City
June 24, 1924
[NL]

Dear Ken:

I notice a struggle to think, which gives the most primary idea a value entirely ridiculous. Also a tendency to kiss the ass of culture, like a woman's clubman. Tonight I read one of Poe's poems to Crane, and he remarked on how nice it was to hear a poem read out loud. You're well out of it, and if you don't stay out of it, I'll be tempted to kick your muscular and overheated arse.

We climbed to the end of a scow at the end of the pier at the Brooklyn end of the Brooklyn Bridge, listened to the black water lapping and watched the Shenandoah float across the skyline of New York, at the point where "Waterman's Fountain Pen" is displayed in enormous letters. Allen Tate was with us. When I came home I found that the person who steals our milk twice a week had washed the bottle and left it outside the door.

Seaver[1] asked me to contribute to *1924*. The timing of his letter (just before the appearance of the first issue with Munson's essay) made me smell politics, though I am probably wrong. I shall contribute anyhow. Hart tells me you are giving him your essay on Pater. I saw a man tonight with a bald head except for a natural monk's tonsure of long black hair, a perfect circle around the bare crown. He was astonishing. I am becoming an eye. Also, I diarize . . .

Yrs.
M.

1. Edwin Seaver, editor of *1924*, a monthly magazine of the arts which appeared in July and closed publication in December.

Andover, N.J.
July 10, 1924
[PS]

Dear Malcolm,

. . . My life has still not become regulated. I am still struggling against natural forces. I lay down my hoe to pick cherries, and climb out of the cherry tree to clean the spring, while in the meantime my woodpile has been dwindling to nothing

. . . And each morning, for better or worse, I sit for at least two hours before a begrudging typewriter and write my own personal little paragraphs and codas for posterity. After this story I expect to try writing some general essays. I also thought of laying out some larger fiction form which would admit of addition bit by bit, day by day. Perhaps I shall even try my five-act drama, my Despot.

How well I shall write remains to be seen; but there is no doubt that I shall *write*. I am now damnably and inexorably under way. The strain is still considerable. But I have one advantage—or is it a disadvantage?—over other poor convicts like Flaubert: that I can sidetrack my story along some other line as soon as the nausea gets too much for me. But regrettably, that in itself produces its own species of nausea, and from this species I am not able to escape. I see in this a new plea for the Shakespearean drama. For Shakespeare could, without violating his mold, skip from peasants to kings; and yet he kept the same peasants and kings throughout, so that the freedom of his skippings did not become in turn an annoyance of itself. The great *artistic* value (or let us say formal value as distinguished from the pure interest in subject matter) I see now in the process of character building is that by building characters one builds potentialities so that one's situations have these potentialities to feed upon. A situation, for instance, cannot *per se* be poignant; but a character in a situation can be poignant.

. . .

I continue to read at Schopenhauer, who is sometimes enlightening, sometimes disappointing, and sometimes downright irritating. I think that most of all he has given me a fondness for the valiant nomenclature of Kant. While Spengler is just as gratifying in this respect. I shall have the first third of his introduction finished this weekend, and shall bring it along with me. Regardless of what one may think of his doctrines as a whole, I believe that he has contributed a new and vital method in history by his consideration of historical events as symbols. Translating Spengler has made me realize just how handy the German language is for metaphysical exposition. And Christ, what a scatterbrained paragraph.

No matter. I put up four banisters between the beginning and the ending of it, and went to the spring for water.

Luck. See you soon.

K. B.

Andover, New Jersey
November 8, 1924
[PS]

Dear Malcolm,

There is a procedure whereby, after several days of sultriness and sluggishness, days too warm for the autumn, when one is exhausted more at the prospect of chopping wood than he is after once getting into the job (primarily, in my case, because I begin in the middle of the afternoon, so that as I progress the chill of evening finally dispels the mist, and the sun sets in a world of sharp outlines), after such days, I say, a wind gradually picks up from the south, southeast, or southwest, fluctuates among these three in fact, so that there is sometimes coal smoke in the air from the main line to Buffalo; we decide that a rain now is definitely scheduled. I specialize in dead chestnut, for it does not matter if I do chop green wood in the rain. After a time, under increasing gales, the rain either comes or does not come. While if it does not, the sky goes through the same gestures as though it had; there is a conflict—I decide that the wind is coming from the west— an hour later I go out to look at the chimney, and the smoke is going south. At such moments the psychophysical parallel becomes apparent. Perhaps I awake an hour before breakfast and go out through the woods with the dog. (Once I shook a squirrel out of a birch tree, and the dog had bitten it before it hit the ground.) I note the solidity of my shoes as they thump over rocks and sod. I stop to observe perspectives. At such times I always reflect that there is no anguish but physical pain, and that so far the good God has pretty well spared me that. I resolve again to bite hard and keep my muscles firm. Tightening my arm, I slip my hand under my coat and rejoice that my tits are solid.

Philosophy is the attempt to increase enjoyment and decrease anguish. In practice it tends to one of two extremes. It either heightens our sensitivity to enjoyment to such an extent that anguish can feed upon this sensitivity with all the greater gluttony, or, in attempting to narcoticize our capacity for anguish, it also narcoticizes our capacity for elation. The philosopher finally turns to things of the spirit, not through a lack of appetite for things of the world, but because here the risk of loss is minimized: here one can sun himself in a species of experiences in which he need not fear lest the very sweetness of them become later the basis of their greater bitterness.

For several months now a strange unnamed desolation has been settling down upon me. I awake in the night, and am desolate. I guffaw, and am desolate. There is nowhere I can go that my self does not go with me. Out of this desolation a few symbols emerge—again and again I think of cold wind sweeping across ice, of glimpses down into pygmy valleys miles and miles below, of opening the door and finding a countryside covered with snow. While what does this mean: that when my brain has been absent and I suddenly recall what I have been doing unconsciously, I discover that I have, by an elaborate system of overlapping strokes, been drawing in my mind the three letters, in capitals, ONE, each square, so that the O is composed of four straight lines and four right angles. That I leave to the Floyd Dells: I mention it, since it interests me so greatly that I thought it might interest you a little.

•   •   •

To cure certain diseases, I believe, medicine has even found the venom of certain snakes of great value. Likewise I feel that a winter in New York, with the *illusion* of wealth, is what I most greatly need. I am going to try getting a part-time job, perhaps sounding MacVeagh[1] at *The Dial*. If you hear of anything, let me know.

K. B.

1. Lincoln MacVeagh (1890–1972), president of Dial Press from 1923 to 1933.

33 Bank Street
November 16, 1924
[PS]

Dear Kenneth:

Now the latest news is that I'm out with *1924*. Not walked out, Kenneth, but kicked. At least so I interpret a tart letter from Seaver, refusing to make two changes I requested in the open letter to [Waldo] Frank. I answered him diplomatically, because I don't want to quarrel. It is an excellent magazine, the most interesting we have at present. What disturbs me is the fact that it is continuing old quarrels instead of ending them . . .

Everywhere I turn, another fight. Meanwhile Hart, Matty, and I had been making plans together. We decided to borrow *1924* for an issue which should be entitled Contributions to a Literary History of Our Times. We wanted to fill the issue with memoirs, letters, anything which bore on our thesis that the Great Literary Politicians of New York were a bunch of worms, afraid of shadows because they cast none, anxious to kiss the feet that trampled on them . . .

Well, Kenneth, it doesn't look to me as if we'll be lent an issue of *1924*. Failing this, Matty and I think an issue of *Broom* is in order. We'll lay off Munson. Hart and Allen Tate will contribute. What do you suggest?

This little rumpus with Frank . . . has been a great education. I find that it is forbidden to say a word against mysticism. Yet I only mentioned mysticism incidentally, in the middle of a catalogue. First Seaver caught me up, asked me what I meant and argued for an hour. Then Frank, disregarding the rest of my letter, devoted a long paragraph to the one phrase "passive mysticism." Then Seaver, as editor, forbids me to add a footnote explaining what I meant. I gather the impression, at secondhand through Tate, that Frank, Munson, and Crane have gone much deeper into Gurdjieff, Ouspensky, etc. than we ever suspected, and that any reference to mysticism outrages not an idea but a cult. Yeats swallowed any number of theosophies and continued to write well. I like Yeats but God knows I can't swallow theosophy. The only solution is to write. I think, if anyone paid me, I'd begin writing, and forget the whole dirty series of arguments . . .

· · ·

Are you working on the aesthetic or writing the new story? When are you coming to town? What do you want to write for the proposed new issue of *Broom*, *1924*, or *Secession*? Hannah[1] is resting easily, the baby is fat, and Peggy is solving a crossword puzzle.

> Yours,
> M

1. Hannah Josephson, Matthew Josephson's wife.

Andover, New Jersey
November 20, 1924
[PS]

Dear Malcolm,

When I say that I do not understand the situation of which you complain, I do not mean thereby to pose in any self-contented aloofness. Yet from what little I know of Seaver, I should imagine that your touchiness has read a certain intransigence into his actions which he does not possess. The conception of someone suppressing a footnote in the interests of mysticism's salvation is enormous. I can much more readily suppose the suppression to have occurred to avoid delay in publishing the issue, which is already quite belated.

I do openly and avowedly, of course, share your distrust of this parlor mysticism. I share your belief that Frank does not write well, although I give him more credit for his intentions than you do. I also share your concession that if he did write well you could forgive the mysticism. Indeed, I could even forgive it if I felt that it were at bottom sincere. Yeats did undoubtedly see things. Yeats got religion. Yeats lived the life of a mystic, disorbited, tootle-voiced, among cranks and horrors. I suspect that the mysticism of Frank is like the emotionalism of Rosenfeld—the reparation by pen and ink of certain lacunae in character. These mystics feed too well for me to take them seriously. Of all attitudes toward life, mysticism most demands denials and suicidal liberties. *I have never, in word or act, seen their mysticism.* And when your correspondence appears in *1924*, I shall take the opportunity to say so, if Seaver will not suppress me in turn.

The last couple of weeks have been in some ways the most idyllic time of my approaching-thirty years. I have lived in that quiet frenzy which is the only real intoxication of writing, waking in the night and memorizing sentences to be written down the next morning, finding a brand new aspect of my subject presented to me while playing a sorry César Franck or while drying the dishes, hurrying to get one notion down lest it be crowded out of my head by the pressure of another. Whatever anyone else may think of the result, this much of felicity has been granted me, I shall have, we might say, lived that much longer. Each morning I go to my room with the eagerness of a young bride to the bridal chamber. Each afternoon I saw wood from three until six. Each evening I read, play the organ, and take notes. For some strange reason, literature seems important to me—I have, at the core of me, forgotten its systematic denigration at the hands of the New York newspapermen . . . I have the assurance of knowing that some aspects of my thesis, although discovered by myself in a halting fashion, have been made clearer by theories from Plato . . .

Plato is the eternal philosopher. If the entire works of Plato were erased from the documents of the world, they would be rewritten in the course of time. Kant, had he possessed sufficient grace, could have rewritten Plato. As it is he very nearly did. My own nebbing in the matter revolves about the displacement of Plato's universals. As I have said before, it is simply the talk of "psychological universals" instead of "metaphysical universals." Situating the arch-types, the ur-formen, not in the universe, but in man. Universale intelligitur, singulare sentitur (a scholastic formula I picked up from somewhere) is the keynote. Art brings the forms of emotion into our organic experience by embodying them in one specific plot. There is but one crescendo (one sense of crescendo in the human makeup) but there are as many crescendos in art as one cares to embody in the particularities of subject matter.

I shall not go into it all now. Form in art becomes defined by this system as the arousing of a desire and the satisfaction of that desire. If I, by so many pages, awake in the reader the wish to see, let us say, a letter which one character has written to another, and at the proper moment produce that letter—that is form. Like the psychoanalysts, I agree in defining art as a waking sleep, but insist that it is a waking sleep for the audience, not for the artist. Modern theories, I point out, too often incline to define the essence of art in terms of the artist's weaknesses.

My principal difficulty is in getting some order into all the subsidiary issues which are entailed in this. An aesthetic, like a metaphysic or an ethic, is one sentence. (*Hamlet*, Emma Bovary, *Don Quixote*—each of these is also one sentence.) So it really should be said all at once. There is no beginning and no end, for each assertion involves some other assertion.

But I close, the woodpile calling me . . .

K. B.

Andover, New Jersey
January 14, 1925
[PS]

Dear Malcolm,

Yesterday afternoon, with fifteen minutes between the end of the day's manual toil and supper, I walked alone in the road, before my property and God's landscape, and took stock. The sky was a consistent blue, though with pinks and purples at the appropriate corners of the horizon, the snow tinkled beneath the heel, in the still air my cigarette smoke followed me as I walked. I observed first that it would be a cold clear night: and sure enough, as I kindled the fire this morning in my bathrobe, I noted that the thermometer registered six below. I next observed that you had somehow, in some intangible, imponderable manner, greatly wronged this country: and I decided that this was due to your never having seen it, as one—we learn—must see a woman, in all its subtle shiftings and its broad complementary phases. I next pondered on the psychology of resignationism, and from amid vague mutterings of the unuttered I extricated this: resignationism is a kind of disillusionment in advance; it is the systematized equipment of a persona whose dread of loss is greater than his joy of possession. The resignationist believes that he will eventually be abandoned, not by reason of a friend's or any enemy's malice, but by the nature of things. Others, sensing this distrust, consider it an implied maligning of their characters, and thus does the fear of estrangement produce estrangement.

Quite inconsequently, I went on to observe things of myself. I decided that I have something of that character in Thomas Mann who peers through the windows at the happiness of others, envying them their happiness but not the mode of life and the type of mind which gave them this happiness . . . I am also a man who has unconsciously, and with great distress to both myself and others, held to the belief that a common interest in the same craft rides above all tact. I have, that is, caused personal pique through the unconscious assumption that it could be erased, not by discussing it in its own terms, but by scrapping it and turning rather to some matter of theory . . .

Concerning yourself, I decided that you are no longer the man you were at high school. It has taken me years to find this out: and my refusal to recognize the change has been the cause of many minor disorders. Jack,[1] you will remember, said that you suffered from a persecutional mania. I, approaching from a different order of experiences, discovered about the same thing in my growing conviction that you must be treated with tact. Now, the very fact that one uses tact with Scofield Thayer or Henry Seidel Canby[2] has always to my mind made that sterling quality a little less sterling. And a factor which you hate in literature, I hate very much in life. To me, the employment of tact is a subtle method of denigration, which, if it implies no absolute discredit to the persons involved, does certainly imply discredit to their relationship. Perhaps character is to a great extent a practical requirement, and to act we must suddenly stop hearing. At any case, in adolescence we heard much and acted little, and in reaction perhaps now, to act, we automatically stifle too many doubts . . .

Between Munson and me, you may be interested to know, there has been a break. Not an absolute break, but one of those imponderables, intangibles, a friendship worn down by attrition. The many rumors, a tetchiness almost diseased, an inexplicable disinclination on my part to clear away again and again an issue which just as often became muddled in my absence . . . by a progress subtle beyond human computation, we gradually and without avowal decided to go elsewhere. In all this, I believe, Munson took the lead . . .

In the meantime, I hope that you will soon get anchored; although even that is without much promise, as I fear that by spring I may be back plugging in New York.

K. B.

1. John Brooks Wheelwright.
2. Henry Seidel Canby, editor of *The Literary Review*.

33 Bank Street,
New York City
January 15, 1925
[NL]

Dear Kenneth:

It is very late; too late to be running a typewriter in an apartment house with thin walls, and I must confine this letter to a page. The temptation is to write several, for I, my dignity, rather, has been subtly attacked. Some statements contain the germ of their own refutation. When you inform me that you feel the need of tact in dealing with me, you are proving that the feeling is not yet wholehearted, else you certainly would not write me that statement . . . I see no special reason for beginning tact; it would only make us very uncomfortable—or is your statement a lefthanded way of saying (or feeling) that I have been extremely rude to you, as indeed I have been?

Each of us, till his end of days, will defend his own manner of life. Each of us will defend his personal dignity, a quality created for the consumption of his wife. Perhaps I have changed more than you since Peabody; it is hard to believe; perhaps you were a little less ready to admit the change; there is certainly in the air a universal tetchiness. Personally, in large part, I am inclined to blame Munson, who has quarreled, successively, with Matty, me, Hart Crane, and yourself, being the aggressive factor in each of these quarrels. One cheering feature which I think I mentioned to you before is the fact that since Munson has quarreled with everybody, I feel much less of this uneasiness in the air. Curiously I now begin to have some respect for Munson, which I never had before. Some of his later criticisms have been excellent, and in theory his lack of compromise is admirable. In practice it has resulted in fault-finding, tale-bearing, and a vast edifice of quarrels which has not yet been undermined.

. . .

It has occurred to you, it must have occurred to you, that you are the only living man or almost the only living man in almost complete sympathy with Epicurus. For this reason you must at many moments despise us vulgar hedonists.

If greatness were the ability to make enemies, they would now be breaking the busts of Poe, Emerson, and Hawthorne in the Hall of Fame to make way for three of their successors.

These notes offered in a state of torpor this Friday of January, preparatory to pissing and brushing my teeth.

M

Andover, New Jersey
January 20, 1925
[PS]

Dear Malcolm,

I enclose my (financial) contribution to *Aesthete 1925* and the greater difficulty of our being patronized by persons whose aid we value more than their opinions . . .

I am still writing my article on "The Margin of Permanence"; and although it is true that I have not looked out of the window much, but have written usually over a thousand words a day, I am only on the second page of the definitive message. The basic proposition has profited by your onslaughts to the extent that, if it has not been fundamentally changed, it certainly has gained in clarity . . . I shall . . . take up the two chief methods of attack on permanency: that of historical changes, and that of psychological types. In other words, permanency is denied across the years, and it is denied across the gulf of personalities. To prove the historical life of art would be to prove its immortality, to prove the validity of art for different types of mind in any one age would be to prove its universality. Sociological criticism deals with the mortality of art from age to age, aesthetic standards being looked upon as the result of sociological conditions. The psychology of the type of Jung deals with art's failure to be universal, in the sense that a pure introvert could not find sympathetic expression in the work created by a pure extravert. Spengler really includes both methods of attack, in that he takes each art to suit a specific set of conditions and to express the typical mind of the culture in which it originated.

My process is, first, to show that the doctrine of absolute mortality and incommunicability is as untenable as the doctrine of absolute permanence, to drive it to its logical absurdity in complete personal subjectivism by showing that no one person expresses the exact concerns of another or uses exactly the same set of symbols. In other words, I shall point out the "margin of overlap," the "reduplication of experience in essence rather than in detail." Once this is proved as the basis of communication between individuals, it can also be extended upward, until the personality of one culture is seen as overlapping in its expression the essential experiences of the personality of another culture. Indeed, by playing Jung's types against historic change, each can be made to neutralize the other. Jung, for instance, says that there are certain basic divisions of mankind which are continually re-individuated. If I, that is, have the type of mind of a Plato rather than an Aristotle, I shall find in Plato a fuller response to my requirements. Thus, my type of mind may find in certain Greek writers an expression which overlaps into Occidental thought, even though I cannot completely accept the Greek mode of thinking (indeed, for that matter, do I completely accept any one person's mode of thinking, or even my own total mode of last year's thinking?). And by Jung's divisions, I should bring a greater response to Plato than to an Aristotelian mind using for its expression the symbols of my own culture . . .

At bottom the theories of change are not theories of communication, but of creation. The creative element in understanding is what we are at bottom assuming. That is, I do not *hear* Plato, I *create* Plato . . . The appeal in such cases is in the nature of the medium: in philosophy logic, in literature beauty (eloquence, form). Thus, there is the dual principle of hysteric response (response to what in past literature most nearly overlaps my own requirements) and technical response (the equipment which I, the more I approach the state of pure art-emotion, of reine erkenntnis, emphasize above hysteric response).

I shall probably end with an analysis of the symbol. The symbol is, of course, the basis of the hysteric response (Byronism leads us to Byron). The symbol has nothing to do with excellence; in itself it is merely the formulation of the representative, or the characteristic. Madame Bovary is a symbol; but the carrying out of this symbol into the total artwork might have been done well or poorly. Thus, excellence does not have anything to do with the symbol per se. Yet, the symbol can be expressed in a paragraph, and obviously if Madame Bovary were confined to such a paragraph she would have had little effect as a symbol. The symbol, then, must be put "into action," and this action involves form . . .

.   .   .

One interesting matter I came upon is that of self-expression defined in a new way. In other words, once one accepts it as self-expression to become a sailor as well as to write a sonnet to the sea, one comes upon a new application of self-expression as it relates to art. The artist, in other words, expresses himself when he evokes an emotion in his reader. For once we define art as evocation, then the self-expression of the artist would reside in evocation. Thus, it is not merely self-expression to utter a cry in distress; it is also a form of self-expression to make others feel this cry as poignantly as one wants them to. There is the self-expression of thinking oneself Napoleon; there is also the self-expression of commanding an army . . . It is absurd to think, with Brooks, that Twain again and again *frustrated* his desire to express satire or tragedy,[1] when the very persistence of his humor showed that he was obeying some inner drive, expressing some force, in choosing again and again to *evoke* humor.

.   .   .

It snows, it snows. Past, present, future. For weeks this landscape has been as immutable as the four horizons of a becalmed ship. Indeed, I often feel that we are in a ship. Especially when I clean the front porch, and go right down to the last step and peer from there at the water beginning at my feet and stretching across hills and valleys. Or at times I look out the window, and see the smoke trailing away from my chimney, and then we are sailing, Malcolm, sailing across barns with a lean-to of snow on the north, and frozen lakes, and half-lost roads, and empty pigpens, empty because the pigs were slaughtered at Christmas and now hang as frozen pork on wires to protect them from the rodents . . .

K.

1. Burke is referring to Brooks' book *The Ordeal of Mark Twain*, published in 1922.

33 Bank Street
February something,
1925
[NL]

Dear Kenneth:

Starting from the assumption that the people who produced *Aesthete 1925*[1] are superior to the people they attack in (a) attitude (b) social amenities (c) production (ad hominem proof—or else I shouldn't be among the attackers); let us seek the reason for this superiority. It is caused, I believe, by the mere fact that they are not yet successful, resulting in the second fact that they are more interested in literature than in success. With a few exceptions I fear that when successful they will be more obnoxious than the Boyds, Menckens, and Shermans.[2] The virtue of *Aesthete 1925* in my mind is that it is going to retard their success . . .

•   •   •

The issue is printed. The advance copies are going to be sent out to-morrow night, and on Wednesday, Thursday, and Friday we shall see a few bookstores. We will probably telephone city editors on Wednesday and see whether we can break into the news columns.

•   •   •

We had a party for *Aesthete* contributors on Saturday night, an enjoyable, not an expensive affair. My own kick against the world is that, if I advance an idea, it is very hard to get people to say what they think of it. They seem to assent, and later I find that they disagree. I am still working on a

Kreymborg review for the *Dial*, and at the office am writing much original copy . . .

No, I am not so downcast as you. It is your evident aim to attempt the impossible, and kick because it isn't accomplished. Nobody except Dr. Frank Crane[3] can live by philosophy or aesthetics. If you believe in your scheme of life, you will have to make a further compromise to maintain it: you will have to come to New York and get articles to write, books to review, and after an interlude of two weeks and a profit of perhaps $75, return to your third essay, having made the world safe for aesthetics for another month . . . I spent 6 weeks writing the essay on Racine, and my best friends did not read it till one year after being presented with copies. We write our best work for half a dozen people. The half dozen are vulgarizers, and eventually our work, in changed form, reaches the public. Or at least that is the ideal . . .

M

1. *Aesthete 1925* was a single-issue magazine published by Cowley and others. It was in part meant as a response to Ernest Boyd's composite portrait of a modern aesthete ("Aesthete: Model 1924"), to which Cowley took great offense. He describes the incident in *Exile's Return*, pages 190–196.

2. Stuart Sherman, the American literary critic.

3. Dr. Frank Crane (1861–1928), American author, minister, and journalist.

33 Bank Street
March 7, [1925]
[NL]

Dear Kenneth:

I am writing this horizontally, eyes at an angle, toes pointed toward the crack in the ceiling, chest in convalescence from a grippe. Tomorrow morning I shall struggle back to work. H. Loeb sails tonight. He has promised to get a bid for and supervise the printing of the next issue of what-you-may-call-it . . .

I could do you a very pretty essay on Groups and Schools in Literature. Let us brief it, and make it autobiographical. Two years ago, walking down the gangplank of the *Savoy*, I wanted to help to start a—something—in New York that would incorporate the better features of Dada. The better features of Dada were its ethics, assertions, and adventures. I hoped also to be able to find somebody to act as organizer, since I find any sort of leadership profoundly distasteful. These were not definite plans—I should be rather ashamed of them as such—but a sort of emotional direction which I can formulate now after two years.

The series of quarrels over Munson, with all the petty backbitings which followed, discouraged me more than now seems possible. This fall I was again cheered up. *Aesthete*, which I do not think was my idea, went through with much less quarreling than any one had thought possible. Everybody worked hard on it. Everybody met at Squarcialupi's, and the discussion was not entirely gossip. Here at last is a Group—but we never really wanted a group, except for social purposes. What we wanted was a direction. A group stares at its navel and lives in an atmosphere of self-congratulation. Its direction is centripetal.

· · ·

But as for groups, their function is more social than literary, and as we grow older—man's brain is keenest at 16—we should limit them more to this social function. Living in Roseville, this question of the group function never disturbs you. Living in the country, it won't disturb me . . .

M.

Andover, New Jersey
March 17, 1925
[PS]

Dear Malcolm,
. . . Since arranging for my immediate financial future, however unsatisfactory the arrangements are, I have dropped into a brute and blissful sloth, reading books in blessed aimlessness and spending the majority of the sunlit hours puttering around the yard. I reclaimed a most forbidding piece of territory behind the barn, a tangle of briars, weeds, rusty wire, old fence posts, pieces of discarded wagons having been converted into a cosmos fertile and orderly. I am now digging a hole which I hope to make about one-fourth the volume of my study, and into which I plan to lower the trash heap on the hill above the house . . . Just how I am going to sandwich in the various reviews I have picked up I don't know, for I am determined to get the entire semi-circle of cleared land about the house in reputable condition before returning to work in New York.

· · ·

I write you as one talks on the train: totally without the pressure of content. I often, by the way, regret that I resisted so strenuously the onslaught you began to make upon me that night when Jack Wheelwright and I had dinner at your place. For I am completely out of touch with myself, and with others' opinion of me. Of this much at least I am sure: that my continual haggling with Matty must originate in something deeper than merely accidental differences of ideology. I trust myself no further than that—for so blind have I become that I believe that any act can originate from any impulse. I sometimes feel that people unconsciously sense that I am in retreat, and spontaneously pile after me like hounds after a fox. I know nothing, except that sooner or later I must begin again trying to write as richly as possible, trying, if you will pardon me, to write as beautifully as possible. I, like all of us, suffer under checked prestige—for some unaccountable thing has undeniably happened, and whatever little we may have attained we now have less. Whether this is an objective or a subjective event I cannot decide: or perhaps it has a share of each . . . I talk at random, and thus discredit myself more than I should by mere silence, whereupon I must rely heavily upon the imagination of the auditor for rectification. I know merely that some subtle thing is all wrong—perhaps because we are all romantics and hate one another for difficulties inherent in the nature of things.

K. B.

R.F.D. Gaylordsville,
Connecticut
July 26, 1926
[NL]

Dear Kenneth:

I didn't write till I was driven to it by the desire to talk and the need for an interlocutor. Slowly our friends assume their wooden functions. Much as I like Bill, and Allen[1] to a lesser degree, I should never think of talking to them except on a limited number of topics. People, yes, and books, yes, and women and plans for the future, but to discuss the adolescent topics of What We're Doing and Where We're Going, never. They would think that I'd suddenly rematriculated to Peabody. Which I have. At certain periods one feels the need for taking stock, a discouraging business. And at these moments I have the two options of writing to you or getting drunk and talking to perfect strangers. The second being disgraceful.

And even with you I feel a certain delicacy. I'll stop to remark that I've spent most of the summer on my back, mapping the rivers and mountains on the ceiling. That I haven't finished translating Valéry and that I'm afraid the job will be a poor one when it is finished. That for all my brilliant financial prospects, a month of sickness has left me dead broke. That I'm reading T. E. Hulme and can't share Matty's enthusiasm, although he does show the possibility of synthetic thought in this chaotic age . . . That I hear you have returned to the *Dial* and this time I cannot congratulate you; the *Dial* is getting Awful.

And then the category of news, which is short. The Fourth of July party was rather less drunken and less successful than last year's, for me especially, because I couldn't drink. Jimmy[2] was there with the manuscript of a new O'Neill play, which Sue says is the best he ever wrote. There was also a delightful flapper, Jig Cook's[3] daughter, who entered the world at the age of sixteen, provided only with a gold pessary [sic] and a copy of the Kama Sutra. She speaks of Her Generation, which makes one feel very old. And it really is a generation, with marked characteristics, chief of which is a total lack of sexual scruples. Caroline got drunk. She and Allen, more than ever, give the impression of babes in the wood, unable to cope with the complexities of modern life. When the grocer refuses to extend them further credit, Allen writes an article, then settles back into inertia . . .

To take stock. Twenty-eight, good biceps, bad constitution, nothing accomplished. Or seemingly nothing accomplished. What frightens me is that I have no margin. Having finished one poem or one essay, I have no plans for another; I am a perfect vacuum, like a man after copulation who is very doubtful whether he will ever be able to copulate again.

Have I ever talked to you of the Instrumental Mind? It is one of my favorite conceptions. The instrumental mind has no objects of its own. Given an object it can attain it quicker than another mind, but it cannot create an object for itself. And without objects it rusts like an unused tool. Sue is an almost perfect example of such a mind. Myself also, to a lesser degree, for there are moments when I have convictions, dark and intense, for which I respect myself with involuntary mysticism, but I haven't the gift of spinning these moments into days or months.

And so, twenty-eight, an instrumental mind which I believe to be of excellent quality, though sometimes I doubt its quality for lack of objects. And to a certain extent the quality of the instrumental mind is determined by the objects given it; a poor object, such as my articles for *Charm*, will blunt the tool, and I wonder whether it hasn't been blunted already. Then add to this inertia. Couldn't one base a philosophy on inertia? Schopenhauer could see nothing between the two extremes of torture and boredom. Personally I am rarely tortured and very rarely bored; I often attain the almost perfect will-lessness which he recommends, and that is a worse punishment than he was able to conceive. To be empty, to rust, to seek for the traces of desire.

And these traces of desires revolve in a circle, a narrow circle whose limits I fixed myself. Sex, money, writing, I can find no others. The first two require no further explanation. The third, at present, is limited to the wish to write a few essays and write them very well. At the same time believing that the essay is a minor form; that only poetry (the creation of emotions) and novels or the drama (the creation of characters plus emotions) are to be considered as final ends. Still, this is not so much a belief as a prejudice; I consider the example of Valéry, who made an end-in-itself out of the instrumentality of the mind; all his poems and essays are exercises, on themes dictated by circumstance . . .

In this state of mind I am seized, of course, by a naive desire for self-improvement. I want to read books which, you know, make you think. One which I have desired for a long time is Richards' *Principles of Criticism.* Maybe you could mail me your copy; is it too much to ask?

Behind my present discouragement lies the idea of the good life as one in which all one's powers are exercised to the most dangerous degree. Here the analysis ends.

Yours,
Mal

1. William Slater Brown and Allen Tate.

2. James Light.

3. George Cram Cook, novelist and playwright, one of the organizers of the Provincetown Players.

40 Morton Street,
New York City
February 8, 1927
[PS]

Dear Malcolm,

A few days ago I sat down to write you, to depose my ungainly and inadequate felicitations at your having come so successfully through the mill. But the engineering problems seemed immense, and besides I tended to bellyache on my own account, so I gave up in despair. My aesthetic paralysis has definitely spread to my letters, and silence seems even gradually to be encroaching upon my speech . . .

But I do not write you because I have to say such things. I say such things because I have to write you. It is because it is so natural for me to complain in letters, that I have ceased to write letters. I prefer to watch people pass, prefer, that is, as one may prefer gas to poison. And I have no memory. I sometimes believe that I have shoved nearly the whole of the last fifteen years out of my consciousness.

In anything so far-reaching, one could hardly expect my relationship toward you to be spared, even had you made great efforts to the contrary. Whereas we have evidence, minutely and unavowedly amassed, to suppose that you have done anything but that. All this, however, must remain un-debated. So long as there is any neutral ground left—and there gradually becomes less of it—we may expect to occasionally hunt it out; and I suppose that is enough to be satisfied with.

.   .   .

Oh yes: Bohemianism has become a big word in my vocabulary. For I discover that if I ever despised it, I despised it through the impurity of its disciples, through its extreme vulnerability to prosperity. But our president has taught me the greater value of these things. And what the socialists cannot do, perhaps the Bohemians can do, in the way of interfering with America's rising efficiency . . . And question: who are the Bohemians? . . .

K. B.

219 Wallace Building,
Center & Highland Avenues,
Pittsburgh, Pa.
February 22, [1927]
[NL]

Dear Kenneth:

Living in the Wallace Building makes me feel sixteen or less; if there were only a piano and volume 1 of Beethoven's sonatas it wouldn't be quite so bad; as it is, I feel soulful, bored, too weak to work; I'd like to write poems, but have no ideas. I am mildly furious with you for not answering my letter.[1] This is the second time, or the third, that I have carefully staked out a portion of my Soul to you and received no reply. I have the impulse to say—well then, let's fight—for I am incapable of preserving an indifferent neutrality. By the simple process of not writing and not talking, we have got ourselves into a situation where we have our choice of talking it out or fighting it out. And if you don't answer this letter, I'll think you're en-couraging me toward the second choice. Really.

It's so dumb of us to be in this situation, this vague dissatisfaction that is worse than hostility. Blame it on me if you want to. I've made several attempts to get out of it; mild attempts, I'll admit, but each time I've come against either indifference, or, what is infinitely worse, your goddamned sense of duty, so that I feel that I've been replaced by Friendship or Loyalty in the abstract. I suppose the truth is that you don't want friends just now (any more than you want to write, for the two go together); you want acquaintances—still, Jesus, I think I understand you—by reading myself into you—and it's all wrong, we're wrong, and we'll either talk or fight it out.

M.

1. The letter Cowley refers to has not survived.

The Dial
152 West Thirteenth Street,
New York City
Telephone: Chelsea 6540
August 23, 1927
[PS]

Dear Malcolm,

. . . A letter from Matty, speaking of the murder of Sacco and Vanzetti, reached me appropriately today. The event has convinced him, as it has me, that our rebellion is after all but around the corner, that we are—categorically—candidates for the door. As is everything with me, so my interest in radicalism is negative, arrived at by a process of elimination, when it suddenly seems so much more logical to eliminate Elliot[1] and Fuller[2] than those two poor bozoes. I should like, and I shall try, to keep today green in my emotions. Perhaps it is too important for a symbol—perhaps it incites less adequately than a downtrodden flag or a shoe on a stick, but it will serve. We are getting fat over here, mong vyooks.

Art? No, art is not literally rebellion. But art is the thought that precedes an act, and as such it is *per se* protest. It would be serving its purpose merely to engender a brand of skepticism, of distrust, which could be an equipment for testing the slogans slung out when interests are endangered. I shall never believe that it is too specifically *Uncle Tom's Cabin*, or even Voltaire; it is the Ninth Symphony that opens the crack for the wedge. Hell—why the Ninth? What I mean is: prepare the mold—and any particular problem poured into it will assume the same shape. And art is always next year's mold, and those parts of last year's which the astute find still serviceable. But now you will complain that I have given up nothing. He kept cross, trident, and rune.

Greetings. We are all bastards, we are all sons-of-bitch—decent only in that we can imagine decency.

K .B.

1. Elliott was the executioner of Sacco and Vanzetti.
2. Governor Alvan Fuller, who refused to pardon Sacco and Vanzetti.

Andover, New Jersey
July 21, 1928
[PS]

Dear Malcolm,

I remember writing you, a couple of years ago, a rather passionate thesis to the effect that friends are friends within certain limits, and that friendships are broken by increasing either the adversity or good fortune under which they originated. How then with us, when adversity and good fortune both have increased over our unpresentable days in Pittsburgh? Meanwhile, however, the concept itself has altered. And a friend is none other than that person whom one treats with all the shabbiness and dilatoriness that he scrupulously rules out of his business relationships. I remember writing you a couple of years ago. What can be done about all these gloomy things, mong vyooks? I feel so desolate sometimes, when I consider how little gracefulness prevails among our disjunct group. That not a single sentence in the various Sears Roebuck catalogues for which we write is given less consideration by the scholar who produced it than is accorded the gravest of our human dealings . . .

· · ·

I confess, I grow uneasy sometimes, when I stop to consider how things are moving at present. For who can feel any security in his life unless he can be sure that he is guiding it in the direction of amenities? Yes, this all means that I stopped translating for a couple of days and began to take the inventory again, and things looked forbidding. I shall return to the grind tomorrow with a keener purpose, but not without first registering this plaint.

Was machst du? Later on in the summer I should like to trek across to your country. When the first faint promise of fall arrives.

Sincerely,
K. B.

R.F.D. Patterson, N.Y.
July 24, 1928
[NL]

Dear Kenneth:

Your plaint received; your mea culpa noted. I should like to repeat our walk of 1927, and not to regard it as an escape (escapes are what one never makes) but as a temporary, undistant, pleasurable goal. Why could we not even set a definite date for the venture?—say Tuesday, September 4, the day after Labor Day, when slaves are going back to their offices and the country districts begin to be emptied of visitors . . . Perhaps you and all the family could visit this neighborhood, Lily and the kids staying behind, we marching forward; or perhaps you would prefer to come northward alone. I'll see you once before then, and we'll arrange an itinerary.

. . . I really descend to the depths of poverty every summer; it's my idle and unhappy season; the other seasons are busy and unhappy. Incidentally, you must read *La Colline Inspirée;*[1] it's really an admirable novel, parts of which you would have liked to write. Is it not time for us to moot the world once more? Would eternal life be desirable if it existed? Who is God? Is space limited? Why literature, and is poetry more to be admired than prose? Is love really wonderful? Now that we have a good five-cent cigar, what does the country really need? If a bandit approached you with drawn revolver and announced that he was either going to shoot off your nuts or blow out your brain, would you kiss him? For answers see next week's *Saturday Evening Post.*

Yours,
Mal

1. *La Colline Inspirée*, by Maurice Barrès, was published in 1913. Cowley was translating the novel, which appeared as *The Sacred Hill* in 1929.

Andover, New Jersey
October 15, 1928
[PS]

Dear Malcolm,

I did not hear definitely until today that the job is to come through with Colonel Woods.[1] Whereby my delay in writing you. Tomorrow I am sending you, by registered mail, five articles. I saw Freeman,[2] told him about you, and he said that I could turn these over to you.[3] I advise that when you receive them you write him telling him you have them, and stating when you will send him the first two or three. Always return the originals with the translation, as they figure [payment] by the French . . .

.   .   .

I don't start working for Woods until next Monday a week—which means that as I have promised to deliver Smith[4] the last installment of the *Saint Paul* in one week, I shall have a week of sublime loafing before the new venture. (Sublime loafing—read: one musical chronicle,[5] one review of Romier,[6] and the Fourth Declamation.[7])

But why continue with this extroversion stuff? Only because I should like to write you a letter. But alas! this is worse than no communication at all! I should like to go into business.

Sincerely,

K. B.

1. Colonel Arthur Woods (1870–1942). Burke became an assistant to Woods, who was doing research into drug addiction under the auspices of the Rockefeller Foundation. He later drew on this experience in writing about Coleridge in *Language As Symbolic Action* (pages 201–222).

2. Possibly Joseph Freeman (1897–1965), Russian-born American journalist, poet, and co-founder and editor of *The New Masses*.

3. Burke had arranged for Cowley to do some translating for *Vanity Fair*.

4. Smith was an editor at Harcourt, Brace. Burke was translating *Saint Paul*, by Emile Baumann. The volume was published in 1929.

5. Burke was a music critic for *The Dial* from December of 1927 through June of 1929. "Musical Chronicle" was the title he used for his reviews.

6. Lucien Romier (1885–1944), French historian.

7. Burke had begun to publish sections of his novel, *Towards a Better Life*, in August of 1928. The first, published in *The Dial*, was called "A Declamation." Nine more chapters were published in *The Dial* and *Hound and Horn* between October of 1928 and the spring of 1930.

R.F.D. Patterson,
Putnam County, N.Y.
October 17, 1928
[PS]

Dear Kenneth:

. . . The five articles arrived safely. I set to work on them last night. Morand[1] is nice to translate. However, I'll have to change the order of submission slightly, because the article on the what-you-may-callem fakes will require a little library work, whereas the article on French West Africa can be finished right here. Thanks for the work. Later, when I know more about it, I'll be able to measure the exact tone of gratitude to assume, but just now it seems to me that the tone will be loud and thankful.

Don't apologize for extroversion. Temporarily, perhaps permanently, I have no soul. People that work pretty hard at a job that partly interests them are apt not to have a soul. Writers are especially apt not to have a soul. All the feeling that goes into what they write is subtracted from what they say, and they are left to cherish such simple emotions as vanity, cupidity, and lust. It would be nice to be permanently adolescent. Still, I should not like to return to the sense of futility that brooded over our own adolescence. We had determined to be writers, and writers, in America, play no part in public affairs. They are specialists, in other words cripples. I should like to have the courage to proclaim that nothing human is alien to my interests. Perhaps it is true that if, like Leonardo, we discover a methodology, we can apply ourselves to everything. If some American writer would take a stand in favor of the widest interests possible—a stand like that of Zola in the Dreyfus case—he would improve the status and resolve the doubts of all of us. But to reach this point he would have to have a long training in pride, in the noblest conception of himself. The pride of a good writer is to be disinterested, to observe everything, to be able to predict economic and social movements, and yet to draw no profit from his powers of prediction. I stop before this chain of thought is lost in the higher altitudes of bombast.

Yours,
M.

1. Paul Morand (1888–1976), French novelist.

R.F.D. Patterson,
Putnam County, N.Y.
December 30, 1928
[NL]

Dear Kenneth:

It is now 11:55, and I'm just sitting down at my desk after having risen at 8:30. For a long time I sat over two cups of coffee. Then I built a fire in my room (we keep three stoves going most of the time, with the dampers down). Then I dressed leisurely. I got two buckets of water, started out to get two more, and stopped to talk with Peggy about abnormalities of behavior. I had just been reading Stekel's[1] book on the subject, which is full of case histories. I advanced the theory that many of our friends would furnish cases quite as interesting—and sometimes as extreme—as those listed in the book. Hart, for example. Finally I got the two buckets of water. Then I sawed and split an armful of wood (we buy almost all of ours, but I like to get a little chestnut and green sugar-maple to supplement the other; it makes hotter fires). I ate a bowl of oatmeal, standing against the kitchen door and thinking of *Vanity Fair* . . .

Our lives are the sum of such actions—I continue after taking a piece of fudge, throwing a stick of wood on each of two fires, adjusting one draft, and rolling a cigarette. Character is a sum of past actions and a potentiality for actions in the future. If we say, "I know that man's character," we mean that we know what he should do under any given circumstances. I am coming round to behaviorism, not as a philosophy—I detest Watson[2] and his allies—but as a handle by which to move the world. Reading Stekel last night, I reflected that the final use of psychoanalysis was still to be made in literature; the novelists who have dabbled in it, like Conrad Aiken, have treated it subjectively, from the angle of the patient making confessions; the interesting angle is that of the doctor giving case histories—in other words, the behavioristic approach to psychoanalysis. There are marvelous episodes to be related—for example that of the man who loved his wife, but deceived her with every servant girl he met. Once he was discovered, and after a scene that moved him deeply, swore he would never be unfaithful again. He picked up a servant girl the next week and made an appointment to meet her in the country. Going to the railway station, he was attacked by qualms of conscience, to which he surrendered, but a deep gloom of virtue fell upon him. A purse was lying on the bench in the station, beside another girl of the servant class, whose attention was distracted. The man stole the purse, and immediately his gloom disappeared; he returned jubilantly to his wife . . .

Love,
M.

1. Wilhelm Stekel (1868–1940), German psychologist who wrote on psychosexual infantilism.

2. John Broadus Watson (1878–1958), the American psychologist who originated the school of psychology called "behaviorism."

65 Bank Street,
New York City
January 4, 1929
[PS]

Dear Malcolm,

I wrote you exhaustively, a letter which seemed inexpressive enough to destroy. But what the hell made you think I don't live in a jungle? Certainties—uncertainties—risks—quixotism: Hart is a little surer of becoming an elevator boy than I am. I subscribe to the biological necessity of the seemingly suicidal, the logic of the apparently arbitrary. But if one plays all his trumps now, what—to borrow your vexer—does he have at forty? Where turn, short of disruption to a great many others, for his second spring? Yes, I am going to need frisking up. But let us linger with humanism, anchorage, melancholy—until the necessity of romanticism, flight, madness. It is my ambition to see the world some day on a business trip—my ambition because this will mean that I have not been compelled to see it the other way: as a cure. Already it would be serviceable as cure—but I know in advance that I cannot meet the obligations of increased dosage.

I'll probably shake loose a little. But not just yet. But safety and hazard are much more subjective than you seem to assume. One can brave the dangers of earthquake in a spot where six million people never give the matter a thought. And surely you are talking about mental events alone. Credit me then with my jungle. In any times but today I should have done much to propitiate deities.

All tangled. But how bellyache? If I were untangled today, I'd be tangled again tomorrow. But it's all worth trying to understand and formulate—and one should try to write a tragedy about it so that he'll be cleared for writing a farce. Half the time I'm quite gloomy—and then I suddenly feel that it really is a privilege to go through the mill, whereat I favor maintaining the same rules that had proved discomforting.

. . . I should like to come up some weekend. Just now I have a great many things which I should enjoy saying to the hills in your presence . . .

K. B.

R.F.D. Patterson,
Putnam County, N.Y.
June 23, 1929
[NL]

Dear Kenneth:

I've just finished the second of two leading essays for Mrs. Van Doren.[1] One of them appeared last Sunday; the other appears next Sunday; they deal, one with "Our Own Generation," the other with "The New Primitives." They speak in generalities, half of which are commonplaces, the other half questionable. I hope you read them, and I'm anxious to get hold of the essay you wrote for the *Bookman*.[2] Our judgments must have coincided except on Hemingway, whose work I enjoy on the whole; out of malice I listed "some of Kenneth Burke's short stories and the long description of the fiesta in *The Sun Also Rises*" side by side in a brief catalogue of what I thought were the permanent achievements of our own generation. My other listings were *The Enormous Room*, the introductory essay to *Goodbye Wisconsin*[3] (and I should have added *The Apple of the Eye*[4] if I had read it in time), *Orient Express*, "The Bridge," *My Heart and My Flesh*,[5] and did I give others? I forget. Callaghan[6] is entirely trivial, so I did not mention him anywhere.

·   ·   ·

I'm thinking of assembling a book of essays. Being visiting critic for "Books" next winter would give me a chance to write four of them in the same direction, and thus give a certain unity to the book. It could be either about French or American literature; personally I should like to make it American and to deal with the problems confronting ourselves. For example, an essay on "The Literary Life" in which I described the opportunities afforded by a career of letters, distinguished between men of letters and writers pure and simple, pointing out that very few Americans have achieved a literary career, demanded a higher code of literary ethics, etc. Some of my pressing financial problems being solved, I feel a little more confident. And incidentally, I've been working like hell this spring; I never turned out so much in an equal space of time.

• • •

I'm going to be in New York Tuesday and Wednesday. There's one chance in fifty, I suppose, that you'll be there. I'll find out, anyway.

Yours,
Malcolm

1. Irita Van Doren, editor of the *Herald Tribune* books section.

2. "Thomas Mann and André Gide," which appeared in the June, 1930, issue of *The Bookman*. It later became a chapter in *Counter-Statement*.

3. A book of stories by Glenway Wescott, published in 1928.

4. A novel published by Wescott in 1924.

5. *My Heart and My Flesh* (1927), a novel by Elizabeth M. Roberts.

6. Morley Callaghan (1903–), a Canadian novelist.

July 3, 1929
[PS]

Dear Malcolm,

. . . I wish here to enter a protest against your synthetic portraits,[1] unless you choose to defend them on the grounds of business. I maintain that they are absolutely meaningless. I expect to see you next writing an article on Anita Loos,[2] Frances Newman,[3] Radclyffe Hall,[4] Smith's brand-new whiz, et al., this article to be given the timely title, The Flapper Generation, and to begin with a respectful and even obsequious refutation of an article in the *Ladies Home Journal*. I expect to see you close this article with a synthetic portrait, a young girl who had a college education and did not have a college education, who aborted and did not abort, who was a Lesbian man-eater, a virginal whore, and who stood sitting on the burning deck of a wintry night in June. I grant that it is all possible, however, so I suppose your synthetic portraits are thus untouched.

I hope that you take the part-time job. And with little zest for your suggestion that I freelance, I as earnestly hope that I do not lose mine. The most precious prerogative which I seek as a writer is that of silence between sallies, of being able to clam up till my dying day if things aren't flowing right. With the demise of *The Dial* I wished to wave farewell forever to the deadline. I prefer that my formal writing be kept, if possible, a little to one side—and that I be as independent as possible of its success. I am prepared, at any moment, to reenter the fray, but only when I am forced to do so. I shall avoid as long as possible. For though aware that you scorn avoidances, and though tending to agree with you in this, I believe that we must always avoid something, and I prefer as avoidance number one to avoid the need of watering the stock. And one cannot earn his living as a freelance without watering the stock. I should rather revert to translation.

I think of all such matters a great deal. For it is my nature never to feel secure, to live in preparation for some vague calamity. These calamities can be financial, they can also be mental. They often seem of the latter kind— and then I decide that I must contrive to write something concentrated, so that I may respect myself. I see no guaranty of such a concentrated article arising out of freelancing. It must be done in free and different hours, like practicing the piano. Or at least, this all seems the most plausible at present.

K. B.

1. Burke is referring to the two articles mentioned in Cowley's letter of June 23.

2. Anita Loos (1893–1981), novelist and screenwriter, is best known for *Gentlemen Prefer Blondes* (1925).

3. Frances Newman (?–1928), American author and librarian.

4. Radclyffe Hall (1883–1928), British novelist and poet.

Room 3004,
61 Broadway
September 24, 1929
[PS]

Dear Malcolm,

If you must go on a jag of irresponsiveness, please pray why choose a time when I have submitted a manuscript? Don't you realize that I have gone back to my carbon-copy public of ten years ago? Or are you ecstatically engrossed, to my utter exclusion, doing field work like all my friends hey nonny nonny well a day.

• • •

If you minded the Declamation greatly, all the more reason for comment. If without ideas, simply grade it and return. The next chapter awaits an invention. For it is to be the one song of the book (it and the last paragraphs of the last chapter). Let this be a song, the with-learning-burdened lyric of one who—of one who, too many of one who's—and should we say simply: the learning-burdened lyric—of one who, then follows a metaphor, still unfound, along the lines of climbing out of sullenness into sunlight (though preferably not so mixed). Thereupon our hero must sing his head off, just sing and sing—and that's pretty hard to manage for the champion bellyacher of New York and New Jersey. So we are looking for another invention, though we may finally be forced to use variations of that discovered in the Declamation which you have these weeks been keeping under your pillow— the discovery namely of having him think of his beatitude in terms of snatching it from others, of guarding it, of reminding himself that others do not possess it. I don't like to work that for another act, but there ought to be one step beyond it (that's what one may learn from the study of Milton and John D. Shakespeare—see if the same screw can be given another turn).

How rides the book?

K. B.

R.F.D. Patterson,
Putnam County, New York
September 30, 1929
[NL]

Dear Kenneth:

I can't understand why it doesn't rain. The weather for three days has been warm and threatening . . . I have been working my head off, first to finish the translation of *The Count's Ball*,[1] God, what a title! and then to write an essay on Hemingway for the *Tribune*, a really terrible essay, so bad that it may queer me even with a tolerant editor. I have written no letters, but I have received a good many, among which are a Declamation and a follow-up letter about the Declamation.

Mr. Burke! Let us catalogue my reactions accurately. The first was one of amusement to think that you were writing a novel in spite of yourself, and apologizing for its being a novel. That was before I had read anything but your letter. On reading the Declamation itself, this feeling was rein-forced; I also felt a general admiration for it (the Declamation), and was impressed by the end, in which you employed a very simple device very effectively. I like the quibble about the cows. I discussed the whole thing with Ivan Beede,[2] who is a realist and admires Hemingway and Nathan Asch. He said, "Well, Burke certainly makes the reader work." On hearing this remark, I decided that you had not departed from your original method entirely. I then put the Declamation and your letter aside for two weeks, so that before making a more detailed comment, I shall have to read them over again. The pause is represented by these dots . . .

I dove into your prose, and I have returned with certain bits of wreckage which were perhaps not taken from the depths. First, I was impressed by your having a nominal, as opposed to a verbal, style. On saying, "could you consider *their abandonment?*" weren't you carrying this process too far. Your style is admirably fitted to expressing abstruse ideas. But when giving a very simple idea . . . don't you run the danger of self-caricature? It has always seemed to me that certain things gain force by being baldly stated. Florence[3] didn't say "And the herd—the herd also is yours." What she probably said was "And those cows—are they yours too?" "They too are mine," the hero probably answered, for he spoke more stiltedly . . .

I like the declamation as a whole; I like it vastly, and I especially like the paragraph on chance, the paragraph on the beauties of nature, the final paragraph, which is full of emotion, and in general the revelation of the hero's character. Yes, I like his attitude toward his family. The whole declamation seems to be preparing for your final religious outburst.

Yesterday I rested. Nothing is quite so tiring as writing a bad essay which one has tried desperately to transform into a good essay, without success. Even after spending a day in nursing my body I still feel whipped and exhausted. It seems to me that his year might well be known as the era of ill feeling. Everybody is quarreling, has quarreled, or is about to quarrel with everybody else . . .

Yours,
M.

1. *The Count's Ball*, a novel by the French writer Raymond Radiguet. Cowley's translation was published by W. W. Norton and Company in 1929.

2. Ivan Beede was, as Cowley recalls, a "midwestern realist with writer's block." He was a neighbor of the Cowleys in 1929.

3. Florence is a character in Burke's novel, *Towards a Better Life.*

Room 3004,
61 Broadway
October 3, 1929
[PS]

Dear Malcolm,

Best thanks for learned comments, which were just and gentle. On the score of self-caricature, I admit that I am vulnerable, though I plead that I cannot accept your proposed solution of the difficulty. In the absolute, your conversation about the cows, as amended, is better than mine. But I do not feel that it is better in my context. I do not have so strongly as you the test of naturalness in writing—for it leads too inexorably to Hemingway, whom I hate as though sent upon earth to hate him . . . There is no particular virtue attached to naturalness, except where it is a hit, where the naturalness is exceptional in its enlightenment. Otherwise, one may have to select the stilted as less injurious to the frame. In my case, the frame which I had intended to make all-inclusive has become more and more selective. My hero, in ordering a loaf of bread, would say: Have you, I asked him, some larger unit of bread—a loaf, or possibly a double loaf? . . .

. . .

Don't neglect to eat avec when you come to town. Shall scan the horizon for dust spot.

K. B.

Sunday morning,
February 16, 1931
[NL]

Dear Kenneth:

Until Tuesday morning I'll be here in Riverton, at an inn designed primarily as a house of sin. There's a bar, there's a quarter slot machine, there's a hardboiled proprietor who used to be a gangster in Hartford and now collects Hitchcock chairs, there's a disposition to ask no questions of the couples who rent a room for an hour or two—that is, if they have baggage. But sin lies dormant in Connecticut during the winter, and virtue is cheaper in hard times. There are no couples coming upstairs, baby, for an hour or two, no drinkers at the bar; there is nobody, in fact, except the town philosopher, a huge man of sixty-five with a drooping left eye, who grandiloquently repeats the news in the daily papers, then goes home at eleven o'clock to study spiritualism until dawn.

The village is dead . . . There's no business anywhere. Even the country-side is moribund, with the river outside my window reduced to a trickle of black water at the edge of the ice and nothing to trouble the stillness except an oak leaf clicking across the snow. I wander upstairs and down, waiting for a telephone call I don't expect, then go walking swiftly along the state road . . . I try to reconstruct a philosophy that will work in periods like this. When you're satisfied with things you don't need a philosophy.

One of my worries, not the chief one, I admit, but real for all of that, is the way you've been acting toward me for the last two months. I suppose it's chiefly on account of the *New Republic*,[1] and partly, too, because you're bothered by my habit of loading my troubles on you and by the nature of those troubles. About the *New Republic*, there isn't much more to say. It's a magazine rendered wooden by the fact that everything printed has to be passed upon by four editors of different tastes (or very strongly endorsed by two or three). It has a sort of group personality, which isn't that of any single editor. If what a man writes agrees with that group personality, and is short enough, it is almost certain to be printed. If it's 3,500 words or over, it's almost certain to be cut, and the cutting job, if it's delicate, comes to me; in case of articles which are straight reporting, Bill Brown does the editing. Bliven,[2] with his newspaper training, has cutomania, but most people write so diffusely that the cuts he orders usually improve the paper. I'm trying to restrain him, however, and have him consult with authors before taking action. In the book department I have almost complete authority; it's limited by space requirements, by the necessity for mentioning certain books, and by the judgments of the other editors on the reviews as printed. I'm anxious, damned anxious, for you to do as much writing as possible for the book department. As for the rest of the paper, if you'll talk over articles in advance with Bliven or Soule,[3] there won't be any difficulty.

What you write, as I told you at Matty's, is always on the margins of journalism. That's what makes it good; it's also what makes it difficult to steer through an editorial board with strong individual prejudices. For God's sake, don't put the blame on the least influential of the four editors.

The second matter is even more difficult to talk about. I'm in a hole; I've been in one for six weeks and I may be in one for the next six months. It isn't merely the bust-up of one affair,[4] and being kept in doubt about what's going to happen next; it's the fact that a whole scheme of life collapsed at the same time, that I've got to find a new one and find it for myself. I haven't been putting enough into my work—with the result that when I needed it, my work hadn't enough to give me. I feel as hollow as a sucked egg. I feel as one has a right to feel at twenty. If I could drop everything, go to Europe, write an ambitious book, I'd be cured quickly; but I don't want to drop the *New Republic*, which seems to me the only paper with signs of life and the only one which gives scope to its editors . . . What's the answer? I'll have to go muddling along in this direction, writing myself out of a hole as well as possible, until next October; then I'll take a two-months' vacation in France or Russia and hope that it gives me a chance to get readjusted.

I'll spend long weekends in the country till May 1; in the city I'll trot about. It's a bleak prospect; don't make it bleaker. I don't think my troubles are peculiar to myself. A lot of people I know have been moving in what now seems to be the wrong direction; they too will have to change or go bust. It's pretty late to change now, but not so late as it will be next year, or the next. But we can talk about that some other time.

Yours,
Malcolm

1. Cowley had become literary editor of *The New Republic* in 1930. Burke had been complaining about the magazine's reluctance to publish some of his proposed essays and reviews.

2. Bruce Bliven, an editor at *The New Republic*.

3. George Soule, another of the editors at *The New Republic*.

4. Cowley and his wife, Peggy, separated and divorced in 1931.

Room 220
April 29, 1931
[PS]

Dear Malcolm,

. . . Well, lil coolie Burke has placed its *Counter-Statement* all right—to appear in the fall. It seems doubtful whether people must eat, but it is certain that publishers must publish.

Do you know, Malcolm, that I sing from morning to night—with trench morale? That I first shiver, and then giggle, to learn that U.S. Steel earns the faithful exactly five cents a share in three months. That I note with hilarity how the real break threatens to begin, a year and a half after the greatest debauch of financial gloom in all history. How long will't be, I ask myself, until we start to nibble at corners of the estate—until this pathetic little Sir Walter Scott dream, so essential to my scheme of self-respect, begins to turn nightmare?

Meanwhile, I compensatorily frisk. Even this morning I frisk, though I should be sour with hangover. And it is clear at least that our definitions of human decency were made in bad times, for people are better in bad years than in prosperous ones. One reads, for instance, that 1930 was the best concert year in the history of American music. I doubt whether any publisher in New York would have as much as considered my remote critical elucubrations (escape mechanism?) in 1929. (New test of human virtue: willingness to hear lil coolie Burke.) . . .

K. B.

Andover, New Jersey
June 1, 1931
[PS]

Dear Malcolm,

Well, well—just finished writing you a three-paged letter, single-spaced; but as it is Old Style, we shall not send it . . .

Let us, then, by way of postscript, simply repeat our request that you do not forget to bring the letters.[1] I count on them to complete the unclean job of orientation upon which I am engaged (I mean that, regardless of this fiction which we are to turn out, I am interested in looking over my story, to see whither I am, or was, going.)[2]

Schedule: to finish up the closing three thousand or so words of *Counter-Statement* this week. Then to write nothing but Declamations until I am through with them or am fed up on them. To write every morning; to swim, garden, and otherwise disport every afternoon; occasionally to write, occasionally to think, occasionally to feel, every evening. The pond is stupendous, heaped high with crystal-clear water. You, who saw it in its drought character ("nuisance character"), when many were walking miles for enough water to boil an egg, will be startled at its swollenness. And the new room, as I come back to it after several months (like leaving a poem to mellow), verges upon the architecturally planful. The gardens flourish, the grass is already two feet high. So there is a summer—there is enough for a "pure present"—and as I did with considerable success in Maine some years ago, I shall devote myself merrily to my tasks and my bodily exertions, thinking of nothing beyond the end of the season . . .

Greetings,
K. B.

1. The letters Burke had written to Cowley, beginning in the early twenties.

2. Burke refers here to his novel, *Towards a Better Life*, which was very loosely autobiographical. The experience of writing it proved a kind of turning point in his life, hence his reference to the "job of orientation."

Wednesday, June 10,
1931
[NL]

Dear Kenneth:

This week, instead of foolishly slaving at the office, I'm sitting in my room at the Hotel Albert working on *Exile's Return*. There's one part of the story that I hate to write—namely, the Boyd episode. I have accordingly put it off till the last, and have instead been writing the two concluding episodes, the visit to Bill[1] at Woodstock and the slow readjustment to New York. There's no fire of inspiration anywhere—a few good paragraphs, and for the rest a plugging away at events.

Your letters I have, the whole fat folder of them. I'll remember to carry them along with me on Friday. Muriel[2] and I will take the 5:30 from Hoboken; I don't think we could make the 4:45. And you'll meet us at Cranberry Lake, will you? I hope the rain stops raining by then so that we can bathe our weary members in the lake.

How are you coming with the Declamations? Give my entire best to the family.

Yours,
M.

1. William Slater Brown.
2. Muriel Maurer. She and Cowley were married in June of 1932.

Andover, New Jersey
August 9, 1931
[PS]

Dear Malcolm,

. . . I look forward to your Memories. As for me, I was halted at chapter sixteen by the necessity of a little research. I decided to try refurbishing, for this chapter, a story which I had written at college.[1] It is very immature, but the essential note of meekness was so genuine in it that I decided to try salvaging it, since my hero at this point becomes very meek, meeker than I can, except in flashes, now imagine. He, it happens, was a lover of Blake; but what he said of Blake was quite negligible, so I must invent some substitute remarks of a little better order. Wherefore, our interruption.

. . .

Now—three chapters to be written. I have enough good notes to ensure that the last two will, by my standards, be passable. But Chapter XVI is still a risk, as I may not be able to undo the essential immaturity of the story. In which case I should be at a loss, for the contrivance of having the hero disclose his situation under the best terms by having him write about a fictive character who is clearly himself is very useful to me at this point. His state of self-pity, that is, would be a little thick if we had to carry him through a whole chapter of out-and-out self-pity. By the imponderability of usage, I believe that the reader could forgive the hero's sorrows as disclosed obliquely through a story of someone else's sorrow, where a literal account of his plight would be too vieux jeu. . . .

Well, when I am through I shall love you all. I shall be contented enough, it seems, to throw myself quite simply upon your mercies and ask, without stint, for help. If only I should be so pleased with myself that I had no dignity whatever for people to tread upon. I rely upon the Declamations to burn away certain very uncomfortable parts of me. "If I could, by a ritual, like the old Jews, load my sins upon a goat, I should beat it mercilessly and drive it into the wilderness to die." Each man can, out of the depths of himself, invent but one new aspect of vice—and no wonder he prizes it so greatly that he makes it cause the destruction of his hero.

Meanwhile, life goes on. Each weekend there are boisterous throngs about. Rice wine is cheap but effective. The pond continues to flourish. Seven oil lamps in one room give the illusion of blazing splendor. Thus do we, by going through the motions, conceal from ourselves the steady march toward zero. For weeks I forget the matter, then I look at a new bank statement, et ça me flanque un coup dans l'épigastre. Yes, I move toward the end of my nether . . . I was in town recently, and a pall of forebodings fell upon me. And after the cocktails and the beer had worn off, even before I had gone to bed, I all inside me sobbed, and I said I can't conceal it, I am getting frightened. Big taxes on big fortunes—it is so obviously the method of reformation without revolution, I don't see how people can talk of anything else. Slogan: "We must be generous with the industrialists' money." We need some insolence in this matter. We must appropriate their funds while snickering . . .

> Briefly,
> K. B.

---

1. Part three, Chapter IV, of Towards a Better Life, entitled "A Story by John Neal" (John Neal is the main character, and narrator, of the novel).

381 Bleecker Street,
New York City
October 19, 1931
[PS]

Dear Malcolm,

. . . Harcourt, Brace have taken my Declamations, to be published under the title of *Towards a Better Life*, and to appear in January if the world lasts that long. They gave me no advance, but in exchange have agreed to give me a fancy edition, allowing me to neb in the choice of type, paper, binding, and format. It is not to be a limited edition (not limited by fiat, that is).

I may spend the next couple of months on a pamphlet to be called Invective Against the Republican Party, using some of the juicier pieces of our history since the Civil War for my potboiling substance, but continually branching into my definitions of the good life, my Summons to Poets, and the like . . . Also, I have a new theory of business cycles by which the current cant about "prosperity followed depression before, therefore it will follow again" can be undermined. I want to show that each depression in our history was remedied not by the "course of events," but by the introduction of a new element that whipped up the old nag, started things going again until this temporary remedy in turn had failed . . . It destroys the comfortable leading-businessman proclamations that things are "bound to come back of their own accord," and shows that we must take a new step to bring them back, as a new step was taken to end every depression in the past . . .

Greetings,
K. B.

Yaddo,
Saratoga Springs, New York
October 20, 1931
[NL]

Dear Kenneth:

A man with less intelligence than Hoover—a man, God save us, with less character than Hoover—could end the present crisis (not restore prosperity, but stop the panic, the hoarding, the runs on banks) if the proper social machinery existed. Under the present system, however, only a man of superhuman ability could do so. This is the answer to several pages of your Program—but of this more later.

·   ·   ·

Returning with relief to your book [*Counter-Statement*]—thanks. I didn't acknowledge receipt of the gift because I wanted to read some more of it before writing you. I have read three chapters—Psychology and Form, The Status of Art, Program. I think that in defining form as "the creation of an appetite in the mind of the auditor and the adequate satisfaction of that appetite" you discovered an important principle, and a true one—and one which in itself negates a good deal of what you say in other parts of the book. Your standards elsewhere tend to be Crocean by virtue of your emphasis on technique, on judging how far the author accomplished what he set out to accomplish. But if art is the satisfaction of an appetite created by the artist, we are driven inevitably to consider the nature of the appetite, to criticize ends instead of means. Art is a form of propaganda—for what? And the lamest part of the book, to my mind, is your consideration of the "what," your program. (Before continuing, I'll stop to render tribute to your illuminating asides, to all the aphorisms scattered about so lavishly.)

I'll try also to define my own position. I'm being driven toward what is known as Marxian criticism by a mental process somewhat akin to your praise of inefficiency, or rather of the situations in which society can flourish even with lazy and vicious leaders. In running a book department, I've noticed that even unintelligent reviewers can write firm reviews, hard, organized, effective reviews, if they have a Marxian slant. There must be something to it, I conclude. It doesn't attempt to reduce all art to its economic, or rather its social, causes, but it does consider art as organically related with its social background, and functionally affecting it. Technique it discusses too, without giving it first place. I can't achieve your overmastering interest in How; the field of discussion seems limited and, in the end, barren. I tend to judge your critical writing by the Marxian elements in it, which are so important that one would almost say you were being pushed into [it] backwards. Certain pages of your discussion—especially when you are discussing the relation of a book to its age, or the value of art as propaganda—are written as if you were continuing a discussion with some communist critic, arguing against some of his conclusions from his own premises.

Granville Hicks has reviewed your book for the *New Republic*, not very satisfactorily. He differs with most of what you say, understands most of it, but simply misses the significance of your central definition of form. (By the way, I think that definition, by its logical implications, is responsible for what I have just called the Marxian elements in *Counter-Statement*.) I'm going to see Hicks on Saturday and argue with him.

·   ·   ·

Your idea about depressions is good but not original with you. It's been mentioned briefly by several economists; I don't remember seeing it developed in full. Talk it over with Soule. What about doing a piece on the benefits of the depression?

Yours,
M.

381 Bleecker Street,
New York City
October 22, 1931
[PS]

Dear Malcolm,

. . . What you say about Marxian criticism, I do not quite understand. When you say that your position "considers art as organically related with its social background, and functionally affecting it," I certainly see nothing in this position with which I could have, or would want to have, the slightest objection. I had thought that my book was devoted primarily to examining some of the implications of such an attitude (I was trying to show, by my elaborate machinery, that even art which is, by the Marxian-psychoanalytic hybrid of thinking, called retreatist or "escape," can have a function of this sort). As for my "overmastering interest in How," it seems to me that, as a critic, one should attempt to put the following cards upon the table: He should try to write a Critic's Credo, at least once in his life. This Critic's Credo should contain (a) an apology for art in the light of any current doctrines which might seem to discredit art, (b) A rhetoric, an analysis of the processes by which a work of art is effective, and (c) a program, a discussion as to what effects might be desirable at the critic's particular time in history. The three issues, if one lives with them as many months as I have, will be found to merge into one another . . . I insist that a man is not, even in this flimsy age, entitled to hang out his shingle as a critic until he can offer a rounded credo containing a rhetoric as one of its divisions. You yourself, strangely enough, defend me as to How in the very paragraphs condemning it, for you announce that you are being won to Marxian critics because they "write better." (In this particular, incidentally, you take a symptom as a cause. In general, the Marxians may write better—incidentally, they don't as a group, though you may have assembled some that do— because their position is the more vigorous at the present time. They are Marxians because they are more vigorous, and they write better because they are more vigorous—they do not write better because they are Marxians. In another age, particularly when, as is fast becoming the case in Russia,

Marxism is enshrined, the more vigorous writers will be the non-Marxians. This you know as well as I.)

. . .

Incidentally, I wonder if it was Marxism in its sleepier moments which led you in an earlier chapter to associate "rhetoric, fantasy, and gesture" with "after-hours" literature . . . Rhetoric . . . has flourished less in "after-hours" literature than in literature which was primarily devoted to the swaying of audiences for specific utilitarian ends. If it later seems empty, and thus becomes discredited, this is because the issue behind it has vanished, at least in the form which the rhetor had in mind, and thus all his antics seem a bit overdone. Please be critic enough (even in your Marxian enshrinement) to guard against such glibness. As for fantasy, a work like *Gulliver's Travels* should be enough to remind us that fantasy is a fundamental weapon of extracurricular education, the only kind of education that is worth considering, since it is the only kind that does not uphold the powers that be.

. . .

Well, dearie, the book moves slowly. . . . Grattan in the *Telegram* last night published a short but very enthusiastic review, the beginning of which may interest you, since it begins: "In the fragments of autobiography Malcolm Cowley is contributing to *The New Republic* he tells us that he found his friends at a crucial moment without an aesthetic that also had political and social implications. It would almost seem that Mr. Burke has spent the years since circa 1923 developing an aesthetic that would meet all the demands one could reasonably make upon it." He later credits me with "the most brilliant essay in technical criticism written in this generation," little knowing that, had he been one of my boon compenyons, he could have disposed of this difficulty quite simply by adding, "but what of it?" Nothing else has appeared that I know of . . .

K. B.

381 Bleecker Street,
New York City
May 10, 1932
[PS]

Dear Malcolm,

. . . The end of this week I remove to the woods. My strange difficulties!—for when I am there, after only a few hours, a new TONE filters into me, and I line up the thing as follows: a sentence that I might write, or might like to write, when in the country; I mean, when it is a sentence apposite to what goes on there and to how the city seems from there. But in the city a sentence, to be apposite, must, at best, be written like head-lines—and who could think, in advance, of sitting himself down to a life of writing headlines? You always hated organ music (which in one sense is strange, for your own way of writing has, if not the virtues, at least one of the major vices, of organ music: it lacks edges)—but there is something distinctly organ-music about the country, and to come back to the city with an organ-music concept is to be aghast at one's old-fogeydom. So, all my city notes must now undergo a sea-change—which may mean that they must all move toward the bottom of the sea. But I took them with city-feeling—and now we shall see whether, in working them over, I get mellowing, or mere neutralization . . .

We both, I think, share the mental inappositeness that comes of dipping, now and then, into our Milton—and my study of the muckraking literature has confirmed me in my belief that this is an inappositeness which one should only relinquish when he has found, once and for all, that he cannot bamboozle the headline-thinking world into accepting even a vestige of it. The muckraking literature is a dreary thing because it thought that the facts were enough. Which they are, I suppose, the first time—but when you have read them three or four times, you understand that they are the mere beginning of an article (and the *New Republic*, which must go over them once a week, must sooner or later take this into account). Ha! they talk about "escape" literature—and lemme tell you, that about a year from now, when one after another the depression-ridden sneak away to dream in Trollope, the pedestrian weeklies will gravely announce that the public is closing its eyes to the dreary spectacle about them, that it is again "evading"—but I will tell you that it is evading something even more fundamentally ghastly than the depression; it is evading the headline, the bare-facts school of Kleenex, use-once-and-throw-away weeklies, those who think that literature is not singing, but signing an affidavit. It will be evading, not the depression in society, but the depression in prose—for I hold this: that if you are to maintain their attention upon things which are at bottom disagreeable, and which people wish were different, you can do this only by making them different, which is to say, only by embedding them in literary happenings, only by making the story of corruption a beautiful and engrossing and fanciful thing. Of course, you know this as well as I . . .

Well, this is buzzing time (the plum trees were silent while the sun was behind a cloud—and the moment the sun appeared, the plum trees were abuzz). This is buzzing time—and I go back for the thirty-ninth showdown—with the most tangled mess of notes yet, and still not even knowing whether

I am going to write an essay or a fiction. I'll toss a coin—which is to say, I'll leave it all up to the first sentence . . .

Ever thine,
K. B.

Yaddo,
Saratoga Springs, N.Y.
June 2, 1932
[NL]

Dear Kenneth:

You remember the story told, I think it was by your mother, about the first time we met—I was three and you were four; I walked around your parlor touching things, and you walked after me saying, Don't touch. Mustn't. Anyone looking at us today or reading your letters to me would think that the same situation was being repeated, that I was plunging into Communism while you were saying, Don't touch, be careful, mustn't. But that's only an appearance. I suspect that you're not really a hell of a lot concerned over my adventures with our comrades of the Left—except in so far as they seem to reflect on your own beliefs. If you are concerned, you've got no right to be: I'm not plunging blindly ahead into anything, I'm sort of feeling my way and trying to fit things into a system that will make it possible for me to define my own attitude toward the world and guess what's coming next. And the truth is that I'm deeply concerned and disturbed about you, that really I'm the one who's saying, Don't touch.

I've got the idea that the path in which you're engaged (emotional plus ideological, they work together) is one which has no issue except that list of refuges you made in the last chapter of your Declamations.[1] I said as much when I reviewed your book, and you got damned sore and produced a much more ingenious explanation of your hero. I also waxed mystical about Society and the Individual, but in a fashion more tentative than you perhaps realized—I'm feeling my way, as I said before; I'm trying to evolve a theory, a hypothesis, that will fit what I see happening—the events come first, then the hypothesis, which in turn has to be tested by future events and revised in the light of them. But God, Kenneth, what I'm trying to say is that whatever the hypothesis, the events are there. You've gone along a certain path and it has produced an extraordinary book, and a theory of criticism which has important implications, and the path may lead you to one more book, the one you're writing—but beyond that you've got to get into another path, another pattern of behavior.

I'm not saying, either, Come on over into our nice Red pasture and play with all us communist boys. That would be swell, but you're not going to do it, so what's the use of arguing about it. There are a number of simpler possibilities. You might simply tear yourself away, go for a trip to Russia or Mexico—that didn't help Hart, but you're not at all like him; you're not in a self-created situation which you are forced to carry with you. Maybe just getting a job, after you finish this book, would be enough—and maybe I'm all wet in what I'm saying: the country, frogs, birds, garden, lake, etc. may be fixing up all your troubles. Going on the wagon for a year would be a damned good step. It's your job to do something. In the meantime, I want to reregister a couple of remarks, because you're always disposed to forget them. (a) I think more of you than of any other living person (read "man" for the sake of strict accuracy). (b) For that reason you can hurt me more than anybody else, when you're so minded. (c) I've got a vast respect for what you write, even when I think you're dead wrong. But of this no more . . .

Yours,
Malcolm

1. "Madness, travel, drugs, the Faith," and "death by one's own hand," are the "refuges" listed at the beginning of the final chapter of Burke's novel.

Andover, New Jersey
June 4, 1932
[PS]

Dear Malcolm,

. . . After a pond-day, deck tennis, sun-absorbing. If there were an eternal hot-day, and I could eternally bask in it, then would I be the most fortified of men. I look forward with confidence to tomorrow's opening battle. "Just what do you have against Communism?" Bob[1] asked me last night—and I had never thought of it so bluntly, but my answer was as blunt: "Absolutely nothing." And then, in the night, I awoke and asked myself the same question, and discovered the following qualifications: "I am not a joiner of societies, I am a literary man. I can only welcome Communism by converting it into my own vocabulary. I am, in the deepest sense, a translator. I go on translating, even if I must but translate English into English. My book[2] will have the communist objectives, and the communist tenor, but the approach will be the approach that seems significant to me. Those who cannot recognize a concept, even [if] it is their concept, unless this concept is stated in exactly the words they use to state it, will think my book something else. Having agreed fully with the communists as to objectives, and having even specifically stated in my sinful Program that I considered nationalization of private wealth the fulcrum of the new economy, I diverged solely in my notion of the tactics for arriving at these objectives (and I am pleased to see, in the recent Communist endorsement of the soldiers' bonus, that they have begun to do the very sort of thing I had in mind).

"So Malcolm, who has made it a practice all his life to bury me, who put me in a narrow house years ago, who once again sees me facing the wall, and who can imagine nothing prettier than a picture of me masturbating myself into extinction at the age of seventeen, so he finds it a grave error that I cannot sign on the dotted line, fears that all my risky cows are fatal herds, interprets as bafflement pure and simple the years of my life which, to date, have been the most crowded years. He bows me out when I am just beginning. Errors I have certainly made in abundance—as with the damage done me by my drinking; but this is social damage, causing me to make blunders where my aunts would not, and impairing my income rather than my understanding. I really do not think I am in a bad way at all. A month of ample physical exercise and sunlight has put me in very good animal shape. I am tremendously interested in a tremendous number of subjects. I have both critical and creative outlets, I have intellectual, emotional, sensuous outlets, I enjoy conversations, I enjoy games, I enjoy being alone, I run my eye over my books the way I have seen a fatty man pat his belly . . . I believe that Malcolm is—as the old saying has it—wrong." . . .

K. B.

1. The novelist Robert Cantwell (1908–1978).
2. *Permanence and Change.*

c/o Henry Meriwether
"Cloverlands,"
Trenton, Kentucky
June 1, 1933
[Postmark]
[NL]

Dear Kenneth:

I've been reading piles of my letters to you and writing on the basis of them—they were most interesting during my last 6 months in France—wish I had yours to reread. The hardest thing now is that we seem to speak 2 languages often. I am living in luxury and kindness 8 miles from a railroad and 2 miles from a telephone, rising at 6 and writing.

Yrs.,
M.

Andover, New Jersey
June 4, 1933
[PS]

Dear Malcolm,

Two lengvich. You spick one lengvich, ah spick nudder lengvich . . . ["]Perhaps we do not realize how thoroughly we have adapted our mentalities to the 'prose-demands' of contemporary social and economic organization. Our basically secular emphasis has so 'taken the props out from under' the poetic, or religious, emphasis that we cannot even imagine how people may have once laid the focus of their interests elsewhere.[1] The keen demands placed upon us by the disorders of the contemporary state, the competitive requirements akin to conditions of drought or famine, effectively restrict our 'serious' efforts to a field of economic cunning bounded on the right by Anti-Marxian Business and on the left by Marxian Anti-Business. Hence, we forget that the *wells of the imaginative* are in the sphere of poetry and music, attempting rather to confine them to certain conflicts which are hardly even 'economic,' but could more accurately be further restricted to the terms 'monetary' or 'financial.' Yet one must not content himself with merely censuring such a way of seeing. If it is here, and so prevalently, it must be here as the 'answer to a need,' and where there is a need to be met, nothing less than glut can set it at rest."

• • •

Granted: there are sewers to be cleaned. To get them cleaned by calling them altars is promotion work. But is it one lengvich to call them altars, and another lengvich to call them sewers? Or is that not the issue at all?

What is to be our job for the summer? Every time I try to state it, I state it differently . . . Pre-evolutionary thought naively overstressed the *constant* aspect of human society—evolutionary thought compensatorily overstressed the *shifting* aspect—a machinery of documentation and logic now seems available for making our century distinctive as the *merger* of these two principles. In particular it leads, I think, with the help of Ogden and Richards'[2] stressing of the nature of symbols, to a *conversion* technique (voilà the catholicistie) for showing that many disputes were terminological rather than basic, disputes over the symbols of reference rather than over the objects of reference. This might further lead (I have tentative notes on this aspect) to a restating of the notion of "The Way," holding that there has ever been only one technique of the "good life," and that it has been restated, at various times in history, within the terminological stressings uppermost at the time . . . This would seem to involve, at bottom, a preserving of the old distinction between "particulars" and "essence," a point on which I am not yet wholly contented. The placing of "prose" and "po-etry," of "economic cunning" as against the "religious," must be amply considered. Fundamentally, I think my point can be stated to the effect that all the resources of prose thought must be developed in order that the poetic can be given its only genuine safeguards. That is: only a thorough body of secular criticism, secular thought "carried all the way round the circle" can properly equip a society against the misuse of its most *desirable* aspects, the *poetic* or *religious* aspects. This is, I believe, practically the same as Eliot's position. I believe that Eliot is right in everything except his *exile*, which is a very momentous thing to be wrong in. He is able to begin too far along, with too many refinements—we must begin with rougher things. And there is a certain advantage in our requirement, for I think that these rougher things should never be neglected, as they can so easily be, once it has become cheap to hire servants to empty your bizbod for you. A cultural scheme that does not empty its own bizbod is a house erected upon the sands. There is then so great a differential to be supplied by the imagination that the imagination often fails to supply it.

Salutes to the success of your volume. If you want me to send you my letters, I'll do so, if you give me the pennies necessary for the registered mailing, and vow to get the documents back to me sometime. They are most useful to me in that they provide something which seems to me an unending source of marvel: documents for revealing the discrepancy be-tween what one once deemed important and what one now remembers. My forgettery being the most distinctive thing I have, I am eternally en-tranced by its workings . . .

Greetings,
K. B.

1. The remainder of this letter, and Burke's letter of June 16, sketch in the argument of *Permanence and Change*.

2. C. K. Ogden and I. A. Richards, authors of *The Meaning of Meaning* (1923), a book that had a significant impact on Burke's thinking.

c/o Henry T. Meriweather
"Cloverlands,"
Trenton, Kentucky
June 13, 1933
[NL]

Dear Kenneth:

I won't attempt at present to answer your letter—I have several things to say, but they're hard to say, and I'm working anyhow on a chapter that has something to do with the discussion. Here are a few pages from it that I've just finished rewriting to make them clearer for the vulgus—expanding the Flaubert episode a little so as to show its significance more clearly. Just before the episode begins, I have quoted my essay on "The Youngest Generation" to explain the ideas that I carried to France. It's all as if I continued the long debate which began in our letters of that year. The section that follows this one will quote the angry letter I wrote you when you said, in *Vanity Fair*, that in America "there is not a trace of that really dignified richness which makes for peasants, household gods, traditions." In the next section, I'll describe my impressions of Joyce, Eliot, Stein, Pound, Salmon, the Dadas—then comes a section on Dadaism, which I describe as the logical and illogical extreme of the religion-of-art movement—then finally a picture of my own ideas in 1923, and the episode of the Dôme.[1] All this—it will be at least 20,000 words—makes up the chapter on the exiles in France. The Exiles' Return chapter is written—but I'll be damned if I know what to do with the rest of the book; I can't carry it through on this extended scale; I'll have to just chop it off somewhere, and end with a personal confession.

Bien à toi,
Malcolm

1. The Dôme, a café on the boulevard Montparnasse, was a frequent gathering place for the Dada group in Paris. The episode Cowley refers to involved the Dada's harassment of the proprietor of another café, the Rotonde, because they suspected him of informing on a group of revolutionaries who met there. Cowley was jailed for punching the proprietor in the jaw. For his account of this incident, see *Exile's Return*, pages 164–170.

Andover, New Jersey
June 16, 1933
[PS]

Dear Malcolm,

Fundamentally, our differences in emphasis, classification, etc. seem to derive from the following initial or informing distinction in purpose: You are trying to write an interpretation of certain cultural trends; I am trying to write on the process of interpretation. The criticism of religion, said Marx, is the beginning of all criticism. And you rightly criticize art as an aspect of religion. But note the unintended joker in Marx's statement: He tells us what is the *beginning* of all criticism. What might be the *end*? Surely someone has said, or will say, that the *end* of all criticism is the criticism of criticism.

Thus, one must try (if it is the criticism of criticism he would write) to rehash the whole business of orientation, of imaginative and ideological symbolism, of "meanings" in their double function of both guiding and misguiding us. One tries to find how meanings arise. One notes that their origin brings one close to the springs of "propriety" which are found in religion and art. And there are many situations in which, to meet some new purpose, we must do violence to an older schema of propriety. Of course, this point of view omits the "escape" concept entirely, accepting it as natural and normal that people should try to escape from dissatisfactory conditions, but holding that certain systems of meaning may misguide them in their choice of *means of escape*. It is, I think, clear that if one approaches the nineteenth century from this point of view, he sees it as enormously and ingeniously preoccupied with exactly the problem that *should* have preoccupied it: namely, the problem of reinterpretation, transvaluation, new meanings. To call some of its attempts "escape" merely because you happen to consider them "wrong" would be exactly like calling one of your first drafts an escape, once you had reached your last revision.

This point of view shows our divergence at its clearest when we come to something like Dadaism. You take it as the culmination of the "religious." I take it as the very opposite, the use of the anti-religious function (criticism), in the attempt to establish what I call "perspective by incongruity."[1] Dadaism was a highly critical movement. Its very central aim was to outrage all the "religious" proprieties (as one finds them, in art, lurking under the name of "taste") . . .

Ever thine,
K. B.

[Postscript] Incidentally, you seem to assume that the artist's "desire to exert an influence on the world outside" is a desire to exert a specifically political, rather than a generally "educational" or "heuristic" influence—a Ciceronian ambition. It may be, if the artist is that kind of an artist, though I see no evidence that Shakespeare had a great frustrate desire to be king. I do find evidence that he exerted exactly the kind of influence he wanted to exert.

1. "Perspective by incongruity" is a method of explanation based on the incongruous juxtaposition of two things usually not related. Burke, who developed the idea of such perspectives based on his reading of Friedrich Nietzsche, conceived of them as essentially poetic or metaphoric phrases that derive their explanatory power from the incongruity of what they juxtapose. Examples include phrases such as "the socialization of losses," the "architecture of thought," and the "bureaucratization of the imaginative."

Trenton, Kentucky
July 15, 1933
[NL]

Dear Kenneth:

Here's another first draft from my ms. Even when very tangential, your criticisms help me by forcing me to define what I am trying to say. The chapter you're going to like least of all is the long chapter on Dada, in which I talk directly about the religion of art (you're right that Dada was the atheism of art, but it is simultaneously the *extreme* of the religion—one has to be Catholic to enjoy a Black Mass).

Your long letter will get, I hope, a long answer—today I'm pushing off for N.Y. and cleaning up my papers. I'll be home Monday night.

Your'n,
M.

78 Bank Street,
New York City
May 29, 1934
[PS]

Dear Malcolm,

. . . Why did I, last night, lie awake until four o'clock, pondering over the puzzles of you and your Goddamned book, while you were probably snoring the snore of the just? Perhaps because the only class war I really know at first hand is the class war between exploiting editors and exploited authors—and you for a few hours were again back in my class.

I have long felt that you were settling scores in that book, though I am by no means clear as to what these scores may be. Such books need to be well received, otherwise the process of "justification" is left uncompleted, or even directly outraged. Similarly in the Declamations I was settling scores, though again I am vague as to their nature. But I am not vague as to the suffering caused by its dismissal, when it was discredited, we might say, in the lump, by a discrediting of the whole genre in which it was written.

In the end, I suppose it is fitting that our self-indulgences should be swatted. But they are never wholly made of self-indulgence by a damned sight—they are also made of work, and when work ceases to be good legal tender, one is simply in hell. For work and socialization are one.

The particular thing with which I should reproach you is a fundamental lack of sympathy with the plight in which so many people have found themselves. I fear that you would have to have books coming out every day for a year, and Gannett's[1] peppering them as regularly, before sympathy could become a permanent part of you. For this conjecture I can proffer no proof.

Greetings,
K. B.

1. Lewis Gannett, a book critic for the *New York Herald Tribune* who had given an unfavorable review to *Exile's Return*.

78 Bank Street,
New York City
June 9, 1934
[PS]

Dear Malcolm,

. . . Strange paradox: a great change is supposed to have taken place. Everybody is supposed in some way to have been reformed. Yet they are all living about the same patterns of life as they ever did (except that Russia has taken the place of France as the foreign ideal). We speak as though we were new—and then we say that what we are saying now we said back in 1922. Perhaps one drops nothing; one simply, as he matures, finds that he must take more into account. For my own part, at least, I think that everything in my present book was implicit in my essay on "Psychology and Form,"[1] which was in turn implicit in an article on "the psychology of a Greek vase" which I wrote three years earlier when discussing the books of John Middleton Murry. I have simply extended a criticism of art until it included areas of production which do not happen, in the language of common sense, to be called art. My book is an elaborate plea for the poetic metaphor, as against the mechanistic metaphor, in the interpretation of human purpose . . .

What next? I think that, once this work is out of the way, I shall lay off "first principles" for a while and go back to straight literary criticism, perhaps reviewing the modern scene in the light of my formulas to date. I guess Americans simply will not read philosophy as such—and since I want to be read, I must again bestir myself to find the rephrasing of my position that might ring the bell. I also think of planning, for work at odd moments, a kind of research-work epic, attempting to establish in four parts and a fifth, the specific imagery, in customs and aims, behind my schema of the "four rationalizations, magic, religion, science, and communism." I see ways of making the thing quite picturesque (particularly by stating so many long discredited doctrines as though they were true, and by interlarding the dogmas with narratives that illustrate the concomitant social texture). The great technical problem to be met is that of a central protagonist. This protagonist should, I think, be writer-and-audience in one, rather than some perennial figure forever being reborn (as the latter solution would suggest overtones which I do not want to suggest). But for the life of me, I cannot see the novel: I can think of poetry, or I can think of critical prose, but I cannot think of that bastard intermediary, the novel.

Greetings,
K. B.

1. In this chapter of *Counter-Statement*, Burke explains one of his fundamental ideas about form, that "form is the creation of an appetite in the mind of the auditor, and the adequate satisfying of that appetite." In this sense, form for Burke is created in "the psychology of the *audience*" (page 31).

121 Bank Street,
New York City
February 27, 1936
[PS]

Dear Malcolm,

Official statement, from the P & C public relations counsel.[1]

Text: "Psychoanalysis as a social theory . . . is fundamentally opposed to Marxism, and no poet or prose writer has ever succeeded in making a synthesis of the two."

Little David modestly offers on this point to do battle.

Little David proposes:

(1) Let MC first convert his assertion of "fundamental opposition" into a completely rationalized account. (In other words, let MC fill out this assertion with all the filling-out he considers to be necessary.)

(2) Let him turn this over to yours truly, for a reply of exactly the same length.

The issue is a burning one. I know of nothing, in the purely critical field, more burning for the NR [*New Republic*]. (Especially inasmuch as many of its readers are old psychoanalysts in training, with economics on top.) For my own part, furthermore, I feel that P & C offers a completely adequate account of the devices whereby Marxian and psychoanalytic fields can be brought together—and I should be happy to engage in honorable combat with you, to see whether I could prove this or whether you could prove your opposite assertion. (Needless to say, I should not have to make specific references to the book at all. I should simply *use* in my reply to you some of the concepts formulated there, and attempt to show why they function as coordinates for putting psychoanalysis and economics together, and for putting them together in ways that lead to the Marxist alignment of foes and friends.)

I ask for but one thing: that you allow me as many words as you allow yourself. I promise that the discussion will be anything but a bore to the general public. . . .

What say?

K. B.

1. A reference to *Permanence and Change.*

> 73 West 11th St.
> [New York City]
> Memorial Day [1936]
> [NL]

Dear Kenneth:

Here are a couple of items for your crapsay ookbay:

Edmund Wilson was very enthusiastic about your verses for the Wrong Occasions.

Marianne Moore asked me to thank you for her for your mention of her poems in the *Southern Review.* This is a long story. She submitted an unsolicited review to the NR. I'm eager to have her do some work for us, but this review was too long and dealt with an unimportant book which, furthermoreover, had a political angle to it that Marianne didn't catch, and anyway I decided to be hardboiled and to ask her to do something else instead. So that meant a telephone conversation lasting for Hours and Hours and Hours.

Marianne said she had tried to write you several times about your remarks on her, for which she was so grateful, but somehow she couldn't do it, she had such a respect for you, she knew that you never did anything except from a sense of duty, but there was this sense of inner shock she had when she heard that you and Lily were divorced, and what she was hoping was just to meet you on the street casually, that [it] would be a great joy to talk to you, everything connected with the old *Dial* made her feel good, but there was that instinct of shock in her that prevented her from writing— and all this I can tell you went on and on, each point being expanded.

Marianne is the very last of the Puritans—no, for the Puritans had the sense of a whole social order behind them, and God standing behind the social order, whereas Marianne feels isolated and apologetic; her conventionality has become unconventional, has become something that sets her apart. A sweet soul. But she turns everyone around her into a hypocrite . . .

As ever,
M.

121 Bank Street,
New York City
August 17, 1936
[PS]

Dear Malcolm,

Oyez, oyez, oyez! Here is the letter I have been planning to write to your firm. Kumminbigh!

I now have enough stuff assembled, of my own and other pippels, to begin writing my book.[1] And as I very much dislike the feeling of sitting down to put a bottle out to sea (that is the feeling one gets when the gravitational pull of a specific *terminus ad quem* is missing), I should like as far as possible to organize the material with a view to magazine publication en route.

To the *New Republic* I should like to offer five articles along the lines of the material I presented at Syracuse. It would be full of *examples*. It would go light on my tendency to over-abstractionism. It has already been tried out on the dog—and as evidence as to how the dog took it, I should be more than delighted to be required to present a letter I received from Leonard Brown[2] (which incidentally breathes contentment not only with my orations, but also with yours and Horace's).

The five articles should appeal (a) to those who are interested in *trends*, in accounts of present trends with relation to trends in the remote past and the near past, and (b) those who are interested in *education*, particularly in the attempts to combat the disintegration of knowledge into a thousand disparate disciplines—in other words, those who look yearningly toward the "integrated program," such as they look yearningly toward in Happy's[3] courses at Dalton. The "flower in the crannied wall" approach.

The subjects of the five articles would be roughly as follows:

"Acceptance and Rejection."[4] How thinkers, of either the imaginative or conceptual sort, build vast symbolic bridges to get them across the gaps of conflict. Our examples would be from myth, legend, ritual, philosophy, religion, theology, science, epic, tragedy, comedy, sentimentality, and satire.

The ways in which, by the rise of new material, such frames of acceptance become irrelevant, and even obstructive.

"Neo-Malthusianism." Where we, somewhat perversely, pick a bad name for our principle, and then try to live it down . . . Basic point: How a given frame of orientation provides its particular opportunities for laxity, for letting down—and how people tend to "move in on" these opportunities, eventually *organizing* their laxities, or liberties, until the frame of orientation itself is endangered . . .

"Authority." My thanks to George Soule, who put me on to Laski,[5] and thereby made some of my blusterings on this subject more precise. Our discussion would gravitate around the psychological concept of "identification." The ways in which the identification process finally heads up in a symbol of authority. (Simplest example: Germans have been building roads for many centuries, but when they build a road after 1933, *Hitler* does it.) . . .

"Euphemism and Debunking." The verbal issues that are tied up with the problem of engineering shifts in the symbol of authority. The integrative nature of euphemistic symbols, the disintegrative nature of debunking symbols . . .

And now, having reviewed the ways in which cultural integers are wound up and wound down, and the problems of winding-up again out of the materials of the winding-down, I should be prepared, and should have prepared the readers, for a discussion of "Metaphor," as the strategic center of symbolic frames and their rebuilding . . . Among other things, the approach to history through this entrance has made me realize, as I never did before, precisely how *revolutionary* was the shift from the feudal *family* concept of authority to the bourgeois concept of *delegated authority* . . .

So much for the five. I have not tried to tell the whole story. I have tried simply to indicate that the articles I am proposing for the *New Republic* are very much in line with the interests of the gazette (the contemplation of historical transitions, and the ways and means of contributing to historical transitions) . . .

Sincerely,
K. B.

1. *Attitudes Toward History.*

2. Leonard Brown was a professor at Syracuse University.

3. Burke's daughter.

4. This article became Part I of *Attitudes Toward History.* The rest of the letter outlines what became other portions of the book. Although the *New Republic* published the book, they did not publish the articles.

5. Harold J. Laski (1893–1950), British philosopher, political scientist, and educator. The work Burke refers to is probably *Authority in the Modern State* (1919).

Andover, New Jersey
October 6, 1936
[PS]

Dear Malcolm,

Greetings, to the editor of a great book review section, from the chap who decided to write a book review of history.

· · ·

. . . [T]hings began to fall together, and I hated to gamble with luck, so I kept on. And now the problem is as follows:

I have bumped out 20,000 words, which makes the first third of my book review, but doesn't match the outline I submitted to the *New Republic*. In fact, things are altered considerably. All the business about shifts of authority, euphemism and debunking, and metaphor is there, but only in an adumbrating form . . . The whole, to date, *focuses* upon "frames of acceptance and rejection" (our reworking of Schopenhauer's "Bejahung und Verneinung" formula?).

I start with an analysis of William James, Whitman, and Emerson as propounders of representative U.S. Bejahung frames. Then I struck an unexpected bonanza. I began analyzing various poetic categories (epic, tragedy, comedy, humor, satire, burlesque, grotesque, elegy, didactic) from this standpoint, and found that they responded with (to me) astonishing relevancies—so the remainder of the section is devoted to an analysis of these categories.

· · ·

So now I am wondering about Section I. I am wondering whether the *New Republic* will find some of it usable. In any case, I shall try to get it revised and typed, and to submit it soon. As an economic interpretation of art forms it is, to my limited knowledge, something new, so I have hopes that the editors will take kindly to it, even though my whole story isn't definitively driven home.

How goes it with the chateau?[1] I shall have to be more apologetic than ever about our own loose-jointed structure, with its springy floorboards, and its airy walls that make it a constant Welcome to the hornet and the mosquito, and its archaic stoves that keep me busy chopping down and cutting up various leafy symbols of authority . . .

Greetings,
K. B.

1. Cowley and his wife were remodeling the barn they had purchased in Sherman.

The New Republic
40 East 49th Street,
New York, N.Y.
October 19, 1936
[NL]

Dear Kenneth:

There is no time or space here at the office to write you a letter, so let's make three simple points:

1. We have been living in the house for three weeks now, but living surrounded with gangs of carpenters, plumbers, steamfitters, masons, painters, and other trades. I think that the oil furnace is installed at last, and the heat turned on. That means that life will be possible in cold weather. I work so hard transplanting lilac bushes, oak trees, and Siberian elms that I don't get a chance to look at the place. You and Libby must come over. Why not make it next weekend?—and this is a serious invitation.

2. There's not a darned word to say about your manuscript, except to ship it in and let us have a look at it.

3. For God's sake, send in your review right away or not at all.

As ever,
Malcolm

Andover, New Jersey
October 20, 1936
[PS]

Dear Malcolm,

What!—no congratulations on our having completed Part One? But maybe I don't deserve any, having tried to "keep my good fortune for myself, while sharing with others my delight in it"—an ambiguous kind of collectivism that mostly serves to warm the heart of the Indian-giver.

Anyhow, the Little Woman (incorporated) hasn't yet finished the typing, so I can't come across for another week or so.

Meanwhile, I batted out the second section, on History proper. And now, while the world goes on its way, I keep trying to decide whether I should offer this section instead. For the first, on maturer computation, seems to be circa 27,000 words in length, while the second is circa 15,000. Or maybe I shall wait until they are both typed, and come around with both, to let the editors pickandchoose as they see best.

I ain't exactly modest about this thing, which seems to have got a very complex message said quite articulately. And if *this* puts you to sleep, like *Permanence and Change*, then I shall have to admit that you set too high standards for me, and that I must *always* disappoint you.

• • •

Did you know that, in your good review of Aragon's book,[1] you made almost word for word the same point as you made when reviewing *White Oxen* in *The Dial*? (We both swept our characters from the scene at a given page, while his "disdain" is matched by my "voice of Swift"—I presumably being more "derivative.") Your remarks led me to note, however, a probable difference in solutions from that point on, as Aragon still continues with fiction, whereas I simply can't imagine writing a story for another fifteen years. The "short-circuiting" via criticism still prevails. I.e., several times I have planned a "curve" of plot development that might require, say, eight or ten thousand words. Then I "conceptualize" what I am after, and find that it can be said, in the shorthand of abstractions, within the compass of a hundred words. Whereupon the novelistic way seems like a long circum-locution. And I guess I am not *lover* enough of the novelistic way (now rarely looking at a novel, unless someone hires me to do so) for the longest way round to be the shortest way home. But I confess that the whole matter bothers me. I keep asking myself why I somehow still *want* to write a novel, despite that fact that I won't even read other people's novels. Is it a mere hangover of childhood coordinates (when I lived in the world of this form that is alas! so akin to the gossip of women, and seems to become "mas-culine" only in proportion as narrative *surrender* is rejected, with corre-sponding breakdown of the frame)? You yourself spoke of the writer's need to "yield." And the incentive to which I was most conscious of "yielding," in my adolescent days of novel-reading, was self-abuse. So I ask whether my resistance to novels is tied with that—and whether your term betrays a similar resistance to *poetry* on your part. An art form certainly *need not* have such connotations—but there are occasions when it *may*—and perhaps, in cases where it does, it has something to do with a turn from fiction to criticism at maturity . . .

Sincerely,
K. B.

1. Cowley's review of a translation of Louis Aragon's *The Bells of Basel* had appeared in the October 7 issue of the *New Republic*.

October 30, 1936
[NL]

Dear Kenneth,

The first installment of your book has been received and read by me. I am passing it on first to George Soule and then to Dan Mebane.[1] I read the first part of it with considerable enthusiasm, and the last part with enthusiasm. You are obviously on the track of something new and quite important in the world of thought—something that might turn out to be a formulation on the order of Freud or Spengler. That is why I read the 20,000 words with real excitement. In the beginning you are clearer than ever before as a theorist. Toward the end of the section, you begin to yield to your old vice, which is that of the very keen-nosed but undertrained hound dog—he starts out a-helling after a rabbit, almost tracks it down, but gets turned aside by the strong scent of a fox, runs into a place where the fox scared up a partridge, hunts for the partridge, feels hungry, and digs up a field mouse. You dig up some field mice too.

My principal prayer to you would be that in writing a book like this you take for granted that none of your readers has read any single author that you mention. This means that you would explain what each author was saying (perhaps even Shakespeare) and would give chunks of quotation from them at crucial points . . . Outside of that, there are times when I don't think that you establish your terms clearly enough. For example, "neo-Malthusian." The same phrase has been used in very different connections. Don't you mean simply Malthusianism in the philosophical world? . . . There are several other points I'd like to talk about if we ever had time to go over the manuscript together. But it's good, damned good.

What *The New Republic* will do with it, I don't know. Maybe we would be able to print a series of articles taken out of the book as a whole. There is unfortunately no hurry, because the book as a whole can't be printed until next spring . . . If we were confined to the present section, I should guess that two articles would be all that would pass the editorial censorship, though this also would require a good deal of further discussion. Dan Mebane will certainly want to publish the book when he sees it.

Isn't there any way that you and Libbie could drive out to see us? We're anxious to have you take a look at the new house.

As ever,
[M.]

1. Dan Mebane was the business manager of the *New Republic*. He was also the publisher of Dollar Books.

Andover, New Jersey
November 2, 1936
[PS]

Dear Malcolm,

Many thanks indeed for your generous comments on "Acceptance and Rejection" (a topic alas! of great concern to editors). And I am most eager to get the advantage of all suggestions you have to make—and I wholly agree with those you make in your letter. I shall probably barge ahead at present (after a week or two layoff, as I was getting too much into the thing, a state of affairs that makes one a bit of a prima donna, which no longer likee)—and afterward I shall do the adding or subtracting. So all that you have to suggest will be gratefully listened to. "Neo-Malthusianism" is, I hope, made clearer when we get to our second section, "The Curve of History." And I have considered it possible that, toward the end of the book, I might introduce a kind of glossary that would also serve as a re-capitulation . . . Incidentally, your remarks on "Neo-Malthusianism" make me realize that "neo" may not mean "neo" at all. The difference between Somethingism and Neo-Somethingism. "Why am I so hipped on this term?" I asked myself. And I got somewhat of a clue by noting that "Malthus" to me always sounded like Methusaleh . . . So I guess I'm saying in effect that I want very much to be talking about the world when I'm ninety. No wonder. In these times of warped emphases, it is quite natural for one to be an ass at least until he is sixty.

. . . As everyone has cleared out except for weekends, I miss company a lot . . . we go long distances in search of *the most trivial* movies, which are somewhat Ersatz . . . I am cutting brush and laying up wood for April. Give me one splendid snowstorm a year, and for the rest of the time I'm ready to cook in the sun.

Best greetings,
K. B.

The New Republic
40 East 49th Street,
New York, N.Y.
August 31, 1937
[NL]

Dear Kenneth:

I have been reading your book[1] with a mixture of emotions, most of them falling into the "acceptance" frame—surprise, agreement, enthusiasm. I get reservations at points where the lyrical element becomes too strong, as in the long dissertation on the mimetic value of words—and didn't it occur to you that you had omitted two of the most important "hard C" words, two of the shortest? You are presenting a philosophy that starts out as a book review and ends as autobiography. "Collectipsism" is my word for it, if you can figure that out.

I have two ideas for exploiting it for *The New Republic*, and both of them will encounter resistance from the other editors. One is to break a *New Republic* rule that has never been broken, and have the book reviewed. It couldn't be done so baldly as that. But if some *New Republic* friend and standby like Charley Beard[2] were willing to do a piece on it, I am pretty sure that the piece would be published. The other idea is to extract from the book a couple of thousand words of aphorisms, extending in length from a sentence to a paragraph, not necessarily intended to explain your central ideas, but rather to give examples of the vistas that you open on the way . . .

Matty got Beard to read the book, and he tells me that Beard liked it very much. Matty has now departed for a week's vacation in the Adirondacks. Everybody else in our section of the country seems to be well or at least convalescing . . .

As ever,
Malcolm

1. *Attitudes Toward History*.

2. Charles A. Beard (1874–1948), an American historian whose broad view of history as a topic which should include economics, politics, culture, and intellectual life made him a logical choice to review the book.

Andover, New Jersey
September 5, 1937
[PS]

Dear Malcolm,

. . . Many thanks indeed for words anent my double-decker canoe.[1] I agree with you that the business on "Cues" is the most vulnerable section. I also agree that the two other hard-C words should be there. The structure of the basic dirty words must have a lot to do with the shaping of furtive puns. Having decided that "f," for instance (and its tonal equivalent, "v"), often means what you are thinking, I have asked myself just what the gruff materialist may be getting [at] when he says, pounding the table, "What we want is *f*acts, hard *f*acts." And I can show you some surprising f-passages in Henry Adams, the Virgin-and-Dynamo man with f-trouble, that should, by this theory, appear exactly where they do appear. Also O'Neill, and his Hairy Ape, Yank (yank!).

I do not kid myself into believing that anything precise could be made of such speculations . . . My main trouble, I think, was in not pointing the section properly. I was trying to show (a) the ways in which one is an "individualist" in even the most socialized of materials, language, (b) the ways in which poetic speech is an "act," a "dance in the pure present," in contrast with the "postponed consumption" of scientific concepts—though I should have to add that, once a man becomes married to even the most abstruse of vocabularies, his use of them tends to become ritualistic, an *assertion in the present*, as with the communist dancer who is getting victory *now* (to borrow a succinct term from our bum father-image, a bleezicks if there ever was one) by dancing the subsequent triumph of the proletariat. Eventually I may be able to make the issues clearer and less vulnerable (though I admit that I consider them with much resistance, and am always on the verge of deciding to drop the whole matter).

I decide to drop it. Then I pick up *Moby Dick*. I note Queequeg. I note that the vague picture of the whale is called s*qui*tchy. The boat is the Pe*qu*od. And then I weaken again, looking for correspondences (and, of course, finding them). (Incidentally, I am now taking notes for an article, "*Moby Dick*; An Essay to Illustrate a Method," in which I would put down my procedures for analyzing the symbolic structure of a book, in cards-on-the-table fashion, for others to inspect, approve, condemn, or modify, as they see fit . . . I have to date charted only the first fifth of the book, which seems to be in the black-mass, sprout-out-of-rot category.) . . .

Best greetings,
K. B.

1. *Attitudes Toward History* was originally published in a two-volume edition.

The New Republic
40 East 49th St.,
New York, N.Y.
October 1, 1937
[NL]

Dear Kenneth:

So far I have just had time to glance at your Axioms;[1] I'm carrying them home with me to read over the weekend. Just in glancing at them I ran into some beauties that I hadn't noticed myself when I read *Attitudes Toward*

History. If we use your axioms we'd use them "as if" they had never been printed before, while giving full credit to the book. That means that there would not be any rows of dots to indicate omitted material. Your suggestion about mostly short passages and a couple of long ones seems excellent . . .

As ever,
Malcolm

1. Burke's "Axioms" were aphorisms selected from *Attitudes Toward History*. They were published in the March, 1938, issue of the *New Republic* under the title "Maxims and Anecdotes."

Andover, New Jersey
October 22, 1937
[PS]

Dear Malcolm,
 . . . Poor-paying honors continue to drift in, but jeez am I broke! The main interest in my stuff seems to come from sociologists—which is beginning to lead me to think that what I once called "metabiology" is pure and simple sociology-without-portfolio. Tactical problem: How [to] proceed with one's attempt to scramble the categories of specialization, when only by specialization can one assemble the kind of curriculum vitae necessary for a job? Some day there will be chairs in "interrelationship" ("coordination," "meaning")—but I suppose that every time I go to knock at the door, there will be a Stew Chase[1] who came late but pushes right past . . .

Best greetings,
K. B.

1. Stewart Chase wrote on economic matters for the *New Republic*.

The University of Chicago,
Department of English
August 8, 1938
[PS]

Dear Malcolm,
 Seven [weeks] down and three to go. Am in the thick of knots (Jeez! what Coleridge's Imagination-Fancy distinction can get you into, if you try tracking it to its lair, with the kids waiting patiently while you wrestle with

yourself, get yourself down, wriggle free again, start over, etc.—fantastically, while the weather slowly rises to the boiling point). Mark sixth week as the toughest—for at the same time the Critical Theory course got into a backstream of epistemology—the similarity of predicament in the two courses having decided me that much of the difficulty came from within—so this is to be shaking-off week.

•   •   •

Am learning a hell of a lot—and have been gratified by the friendliness of the kids, who don't seem to mind that I am better at flushing game than at bagging it. They have come around to offer me many testimonials—so I have, up to now at least, remained in fairly good repute with the administration, despite my departures from the norm. In fact, there are tentative negotiations in the offing, though I feel that I should try to stick with agro-Bohemianism, for all its financial rigors, as a prolonged training in this sort of effort would lead one gradually to reshape both his methods and his interests (getting increases of clarity by channelization—said channelization prompting one to make a restricted ordering into point 1, point 2, point 3 equal maturity, which it very much ain't).

Anyhow—twelve more days devoted to public prayer—and then may I have a few languid weeks in which I am the strong, silent man . . . I am sure that I must be working much harder than they work who know this trade—for each time I awake in the night, I discover that I have been dreaming lectures.

Best greetings,
K. B.

R.F.D. Gaylordsville,
Connecticut
October 7, 1938
[NL]

Dear Kenneth:

I have been laid up for nearly three weeks—first twelve days in the Midtown Hospital, then here in the country. The trouble is a bad case of tonsilitis that still hasn't healed, though the two big abscesses that kept me from swallowing were both lanced before I left the hospital. Now I merely feel weak on my pins and unable to walk more than a couple of hundred yards. I don't mind the sensation of being weak as a baby. Is that womb hunger? I think it is rather a reminder to me of human limitations, of how little we can do in this world and how we have to conserve our forces. At forty I wish I could get to work on some enterprise that would advance little by little, maybe only a paragraph or a stanza every day, but would go ahead remorselessly until, at the end of years, I would have piled up a monument. Instead of that I still fiddle around.

I wonder what is going to be the, call it spiritual effect, of the big sellout in Munich.[1] To me the world situation resembles more and more the civil wars in the classical world that lasted from 300 B.C. till the reign of Augustus, with an aristocratic and a popular party in every state and the aristocrats always ready to sell out to the Persians, the Macedonians, or the Romans. Then the popular party too is driven to extremes, as under Marius in Rome and Stalin in Russia; and the philosophers retire to Tusculum, till they are interrupted there by soldiers and politely asked to cut their throats. I can't set it all down in an orderly manner. We were betrayed, we were sold behind our backs. I almost feel like going into the service of the Comintern, like the hero of Hemingway's play (not a very good play) on the theory that it's better to fight for something half right than to lie down and let the bastards walk over us. I wish I knew how to fly or to operate a machine gun.

. . . We haven't been seeing enough of each other, and it's a very bad idea to let friendships lapse through taking them for granted. Maybe you could arrange for a visit later this month or early in November—but preferably before the leaves fall, for the country just now is wonderful and marvelous and it would be great to take a long walk over the back roads.

As ever,
M.

1. The Munich Pact had been signed on September 30.

Andover, New Jersey
October 14, 1938
[PS]

Dear Malcolm,

Was sorry to learn of your illness, the which I trust is by now well abated. And as your letter attested, the news of then gave a sick man the most perfect sort of objective materials to match. My great discovery re valetudinarianism in my own case is that the very slightest of errors make all the difference between feeling quite O.K. and being a wreck. Let me obey the schedule for two days running, and I am O.K. But let me even so much as wake up sleepy, and I am a wreck. Put me on one side the watershed, and I can't even read without jumpiness (revise as: and I go cascading down over cliffs and boulders)—put me on the other side the watershed, and I go forth with scythe, brush hook, and axe, carving out an empire, in accordance with my theories of cultural imperialism . . . All told, I suspect that you have simply not yet given formal recognition to this principle of amplification with which nature pursues us . . . I pass along this proverbialism as particularly serviceable for all ages beset by an overall ailment in choreography (ages in which the incantatory imagery of the state threatens to give subjective ailments objective materials to match—ages, I mean, in which the intelligence of events makes you sick) . . .

> Best greetings, and
> hoping you
> are in trim again,
> K. B.

> Gaylordsville,
> [Connecticut]
> October 14, 1939
> [NL]

Dear Kenneth:

Here's a letter begging for advice in regard to a project I'm undertaking or at least considering. I want to do a series of articles for the *New Republic* under the working title of "The Religion of Science." That's a poor title, because part of my idea is that most distinctions between "religion" and "church" are hooey—that a church is a body of customs, etc. which institutionalize religious feelings and is the only practicable angle from which to study them. Moreover, my series won't have anything to do with the Faith of a Physicist and all that junk—it is concerned purely with the social sciences and what they have discovered about the nature and origins of religion. Even that is too big a subject to be treated in less than a lifetime, but hell, I work for a weekly and know how to bat the subject down to manageable dimensions. My working outline runs something like this (to date)—eight chapters to be boiled down into five articles, thus:

I. This is a period of religious wars. Communism, fascism, Catholicism, perhaps Protestant capitalism, all have their churches, which are now in conflict, with shifting alliances. The question is whether the western liberals have or could have a faith worth fighting for.

· · ·

II. Auguste Comte—a honey for this series because, as you remember, his girlfriend died and he tried to invent a synthetic religion with the lady as one of the saints. He is also the precursor of modern sociology, so we get a beautiful tie-up.

III. Frazer and *The Golden Bough*. It's essentially an anti-religious book, but his anthropological basis of Christian doctrines like the Crucifixion and the Resurrection gave them a validity that had been destroyed by the Higher Criticism . . .

IV. Durkheim and his *Elementary Forms of Religious Life*. That's a book you certainly ought to read.

V. Breasted and *The Dawn of Conscience*.[1] Important largely for its effect on Freud.

VI. Freud, *Totem and Taboo* and *Moses and Monotheism*. Again an attempt to find a historical basis for religious rites and attitudes.

VII. Communism as a religion, or rather as a church. The parallel between the Party and the religious orders (it has its Franciscans, its Benedictines, its Dominicans, its Jesuits). Stalin as pope. Christian rites like conversion, public confession, communion among the Russian communists. The weakness of Communism as a religion—i.e., its failure to check individual pride, its weak rituals, and its lack of gratitude, though that's a poor way of putting it. Trotsky's notion that history is God.

VIII. A personal credo, drawn from several of these sources.

From this outline you can easily see why I'm begging for help, because a lot of this stuff lies in territory that you have traversed already. Have you any suggestions, particularly about the first and the seventh chapters—though I'd be very glad to listen on the eighth chapter also? I think the subject is pretty damned important. The effect on me of the Russo-German pact was not to make me think any the less of Stalin—nothing succeeds like success—but to make me feel that I and all the other western liberals had been thrown overboard; in other words it was a phenomenon of alienation, of feeling that Russia is pretty damned good but isn't our country. For that matter, Russian communism has gone pretty far beyond Marx and I never liked a lot of the developments, especially those in the field of art, which ought to be an index to a lot of other fields.

The League of American Writers, prompted by me, is about to issue a statement to its members stating that it won't make a statement on the Russo-German Pact but feels that we had better get busy at home. The idea is to hold the League together and offer a common basis for its liberal and communist members . . .

> As ever,
> Malcolm

1. James Henry Breasted (1865–1935), American Egyptologist and archeologist. *The Dawn of Conscience* was published in 1933.

The New Republic
40 East 49th Street,
New York, N.Y.
November 24, 1939
[NL]

Dear Kenneth:

There are two possible dates for the dinner I wrote you about[1]—Thursday, December 7, and Monday, December 11 . . . .Could you let me know whether you could come on either of these two evenings?

I mentioned the general subject of the dinner, which is the crisis in progressive thinking. In order to carry the discussion one step further, I am enclosing some propositions that state my own reactions.[2] They sound pretty commonplace when stated so briefly, but at least they offer a basis for argument . . .

As ever,
Malcolm

1. Cowley had written earlier about a dinner he was organizing to discuss how progressive intellectuals ought to respond to the developing crisis in Europe and the failures of the Marxist experiment in Russia.

2. Cowley's enclosure states that "during the last twenty years, faith in socialism has tended to become identified with faith in Russia," but that while that faith was "justified" in that the Russians had shown that socialism "is possible and that a party of socialism is a necessity," it has "not been justified" for a number of reasons. They include its failures as an economic system, its failure to "make a place for opposition groups," the famine of 1932, the purges of 1937–1938, and its exclusion of "discoveries" in psychology, anthropology, and religion. He concludes that while "these facts are no justification for defending older forms of society based on inherited wealth and revealed religion," what "has happened in Russia" requires that "a *democratic socialism* continues to be our basis for action." The statement was published in the *New Republic* on February 26, 1940, under the title "Sixteen Propositions" (it was unsigned).

The New Republic
40 East 49th Street,
New York, N.Y.
December 16, 1939
[NL]

Dear Kenneth:

. . . Sorry you missed the dinner. An interesting discussion. We didn't agree on exactly the theme of the symposium-series we should run as a result of it. My own feeling is that it should be something called, "What is

Worth Keeping in Marxism?" and should be a dispassionate evaluation of Communism, preferably by people working in the different social sciences, in view of what has happened in Russia. But there are objections to this. Have you any ideas on what we should do? . . .

As ever,
Malcolm

Andover, New Jersey
December 24, 1939
[PS]

Dear Malcolm,

Only yesterday the dreary news reached me about your father. And I would state my condolences, bunglingly but earnestly. As with our long tradition, dating back to the days of Jake Davis, I do not know what more to say. To me your father means the apartment in East Liberty, Chopin waltzes and Beethoven Sonatas, and the annex: the room across the hall, where we talked in expectation of literature as enchantment.

Last night, circa three o'clock, my fifth child awoke us, crying from gums bursting with teeth—and I lay awake for a long time, with my customary Christmas-cheer gloom, plotting curves of development over the years, and wondering just what were better dropped, what better recovered.

I share your feeling that there is another cultural recombination (or dispersion?) taking place now. Yet I can see no great hopefulness. For the most we could conceivably hope for would be some surprise whereby men were found capable of running their factories without having a factory model of the state. Even if this were got, we'd have the barren norms of book-keeping, machinery, and journalism necessarily taking up far too large a segment of our cultural frame. I guess I am slipping back toward Spengler, and feeling that the most we can aim at is our own peculiar brand of Hellenism. Alexandria—until it gets burned down. Anyhow, the attitude, as I manipulate it, has this one advantage: It provides authority for one to try to write as well as one can, and with such independence of our insti-tutional structures as not even wholly to despise them . . .

[K.]

R.F.D. Gaylordsville,
Connecticut
August 23, 1940
[NL]

Dear Kenneth:

Being at home, though not on that famous leave of absence, I'll sit down to write you a not dictated letter . . . During the last few years I have learned a lot about the institutionalization of human relations, and although all knowledge is supposed to be admirable in itself, I'd just as soon not have acquired that particular knowledge. An editor of a liberal weekly, and particularly a book-review editor, is not a man but an institution, a name to be signed to petitions, a possible speaker at meetings, a leg-up in other writers' careers, a sinister Stalinist or reactionary influence, a whole list of abstractions. He may end by finding himself dehumanized by other people's attitudes toward him. Even his wife gets to judging his actions as those of a public figure. He is loved as a human being by his child and his dog, being lucky enough to have a child and a dog.

That's how I feel when I feel low. I begin to have a great pity for politicians and movie actors and other people whose lives are even more public. I understand why a lot of institutionalized people take to drinking a great deal, so they'll have an excuse for confiding in people, and why others are capable of totally false remarks like, "You know I like you," said with an assumption of simplicity—they're just trying by fraud to reestablish human relations.

All this might sound as if I were getting an exaggerated idea of my importance. Nothing of the kind. The editor of a liberal weekly is worth damned little except in a restricted world of radical politics and literary politics. But he's certainly institutionalized. Practically everyone who comes to see him wants to get something out of him. Social service workers must have the same experience. What do they do when they're at home, away from their clients?

It will be nice to take that three-months' leave of absence. It is going to begin on September 15. Edmund Wilson will take my place October 1 to December 1, then I'll be back again December 15, if the book is finished . . .

Wilson by the way is tremendously acute in some ways, dumb and thick-skinned in others, which is lucky for him. My theory is that it takes an area of insensitivity to keep writers going and keep them from being corrupted. If I had realized at the time the meaning of some opportunities I had in the 1920s I would have taken them and might have been finally corrupted. For example, if I had taken the job with the Literary Guild that was practically offered me, and that I had only to do a little flattering of Carl Van Doren to get, I would have come to depend on the salary and how the hell could I have remained honest? And don't I realize the delicate infringements of honesty that are now involved in working for the *New Republic*, never any big choice, but so many little compromises? It's really easier to give your life for a cause then to hold out for a particular sentence that embodies your way of looking at life—yet if you surrender on the wording of a sentence, and another sentence, pretty soon you find yourself living for the opposite cause to the one you had intended to die for.

I also get sore, every once in a while, at the people who approach me as an institution. Scores of them call me by my first name. That is a sort of intellectual folkway—I can't even remember last names any longer. But how many of those same people would help me out if I got into a jam? I don't have any illusions about that.

About my resignation from the League: it was connected with this process of being institutionalized. On account of the *New Republic* and the use of my name by the League, I couldn't just resign; I had to make it public. And I tried to resign on an issue, not just a squabble. The present CP [Communist Party] line, which the League is following, seems to me not merely mistaken but crooked.

·   ·   ·

Too much of this yammering. It sounds as if I were sitting in my study weeping on this 23d day of August, 1940, the eve of my forty-second birthday, the anniversary of the two heaviest blows that American liberalism has suffered, I mean the execution of Sacco and Vanzetti and the Russo-German pact. As a matter of fact I'm feeling lustier than I have felt all summer, and quite eager to get down to work. And hope you're feeling the same . . .

> As ever,
> [M]

> Prince Edward Island
> Monday, October 14,
> 1940
> [NL]

Dear Kenneth:

. . . Lower Montague, where I'm staying, is at the eastern end of the island, almost at the jumping-off place. The funny little newspaper from Charlottetown gets here a day late, the Halifax papers are two or three days late, the *New York Sunday News* arrives on Thursday morning (the bulldog edition at that), and letters from Connecticut take five days. With the island emptied of all its summer visitors, I am as undisturbed as I can possibly be. And here I came to start work on a new book.[1]

Definition of it: I'm trying to do a sort of *Exile's Return* of the 1930s, but more impersonal, in no sense an autobiography this time. I suppose the old wish to kill one's past and be reborn is working obscurely once more, but I haven't been able to bring it to light, because I haven't been baptized into any new existence. The result is that the narrative will be somewhat more pedestrian . . . My ticklish point will be dealing with all the quarrels of the decade. I simply can't leave them out, because I'm telling the story of a movement that was badly weakened by internal differences before it got slaughtered by external events. On the other hand, I'll be touching some sore spots on my own skin, and had better watch out.

In the case of this book, I'm doing something that I never tried before . . . I sat down, or rather walked about, and outlined the whole thing, chapter by chapter . . . My main idea was that the writers' crusade of the 1930s (which is my subject, although I think Norton will try to sell the book as a literary history) was divided into three stages, and that these stages can best be understood by a religious metaphor, since the experience itself was fundamentally religious. The first stage was conversion to what was, in effect, a primitive church. In the second stage, the church broadened and softened its doctrines in the effort to become universal; that was the period of the People's Front, from 1935 to 1938. In the third stage, the church was weakened by internal schisms and external disasters, so that all but its most stalwart members and most honored priests were alienated. And the whole experience was closed by the Russo-German pact and the war. It makes a neat pattern. Any suggestions here?

I reread a good deal of *Exile's Return*, admiring the writing of it and feeling sore again at the treatment it got . . . Your analysis of the book has a big hole in it. The death-and-rebirth pattern is there, all right, but is complicated by the fact that the book was written at different times and tempos. Up to page 214, I was telling the story of my own adventures in ideas, writing a sort of autobiographical *Bildungsroman*, in which you play a great part, the last reference to you being on page 211. All this section, complete in itself, was written by July, 1933. But I had to do a longer book and I had to bring the story up to date. So, in the winter and spring of 1934, I wrote another hundred pages, in which you are not mentioned once—but neither am I. The author disappeared from his own story. He was now trying to do an objective narrative on the end of the 1920s, in which the chief characters are Scott Fitzgerald, Harry Crosby (two men he knew hardly at all), and Hart Crane, whose figure is in the background, Crosby being a mere surrogate for Crane. The Harry Crosby stuff is some of the best I ever did. One thing that reviewers went wrong on was this lack of connection between the two parts, and that was my own fault. I should have inserted a couple of autobiographical passages into the objective stuff to give the book unity, and I should have explained why I omitted myself from my own story, the reason being that my life after 1923 was indeed quite interesting to me, but not especially significant—or at least I hadn't as yet digested its significance. In the new book, I'll appear only in scattered passages.

Well, that will do for this evening. It's after ten o'clock, and on Prince Edward Island ten o'clock is bedtime . . . Prince Edward Island is dry, by the way—my last bottle of ale will be finished tomorrow, and then I'll drink nothing at all until reaching the states.

Bedtime positively.

As ever,
Malcolm

1. Cowley worked at length on a book about the 1930s, but finally abandoned it. He returned to the project in the late '70s, and published *The Dream of the Golden Mountains: Remembering the 1930's* in 1980.

Andover, New Jersey
December 1, 1940
[PS]

Dear Malcolm,

. . . I, who used once to be *essentially* a letter-writer, have become a rotten correspondent for the most ironical of reasons: I write no letter at all because I plan to write a very long one. There is also another little dialectic, thus: when my work is going well, I am too engrossed to write letters; and when my work is going poorly, I am so low that I lack the vitality to write a letter, even the vitality to say uh-huh or huh-uh.

But in addition to all these "categorical" obstructions, there is the fact that, in the case of this particular letter, I don't know what to say. Your plans for the book were not, in the first letter you wrote me, in a stage whereat anyone else can be much good. I.e., you give what I might describe as a list of "chapterheadings." . . .

The one feature which I most resisted in the whole project, as it *seemed* to be shaping up, was that it was too much journalism and diarism, and not enough criticism. I.e., you might, en route, make observations about literary structures, but they would certainly be extrinsic to the theme of your book. You may answer that, since the whole book hinges about items of literary criticism you have already written, the day-by-dayness is what shows up only in the outline (which represents the *rest* of the book). I am not sure whether that would answer my criticism—but I hesitate to say all this, for usually when he makes such remarks, practically all he means is that somebody else's book could be "correct" only if it were written as he himself would write it.

I do feel, however, that you should try, in filling out your chapterheadings, to outstretch the extreme localism of "the decade." The book, as you outline it, suggests not so much *literature* as *finagling among literary politicians*. Literary history here seems more like the story of how somebody got hold of some committee . . .

As for the red-baitingish quality which your outline suggests: perhaps that will dissolve in the writing, as your interest in other matters crowds it out. Why in the hell the *New Republic*, after thundering for years against the Russian proposals for collective security, should feel that Stalin had done the awful thing of letting Bliven down when he managed to shift Hitler from Russia's neck to Britain's—oh hell. In any event, I wish (as I have said to you on other occasions) that if you must make everything hinge about these matters, I wish you could make the hinges bigger. It was, I grant, a matter of significance to the self-esteem of the typical U.S. intellectual when, by reasons of shifts in international politics, he could no longer simultaneously enjoy the fruits of his salary and think of himself as a rip-roaring advance guard revolutionary. And I do think that a good *funny* piece could be done on the sort of thing that was going on when the *New Republic* was thinking of changing its name to Universal Recantations, Inc. But so far as I personally am concerned, I get pigheaded about the whole business. God knows, I was sluggish about making the change from aestheticism to the social emphasis. I never did make it completely. At the beginning of it all, I used to say that I'd never join the Communist Party because, so long as I didn't, they'd never throw me out—and now, at the end of the decade, I might rephrase it by saying that, through never having been hunkydory with the Party, I now find no occasion to welch. I am grateful to the Party for this much: that at a time when I was in pieces, they upheld a program that enabled me to put myself together again. And because of this service, at that time, I simply feel a slight distaste for this whole business of copy-making out of the welching act. I saw enough of their finaglings to be discouraged long ago (not only with them, but with you). But I feel that, whatever reservations there are to be made about the whole alliance between art and politics, one should make these at a time, and in a spirit, when they can be made for purposes of *enlightenment*, and not when the writing of such stuff is just one last final bit of the same sort of tactics, angling for position, etc.

Maybe all I have said will have only the effect of getting you sore, in a creatively "I'll show the bastard" sort of mood. O.K.—that's at least one way to help a man write a book. Also, I recognize that what I have said may be totally irrelevant, through an erroneous interpretation of your chapterheadings.

. . .

In Florida, I am going to try once more carrying out my resolve to do no further development of my ideas for the Human Relations book,[1] and simply to edit the notes already taken. I see a way of making a very neat monograph on my five terms, "act, scene, agent, agency, purpose" and how they behave implicitly and explicitly in all the ways in which people attribute motives for one another's acts. I think that this might prove to be as fertile an essay for me personally as my "Psychology and Form" one was (incidentally, I was always disgusted at your suggestion, in the Daiches article on Richards, that I got that theme from Richards: note that my essay appeared in *The Dial* in 1925, was written the year before, and that Richards' book appeared in, I believe, 1927.[2] What actually did happen was this: that winter I stayed at Andover, I wrote two essays, "Psychology and Form" and "The Poetic Process"; it was my intention to round these off with a third, "On the Sublime." I began it, then ran into *The Meaning of Meaning*, and was so knocked over that I was unable to write the third essay. And it was not until the "Philosophy of Literary Form" item, the monograph by that name in the forthcoming collection, that I was able to treat of the material for that third essay, though it is there in a much altered state, affected by all that has intervened. The germ of the "Psychology and Form" essay was, in turn, in a review I wrote on Murry,[3] in *The Dial*, 1922, making a distinction between "the psychology of form and the psychology of subject matter," or "between the psychologism of Dostoevsky and the psychologism of, say, a Greek vase"). Meanwhile, as we both are saying: "What the hell? It doesn't matter!" . . .

Sincerely,
K. B.

---

1. *A Grammar of Motives*, in which Burke proposes a method for the study of human motives which he calls Dramatism. In it he argues that any explanation of motive must focus on five things: the *act*, the *scene*, the *agent*, the *agency*, and the *purpose*. He calls these five key terms his "pentad."

2. I. A. Richards did not publish a book in 1927. Burke may be referring to his *Principles of Literary Criticism*, published in 1925, or *Science and Poetry*, published in 1926.

3. Burke reviewed two books by J. Middleton Murry in the December, 1922, issue of *The Dial*, *Still Life* and *The Things We Are*.

R.F.D. Gaylordsville,
Connecticut
December 17, 1940
[NL]

Dear Kenneth:

After Muriel got out of the hospital on November 20, we moved back to the country, and that's where we've been ever since. The Blumes had moved into the house and had taken care of Robbie. They had taken very good care of him too, but he is tremendously attached to his parents, as I suppose most children are, and he was terribly worried about his mother's illness, so that for the first two weeks after our return he looked sickly and nervous and used to have a nightmare regularly at ten o'clock every evening. Now he's back in shape again . . . Muriel has been getting better too, at a fairly rapid rate, considering the nature of the operation. She still has to go into New York twice a week to have a dressing, but that will be over soon.

While she was in the hospital I took a room in New York, on East 71st St., not far away, and tried to go ahead with the book. I made a little progress, not much. For that was just the time chosen by the *New Republic* to have a great shake-up and shakedown. For a time the atmosphere around the office was like Moscow during the purges. Our backers had got tough with us, that was the root of it, and they decided to put Bruce in absolute command and get George[1] and me out of the office. The net result for me wasn't as bad as it might have been. My job from now on is to stay home and write a weekly book page at a decline in salary of $50 a week—but then it costs me about $25 a week to spend three days in New York, if you include city clothes and laundry and hotel bill and general disorganization. The real trouble—I'm telling all this to you in strict confidence— is that a man outside of the office is in a much less secure position than a man inside. For the moment, however, I'm content—I'll be able to go ahead working on the book, taking off two days a week to earn my beans and bread.

So the book becomes even more important than it was before. So I'm even more disturbed by the imperfections of it. Let's take up your yammer and consider all sides of it.

Anyone who was as close to the radical movement as I was is going to be deeply shaken by breaking his connections with it. At that point the religious metaphor is absolutely accurate. You leave a church, and like a defrocked priest you can't think about anything else for a while. You want to justify yourself while blaming yourself—the double drive that one finds in all books by ex-radicals. And at that point you ask, why be an ex-radical?

Here it isn't a question of the religion, which may be good or bad, I haven't decided yet, but of the church, the religion as institutionalized. The church is bad in its effects on people. There's no getting around that point.

And so I write a book intended to deal with the literature of the last ten years, and the Communist Party keeps working into it—and especially into the outline for it. I'll have to bounce it out again. But I can't bounce all of it out, because the Party did play a central role, not by giving all the answers but by stating the problems that people argued about. A difficult job here, to be solved only in the writing.

Meanwhile I adopted one simple formula that may answer some of your objections. No names! No inside revelations! If I want to document a point, I quote from somebody's novel or essay or poem, which is easy and hurts no feelings. If I want to tell a story that might reflect on somebody, friend or enemy, the story's hero is anonymous and some of the details are changed.

And I'm trying to get at something which is the essence of the decade but which has an application beyond immediate timeliness. I want not a series of events or actions but the motives and moods behind them. I want as far as possible to open doors, to let people see that a whole lifetime and very deep feelings are necessary to explain a single speech. What I am really trying to write is a collective novel. The last decade lends itself to just that—having a beginning, a middle, and an end, and having an inner logic that was timed to coincide with external events. In that sense, it's a damned ambitious project, more ambitious than I can carry out with my terrible habit of writing a page or two a day.

.   .   .

It's my sort of book, not yours, because I'll be sticking atmosphere into it—that's what I do easily and do well—but I hope and pray that there won't be anything cheap about it, or journalistic. It's in the later sections that I run into those dangers, and, boy, won't I have to be careful. Maybe the trouble is that once more I am trying to combine literary history with autobiography, and perhaps not making myself clear. But I'll play a much less important part in my story than in *Exile's Return*.

What I'd be grateful for from you is not only comments on the project but also memories of how you felt and thought at different stages of the 1930s, documentation in other words. I can use it all without incriminating you. In the course of conversations lately I have run into some very strange people—none stranger than Bob Cantwell's[2] friend Whittaker Chambers, who used to work for the GPU,[3] and who now proclaims himself as an agent of the counter-revolution, "Christian and democratic," he says, but mostly counter-revolutionary.

Muriel has been wrapping up Christmas presents, all for the kiddies. Time for me to knock off and listen to the late evening news.

As ever,
Malcolm

1. George Soule.

2. Cantwell was active in Popular Front causes and worked with Whittaker Chambers at *Time* magazine.

3. The GPU was the U.S.S.R. secret police organization, 1922–1935.

Melbourne Beach,
Florida
December 21, 1940
[PS]

Dear Malcolm,

'Tis my absolute contention that you have nothing but the abbreviation of income to regret, as regards the new occupational arrangements. The book should gain greatly in continuity—and certain traits, which shall be nameless, but which haven't exactly graced you, whould be given a chance to abate.

. . .

Concerning my own reminiscences of the period: if you're still concerned with such, when I get back, I can give you certain documents that have "symptomatic" value. And the episode of my punishment at the first writers' congress had many twists.[1] If I am in any way a representative case, the important point is this: That I was never merely handling a political issue— that, whenever I was trying overtly to patch something up on the political plane, I was covertly making symbolic passes designed to patch up personal problems totally not-political. (It has always been my conviction that all political symbolism is of this sort—which is both the very basis of my analysis of literary action and the fundamental reason why the officialdom always felt there was something phony about my approach. The officialdom has always held to a very rudimentary and naive kind of realism. I could understand the lure of this position, but I have never for an instant believed in its accuracy, as a statement about human motivation.)

Maybe I could get at, in another way, the sort of thing I have in mind when I want you first to solve some problems to do with "principles." You write: "It isn't a question of the religion, which may be good or bad, I haven't decided yet, but of the church, the religion as institutionalized. The church is bad in its effects on people." If you'd stop here, for instance, and first decide in your mind just what you consider the relationship to be between *any* religious motive and its bureaucratization in institutions, you'd be doing the thing I have in mind. What kind of institutions, if any, are "good" in their effects on people; what kind "bad"; are your objections objections to *this* party; or would they apply to *any* party; what measures did you ever propose, publicly or privately, that might have made for a greater sophistication on the part of affiliations? In brief: what alternative kinds of action did you, or do you, have in mind—and what did you do to try to bring these alternatives about?

· · ·

Perhaps all this hemming and hawing is simply to do with the fact that I haven't yet got the notion of what you're after. I don't flatter myself that anything I say will be of any worth as it is—but it might be useful in suggesting to you something other than it meant to me. I think what I'm pressing you to do is to try, just for once, the experiment of *developing* an idea until it becomes something other than a headline. You speak of your attempt to get "atmosphere"; maybe that's the clue; maybe you prefer to use ideas too much for purely atmospheric purposes, which often gives your presentation what I might call, in the purely technical sense, an "unprincipled" appearance. You speak of the importance of the Party, for instance, in setting the questions that people argued about . . . But there is a still more important matter than questions—or at least just as important as. I hate to say it, because it is so obvious as soon as it has been said, yet you make no mention of it in your letters. I refer to the matter of *terms*. Terms are interrelated; once you select a few, you are no longer free simply to apply them like labels to external situations, but must also follow through all sorts of internal battles, as the terms bring up obligations with relation to one another. What I am asking you to do is, as a kind of preparatory chapter (even if you don't use it), to write a kind of paradigm, stating to yourself just what the anecdote is, what kind of terms you would employ for discussing it, what are their virtues and their limitations, what are their internal relationships, and above all, *what further possibilities you see flickering about the edges of your terminology* (sometimes I have felt you are much more interested in trying to kill things than in trying to make things grow). The *atmospheric* quality of ideas, I think, should be got merely by tinkering with their *names*. That is, I too think of myself as trying to get atmosphere, as for instance when I designate as "the bureaucratization of the imaginative" what you designate as "the institutionalization of religion." . . .

· · ·

Frankly, I think you were on the road to becoming a simply awful person. (And distrusting always my own views on the subject, that would be warped by expectations going back to our walks on Ellsworth Avenue, I base this statement purely on the stories that "went about," the general attitude that people seemed to have toward you—whereas, you had not been out of the place six weeks before I began hearing a different kind of story.) For some damned reason that I can never understand, you *seemed* to demand kinds of tribute or servility that made it very hard for any man of spirit to work with you. I recognize that you had a tough job, dealing always with a race of prima donnas—but things weren't helped any by your becoming a tobacco-chewing, hard-slugging prima donna yourself. So, if you can hang on at this stage, by all means consider yourself lucky (a much greater percentage of insecurity is the average today—and a still much greater percentage is mine). Just drop the idea that the world is demanding any official statements of you (I assure you that it never was, to the extent you seemed to think it was). Accommodate yourself to the much more humane notion that a statement is worth exactly what it is worth as a statement . . . I welcome you, for a season, into the Grand Order of Agro-Bohemians, the Last Cultural lag of the Vanished Frontier, the Horseless Chevalier, the Flying Pedestrians, We Who Are the Very Antithesis of Bureaucracy (hence who, by the rigors of the dialectic, if we get into office, are likely to become the Very Soul of Bureaucracy). I don't know how long the interregnum will last—how long will be the respite before you are lost again beyond the barriers of officialdom—but in the meanwhile, though you take it with a wry face, welcome to our sorry, scattered fraternity of those who are trying to invent things that others cash in on. The one advantage of our trade is that we can, alas, be here when others must be there, be out when others must be in, sleep when others wake, keep vigil while others sleep, etc. . . .

Sincerely,
K. B.

1. At the First American Writers' Congress, held in April, 1935, Burke delivered a talk called "Revolutionary Symbolism in America," in which he argued that the phrase "the people" would be more strategically appropriate than the word "workers" in addressing the lower middle classes in America. He was publicly attacked for his remarks by a number of other participants, and went away shaken.

R.F.D. Gaylordsville,
Connecticut
January 9, 1941
[NL]

Dear Kenneth:

No further progress to report on the book. I began writing the weekly *New Republic* pieces on December 29, twelve days ago; I have done two of them so far and nothing else, except a little woodchopping and whittling and a trip to New York. Damn me for a painfully slow writer, always carrying water uphill in a leaky bucket, always feeling that my next piece has to be "better" and therefore getting an attack of stage fright before starting it. Then after starting it, the continual necessity to change, and change again, and go back and start over.

. . .

You asked what sort of book I planned to write, saying that it still wasn't clear in your mind. Well, I want to write a story of the writers' crusade of the 1930s. Almost every word in that statement is important to me. "Story" in particular is important, because it places the emphasis on movement and sequence and the reasons for both. "Crusade" is important, though slightly inaccurate, because it brings in the religious element that I have been talking about. "1930s" is important because—this answers another of your questions or complaints—I personally can only get at permanent and eternal truths in their temporal manifestations. Actually almost the whole experience of the 1930s happened before—notably in France from 1830 to 1848, though large parts of it also parallel the experience of the early Christians, of Milton, of the English Romantic poets, and of the little American renaissance from 1910 to 1919. But I don't want to touch the permanent motives till I have the whole thing situated in its own time. I can't. I don't think that way.

The writers' crusade of the 1930s is again a morality play to me, or at any rate a story with a beginning, a middle, and an end. Beginning: the depression. Middle: the People's Front era. End: 1939–1940, when everything ended—the Spanish republic (February), Czechoslovakia (March), the Federal Theatre (June), the People's Front (August), the long armistice (September)—then Poland (October), the illusion of Russia as a non-imperialist power (November), free Norway and Denmark (April), the French republic (May and June)—did you ever stop to think how all our world crashed in those few months?

. . .

I certainly haven't worked out my ideas on religion. But as I told you long ago, I think Durkheim had the clue to it—God being in one sense the representative of society. Or putting the matter in a different way, the human being is incomplete. Remember the myth about the two-backed beast? Well, the truth of it is that man is a beast with a million backs and arms and legs and eyes; that he can no more exist by himself than one ant or one bee can exist by himself. Society, however, is not a visible reality in the ordinary sense—that is, a man can be alone walking in the woods and still be part of society. That is why he has to celebrate its reality by religious rites and legends and mysteries. If he tries, however, to act absolutely independently of society, then he is punished in various ways, sometimes by being put in prison, sometimes by mental troubles that become physical ailments. He can be completely happy only by forgetting himself—this is the truth in the Sermon on the Mount and also in the customs of the Communist Party . . .

·   ·   ·

A tendency during the 1930s was to carry much too far the separateness of churches—thus, there was not only a proletarian—i.e., communist—literature and a Fascist literature, but also proletarian heroes, marriages, love affairs, courage, discipline, etc. Hemingway has at present got himself into that other frame of mind where the emphasis is on identity of actions in different faiths—thus he keeps shifting from his [Spanish] Loyalist hero to the Rebels and describing them also in terms of courage, devotion, etc., as if to indicate that the devoted men of all faiths are alike . . .

Remember that I'm not explaining my book at this point, but merely trying to explain my own ideas, not all of which will get into the book. I don't want to be too hard on the communists. That is a tendency I'll have to avoid. It has to be remembered, for example, that they seemed to me the only men immune to corruption. But that was corruption in the vulgar sense, the taking of bribes, and their immunity to this one form of vice made them fall more easily victim to temptations on a somewhat higher level.

Meanwhile I have definitely turned against the monolithic conception of society represented by all the new political religions. If we haven't learned anything else from Russia, and from Germany too, we should have learned that a country is in a pretty desperate pass when its political governor is also its pope, able to enforce a given world view with his political police . . .

About your, what did you do in the Great War, Daddy? question—well, I didn't do enough, not nearly enough. I tried pretty hard to introduce an atmosphere of tolerance and humanity into the actions of the left-wing writers with whom I was associated; I tried to keep them back from reducing everything to politics, though I found myself falling into the vice I was trying to get others to avoid . . . I found that I wasn't doing very much outside my job, which was becoming a bureaucratic job. And since I was doing a very little and saying so very little, I was in a false position—it was taken for granted that I was a Stalinist when, Jesus, you ought to know that I was a long way from that.

I knew that I wasn't getting any too damned popular. But since you started that topic, I wish you'd carry it a lot farther. I had some damned persistent enemies, notably Sidney Hook and Jim Farrell. There is reason to believe that one or the other of them helped to make trouble for me at the *New Republic* by writing to the Elmhirsts.[1] But of course even very faithful enemies like that can't make really bad trouble for you unless other people agree with what they say—and evidently that was my point of weakness. But it's pretty damned important for me to know as much as possible of what was being said, in order that I can mend matters as far as possible and avoid similar mistakes in the future. So keep talking, kid, I'm listening and learning . . .

As ever,
[M]

1. Dorothy and Leonard Elmhirst, owners of the *New Republic*.

Melbourne Beach,
Florida
February 14, 1941
[PS]

Dear Malcolm,

All sorts of interventions (including even time off for a bit of hack, a translating job, to say nothing of my fabulous upsy-downsiness as to health) have intervened since your last letter.

As to your remarks about religion, its variants, etc.: since religion is by definition a kind of Rome, to which all roads lead, I guess one cannot very profitably disagree (or even agree) when somebody wants to talk about this road or that road. One may say that in religion we have a communion merging the individual with the group. Or one may say that "the religious man thinks only of himself." Or begad, I believe that one may say, "dialectically," both of these at once. And in all three there will be much justice, though I should tend to put most store by the third. At least, in acts of communion there is conversion, transubstantiation—and there must be some isolated individual center that is undergoing this process, however intensely the reference is to participation in a group. At least, there is no more typical saint of the Western church than Augustine—no one with a more intense reference beyond the self—but there are few men in all history who have been more intensely individuals . . .

Best greetings,
K. B.

R.F.D. Gaylordsville,
Connecticut
February 22, 1941
[NL]

Dear Kenneth:

The fields woodmouse-colored, with patches of rather dirty snow. A few snowflakes in the air. The elm trees dust-colored in the bottom lands along the brook, but with a few golden-green willows among them. This is the period when the willows and the red osiers begin to change color. In a week or two the pines will begin to get greener too. It is a transition period, of staying in the house and thinking what to do when spring comes, a period when there is nothing to do outdoors but chop wood. I don't think we'll get to Florida—on account of simple inertia (and limited funds), but living here is not so bad, in a warm house, and the family draws closer together in winter . . . Health in general quite good—Muriel has begun to laugh again. Her experiences make her wonder how much the doctors know about cancer . . . I'm more and more convinced of the hypothesis of psychophysical parallelism embodied in what is known as psychosomatic medicine. One example of it: you don't know what to do, so, with a great feeling of relief, you get sick. (Or in terms of international politics, a nation doesn't know what to do, so, with a great feeling of relief, it has a crisis in which everybody is starved or bombed and everybody's next action is automatic.) I had been unhappy at the *New Republic* for the last three or four years; I developed a bad heart and the beginning of stomach ulcers—now I'm looking and feeling a hell of a sight better, though I'm not out of the woods yet. (A great example of what I've been talking about is Trotsky, who used to get sick at every crisis in his own political career; the doctors never did find out what was wrong with him. Dr. Stalin cured him before killing him.)

•   •   •

On a more serious subject—for the dialectical nature of the religious experience, of course you're right. The mystical experience of unity with God is of course unity with society, according to Durkheim's principle, yet it is an experience generally enjoyed in solitude and one that strengthens the individuality of the one by whom it is experienced (while partly destroying his sense of individuality). On the other hand, people lacking in this sense of communion, people who try to develop their personalities, end by being just like all the other people trying to develop their personalities—as note the artists of the 1920s, who might have been turned out on a production line. That much was expressed in the Sermon on the Mount—"He who loseth his life, etc."

As ever,
Malcolm

Melbourne Beach,
Florida
March 8, 1941
[PS]

Dear Malcolm,
    . . . I object to your writing me as though you were trying to get me to wake up to the lore about psychogenic illness. Jeez! haven't I been worrying about it, in all sorts of theological and psychological guises, ever since my days as a Christian Scientist? But I do grant you: there is a tremendous amount that is still to be learned in detail about such processes.

·   ·   ·

    Spring is with us, though a March-blowy one. Sorry you couldn't drop around, as I'd like to interest you in this place (which I think has many possibilities, just the way an old house has, when you look at it and somehow see the possibilities in their latency). Even as it is, I have nothing to kick about, having found enough people friendly enough, and having been able to knock my monograph on motives into shape (windup still to be contrived). In this I think I have managed to be more orderly than in the case of any other complex subject I have treated. But God knows what I'll do with it. I correspond on and off with various college teachers, and may send a copy around to them, for possible use in some academic publication. I seem to be shifting my linguistic analysis from a *rhetoric* to a *grammar*. And though I won't guaranty that I have yet been able to prove that the "dramatic or dialectical perspective" is the proper "scientific" instrument for the analysis of human motives, I think I can at least prove that any other perspective is pseudo-scientific (scientific only in the simplest sense).
    I suppose someday when you're around I'll be trotting it out, to let it

get one of those humiliating skimmings-over for which you should be justly famous. (But hold on! it's too near bedtime for exercise now!) . . .

> Sincerely,
> K. B.

> R.F.D. Gaylordsville,
> Connecticut
> April 28, 1941
> [NL]

Dear Kenneth:

Having mislaid your last letter I'll have to answer only part of it and only from memory.

What you said about Hart is a new slant that hadn't occurred to me.[1] I'll think about it and see whether it suggests anything. To be used, it would have to be documented. Another slant—and one that I have documented already. Hart had the impulse of a prophet, spoke in the voice of a prophet, always wanted to be "opening spiritual gates." But at heart he didn't believe in anything. That explains his various prayers and commands—"Lie to us, dance us back the tribal morn!"—"Hasten while they are true, life, death, desire." The world to him was a promise of something, he didn't know what, but a promise that wouldn't ever be fulfilled. That explains why he called the first flowers "twanged red *perfidies* of spring." Later as he drank more, he became able to deceive himself, thought he really had a message, and that is when his poems (cf. "Cape Hatteras") became bombastic. He was furious at Eliot, but furious, for writing "That is the way the world ends, not with a bang but a whimper." He was furious because at heart I think he believed that Eliot was right.

In all that, Hart was typical of our world, the world in which we came to manhood. And now we see the next stage, a violent search for faith at any cost. I have just been noting the symptomatology of the disease in Archibald MacLeish. But it is a disease that, to be honest with myself, I know I share, though with a great deal more self-consciousness and self-criticism. The rack and ruin of the 1930s comes from the fact that for a time we believed something, believed in Communism, still believe in it as a religion (or purpose or ideal) but have ceased to identify the religion with the institutionalized communist Church. Hence a vacuum. It was into this vacuum that fascism rushed in Europe. . . .

·   ·   ·

. . . In the course of the political quarrels I made a couple of deep and sincere enemies—Sidney Hook, James Farrell to begin with; Morrow[2] (since dropped from view), Solow,[3] the *Partisan Review*ers. In some of the attacks on me, the hand of these individuals was evident . . . But it's entirely too comforting to think that one's misfortunes are due to malignant forces or people . . . The question is how much of the trouble was due to definite people and how much of it was justified by my own course of action (or chiefly inaction). Data appreciated . . .

> As ever,
> Malcolm

1. In his letter of April 18, Burke wrote about the place of slang in the "complex superstructure" of Crane's poetry, and speculated in a vague way about its relationship to what "the critics call his 'mysticism.'" This was in response to Cowley's article, "Remembering Hart Crane," which had appeared in the April 14 issue of the *New Republic*.

2. Felix Morrow, who attacked Cowley as a "Stalinist intellectual" in a 1936 article in *New Militant*.

3. Herbert Solow (1903–1964), American editor and writer. A contributing editor to *Time*, 1943–1945, he had been active in Popular Front organizations.

> Andover, New Jersey
> May 1 (where did I hear
> that expression be-
> fore?), 1941
> [PS]

Dear Malcolm,

Back at the old stand. We traveled from Sunday morning until the middle of the day Wednesday. And throughout the entire trip, not a single burp or wheeze out of the old Blunder Bus (I am here referring to the Cadillac, not to myself). True, she consumes four gallons of oil per diem, but that's only two dollars, if you buy the two-gallon tins—and we get but eight miles per gallon of gas. Yet even so, she is a roomy bitch, almost a Pullman, and we carry more luggage than is in many a trailer. I would do a minimum of two hundred miles a day, and Lib a minimum of one hundred, with plenty of snacks and snoozes had by all . . .

. . . . . .

I don't know of any maneuvers against you. If I had, even in my most disgruntled moments I would have told you of them. There was, it is true, another type of admonition that I did consciously withhold—i.e., my old bellyaching, which I relinquished after you had given me plenty of evidence that you considered yourself well rid of it. I felt that you demanded tribute (flattery) rather than criticism, and you seemed to be finding plenty of scriveners who were willing to pay the tribute—so Kassandrus Burp, with no one else to plague with his dire misgivings, was restricted mainly to the austere practice of plaguing himself . . . There were, now and then, inflections, tones of voice, parenthetical remarks adverse to you, that turned up in literary conversations with one person or another, but one cannot remember any of that sort of thing five minutes after it has happened—nor does it ever mean much, as it is usually a part of the flora and fauna of the literary jungle.

· · ·

. . . You *gave the impression* (I leave it to you to decide how justly or unjustly) that you wanted, not a world of equals, but a world of superiors whose positions you might aim at, and underlings who would admire your orders . . . [Y]ou did always seem to think that the *New Republic* was some kind of superior state of consciousness, rather than a project for milking a cow, which said cow has now become unruly and has reminded the milkmaids where the milk comes from . . . The fact is that you did somehow give the impression that you like to think of yourself less and less as some kind of good fellow and more and more as some kind of power—and when someone starts looking like a power in and about the New York Scramble, depend upon it that in time he'll organize an army of little would-be Counter-Powers. One man who is by no means an enemy of yours, but does indeed have great respect for your abilities, once told me that you were becoming a Bouncer . . . All of us tend to hate most in others our own major vices, but you seem to exemplify this pattern more symmetrically than anyone else I know.

· · ·

. . . As to the bang-whimper line in Eliot: I could exegetize that too as per my suggestions on Hart and the Bone of Contention. Remember how Hemingway tells us how Mr. and Mrs. Eliot tried and tried. I always supposed it was because the weapon wouldn't go bang. Such matters I should not consider as the *essential* motivation, but as an important member of the motivational cluster.

Best greetings,
K. B.

R.F.D. Gaylordsville,
Connecticut
May the what? 1941
[NL]

Dear Kenneth:

Il faut cultiver son jardin. That's what I've been doing, cultivating my real garden to the neglect of my metaphorical garden. Escapism, of course. With the social world crashing around us, digging in the earth and moving plants gives a sense of power, that essential feeling of potency, which seems lacking elsewhere. The law of cause and effect can still be applied among plants, whereas among men it is only the Germans who can apply that law, having borrowed social levers from Ford and Lenin and combined them with Bismarck's army. So, after listening to the radioed accounts of twelve thousand parachutists landing on Crete, men from Mars in the land of the Minotaur, I move thirteen tomato plants into lily cups before setting the lily cups in the garden and feel very well satisfied, because I know the plants will grow safe from cutworms or sun-wilt . . .

As per your remark about my hating the things I was destined to become—it's no news to me . . . One might also say that my quarrels with the anti-Stalinists were prophetic, were made worse by doubts I was trying to repress—but in that case the judgment would be external, since I wasn't trying to repress the doubts and since there is a Trotskyist mentality that existed anterior to Trotskyism, and that is not my mentality at all—the quarrel was a renewal of my high school and college quarrel with the grinds, the people who made no higher marks than I did, or not much higher marks (remember I was ninth in my class at Harvard) but hadn't cultivated the ironic attitude that study was unimportant, whereas I made my parade of drunkenness and did my studying in private.

The *New Republic* under Bliven's editorship seems to me a pretty sad mess, an emotional and propagandistic sheet directed toward people who have to be emotionalized and propagandized by logical arguments, a lowbrow sheet for highbrows.

As ever,
Malcolm

621 East Capitol,
Washington, D.C.
January 11, 1942
[NL]

Dear Kenneth:

For a little more than a month, I have been staying in a tourist non-home—a medium-sized room with two double beds in it, two radiators but not enough heat, so that my fingers at the moment are pretty nearly frozen to the keys. $10 a week; worth fully $6 by the standards of other countries. Much loneliness, much looking forward to the day two weeks from now when Muriel and Robbie come down and we get established in what seems to be a comfortable apartment.

It's a strange place for me to be; I mean Washington, not the room. I'm a Chief Information Analyst (but my office is full of Chief Information Analysts); I get what seems to me the lordly salary of $8,000, which is too much for the work I'm doing; the FBI is of course trying to get me fired—you ought to read the long dossier they prepared on me—and I have to depend on Archibald MacLeish[1] to save my job; the whole information setup here is uncertain, so that our organization might be abolished or merged, and altogether it's a lot of sand on which to build a house where I don't want to build a house. Meanwhile it seems that every second writer in the country wants a job like mine to preserve the American Way of Life.

. . . . . .

. . . On the whole, it's better than I thought it would be. The worst feature of a bureaucracy is the struggle for power that has taken the place of a struggle for money. Bureaucrats here can't draw down more than $10,000 a year, because that's how much the congressmen get, and congressmen hate to see anyone else getting more. But they can, like Russian bureaucrats, find other satisfactions, in terms of long-distance phone calls, admiring subordinates, orders obeyed in Honolulu, decisions reflected in victories or defeats in Asia. They can get to feeling pretty good about themselves.

You can get a vague picture of a government agency by imagining the business of General Motors being run by the faculty of the University of Chicago, or better of Columbia—which has now contributed 95 of its faculty members to Washington . . .

As ever,
Malcolm

1. MacLeish was head of the Office of Facts and Figures, where Cowley was working.

Andover, New Jersey
January 27, 1942
[PS]

Dear Malcolm,

Many thanks indeed for yours of recent date. With your considerably interesting report on local conditions. I have also been hearing of you in the metropolitan press and over nation-wide hookups. And even in dark alleys—as a friend who had been seeing a publisher told me that a faithful phoebe[1] had been going the rounds, presumably begging to be told that you were a C.P. because you didn't support Franco. However, I think I can safely offer you congratulations on having successfully passed through the mill—as it is my notion that the stir was mainly for the record (in case, at some future time, the whole situation so changes that a change of administration is possible, whereupon a vast list of such complaints would add up to a campaign plank).

.   .   .

At the moment, am trying to do an essay on Marianne Moore. Then I want to lay everything else aside and try to get my Grammar (on motives) revised (for God knows what, except that I'd like to have it all cleared away before God knows what). Am mildly humiliated at the thought that, whereas I have been digging through this stuff since *Permanence and Change*, my government wants me not at all while embracing fifth-rate college hacks by the trainload. But so be it. If only they don't dry up the sources of my meager income, or make me lay everything aside and go through some kind of mere motions, I guess I have no cause to complain. And one can always be sure at least that, if he can but get his book out, there will be somebody in the officialdom to at least lay eyes upon it long enough to swipe from it . . .

In all that I say, I might seem indifferent to the national necessities. God, I very much am not. Indeed, I am gloomy not only about our own country, but about the whole damned human race. For the more I think things over, the more inconceivable it seems to me that a decent peace can be the outcome of all this. At times I foresee so much destruction of the world's productive and distributive equipment that, when the war is over, the conquerors will have to plunder the conquered in order merely to exist. And the other possibility is a makeshift peace that, coming as a compromise before this drastic stage is reached, simply leaves everything unresolved. Technology has reached a point, physically, where it demands a world order—and people, mentally, politically, are far, far behind the stage of development where they can have a world order (except perhaps as the gradual outgrowth of some vast imperialist conquest). Human history, I fear, is going to follow the curve of a Greek tragedy—with science, technology, as the hybris [sic] that rides to a fall. Meanwhile, all I know is, so far or so long as I am able, to go on trying to increase our awareness (my own and others') of the ways in which motives move us and deceive us, and what kind of knowledge the nature of motives demands of us, if we are not to goad one another endlessly to the cult of powers that can bring no genuine humaneness to the world. It would be silly to think that any book, or even a whole library of books, could solve such difficulties. But such books are, I know, one of the steps in the right direction. Until the steamrollers flatten out all.

. . .

. . . On Sunday, the Tates, the Blackmurs,[2] and Zabel[3] turned up. Tate and Blackmur have been having career dreams, since it is now being decided whether they are to stay on at Princeton. Blackmur, quite pragmatically, dreamed that he caught Gauss[4] with his pants down. Tate seemed happy with the thought of a new neurosis—a feeling that he had gas pockets in his head—until I reminded him that his literary enemies could do wonders with that one, which I think will cause a quick recovery. My own triumph is a recent dream (I had been reading Henry Miller) of Hitler as a kind of Belle Dame Sans Merci. I was to be strung up for torture, and at Hitler's orders. He was present; but as the Führerin, a beautiful young girl. I pled with him (her?) to be saved, receiving no answer but a gentle, Madonna-like (à la Da Vinci) smile. So kindly, so charitable—and all the while the fact remained that nothing was going to be done for me, and I would be strung up and tortured until I died. During my pleading, I took occasion now and then to pass an amorous hand over the firm, girlish breasts. Meanwhile, consider me
puzzled . . .

Sincerely,
K. B.

1. An FBI agent.
2. R. P. Blackmur, a literary critic and professor at Princeton University.
3. Morton Zabel, professor of English and editor of *Poetry*.
4. Dean Christian Gauss of Princeton.

R.F.D. Gaylordsville,
Connecticut
June 28, 1942
[NL]

Dear Kenneth:

What the devil, no letter from you for a long time, no answer even, so far as I can remember, to the screed I wrote you from Washington when I was first living there in a furnished room with two double beds (if you ever want to be really lonely, live alone in a room furnished with two double beds), and I'm wondering whether Something Has Gone Wrong. I hope not because I would like to see you one of these days and tell you some of the things that happened. Things are really pretty bad in Washington as regards the people who belonged to united-front organizations. My trouble largely came from ex-communists (J. B. Matthews,[1] Whittaker Chambers

of *Time*, Eugene Lyons[2] and somebody close to Sidney Hook, if it wasn't
Sidney himself)—but in the background you get the Catholic Church, which
furnishes the popular basis, the day-in, day-out preaching against the Red
Menace that gives people like Dies[3] their support. The FBI is staffed with
Catholics to an extent that nobody recognizes, and doesn't the Church love
to work with them and give them spiritual support and honorary degrees
at commencement time; and don't they love to track down Reds.

Well, I'm back at home now, working in the garden more than ever,
doing my little pieces for the *New Republic*, feeling pretty low but not so
low as last month or the month before, and I think that by fall I'll be writing
again. A magazine called *Chimera* arrived from Princeton with a piece of
yours[4] in which your new slant was better summarized, more briefly and
systematically stated than in the longer essays where you were discovering
instead of merely explaining.

As ever,
Malcolm

1. J. B. Matthews had been active in People's Front organizations in the 1930s (he was chairman
of the American League for Peace and Democracy). He later renounced these ties and became
active in anticommunist organizations in the 1950s. He was hired by the first House Un-
American Activities Committee as a researcher.

2. Eugene Lyons had been a United Press correspondent in Moscow in the 1930s. His book,
Assignments in Utopia (1937), was harshly critical of the Soviet system.

3. Martin Dies (1901–1972), congressman from Texas and the first chairman of the House
Un-American Activities Committee.

4. "The Study of Symbolic Action," which appeared in the Spring issue of *Chimera*.

Andover, New Jersey
July 6, 1942
[PS]

Dear Malcolm,

It was your move—though, what with all the goings-on that must have
been going on at the time my letter reached Washington, your stand on
the matter would be quite understandable. Besides, an inspection of the
curve makes it clear that I, who at the time of the last war was writing five-
paged single-spaced letters, typed on both sides of the paper, am now given
to letting things pile up for months, until I can muster whatever it takes to
epistolate for as much as a paragraph.

·   ·   ·

Garden is in proud shape this year. Have battled back the jungle quite
a bit farther (the old apple trees now being once more an orchard, and at

the edge of them we have a rough stone fireplace where we now and then prepare meals outdoors). A dump heap near the house has been by me terraced. And, all told, things look much better (the sight also having a good incantatory effect upon me). Internationally, I suppose I have the customary point of view—an ever keener grouch on technology and its priesthoods. Every once in a while I note that the editorializings in your gazette are still devoted to the higher-standard-of-living racket (and whenever I encounter this mid–nineteenth century attitude still flourishing, I of course consider it enough to subscribe once more to Flaubert's counter-attitude). Was in town last week, looking at the America (as per Sandburg) photographs at the Modern Museum. Go look at them if you would. Be impressed with what depressed me as a futuristic present shallow in futurity (unless it can somehow manage to reverse itself) with Sandburg contributing some official mouthpiece verbalizing (of the kind that happens after Whitman's catalogues, as tempered by Sears Roebuck catalogues, have been transformed into a kind of proto-material from which one may in turn get such re-transformations as Corwin[1] or MacLeish). But the technical work on the photographs was very impressive, as was the progression from the rural, to the industrial, to the military. And some of the folk subjects . . .

Best greetings to all,
K. B.

1. Norman Corwin was an American radio dramatist known for his unusual adaptations of current topics.

PART THREE

1943-1966

Cowley's prediction that he would soon be over the debacle in Washington and be writing again turned out to be accurate. In fact, his fortunes took an extraordinarily good turn in 1943 when he was offered a five-year Mellon Fellowship to support his projected work on American literature. The fellowship allowed him to devote his full energies to editing the Viking Portable editions of Hemingway, Faulkner, and Hawthorne, and to write essays and reviews on American writers. Although he never lost interest in French literature, Cowley's work as a critic was to become identified from this point on with American literature. When the Mellon Fellowship ran out in 1948, he took a position as literary advisor at Viking Press, and began to accept a number of temporary teaching positions (at the University of Washington, Stanford University, the University of Michigan, U.C. Berkeley, and Cornell).

While Cowley's work led him more deeply into literary and cultural history, Burke's work as a critic continued to broaden, so that by 1950 he had synthesized elements of poetry, philosophy, rhetoric, and linguistics into a system for analyzing human behavior and motives, which he called Dramatism. His earlier observation that Cowley was interested in interpreting "cultural trends" while he was interested in the *process* of interpretation and the criticism of criticism thus proved to be extremely accurate. Burke's *A Grammar of Motives* (1945), in which he elaborated his formulation of the five terms necessary for the analysis of virtually any motivated action (act, scene, agent, agency, and purpose), is a complex interdisciplinary work whose propositions and analyses range over issues in philosophy, economics, linguistics, and literary criticism. As such, it extends his analysis of the process of interpretation until that analysis becomes a system. But as he outlined its broadest aims to Cowley, the book was also concerned with "cultural trends," for it was meant to "increase our awareness (my own and others') of the ways in which motives move us and deceive us, and what kind of knowledge the nature of motives demands of us, if we are not to goad one another endlessly to the cult of powers that can bring no genuine humaneness to the world." Burke originally conceived the book as part of a trilogy, with a "Rhetoric of Motives" and a "Symbolic of Motives" to follow. *A Rhetoric of Motives* was published in 1950, but the book on symbolism, while virtually completed in manuscript, has never been published.

As they did in their earlier letters, Burke and Cowley continue in these years to edit and criticize each other's work, with Cowley trying to get Burke to be less abstract, to temper his tendency toward proliferating terms and systems, and with Burke trying to get Cowley to write less about people, and more about ideas. "I think you should try for a year laying off the obits," Burke wrote to Cowley in December of 1943. "Quit worrying as to whether the other guy is writing important literature," he continues, "and start instead trying to write some yourself . . . The study of linguistic action," he points out, "is still in the stage of the maps that Columbus had." Cowley responds that he likes "writing about people, even if they're dead . . . And I'll probably go on talking from time to time about literary trends, because I'm a literary historian and therefore can't get away from them . . . I write more easily when describing the past (often in an elegiac tone) than when I'm maxlernering about the future."

The postwar years began to bring recognition and a wider audience to both men. In 1946 Burke was elected to the National Institute of Arts and Letters, and Cowley's election followed in 1949. Cowley was elected president of the Institute in 1956, and again from 1962 to 1965. Both received regular offers to teach and lecture, and during the McCarthy era they exchanged a number of letters about how their political affiliations of the 1930s were causing some of these offers to be withdrawn (there were incidents at the University of Washington and the University of Minnesota). During the late fifties and sixties Cowley continued to write about American literature, editing Sherwood Anderson, Fitzgerald, Whitman, and publishing *The Faulkner-Cowley File*. In addition to his two books on motive, Burke also published *Book of Moments: Poems 1915–1954*. His analysis of the language of religion led to the publication in 1961 of *The Rhetoric of Religion*.

By the mid-1960s both men began to feel the need to, as Cowley wrote in 1964, "round things off." He began the task of getting his unpublished essays and reviews collected in book form, while Burke published another book, *Language as Symbolic Action* (1966), and began to focus his attention on refining in a series of essays his theories about language and symbols, and his increasing concern about the perils of technology. Their friendship had now lasted some sixty years, and in 1961 Cowley observed to Burke that they were both "pretty obscure persons until we were fifty years old." He himself had felt the impulse to "*not* become a celebrity," and suspected that Burke had made the same "conscious decision." "I feel now that the decisions were sound, though we were running the risk of bucket-kicking prematurely." It was a "great advantage," he concludes, "that we *were* obscure, that the vast fickle public didn't get tired of us, that now we have the experience and part of the freshness too."

Andover, New Jersey
August 23, 1943
[PS]

Dear Malcolm,

. . . Did you select the verse in the last *New Republic?* I thought it, as a batch, quite good. Also, having long been a student of Marianne Moore's elephants, I thought it notable that she is now asleep thereon.[1] Would like mayhap to compare and contrast this ratio with Louise Bogan and her Fury.[2]

Have been revising my book (and on the whole, I believe, amaking it as clear and orderly as a filing system, plus the *development* of which a filing system is not capable). Who knows? maybe my impatience has taught me how to be patient. At least, I hope it will show up that way. However, in a week or so I am to begin Commuting in the Grand Manner—between New Jersey and Vermont. I made a part-time arrangement,[3] trusting that I'd be able to continue with my revision. Am trying it for one year—from end of this month to middle of December, and from beginning of April to end of July. So, even if it turns out that I can't get much of my own work done when I'm at home during the season, I'll have three and a half months in the winter to finish things up. But must admit, I wouldn't like to be starting out two months from now, with a Sniffle like that of today . . .

Sincerely,
K. B.

1. Burke is referring to Moore's poem, "Asleep on an Elephant," which appeared in *The New Republic* in August.

2. Burke is referring to Louise Bogan's poem "The Sleeping Fury."

3. Burke accepted a part-time position at Bennington College, where he would teach until 1961.

R.F.D. Gaylordsville,
Connecticut
September 5, 1943
[NL]

Dear Kenneth:

So you're going to teach in Vermont. Does that mean Bennington and the beautiful young ladies? And what do you mean when you say you're going to commute: are you actually taking a train back and forth each week? I suppose the pennies will be not unwelcome . . . This month I'm taking a vacation; I'll be at Yaddo[1] until October 1, probably working on Louis Aragon's poems, which Rolfe Humphries has translated but not very accurately. I usually have a nice time at Yaddo; sometimes there is good company, and Saratoga, I discovered last year, has a wonderful tenderloin, a Harlem-plus-Montmartre called Congress Street, full of crap joints, night clubs, and nigger whorehouses. But I'll miss Nathan Asch, now a sergeant in Air Force Intelligence, and his wife now in the WAC.

I listen to the radio and read the *Times* all the way through, as usual, and get bluer and blacker about the next few years. We're certainly fixing to have a nice little war with Russia, besides planning to restore capitalism in Europe. Some things were mighty funny when I was in Washington last year, and one of them was that although most people in government service agreed that we ought to state our war aims, any suggestions to the Chief were disregarded by the Chief. Once, for example, I wrote a radio address that Mr. Big was to deliver by shortwave to the common people of Germany and Italy, but nothing came of it. We also did a pamphlet on the Four Freedoms, and there seemed to be one objection after another to having it published. Finally it came out, in a very innocuous form, eight months after it had been written. I feel now that the war in Europe could be over by Christmas if we laid down a sensible political program, and I sometimes feel that the big people know it could be over by Christmas and don't want it to end—not while the Red Army is still a going concern. Of course their big nightmare is that the Red Army will lick the Germans all by itself. If it crosses the Dnieper line, we'll have a second front PDQ, but not to help the Russians; just to keep them out of Berlin . . .

As ever,
Malcolm

1. Yaddo is a writer's colony in Saratoga Springs, New York.

Andover, New Jersey
November 19, 1943
[PS]

Dear Malcolm,

. . . In these recent months, I have cast into the air as many words as were they spermatozoa and I an adolescent. Were these words the sin of Onan, spilt upon the floor? Or were they—as per Yeats—an annunciation of the holy spirit, an impregnation received through the air?

There have been some good kids about [at Bennington]. Others are wheedlers and finaglers of all sorts. On the whole, I think the project has been going along fairly well. Yet already, in these few months, I have developed the dreadful sense of insecurity that goes with having a job.

Never was anyone more eager to write than I am now. I do so yearn to start, on December 12, revising my Grammar at a fast clip, and getting it definitively cleared away before the end of March. I have been trying it out, in little bits here and there, on the class, and it seems to go quite well. There is an application of it to a Keats Ode in the last *Accent*. You really ought to look it up . . .

. . .

Yours professionally (that is, ask me something, and if I don't know I'll tell you anyhow),

K. B.

c/o Coates,
255 E. 72nd St.,
New York City
November 21, 1943
[PS]

Dear Kenneth:

We came into New York to repair our ravaged fortunes—I couldn't live any longer on my *New Republic* salary, with wartime deductions, and apparently I couldn't earn more money as long as I lived in Gaylordsville-Sherman—(a) because I wasn't in town to get jobs and (b) because if I did get them I was damned slow about finishing them as long as there were nicer things to do outdoors. Well, I edited a war book for Ben Huebsch,[1] getting money enough to move into town, and now I'm trying to finish a profile for the *New Yorker*.[2] We're living with the Coateses in a five-room apartment with a line forming to the right outside the bathroom door, and I'm working during the day at the New York Society Library—not bad, for I have a room to myself, but unheated and therefore impractical as soon as the temperature falls below freezing . . .

As ever,
Malcolm

1. Benjamin W. Huebsch, a publisher. He later became vice president of Viking Press.

2. Cowley's profile was of Max Perkins, and appeared in April, 1944. It was published as a book, *Unshaken Friend*, in 1985, by Roberts Rinehart, Inc.

Andover, New Jersey
December 30, 1943
[PS]

Dear Malcolm,

. . . I think you should try for a year laying off the obits, just to see how it felt. If I were you, I wouldn't even (for quite a season) do any articles along the lines of trends, tendencies, newest tailoring for market or soul, etc. It's beginning to be said that Grace Conley[1] is at every wake.

Instead of grading papers all the time, why don't you get in on the attempt to line up all the new stuff there is to be lined up? I mean, quit worrying as to whether the other guy is writing important literature and start instead trying to write some yourself. And quit admiring so much the pilferers and the peddlers for being so successful in peddling their pilferings. The study of linguistic action is still in the stage of the maps that Columbus had. There are all sorts of vast possibilities to be worked out. And you go on bellyaching as though it were the end of the world. The end of the world comes for us only when we get shut up, wither by destiny or by the authorities. As for the rest, if any writer wants a renaissance, it's up to him to get busy and try to make one.

Down with revolution, up with resolution. (I rhetorically exaggerate.)

Nevertheless, sincerely,
K. B.

---

1. In their correspondence, Burke occasionally refers to Cowley by the name "Grace Conley."

255 East 72nd Street,
New York City
January 9, 1944
[PS]

Dear Kenneth:

What are you trying to do, shake up this bag of bones and rejoint the skeleton into a new man? There comes a time when vast changes are still possible, but you feel that they might be a mistake . . . I'll probably go on writing obituaries from time to time (let's hope not so frequently as this year) because people die and because I like writing about people, even if they're dead, though I like them better living. And I'll probably go on talking from time to time about literary trends, because I'm a literary historian and therefore can't get away from them. It's a weakness of mine, I know, that I write more easily when describing the past (often in an elegiac tone) than when I'm maxlernering about the future, but I also suspect that it might be wrong not to follow my bent, and follow it a lot more determinedly: what I'm working on in my mind is a history of American literature since 1918, in terms of what the writers were trying to do, under what handicaps and with what results . . .

. . .

This being Sunday, I'm writing from the *New Republic* office, but usually, these days, I'm at the New York Society Library on 79th Street, where the librarians are very nice, the books all at hand—you wander through the stacks—and where I have a room and a table for my typewriter, so that I write deathless prose (i.e., that will still be legible next week) wearing my overcoat and pounding my feet on the floor to keep from getting chilblains . . .

I hope you can make a trip into New York, or if not before February, I hope we'll still be here. Please put up with my vices of deafness and wandering attention, knowing that they don't indicate indifference or lack of affection, they're just the character that I have to put up with too, *Hier stehe ich.*

As ever,
Malcolm

Andover, New Jersey
March 6, 1944
[PS]

Dear Malcolm,

Was delighted indeed to receive the hone. Very many thanks, Henceforth, such is magic, I shall always be shaving in your name.

. . .

Anent Dostoevsky: am becoming interested in the possibility of matching "sin" and "crime." I.e., it seems to me that Dostoevsky still sees transgressions fundamentally in terms of "sin," whereas the modern thriller takes the more "enlightened" perspective, in terms of "crime." (Such a distinction cannot be absolute, of course, since there are all sorts of subterfuges whereby the religious motives can be discerned behind their secularized equivalents. But one can see the difference clearly in the attitude toward punishment, which Dostoevsky interprets as a necessary step in cleansing and redemption, and to be voluntarily sought by the criminal, as Dante shows us Arnaut Daniel being careful not to step beyond the borders of the purifying flames.) What I want to do now is to look over a couple of representative modern crime stories, for purposes of contrast and comparison. Do you have any to suggest? I believe that I have read exactly none.

. . .

Guess I'll go in and play the piano.

Play what on the piano? Well, it's like this: I have gone on now, for a couple of years, partly by theory, partly by trial and error, contriving some new sounds, with progressions from one to another, and so on to the next, etc. They are a kind of reversion to the days of my short stories, except that they aim at that sort of thing this time sans paroles. I gravitate between two styles, which I have labeled "faiblesses" and "sournoiseries." The sournoiseries threaten to become odd and sullen; the faiblesses threaten to become so sweet that I sometimes don't even write them down. But there are also some faiblesses sournoises and vice versa—and these I have eternized. So usually, for several hours a week, I pound away at these, thus indirectly repeating, "I am I," until I wonder who am I . . .

Sincerely,
K. B.

R.F.D. Gaylordsville,
Connecticut
March 9, 1944
[NL]

Dear Kenneth:

. . . About sin and retribution, crime and punishment:

Of course by the terminology you (and I) prefer to use, Dostoevsky's novel has the wrong title: it should be "Sin and Retribution." And the "sin" idea is uppermost in every good contemporary novel that ends with the execution or punishment of the hero. It wasn't Dostoevsky's idea, of course— it was Christian and, in the nineteenth century, it was restated by Hegel, who said (though I forget his exact words) that punishment was the *privilege* of the criminal. You ought to look that up.

And think about two novels of the last five years, one of which I know you read. *Native Son* begins with a crime that wasn't a sin, because it was explained sociologically by Bigger Thomas' background. And Wright hasn't very clear ideas about the philosophical meaning of what follows—yet, being a man of strong and rather Christian instincts, he has Bigger Thomas finally *accepting* his execution; it becomes a just retribution instead of a punishment. *Darkness at Noon* is a little clearer on this point. Rubashev (I think that's the hero's name) is an Old Bolshevik who is arrested on what seem to be ungrounded charges. He goes through a series of examinations, and is finally led to make a confession, through the logic of his own position—he sees that he had committed no overt crime, but that nevertheless he had *sinned*;

the crime was implicit in the sin, even if it never became explicit; and in the end he too accepts his punishment as a deserved retribution.

You wanted to know about detective stories. They are full of crimes, and the crimes are always punished; but I cannot remember a single detective novelist (except possibly Graham Greene, who is a Catholic) who introduces the idea of sin and retribution. Punishment is a convention of the detective novel, and therefore the criminal is caught and punished; "crime does not pay." But the reader is never or almost never made to feel that the criminal has sinned and that a moral drama has taken place . . . (If you want documentation, stop into a drugstore and buy detective stories in Pocket Books for a quarter. *Red Harvest*—Dashiell Hammett—and *Farewell, My Lovely*, by Raymond Chandler, are good ones that will keep you awake. Carter Dickson is a more orthodox writer, not extremely good.)

I close, with best wishes.

Malcolm

R.F.D. Gaylordsville,
Connecticut
February 16, 1945
[NL]

Dear Kenneth:

First it was a sprained ankle from skiing, then a worsening of my chronic indigestion, and now for three days it has been an attack of grippe. God how time drips away from me without anything accomplished except a few nicely written essays, based on too much reading because I keep putting off the writing of them. But this morning the old bean seems to be functioning in a slow way; and so I'm writing with the typewriter on a pillow on my knees. Your reprint from the *Sewanee Review*.[1] I had read the piece in the magazine also, but I read it again, with admiration. And certain critical remarks, z.b. Wouldn't "action" be better than "act" as the first of your five terms, considering that you are thinking in terms of drama and must often stop to explain that you don't mean one act in a play? And do you mean one act in a play, or the action of the play as a whole—what is an "act" in your scheme, outside of its not being a mere motion: is it an isolated deed, or a deed plus its antecedents and consequences? That trouble comes up again, in a different form, in your disposition of words like hodos, tao, yoga (which you call "acts") and attitude (which you assign to *agency*); and would come up with the term "pattern of action" or "behavior pattern," which you don't consider. I should think they would all go in the same bin—and what bin? That is, if one says of a man that he has the wrong attitude, one means that his past actions have revealed a pattern leading one to believe that his future actions will be undesirable, or that in theological terms he hasn't found the hodos, etc. In other words, there is something here undistributed among your terms.

What I really want to know is the application of your scheme, your grammar, beyond the interesting examples you have given—what is the terminus of the terminology?

·　　·　　·

I wish you didn't live at such a distance, multiplied by war. Has your teaching begun again, and if so what days are you in New York? For the record, I'll set down what I've been doing, which is always about twelve and a half percent of what I had hoped to do. Since the Hemingway piece last summer, a 5,000-word essay on Robert Frost, 12,000 words on Faulkner, over which I spent more than two months, and which finally I had to get published in chunks as if I had butchered a beef and was selling it off in roasts and steaks . . . 5,000 words on Henry James, printed in two installments in the *New Republic* . . . it all doesn't add up to much, does it, even if we throw in a couple of shorter pieces for the *New Republic*. I think I told you about resigning from the *New Republic* but keeping a drawing account of $20 a week for one 2,000-word article per month. My general plan is to write a book on American literature since 1910 for Doubleday, Doran before doing the book on American literature as a whole. But I don't get much forwarder even with this shorter project—I mean, there are great gaps in it, like O'Neill, Dreiser, Robinson, all the authors who don't greatly attract me . . .

Wish I could talk with you about these various authors and projects. Well, let me know when you're getting into New York, a very unsatisfactory way to see you . . .

As ever,
Malcolm

1. "Container and Thing Contained," published in the Winter 1945 issue of the *Sewanee Review*. This article later became the first chapter of Burke's book *A Grammar of Motives*.

Andover, New Jersey
March 12, 1945
[PS]

Dear Malcolm,

Anent your suggestion, "there is something here undistributed among your terms," right you are. My five terms are the undistributedest bastards you ever saw. When you see the whole venture, I think you'll realize that that's the point. Every one of them merges into the others.

Anent application: Am analyzing the nature of language, as I see it. The pentad is used as the way into the subject.

An "act" is "what somebody does." Every specific philosophy will have its own *particularized* definition of an act. If my term could define it thus particularly, I'd have to throw it over for a term still higher in generalization—and then your objections would apply to this higher term. But I can't have a term for *all* philosophies that will at the same time meet the requirements you would set up for that word as it appears in *one* philosophy. I use "act" sometimes, "action" sometimes; but couldn't very well get along without both, since philosophy uses them both so much, and the Grammar talks a lot about philosophy.

Every once in a while, have wished you were handy, and it were easy to arrange for a walk, of a day or two—on the spur of the moment. Have been working at quite a clip this winter. Instead of revising as I had planned, I have been practically rewriting the middle section—and have thus so far spun a planned 12,000 words into nearly 60,000, with about 10,000 or so still to go. That leaves me a section of about 15,000 still to write for my ending (the gist of two lectures I gave at Bennington last term, requiring no new thought but quite a lot of typewriter pounding). Then, every once in a while, I want to throw the whole business aside and just walk. But those are always spur-of-the-moment matters. By the time one could arrange something across three states, both the internal and external climate would be wholly different.

• • •

How I'd love a good loaf now. But am under the sign of the deadline. And already the kids have started sending me the essays they have written over the winter. Well, have resolved at least that, for a month or so, I'll do little more than read them passages out of my book, with some discush interspersed here and there to keep us all from suffering too much.

Best greetings,
K. B.

Andover, New Jersey
April 16, 1945
[PS]

Dear Malcolm,

Slapping the belongings together for week's trek to Vermont, would take time out to say that we look forward zestfully to arrival of Conleys.

Book was to be done on the fifteenth. Today finds me with about 3,000 words of grand finale still to add . . .

Never was a book more rewritten. It had been accepted. All that was required was a bit of stylistic touching up here and there. Actually, what I have done is to throw out big chunks of the accepted version and add bigger chunks of a totally new version. What we now have is a book which was written before I taught at Bennington, and has been rewritten entire after I tried it out on the dog.

We now have a position, and a method, illustrated with copious examples. But I suppose, despite the extent of the effort, we can look forward to the usual reception: i.e., my noble colleagues will pilfer bits here and there, and scrupulously give credit to dead Frenchmen or half-dead Harvard professors. A tiny pooplet of a succès d'estime, carefully bitched by dumps like the *Nation* and the Fartisan,[1] reviewed in the *New Republic* by somebody who talks about some other book, and omitted even from the annual list of a hundred that includes no less than three titles by Wilson.

For I got infloonce.

But nonetheless and however—one continues, one knows no better. One somehow believes, despite one's knowledge of the racket. One still dares hope. And there's still the woodpile to take it out on, when the stinkeroos get to work, and the reports start coming in.

Meanwhile, best greetings. Tennis court may be in shape by weekend, if weather is right this week. I say this just in case. Until Saturday.

Sincerely,
K. B.

1. Burke was in the habit of referring to the *Partisan Review* as the "Fartisan," owing to his many disagreements with its editors and those who contributed to it.

R.F.D. Gaylordsville,
Connecticut
July 14, 1945
[NL]

Dear K:

Bastille Day, and it may be that something is happening in Paris and elsewhere in the great world; but if so I wouldn't know it. Yet life does move along in the same fashion even without the *New York Times*; and I listen to the radio less than I used to; fifteen minutes of news per day is more than enough. Anyway the news that comes over the radio is never real news; I don't believe it until I have read the headlines. We are probably entering another era of private lives; in other words, we are entering an era of political reaction. The political pendulum doesn't swing from left to right, from radical to conservative; what happens is more like the expansion and contraction of a membrane, like the systole and diastole of the heart: when the membrane expands, when more people enter political life, we have a radical era; when the membrane and the governing class contract, when fewer people vote, attend meetings, write letters to the newspapers, we have a conservative era. In private life I have plenty to worry about. It occurs to me that if my letters to you were laid end to end they would form a chain of complaints and catastrophes. I'm ceasing those complaints as I grow older; I'm making peace with my own bad habits of work, my lapses, my inadequacies; so that if, for six months, I haven't accomplished anything (and I have accomplished a little) I accept it as a fact and that's that . . .

I've been turning my work on the literary history into magazine articles, as you must have noticed, and I finally reached the dizzy summit of 15 cents a word for a book review (from *Time*); but I think this easy-money era for critics is drawing to a close. You should get in on it while there is still time—do a little selling. I ran into Mrs. Slochower[1] at the dentist's and she said that as matters now stand you hadn't definitely resigned from Bennington, but were taking the year off, with the final decision to be made afterward. That sounds reasonable. When is your book coming out? Finishing a book is always a strain on you—on me too, but I don't usually finish them. Write and let me know how you are—and love to all of you.

As ever,
Malcolm

1. Wife of the psychoanalyst and critic, Harry Slochower.

Andover, New Jersey
August 9, 1945
[PS]

Dear Malcolm,

Your letter reached me during the turmoil of the closing days at Bennington, which does spin then. And only now I am gradually beginning to get ready for the Next Phase (though not quite ready, as I am still undecided whether to plunge into the Rhetoric book in all thoroughness, or first to do an unexpected quickie, a treatise on Education, mixing the ideas of the last two years with the personalities of the last two years (the sort of combination that has heretofore been much more your meat than mine).

· · ·

Has the recent inauguration of the new Power Age disgusted you as much as it has me? The era of the Mad Scientist of the B movie now seems with us in a big way. There seems now no logical thing to do but go on tinkering with this damned thing until they have blown up the whole damned world.[1] They may as well blow it up in one big chunk and be done with it. For the fantasies of power (as per money and technology) are now given a whole new vigor in their appeal to the imagination—and so the life of dessication must move to its finish, and all the better if it all vanishes with one big bang. I piously love the world of the animal appetites and the natural affections. I have really learned to thank God for it. And the damned ingratitude of human greed, as reduced to terms of money and scientific power, is gradually implementing such motives as make life not worth the living . . .

Well, whence poppeth up all this? I am grouchy these days. I want to swat something, and I'd rather it weren't myself. But I had no notion that I'd of a sudden swing into a tirade. The irony seems to be that, whereas my study of human motives was begun with the idea of helping me to make my peace with life, every once in a while I surprise myself by a sudden rage at human stupidity. Our modern civilization looks more and more as though it were designed by some cunning efficiency expert in hell who had found a way of introducing a strategic embarrassment at each articulation. I may end up where I began: with Flaubert . . .

Sincerely,
K. B.

1. The second atomic bomb had been dropped that day on Nagasaki.

R.F.D. Gaylordsville,
Connecticut
August 24, 1945
[NL]

Dear Kenneth:

It's my birthday and a slow cold rain is falling and in general it's a good day to write a letter, except that I haven't anything much to say. The atom bomb. We can't keep it out of our minds. It gets worse as time goes on and we learn more about its effects. The Japanese say, of course they may be lying, as today's radio announcer piously suggests, but then again they may be telling the truth, and they say that people in the Hiroshima area continue to die from radioactivity—they lose their red corpuscles and peg out—and the Japanese say they can't afford to send their doctors to Hiroshima for fear of losing them too—and they say that people just a little burned by the bomb found the burns growing worse as time passed, and pegged out, so that the death toll (what a horrible phrase) was 30,000 in the first week and 30,000 more the second week—and you get a new picture of the way radioactivity will wipe out our world, not in a good healthy smash, as you pictured it, with a new sun appearing in this constellation, but rather in a slow leukemia, the world simply made uninhabitable. Some people will certainly get so frightened by this picture that they'll go off into the jungle or the mountains and live by raising roots, in the hope that when the next war comes it won't be worth while wiping them out. Ninety-nine people out of a hundred will want never to use the atom bomb again, but there's always one bad apple in the barrel, always one mad scientist or mad dictator, and in the long run I don't see much hope—but in the short run we're living in the great imperial republic of the twentieth century, we'll be rich, we'll all have three automobiles, we'll have to have them, by law, whether or not we want to sleep with Mae West, we'll have to sleep with her, we'll have to eat too much and then take expensive cures to be slenderized, we'll have to eat expensively denatured food expensively renatured with expensive vitamins, we'll have to have a good time, by God, so we might as well grit our teeth and eat, drink, and be expensively merry, for tomorrow we'll be blown sky high.

·　　·　　·

I'm more disturbed by certain moral qualities in the American world at present than by the triumph of capitalism. I mean the sudden ending of Lend-Lease, though it means breaking up the machinery by which Europe has been supplied with a little food, and I mean the curt words with which Truman dismissed the French newspapermen. There are a lot of other signs like that, all pointing to the want of sympathy and the want of imagination that are coming to distinguish this country. But we had goddamn well better have sympathy and imagination, for now we're on the top of the heap and all the envy of an envious world is going to be directed toward us—and the world will whoop when the first atom bomb falls on New York. Ah, we have triumphed, we have given the Germans and the Japanese lessons in cold-blooded, abstract, self-righteous cruelty, in the names of freedom and democracy. But people who triumph in this world don't last long . . .

And me, as ever,
Malcolm

Andover, New Jersey
October 13, 1945
[PS]

Dear Malcolm,

. . . Have just about cleaned up the last odds and ends of work to do with the *Grammar*. So I think I shall start writing next week on the Rhetoric. If things go as planned, we shall probably linger on here until the beginning of December, and then wend south.

Booksellers show an encouraging advance interest in the *Grammar*. What they seem to like most about it is, surprisingly, that it is part of a three-volume enterprise. I guess trilogies appeal to their instinct of workmanship as booksellers . . . The middle section, analyzing philosophies as languages, is what the semantics gents have been trying to do, without exception bunglingly (since their terms were too inaccurate and inapposite). The last section, On Dialectic, comes just at a time when all the criticasters and horseasters had decided to dismiss the word with a shrug (without having the slightest idea what they are dismissing, beyond the fact that it had a smell of Marxism about it—and this made about as much sense as dismissing words in general because Marx also used words). The first section introduces the five key terms and puts them through their paces as "Ways of Place-ment." And the appendix has four essays: the Four Tropes, the Keats Ode, the Marianne Moore, and the semi-tiff with the Chicago Neo-Aristotelians. There are three tough places: on theories of the Creation, on Spinoza, on Kant. And for the first of these, I put a footnote authorizing harried reader to skip it if he must.

And I believe I do manage successfully the problem of making this a wholly self-sustaining book while at the same time showing how it leads into the other two. All told, over five hundred octavo pages (our ultimate trick being, I guess, that we equate linguistic *appreciation* with linguistic *skepticism*, or if you will, treat both as species of linguistic *quizzicality*).

On the side, I have been mowing the fields about the house, mowing them with a possibly psychotic fervor. I have driven back the wilderness quite a ways, and brought out hidden contours. At one point, I can stand on the edge of the woods above the house, and look across a perfectly cleared surface down to the barn, and through it when the doors before and behind are open. My muscles are firm, though I sometimes feel that I may be splitting my heart (and sometimes even vaguely wonder if that's what I'm trying to do).

The Rhetoric should be the easiest volume of the three to write. My main problem is to keep the book from disintegrating into particular cases (so that it becomes in effect a disguised way of saying repeatedly: "another instance of this is . . . and still another instance is . . . " etc.).[1] I want it to be rather a philosophizing on rhetoric (as the main slant), though the particular instances should be there in profusion.

But the postman is due. How go all things with you, and your family?

Sincerely,
K. B.

1. Burke's ellipses.

R.F.D. Gaylordsville,
Connecticut
November 22, 1945
[NL]

Dear Kenneth:

Beware, beware of your sacroiliac (rhymes with necrophiliac). You've been lifting heavy object with not a single little rupture—then suddenly you bend farther to pick up a penny or a nut or something, and crack, you're laid up in bed for a week with what used to be called a sprained back. What you don't realize is that it's practically incurable. Some people do cure it, by going into a canvas corset right away and staying in said corset for five or six months, but most people get out of bed after the week and go back to digging and lifting, and then, crack again, and this time it's really painful, and this time you realize that you won't ever again be able to touch your toes with your fingers without bending your knees, and you'll be lucky if you can touch your toes at all. Dying is a process of getting farther and farther away from your toes. Anyway I've had this sacroiliac trouble, I've cracked it twice, and the second time was so damned painful that I don't want to ever crack it again. I went down to Lawrenceville, N.J., to give a speech to the boys, and found that four out of five men in the room with me had sacroiliac trouble; and the headmaster, who put me up for the night, had it so bad that he was all prepared to help me with a bed board and an electric heating pad.

·   ·   ·

Infirmities of age: how are they with you? I am now (1) deaf, (2) so farsighted that I can't read ordinary print without glasses, unless I hold the book at arm's length, and even then it blurs; (3) stiff in the back. Not yet impotent, but we're waiting for that.

·   ·   ·

. . . Tomorrow I go back to work on Faulkner;[1] that job will be finished in a couple of weeks; the Aragon is coming out November 28;[2] then, before working on my own book, I have to write a couple of chapters for the

Literary History of the U.S., the symposium. No more now. Except this. Will you ask the publisher to send me, here, not at the *New Republic*, a copy of the *Grammar*—I'll do something about it, either in the *New Republic* or elsewhere. And send me your Florida address before you start traveling.

As ever,
Malcolm

1. Cowley was working on the Viking Portable edition of the works of William Faulkner, which was published in 1946.

2. "Aragon: A Little Anthology," which contained translations by Cowley and others of some of the poems of Louis Aragon, appeared in the Autumn issue of *Sewanee Review*.

Andover, New Jersey
November 25, 1945
[PS]

Dear Malcolm,

Ailments? It has been many years now since I proved myself able to out-ail anybody twice my age. I got a head start at that sort of thing, when at the age of three I broke my neck. As for my sacred ilion, I don't know. But I do know that I have been hectored, on the sitting end of my spine, ever since an occasion in Pittsburgh when, walking with you and Jim, I jumped from a height to a manure pile that happened to be frozen, so that my feet shot from beneath me, and my can went smack against the frozen pinnacle. Sometimes I must squirm for a couple of days, until something snaps in a certain way—and then all is peaceful for a while.

· · ·

All my life I have thought of death. But when I was young, I thought of it as something that came from without, like an attack, or a blow. In recent years, however, it has gradually come to be something within, not so much a disease, or even an ailment, but a state of mind. Or even an extension of certain aspects of language. That is, one gradually comes more to realize that certain ways of developing into the future were, by the same token, ways of dying to the past. So one begins to think of new ways of living—by going back to gather up all the loose ends of experience that one did not pay enough attention to. Is one then beginning simply to reminisce? I have often been chagrined to discover that I am humming old popular songs that I had not thought of since I was a kid.

· · ·

Your 17-hour stretch at writing is far beyond me. Not only would I be floppy-hearted, but also I'd be somewhat crazy. I can go all day, all night, and all the next day, so long as the verbalization is *directed outward* (i.e., at school, an all-night party, rushing home just in time for a bath, sans breakfast, before my two-hour lecture, and then conferences, etc. for the rest of the day), but I can stand only a few hours when the verbalization is by "procession within" . . . Also, I have begun to fear that moment when the writing moves to another room. For though not many readers are susceptible to my magic, *I* am—and the surrealist ideal of writing that writes itself works dismally with me. Instead of aiming at that stage now, as soon as I feel it getting a hold on me, I knock off for the day. I want *me* to do the writing, not *it* to do the writing . . .

Sincerely,
K. B.

R.F.D. Gaylordsville,
Connecticut
March 13, 1946
[NL]

Dear Kenneth:

Today I have to review E. Wilson's new book,[1] and because he's dealing with a society in which the hero feels more and more to have fallen into a groove from which he doesn't realize that he has to emerge by some violent change—"madness, travel, drugs, the Faith, death by one's own hand"— I went back to read, with great admiration, the final chapter of *Towards a Better Life*, where you say it much better, where you face alternatives that Wilson doesn't quite ever see. And I came back to an idea I have mentioned to you several times and want to mention again—why don't you get together the lyric passages in your own writing, not only all the poems, but also the passages like the end of TABL and of "Prince Llan" that are essentially lyric cries? You could get that book published easily, no problem, and it would give a different impression of your work than the present Trivium, I mean a broader impression, because your ideas in the *Grammar*, for example, are there in germ, and readers would begin to see how you had fleshed the ideas, and how they came from personal experience, not from the void.

I'm working on Whitman, the old cocksucker. Very strange the amalgam he made between cocksucking and democracy. Meanwhile the sun shines, the frost gets out of the ground, and I have a hotbed now where I'm trying to start plants for the garden. And I have ordered (did I tell you?) an expensive garden tractor, supposed to do everything, so that instead of working to swing a hoe, you work to tighten a bolt or start a balky motor. Can't imagine you buying such, although it would greatly simplify your lawn problem, which, I suppose, you don't want simplified. Finally the moral lesson that stands out of the *Grammar* is, Don't use machinery!

'Zever,
Malcolm

1. Cowley's review of Edmund Wilson's *Memoirs of Hecate County* appeared in the March 25 edition of the *New Republic*.

Andover, New Jersey
April 3, 1946
[PS]

Dear Malcolm,

. . . Don't know what to say concerning your suggestion about excerpts, etc. You turn my plans around. I had always said that, by the time I got through with my critical writings, people would see what I was doing in T.B.L. You now seem to suggest that excerpts from T.B.L. might help them to see what I am doing now. I intend showing your letter to Munson, on the chance that it might set up a vibration in his musically responsive soul; but I haven't seen him since receiving the letter . . .

Anent Whitman as a coxker: I think the same equation flickers around the edges of Read's[1] anarchism. In sum: the democrats' father-rejection via killing of the king means that they all piss in the same pot (hence the invitation for brother-solidarity to become homosex). As for your remarks on Calamus in NR[2] (incidentally quite readable indeed, they are): I remember once a Weehawken hokku of mine which ran: "Quick! Seize your pen! A pretty girl is passing." And Wilkinson thought I had consciously been punning on "pen," which in Latin, he said, meant also the membrum virile. I realize now that he referred to L. *penis*; but I always thought he referred to L. *calamus*. My Harper's gives no such meaning for calamus, however; but it does list reed pen. So, if you ever happen to run across a passage where Whitman also explicitly recognizes pen as one of the meanings, do depose.

• • •

First draft of the *Rhetoric* goes bumping along. Instead of writing it from start to finish, I seem to be writing it from the middle out. Each day I drive in more wedges that push the two ends farther apart. And there's just the possibility that I may, this time, be lambasted for being too easy to read. The book is as anecdotal as T.B.L., except that this time the anecdotes are strung along an idea instead of a story. The clothesline method. Except that there is a shortage of clothespins, so that you have to hang several items at each spot along the line. The anecdotes treat everything as of equal importance: what two diplomats solemnly announce at an International Conference is valued no higher than something that Butchie and Michael say at the sand pile. I gave as the formula, "benevolently caustic," but out of some correspondence with Knickerbocker[3] I have found a more tonal way of expressing the same design: "ironically ironic."

Why not drop around this spring? Before the battles with nature begin. (Yesterday I did my first lawn-mowing.)

Meanwhile, back to the grind.

Sincerely,
K. B.

1. Probably Herbert Read, whose book *Art and Society* Burke reviewed in 1937 for the *New Republic*. In *A Grammar of Motives*, Burke discusses Read's *Poetry and Anarchism* (pages 344–349).

2. "Walt Whitman: The Miracle," a reevaluation of *Leaves of Grass* published in the March 18 issue of the *New Republic*.

3. William S. Knickerbocker, English professor and critic, editor of *The Sewanee Review*, 1926 to 1942. He wrote a favorable review of *The Philosophy of Literary Form* in 1941.

April 5, 1946
[NL]

Dear Kenneth:

. . . About Whitman's *Calamus*:—He didn't know Latin, had only six years of public schooling, though later he taught himself a little French. So to him the word had only the American meaning of "sweet flag" (which is not a reed), and he built his emblem or token or symbol on the root, not the leaves, or the stem. One of my theories about American literature is that Americans turn naturally ("instinctively") to symbolism. Why, I don't know— I note the great influence of Swedenborg here, but I think that influence is more the manifestation of an already existing tendency than it is the cause of the tendency. Do Puritans naturally search for inner meanings (since the tendency seems to be connected with Puritanism)? As compensation for a bare external life? Anyhow, it is a fact that American realists or naturalists, when they are good, keep lapsing instinctively into symbolism—yes, even Dreiser. Emerson's *Essays*, especially "The Poet," would seem to be indicated as reading for you, in connection with the *Rhetoric*.

Muriel and I would like very much to see you. Whether we can get down to Andover during the Easter vacation is a real question . . . Also there's the thought that you and Libby haven't been in these parts for years. Couldn't we tempt you up here with your whole family, around Easter time, with a promise of ping pong, talks, walks, and drinks?

> More later,
> Malcolm

> R.F.D. Gaylordsville,
> Connecticut
> April 1, 1947
> [NL]

Dear Kenneth:

. . . I want to ask a question about what's his name, the six-foot poet from Bennington and Penn State[1] (God, I can't remember names after ten o'clock in the evening), but now he wants to go to Yaddo. Tell me, should I recommend him? I would on the basis of his work, but he seemed so nervous the last time I saw him and I wonder how he'd bear up in that hothouse atmosphere of geniuses eating at the same table. I sent them a guy last year who made all sorts of trouble by sleeping with Mrs. Ames' secretary, then jilting her, and I don't want to make trouble for her again.

I'm going downstairs now to listen to the radio and take one more step toward nervous prostration. These are wonderful days for a semanticist who doesn't give a damn whether the world is going to be blown up, so long as he can point out the techniques of propaganda. All the old techniques are being shamelessly employed, day after day, and I hope you've quit reading the *Times*—the *Herald Tribune* is bad too, but not that bad. For me, the worst is the feeling of helplessness in a crisis—I can't do a thing, can't even find a magazine that would publish what I think. Wallace's (Mike Straight's) *New Republic*[2] is trying to do a job, but it's not my paper any more.

> As ever,
> Malcolm

1. Theodore Roethke.
2. Henry A. Wallace, editor, and Michael Straight, publisher.

> Andover, New Jersey
> April 14, 1947
> [PS]

Dear Malcolm,

I think Roethke will be as law-abiding as the next guy. I think he's looking for a hole in the ground to crawl into for a while. He's one of the kind that would do best in a studio off by himself. As he does his writing in the odd hours of the night (yet not noisily, as I know, having lived in the same cottage with him for a couple of years, and being awakened each time a cat would tread too loudly in the next valley).

If you have any doubts about him, what I'd suggest is this: whatever time you plan to recommend him for, you tell him at first that you can only positively guaranty half that time, but you hope to make it longer, and can do so if other plans turn out as intended, etc. This would put him in the most apologetic mood imaginable, and he'd go cringing about like a wounded bear, and he'd be self-effacement itself, and would produce produce produce.

As for his morality: I'm sure he'd be no less circumspect and austere than the Authorities themselves.

I continue to be in the thick of things for the *Rhetoric*. The new twists I have done to the neo-substantive business are my pride . . .

. . . [T]he neo-substantive racket: the study of all the roundabout *narrative* ways in which language, without the speaker intentionally doing so, or even knowing what I mean by so doing, finds equivalents for the philosophic terminologies of essence. (How does a primitive tribe, for instance, work out a vocabulary of essence, when such vocabularies in the formal, philosophic sense are not found until a society reaches a very sophisticated stage? It is all part of my continuing battle against positivism . . . Positivists, in the formal sense, are not very ubiquitous enemies. But positivism, in the half-assed sense, is all about us, and thus is properly one of my major concerns.

For a while I had hoped that my *Rhetoric* would be a fairly easy book to read. And much of it will be, as compared with the *Grammar*. But alas! there'll be much that is quite tough, too. So once more I've abandoned my hopes of writing a book that would both be written just as I want to write it and fairly popular. I was particularly anxious to wangle a maximum of readers for the *Rhetoric*, because it bears upon the immediate fallacies of politics, etc. But, hell, it takes all sorts of people to make a world. And I guess what I am most interested in doing is to write a trilogy into which one could immerse himself, in case there should ever be a time again in which people wanted to immerse themselves in protracted contemplation generally and in the protracted contemplation of the Logos particularly. So, Deo volente, I'll go on trying merely to round it all out as structurally as possible. And if there is anything in it that could, if played up by itself, be more popular, it will get about. No matter how "obscure" one may be, and how few readers he may have, he need never lack "collaborators" in this sense: the pedlars, the plagiarists, etc. And there are even signs that a certain modicum of credit will come our way—though I have studied enough

Rhetoric now to take it for granted that an imbecile, with favors to dispense, will get credit for a two-page squib without one jot of originality in it, but the most momentous book imaginable, written by someone without favors to dispense, could hope at most to be pilfered, sans mention. (Another device I have noted is this: Preen would pilfer from Prone; he pilfers a really good thing, and says nothing; then, to make amends, he scrupulously gives Prone credit for something trivial.) . . .

Sincerely,
K. B.

Andover, New Jersey
April 26, 1947
[PS]

Dear Malcolm,
Again back from the wars.

·   ·   ·

. . . The class having done rhetorical analyses of plays, each of the fifteen members having chosen a different play, we are now considering these one by one, and attempting to work out a set of overall critical categories for the lot. (The instructions had been merely that the play should be considered as a recipe for affecting an audience.) This last enterprise just happened by itself. These papers were written last term, and several students asked to have them discussed in class. So we began—and it immediately became apparent that the enterprise would be formless, a mere turning from one thing to another, unless we started a new project, in looking for a set of terms sufficiently generalized to encompass the whole batch. And lo! Papa discovers that, of a sudden, he has thus been driven by his class into discovering exactly what he needed for this section of his book, the treatment of plays from the rhetorical point of view. I have, of course, written on this subject before, as with my analysis of *Julius Caesar*[1] from the rhetorical point of view, and the "Lexicon" in *Counter-Statement*. But I never attempted a set of purely "Aristotelian" categories. But we seem to be working them out now: hence, good criticism, for we're doing close textual analysis, but along with it we are working with a more generalized vocabulary—or better, we are building up a more generalized vocabulary.

The explication-du-texte racket in itself, I have discovered, is a little better than what we, at Peabody, used to call "bulling." It is hardly more than a burlesque of the American craze for empiricist, positivistic "factualism." But if you start putting a lot of such explications together, each written by a different person on a different text, yet all aiming at the same thing (the analysis of works from a particular point of view) then you inevitably come upon the need for a generic vocabulary that will prevail above or beneath this jumble of particulars. And lo! you've got good criticism. For you've kept your eye on the text at every point, you have constantly observed, yet at the same time you have transcended the particulars through your overall vocabulary. And pedagogically, it's in many ways more instructive to be working *toward* such a vocabulary, with the students participating in the search, than it is to have a pedagogy already worked out, and offered to them at the start. In this latter case, they may never quite know what they have, through not having quite earned it. Thus, with my brave Five Terms. It took me about thirty years of fumbling to arrive at them. For me they are like getting to a cleared field after stumbling through a thicket. So I offer them in triumph; but the class just takes them for granted, and lets the cleared field go back to brush.

· · ·

But the battle of the grass has begun. I must to the front.

Sincerely,
K. B.

1. Burke is referring to his essay "Antony in Behalf of the Play," which appeared in the Autumn 1935 issue of the *Southern Review*.

December 3, 1947
[NL]

Dear Kenneth:

. . . One change in the life here: I bought a secondhand piano, an upright, big and ugly and not really loud enough to satisfy my taste for noise. It stands in the cellar, and thither I retire at the hours when I would usually be working outside or taking a nap. I've returned to adolescence and Beethoven, even to Chopin waltzes, and after a month I play as well, which means as badly, as I ever did. I've been actually working on the last movement of the "Moonlight" but there are still passages of it I play like one of Uncle Joe Giddings' second-year pupils. (Allen Tate went back to his violin—is it something in our autumnal range of life?)

Otherwise working on Hawthorne. He's harder to take hold of than Whitman, being smoother and having a vice he could keep secret. But he said at the end of *The Scarlet Letter*, "Be true! Be true! Show freely to the world, if not your worst, yet some trait whereby the worst may be inferred!" So the trait that keeps recurring in his work is the looking at reflections—

you know about that. But did you note a couple of juxtapositions? One of his heroes, David Swan, looks into a spring and instead of his own face sees that of a beautiful girl (Hawthorne himself was beautiful, with eyelashes, as one of his female relatives said, "half a mile long and curling up at the tips"). And this?—the other recurrent image, outside the mirror or mirrorlike water, is the snake. And he mentions mirrorlike brooks that glide "like snakes"; and in "The Bosom Serpent" the snake when finally dislodged from the hero's breast—by his wife—glides away into the fountain. And this?—that in the wonderful "Young Goodman Brown" and in "The Bosom Serpent" the hero accuses everyone else of having his own evil, of being sold to Satan. Otherwise one notes precipices from which people jump or are pushed; fires that burn in their bosoms or into which they cast themselves; old houses that are torn down little by little and consumed in the kitchen fireplace. And the search for a father that becomes a search for something nonexistent or evil, as in "My Kinsman, Major Molineux."

I'm getting a free trip to Havana, for *Life*, to do a piece on Hemingway, and decided to take the family along. That will be March 1–15, probably. Would it be possible for us to stop off and say hello to you at Melbourne [Florida] on the return, if things worked out so that we could travel that way?

As ever,
Malcolm

Melbourne Beach,
Florida
December 12, 1947
[PS]

Dear Malcolm,

Glad to hear from you. And it would be splongdeed if you all could arrange to stop over here. There are all sorts of extra couches, lounges, settees, divans, and sofas in this place, though a dearth of bedding and rooms. But we could decide all those matters when you got here, and looked things over . . .

So far, the sea has been so viable, we have not once used the sulphur pool. Every day has been sunny and mild. (Tomorrow, it seems, will be cloudy, perhaps even not swim-worthy.) I have resumed my writing again, so my ailments are returning—but for the first week or ten days, I lived in such Perfect Relaxation that I can go for years on the mere memory of it. I had come to fear that such a mood was no longer physiologically or psychologically possible. I slept like a brute. I let the sea do everything—I merely gave to it. I had one of those attacks of sheer appetite (though milder, milder) I used to have at times in adolescence. Life on the seashore is so vital, because all one does is bask in the sun, roll on the waves, and pick up dead things. Standing on the seashore, one is on the peak of a very high mountain. Scoop out the water, and the depths would make you dizzy. Or is the sea a jungle? I can shiver at the thought of the times when my ancestors had no place to hide, when one was pursued, not by inflation, but by jaws. As for the dead things, or the dying things: they often have dirty Surrealist shapes.

· · ·

Internationally, after becoming almost fantastically disturbed, I suddenly shifted to a kind of entre-deux-guerres attitude, carping the diem where it listeth. And I have told myself that the Russians, in the last analysis, will be shrewd enough to stop short of the point at which our War Party can start the Ultimate Holocaust. For though, the more I study the imagery of late capitalism, the more I believe there is a positive *demand* for universal suicide bubbling at the bottom of it, I think the cult of machinery in Russia is still at a stage corresponding to the popular attitude toward the Crystal Palace in Victorian England. And whatever may come of this optimism eventually, for the time being it at least removes the *psychotic* impulses toward war. The Russians don't want to be punished, they want to succeed. But we, rotten with the guilt of two profiteer-making wars, plus the gradual crystallizing of social status (hence, the guilt that comes of trying to make inequality *permanent*), probably have just enough sense of justice to demand that we be destroyed (while being uncritical enough to think that we are trying to *save* something). Can the Rooshians be shrewd enough to deflect all this? . . .

Sincerely,
K. B.

R.F.D. Gaylordsville,
Connecticut
February 1, 1948
[NL]

Dear Kenneth:

Two days ago I went to the *Life* offices, which are as hard to get into as the Pentagon, and collected our tickets for Havana, about $360 worth. They made me feel very rich, even if my bank account was at the moment overdrawn, not to mention an outstanding note for the new car. We take the plane from Newark on Sunday morning, February 29, arrive in Havana that afternoon, leave for Key West the following Sunday—and I think we can get to Melbourne Beach by train some time on Tuesday evening, Wednesday at the latest . . .

Of course Hemingway, with his suicidal instincts, might overturn his car (he's done that about eight times, but his son reports he's driving slower now) or otherwise blow his top so that the whole trip would be canceled or delayed. We have to expect those things. But if everything goes according to schedule, those are the dates we'll be keeping . . .

. . . I keep fussing over Hawthorne, who's pretty interesting in his fishlike way, and over the problem of writing about what you call his reflexiveness without saying that he jerked off and felt very sinful about it—why, probably he didn't jerk off more than anyone else, but he had a sharper conscience, so that he thought he was attending witches' conventicles like Young Goodman Brown and committing the Unpardonable Sin like Ethan Brand. Then when he married and became normal he also became less interesting. Well, by the time I see you I hope my Hawthorne work will be finished, introduction and all—everything else is in the printer's hands . . .

As ever,
Malcolm

R.F.D. Gaylordsville,
Connecticut
February 14, 1948
[PS]

Dear Kenneth:

Long delay in answering your letter, in spite of the need for haste—but E. Hemingway has kept me hanging by my thumbs; not a word from him since he started back to Havana. Well, I've simply got to take for granted that everything is all right and go ahead with the arrangements . . .

. . . I work on Hawthorne—find more of his deliciously narcissistic figures of speech and symbols. Mirror equals fountain or pool or brook; snakes live in pool ("The Bosom Serpent"); brook winds like serpent; once Mr. Bullfrog thinks of marrying his own image in the mirror. Through self-absorption the outside world grows unreal (many passages on this point) and the heart itself grows chill, sluggish, torpid—he abounds in such adjectives. His wife ("The Birthmark") has a birthmark on her face in the shape of a little hand! My guess is that Hawthorne masturbated much less than the average college-level male interviewed for the Kinsey Report; he simply brooded more over the fact, had a sharper conscience, felt himself more utterly damned. Then he became *real* through marriage and tried to build himself a new factual life on the crust he formed above his quagmire—that failed him because he buried his Demon, finally. I shouldn't spend so much time on this bedroom peeping. The more important fact is that Hawthorne was really the first artist in American fiction—much more conscious of his own aims than Poe, who chiefly made a parade of consciousness.

As ever,
Malcolm

R.F.D. Gaylordsville,
Connecticut
August 16, 1948
[NL]

Dear Kenneth:

. . . News here? Oh, plenty of it, but not very consequential . . . After four years of very easy living, during which I have paid off debts but saved nothing, living is already beginning to be harder, with the inflation—and by next May, when I get my last check from Mrs. Mellon's estate,[1] it is going to be hard, hard. I've run into that trouble you had when working for Rockefeller—I work ten times as long at every job as the job in itself justifies, and therefore finish very little. Just now it's Hemingway, and as *preparation* for writing the piece in *Life* I have been writing a biography of Ernest from the cradle, not quite to the grave, and working up a considerable admiration for the Great Man—as I told you, he pays the price for greatness, as if he went up to the cashier's desk after making his purchase; he pays the price by setting up a code for himself and living up to it, and by being extraordinarily attentive to everyone around him so that they have to be attentive and admiring in return, just so that each of them can keep his self-respect. The interesting thing I discovered that he won't talk about is that he was a lonely and awkward boy bullied by his schoolmates, who were richer, better at sports, better liked by the girls. I think he's been revenging himself on his schoolmates for the last thirty-five years. He overcompensates—he started out by boasting and being a little bit of a four-flusher; now he does his boasting by indirection, and if you call his four-flush you find it's a straight flush.

. . . And what else? *The Portable Hawthorne* came out and hasn't been reviewed except in "out-of-town cities," as Muriel calls them. I'll send you a prescribed copy next week when I get back. The Whitman is coming out very soon . . . It's funny, I wrote a piece on Hawthorne for *Sewanee Review* and used the blunt word "masturbation" and *Sewanee* insisted on having the word changed—but by that time I didn't care so much, because I had made the point for anyone who wanted to read carefully.

Love and twitches,
Malcolm

1. In 1943 Cowley received a five-year grant from Mary Mellon to work on American literature. It paid $5,550 per year.

Andover, New Jersey
September 14, 1948
[PS]

Dear Malcolm,

Home this week, on furlough from the wars. Was delighted to find the Hawthorne volume. Many thanks indeed. I shall read it through, fairly soon, and shall write you about it. Glancing over the excerpts from the notebooks, I seemed to hear the tonalities of the last chapter in my own TBL. I guess Hawthorne and I were brothers in the fine art of mirror-writing. Am thinking that this might be a good book for me to use in the second term of my class. Looks as though Hawthorne would be as clear as Emerson and Henry Adams, for use in charting "equations." More anon.

A few months ago, I feared I was in for a dreadful siege of gloom. But though there is something wrong (some kind of catch in my breathing, a form I fear of pumpitis), and though I find new automatisms creeping up on me (the family complains that I go on muttering under my breath after I have finished saying something, though every time they caught me at it I found I was humming), and though right in the midst of things I sometimes feel as if I had returned from the dead (a mood that comes over me at school, where so many I knew have departed, and thus give me the sense of having departed, since reality for those there now has no such quality in it, and those there now obviously set the tone for reality there now)— well, I'm making myself at home in such—I too, though with connotations other than Hemingway's, call myself "papa." Though certain competent bureaucrats with whom I come into contact make me feel like a child, the young make me feel very old, and I salute them, but as a moriturus [sic]. (Always the same principle: if one can only be old soon enough, and if one can only say goodbye long enough, if one can go on ailing and ailing, he might live to be ninety. I'm not sure that I would vote for living to be ninety. But at least one must live *in that direction*) . . .

Sincerely,
K. B.

R.F.D. Gaylordsville,
Connecticut
December 9, 1948
[NL]

Dear Kenneth:

Here I am faced with the problem of writing a piece on Myths in American Literature and the piece refuses to write itself and so I'm thinking aloud in a letter as if I were walking east along Ellsworth Avenue after the library had closed and telling you what I was vaguely planning to do.

Myths, I want to say, are permanent archetypes of human character and experience. Myths are the wise Ulysses, the dutiful Aeneas (is that the best reading for *pius?*), the courtly Lancelot and—leaping over a few centuries—Daniel Boone in the forest, Huckleberry Finn on the river, and Buffalo Bill on the prairies. Myths provide a pattern for our emotions; they are variously shaped windows through which we look at the world.

A country without myths is a country naked of human associations in which we are intruders, not residents. A central concern of American writers from the very beginning has been to create or give a final form to myths that would make this new country our home. Many of them (Irving, Hawthorne, Poe) started by writing ghost stories. They were acting on the sound instinct that a house has to be a little haunted before we can feel at home in it.

In older countries the myths had a basis in folklore; they were repeated time after time at the fireside on winter evenings before they were copied into manuscripts. But this country was the first to be settled by men and women who were, in the majority, literate, so that they worked with printed words from the beginning. Oral traditions have played a great part in our myths, but they were quickly seized upon by professional writers, so that a figure like Paul Bunyan, for example, is one-tenth an invention of the lumbermen and nine-tenths a literary elaboration . . . And when one thinks of the heroes of the American myth, it seems to me that more of them—Leatherstocking, Evangeline, Captain Ahab, Huck Finn, the Connecticut Yankee, Babbitt, Daisy Miller, and the Hemingway hero among others—come from literature than come from history (Washington, Boone, Crockett, Lincoln) or from folklore heroes who have the dust of scholarship. Skipper Ireson (literature) is vivid where Captain Stormalong (folklore) seems academic.

Whitman was writing about the importance of myths in "Democratic Vistas." He said, "The central point in any nation, and that whence it is itself really sway'd the most, and when it sways others, is its national literature, especially its archetypal poems . . . Few are aware how the great literature penetrates all, gives hue to all, shapes aggregates and individuals, and, after subtle ways, the irresistible power, constructs, sustains, demolishes at will."—"The literature, songs, esthetics, &c., of a country are of importance principally because they furnish the materials and suggestions of personality for the women and men of that country and enforce them in a thousand effective ways."—"All else in the contributions of a nation or age . . . remains crude . . . until vitalized by national, original archetypes in literature. They only put the nation in form, finally tell anything—prove, complete anything—perpetuate anything." And Whitman wrote the essay, not only to justify his own career, but to summon other "orbic bards, with unconditional, uncompromising sway," to create new myths for the nation.

I have a lot to say on the subject, and some fears that I might fall into nationalistic hurrah. I don't think most people realize how consciously our nineteenth-century writers set about the task of creating or transcribing American myths. They had found what they called romance in Europe and wanted to transport it to the American scene, so that it too would "serve to make our country dearer and more interesting to us," as Hawthorne said, "and afford fit soil for poetry to root itself in." By 1890 they had actually created a unified tissue of nationality—but then the country began changing from agricultural to industrial, rural to urban, and the new generation required new myths. The battle between idealism and realism that raged from 1886 to 1910 and after (to be revived in the Humanist controversy) was also a battle between two mythologies. Now the country has changed again and we are looking for new myths to express a new time.

And more and more to be said—but still I don't know how to begin or how to phrase my remarks, and I'm writing this letter chiefly in the effort to clarify my own muddy mind. But so far the mud refuses to settle . . .

> As ever,
> Malcolm

> 4111 36th Ave. NE,
> Seattle, Washington
> January 5, 1950
> [PS]

Dear Kenneth:

. . . Just now I'm a *cause célèbre* at the University of Washington.[1] The worst of it is, I can't go to the bastards and ask them what they want, because the bastards are fighting in the dark and refuse to come out from behind the wainscoting. All except one of them, a regent of the university named Stuntz, and I think I know what he wants, which is to get the president of the university fired and a Catholic named in his place. I think (but am not yet sure) that I wandered as if between the lines of a deadly battle, and came under fire that was intended to go beyond me (or my corpse) and hit somebody else.

The way it worked out was funny. They had intended to attack me on the ground of having belonged to subversive organizations in the 1930s; but I got ahead of them by writing the university and telling them what subversive organizations I had belonged to and authorizing them to release the letter to the press. Then they went through my books fine-combing to discover something subversive. Nothing did they find of that nature, but they ran across some dirty words in my poems (including one honey of a line from a poem in *The Dry Season*,[2] about a girl diving into the East River—

> . . . bright with gulls,
> Used condoms, turds and grapefruit rind.)

Thereupon they made a list of all the dirty passages they could find in my poems, or all the passages that by a long stretch of the imagination could be interpreted as being dirty, and secretly distributed the document to the American Legion, the Veterans of Foreign Wars, the Parent-Teachers' Association, the DAR, and God knows what other organizations. That produced a real scandal, although the worst of it was over before I arrived. The result is that I have 150 students in a course planned for 50 . . . Week after next I start a series of public lectures, and I think the first of them will be devoted to my own poetry, a defense working into an attack on the underhanded methods of whoever circulated the document. That should be fun. I'd like to build a fire under the sons of bitches . . .

As ever,
Malcolm

1. Cowley was appointed Walker-Ames lecturer at the University.

2. The poem Cowley refers to is "Roxane." It appears on page 97 of *Blue Juniata: Collected Poems*.

4111 36th Ave. NE,
Seattle, Washington
January 10, 1950
[PS]

Dear Kenneth:

This last October Ted Roethke had a complete breakdown, went to a local sanitarium. It's bad, paranoia with some schizophrenic symptoms. He was crazy enough to persuade some of his students to effect an escape for him, got down into Oregon, realized he could go no farther and returned. Now he's in another sanitarium, not allowed to receive visitors (except Jim Jackson and another faculty member named Leota Willis), and his mail censored. They aren't very sanguine about his recovery, but are so far trying to avoid giving him the shock treatment. He wrote an introduction to some of his poems and sent it out to me by a student attendant named Jespers, no, Jepson. I'm sure the prose introduction couldn't be published without the poems it is intended to elucidate, and those have been published already, so after consultation with Jepson I'm sending it on to you . . . Any letter sent to him should be non-exciting if it is to reach him. Their chief aim at present is to give him a sense of protection and security (womb?) . . .

As ever,
Malcolm

The University of Chicago
Chicago 37, Illinois
The College Faculty Exchange
January 23, 1950
[PS]

Dear Malcolm,

Many thanks for info and data anent Ted Roethke. I have written him, in the usual semi-bantering tone in which I always wrote him. I hope the savants in authority will not decide that I should be banned as too exciting. (Strangely enough, I most pigheadedly believe that I could do as much as anybody to talk him out of some faulty system-building, if that's his ailment, and if it's still susceptible to haggling. But there is the dangerous side in his poetry, certainly, the side that makes him want to develop backward. And he has quite an investment in it. But if there is anything I could do, I'd like to try; for I remember with great fondness our times at Bennington. In fact, I guess I sometimes read the whole of Bennington, at its most magic moments, into some of his lines—and it does have magic moments, as do some of his lines.)

And how goes it with you and the Welcoming Committee? Did you read your poesies, as planned? When I told Rago[1] here that you were being pursued for a few references that caused a deep crimson blush on the cheeks of the American Legion, he recited the poem, right off, and praised it for its *morality*. So, you should consider yourself lucky. For, your verses having been so good anyhow, they should look positively dazzling when presented in the light of such agitation.

One month of winter gone, no hay. And so far, nary a really tough climatic moment. Working my damned head off, talking my damned head off, every minute yearning with fervor to be dolce far niente-ing in Andover, simply because I don't know how to do anything midway between boom and slump, so far as this word-slinging racket is concerned. So I am slump-yearningly booming . . .

Sincerely,
K. B.

1. Henry A. Rago, an assistant professor of humanities at the University of Chicago and editor of *Poetry* magazine.

Sherman, Connecticut
May 1, 1950
[NL]

Dear Kenneth:

"One of the few truly speculative minds that exist in this time and country. He opens perspectives for other writers in all fields, from poetry to journalism to theology, because he is able to find in all fields the symbols that express the drama of human destiny."

Look, Kenneth! Shit, Kenneth! I've opened the mouth of a sewer. If you want to use this fecal matter, you and Prentice-Hall are welcome to it (maybe the first sentence alone would be helpful).

I've just finished reading the *Rhetoric,* and I've been going back over other volumes. I'll offer a few practical kicks, as a reader. Too many words of Greek derivation (chiliastic, charismatic, dyslogistic, heuristic, etc.). Those four I remember because you use them so much, and we can expect your readers to look them up; but there are other Greek words that you will just throw in from time to time—wouldn't it be better to define them unobtrusively? Too many sentences begin with a strong, isolated accent: *"Thus,* we conclude . . ." *"True,* it is not only . . ." *"However,* a second thought would lead." Your writing is more crabbed now than it was even in the *Attitudes* (which wasn't really crabbed, but only dispersed); it has lost the grace of *Counter-Statement.* I suppose this is the natural result of putting your emphasis on ideas rather than expression, and I wouldn't want you to become a stylist again, since that might mean less emphasis on ideas—but it wouldn't hurt to vary your sentence structure more than at present or to be more strategic in your division of paragraphs.

On the other hand, this book seems more tightly composed than some of the preceding ones—it is easier to grasp in its general outlines; and I do think that it may become considerably more popular.

．　　　．　　　．

One important part in the argument wasn't sufficiently developed, I mean the integral connection between mystery and hierarchy; not that I doubt the point, I just feel you should have devoted more space to it.

I'm carping in a small way, but I like the book enormously as a whole, like your method of attack and the light you cast on dark places. My strategy (your word) will now be to write a review of it for the *New Republic,* putting in the eulogistic adjectives that I omitted when reviewing TABL, but not even attempting to say anything of moment; I'll just do an honest journalistic blurb with cute touches of personality in an attempt to get more readers for the book. If you have a moment on receiving this letter, I wish you'd sit down and write one page for me (and later for others) on the curve of your thought from *Counter-Statement* through *Permanence and Change,* through *Attitudes Toward History,* through *The Philosophy of Literary Form* (of which I haven't a copy, remember you just lent me one), through the *Grammar* and the *Rhetoric* to the next stage—what you tried to do in each book . . .

> As ever,
> Malcolm

> Andover, New Jersey,
> May 3, 1950
> [PS]

Dear Malcolm,

In re yours of inst., anent the stations of my cross, as regards literary criticism:

Counter-Statement. Emerging out of aesthetic criticism. Centered in definition of form: as arousing and fulfilling of expectations. Principle stated somewhat dithyrambically (inspirationally) in "Psychology and Form" essay. Codified in "Lexicon Rhetoricae." Book destroyed about time they were plowing under the little pigs. (Hickville Granny [Granville Hicks] wrote an article, in *Partisan {Review}* I believe, on "The Crisis in Criticism." *Counter-Statement* was the crisis.)

During dismality of last Hoover years, first wrote a short book never published. Called "Auscultation, Creation, and Revision." Ended on ecstatic appreciation of poem by Li Tai Po, on dancing with his shadow in the moonlight. Good poem, but not a very comfortable one to end on, those years.

Became economics-minded. Decided to write a book on the devices of businessmen. Began to take notes. But gave up the project when I came across the report of the Pujo Investigation.[1] For there it all was, summed up to perfection.

Began then asking about the motives behind the level of such devices. Thence, got to problems of interpretation, communication, cooperation in general. Out of this came *Permanence and Change* (which was originally entitled Treatise on Communication—title being changed because publisher thought it sounded like a report on telephone and telegraph). Looking back, I discover an unintended form in the book. The middle section is the transition (and deals appropriately with a term that befits the intermediate: perspective by incongruity, vistas got by a stylistic device for bringing disrelated categories of things together. I think that it corresponds, in the essayistic form, to what would be called the stage of rending or tearing [sparagmos] in Greek tragedy. One lady reader who took a shine to it described her sensations in ways that suggested deflowering [she was pretty, too]). A somewhat surrealist notion—or what Coleridge might have done with his term "fancy," if he had been aligning it with "imagination" now instead of a century ago. Book written in 1933. Published in 1935.

Then came the united front period. League of American Writers, etc. Became interested in relation between culture in general and political organization in particular. Hence, *Attitudes Toward History.* Centers in one particular perspective by incongruity: bureaucratization of the imaginative (to do with all the problems, paradoxes, etc., that arise when men attempt to carry out a plan by organizing it, embodying it in materials that must to some extent introduce unintended effects, since the materials have a genius of their own, over and above their nature as means to any single man-made end). Also: whereas P&C had dealt with orientation generally in philosophic terms, ATH attempted to look at orientations historically. Hence, middle section on Curve of History, which I don't think is such a bad survey. (First section aims to distinguish literary *genres* in terms of "strategies.")

Next book, *The Philosophy of Literary Form,* had another sort of problem to solve. Had begun teaching now. New School, Syracuse in summer, Chicago one summer, scattered lectures, etc. Problem of circumstantiality in critical analysis. There was the old school, immured in the text. There were the leftists, strong on talk of relations between literature and society, but weak on internal analysis. Tried to bridge this gap. To this end, the theory of "clusters," "equations." To find out *what goes with what* in a book, so that one's analysis is internal; yet to note the social relevance of such "equations." . . .

Had originally intended to write a third volume to P&C and ATH. It was to be called On Human Relations. Had been taking notes (social strategies, diplomatic devices, ways of outwitting others and oneself, etc.). Began to write these up. Found that they needed a general theoretical introduction. Thought a few thousand words would do the job. But the project grew into the *Grammar*. The five terms with which the work now begins were settled upon toward the end of the first version, and the book was turned around accordingly. Also, had begun teaching at Bennington, where students who know no philosophy had asked me to tutor them in philosophy . . .

The terms, in accordance with our methodological interest, also had a theory behind them, which we sloganized as "dramatism." Relations between the terms (as functions): the "dramatistic ratios." *Grammar* tries to show how these terms can serve to elucidate basic methods of placement and expression in different literary orders: (treated as aspects of "symbolic action") drama, poetry, theology, metaphysics, law, etc. Aims to show the transformations needed for turning them upon different kinds of subject matter (transformations needed to keep the analysis from being a mere analogizing, as were one to treat *all* forms purely and simply as "drama").

Symbolic is, roughly, to carry further the sort of problem treated in *The Philosophy of Literary Form*. As things now look, it will begin with an analysis of tragedy.

As for *Rhetoric:* last section is not, I think, as purely coda-like or appendix-like as you would suggest. Since the *Rhetoric* hinges upon two principles, persuasion and identification, in keeping with my philosophic hankerings I wanted to carry each to its farthest stage: hence, "pure persuasion" as the "meta-rhetoric" for "persuasion"; and as the "meta-rhetoric" for "identification," one should have for a windup "absolute identification."

• • •

Anyhow, many thanks for comments. I've tried again and again, by the way, to drop the beginning bumps, "true . . . thus . . . hence . . . however . . . in fact . . . that is," etc.[2] But my point-by-point method makes them inevitable, I am afraid. A style without therefore's, however's, and even "and's" lends itself best to an "impressionistic" subject matter, or one in which a theme is restated in various images that simply coexist as a conglomeration: "It was an x-like day. The clouds did such-and-such. The birds were whatever. Old Mr. Q, on the verandah, was something over trying to something with the what-is-it. Above the thingumbob, beautifully interrupted by the longly-adjectival brief-noun, an inanimate object in the same class of mood-evocation, etc." . . .

• • •

Thanks for the blurby-wurby. I'll send it along, and let them use their judgment. I agree with you that the first sentence might be best by its honorable self . . .

Sincerely,

K. B.

1. The Pujo Investigation, headed by Representative Arsene P. Pujo, delved into the complex workings of American finance, uncovering evidence that a small number of financial leaders controlled money and credit in the United States.

2. Ellipses Burke's.

Sherman, Connecticut
May 11, 1950
[PS]

Dear Kenneth:

I'm having trouble writing the review, in spite of your sending me the Stations of the Cross of Jesus H. Burke. They were helpful, and they also sharpen my dilemma, which is, in your language, whether to approach your system by the temporally prior or the logically prior. I could start with man as a symbol-using animal, since that has become the central concept in your system—but temporally it comes fairly late in the development of your thought. But my real problem, in writing a short review, is how to keep it shallow and yet useful; I can't go deep or else the review will do more harm than good, by frightening readers with its difficulty. And starting with the temporally prior—writing a story—is a more interesting way to treat the subject (I mean more interesting in the sense of easy to follow) than starting with the logically prior.

Doing Burke in 1,200 words is a problem and you can't solve it for me.

I won't have much space, if any, for your concept of mystery. Just now I think it is the weak point in your system. I'll be dogmatic: mystery arises from the conflict between man as an individual and man as a member of society. You know that. You say as much at the top of page 21:

"Here are ambiguities of substance. In being identified with B, A is 'substantially one' with a person other than himself. Yet at the same time he remains unique, an individual locus of motives. Thus he is both joined and separate, at once a distinct substance and consubstantial with another."

You return to this theme on page 130, in talking about another ambiguity caused by the biologic drive toward amassing property combined with the fact that production is public or communal. "Ambiguity" or "rhetorical situation" is the term you use—but how is this to be distinguished from mystery? No, the underlying mystery is how, as separate organisms, we are still tied to other organisms in invisible ways. Religion is the attempt to eternalize the invisible. The underlying dialectic is *I* (thesis), *they* (antithesis) and *we* (synthesis). The greatest of the rhetorical mountings is the expansion and finally universalization of the "we" (you discuss this subject on p. 312).

What about the mystery of hierarchy? It *is* mystery. On the other hand it is the second, not the first, mystery, and sometimes you confuse it with the first. For example, I think that most initiation ceremonies are part of the first mystery—they are a change of group, a change of "we," of identification, and therefore a sort of rebirth. Fast, cut off the foreskin, suffer pain, child dies, man is born. There's hierarchy involved here, so far as man is more powerful than child, but there's also the deeper mystery of consubstantiality, first with other children, then with other men.

In hierarchy there is another mystery you don't discuss, I mean the opposition between man and office. The Kansas City haberdasher receives our respect (or does he?) in so far as he is President. In so far as he confuses himself, in himself, with the President as hierarchic symbol, he becomes a twerp. I think it will be important for you to think along these lines, or simply read theorists who have discussed them, because so far you haven't said whether the hierarchy was good or bad, you have simply said that it was inevitable. If it is inevitable we tend to think that it is therefore good, natural. And a hell of a lot of phony business, mystification, can be put over on us in the name of hierarchy. I think the distinction between man and office, developed in the Roman Church and applied by almost all the democratic theorists, points a way out of this difficulty . . .

As ever,
Malcolm

Andover, New Jersey
May 12, 1950
[PS]

Dear Malcolm,

I most certainly wouldn't object, head on, to your proposed individual-society alignment for the discussion of mystery. For, as you correctly note at some points, I use it myself. (You could have quoted many other spots than the one you do.) I'd say the individual-society alignment is good "first rough approximate," serviceable for many purposes; but it's too blunt for use when dealing with such concerns as we treated with respect to H. James, Castiglione, Kafka, Venus and Adonis, etc.

· · ·

Technically, your error consists in plumping for a definition not sufficiently generalized. You say, "Mystery arises from the conflict between man as an individual and man as a member of society." Then, after citing me, you go on to expand your statement as though you were saying things counter to the things I said. My basic statement was more highly generalized (as it should have been): "The conditions for mystery prevail when there is communication between different kinds of beings." You will note that, when the situation is so stated, either the individual-species alignment (man and society) or the individual-species-genus alignment (man, class, society) fall under the definition. When I am talking about the "fall in general (separation as de-termination), the individual–society alignment is adequate. When I talk about "order," it is *not* adequate.

In speaking of the rituals for initiating the child into the state of manhood, you seem to imply that the element of hierarchy is slight. But I take the existence of a priesthood to be per se the evidence of social classification (with magic for promoting tribal cohesion over and above the differences in tribal status). Also, I have explicitly stated: the differences that are ritualistically bridged can be real or imaginary, social or physiological. (For instance, the "sexual mystery' is rooted in a real *physiological* difference between men and women; but when you begin to analyze its manifestations in complex literary works, you readily see how much such magic has been accented by purely *social* differentiations.)

As for your point about temporal and logical priority: I can't see the difficulty. My present formula about the "symbol-using" animal is not a new thing at all with me, but is a quite natural development of my concern with communication, in every one of my books. This takes one form in *Counter-Statement,* another in P&C ("man a communicant"), another in each of the books. What is now called "hierarchy" was treated in ATH in terms of "bureaucracy."

But you do have one unanswerable statement: The problem of dealing with all my books in 1,200 words. For that reason, I do hope my over-zealousness in lining up my past works will not interfere with the proper proportions of the review. For it would be ironical indeed if, in presenting the works which are *not* available for reading or purchase, you thereby had to slight the two that *are* available . . .

Sincerely,

K. B.

Sherman, Connecticut
May 25, 1950
[PS]

Dear Kenneth:

Finished the review. I had undertaken to do a tough job of work, to talk about all your critical and philosophical books, but especially the last two, in a review short enough so that the *New Republic* would print it, and at the same time give prospective readers some guideposts and encourage them to go to work on you. Had to face squarely the problem of your being sometimes difficult to read and turn it into a sales point. Anyhow the review is now in type, as written, and yesterday I rescued the ms. and here it is.

By the time it was finished I could just as easily have written a 6,000-word essay, filled out with quotations. You will note how little I said about the Burkean dialectic of transcendence and how I omitted the whole question of hierarchy. I'll mention now some matters that didn't go into the review, mostly qualms and questions . . .

.   .   .

On the subject of the essential mystery I have so much to say that I'm hopeless about putting it into a letter. I didn't at all mean the conflict between the individual and society (which is old and crude stuff)—I meant the conflict between the individual's idea of himself as an individual and his idea of himself as an incomplete part of another entity. The group, the family, the totemic phratry, the tribe, the nation—you can't *see* it, touch it, smell it, but nevertheless it exists and we are consubstantial with it—you know all this stuff, have discussed it; but now you would put it as a secondary thing, whereas to me it seems to be your real subject when you talk about symbols—the language itself is the group medium and religion is a ritualization and rendering visual of what is to me the central mystery in human life. "Difference" is such a broad thing that it becomes meaningless as an explanation of mystery; I am different from a stone or a tree or a house, but that doesn't arouse any sense of mystery—and you're objectively wrong about one thing, there can be and are many, many initiation rites without a priesthood, or with amateur priests (as among the Navajos) who draw no advantage from their function. And another remark: the danger of your socio-anagogy is that it may lead to another debunking: "He's just saying that he's better than we." . . .

As ever,
Malcolm

Andover, New Jersey
June 5, 1950
[PS]

Dear Malcolm,

As regards review of *Rhetoric* as "hard to follow." (As attested by expert reader who has known author since age of three.)

We cite (from review by Texas newspaperman in *San Antonio Express*):

> *"The Rhetoric of Motives* is a profound and rewarding book. Despite the newness of its concepts and its unconventional organization, *it is not difficult reading."*

Down with Babylonic ease; up with the vigor and wholesomeness of the cattleman.

Otherwise, ailingly,
K. B.

Sherman, Connecticut
August 30, 1950

Dear Kenneth:

Wrote a review of Hemingway's new one[1] the day after the verbalization. It probably means the end of a beautiful friendship, although I said as much for the book as I could find it in my conscience to say. What I'm afraid of is that the guy has been living for ten years in an alcoholic haze and can't write any longer except an occasional paragraph—while he's been earning close to a hundred thousand dollars a year as a writer. One quote I loved because it expresses something I feel about our situation:

> *"Now we are governed in some way, by the dregs. We are governed by what you find in the bottom of dead beer glasses that whores have dunked their cigarettes in. The place has not even been swept out yet and they have an amateur pianist beating on the box."*

He's wonderful at making those sweeping remarks, as if in a bar late at night, but there are too many of them in his novel and there is no sustained episode—one chapter is of 300 words, and anybody knows that when you get to writing 300-word chapters the brain isn't working. After his breakdown Scott Fitzgerald could at least do the early chapters of *The Last Tycoon*—but then he'd got to the stage where he had to go on the wagon for months and had time to think.

No, I don't think I handed too much to Cleanth Brooks.[2] He's wonderful at close reading—and if he isn't so good, isn't good at all, when he tries to construct a system of criticism, let us be thankful for what he has done to make our appreciations more complicated. In your letter to Haydn,[3] which does put your remarks into more perspective, your criticism of the New Critics for too much uniqueness of interpretation, too much attention to the individual work *sub specie* itself instead of *aeternitatis,* is absolutely justified. I said in a different way that they leave the *choice* of works to the journalistic critics, have abnegated the critic's function of discovery. But the best of them are good in their own fashion . . .

As ever,
Malcolm

1. Cowley's review of Hemingway's *Across the River and into the Trees* was published in the September 10 issue of *The New York Herald Tribune Book Review.*

2. Cowley is referring to remarks he made in a forum entitled "The New Criticism." Burke was one of a number of other participants, and the discussion was published in the April, 1951, issue of *The American Scholar.*

3. Hiram Haydn, an editor, was one of the discussants in the forum on the New Criticism.

Sherman, Connecticut
October 26, 1950
[PS]

Dear Kenneth:

. . . Remember my saying that I doubted whether I would get many invitations from universities this year? And your agreeing? Then you got the bid from Washington, which you didn't want, and I got a very nice one from the University of Minnesota for five months, January to June. $5,333.33, or just about $1,000 per month (I start January 7 and am through June 6). Three afternoons of teaching, or seven hours per week. Well, this sounded so good that I couldn't resist it, after writing a long letter about my past record as a joiner of Communist fronts and after their saying, "Come on anyway." But I haven't yet received formal notice of the appointment and there may be shenanigans on the board of regents. I think my name is on some sort of Catholic blacklist.

Three weeks ago I caught the "x" virus that is miasmating around New York—and Sherman . . . Nevertheless I wrote a lot of stuff about F. Scott Fitzgerald, who is a perfect example of your theory of social anagogy. In all his early work the hero represents the rising middle class, the heroine represents inherited money, they kiss as if he were embracing a pile of stock certificates—and then, since Fitzgerald distrusts the leisure class and thinks they are mysterious, her relatives kill the hero (that's the plot, the real plot of *Gatsby, Tender Is the Night,* and "The Diamond As Big As the Ritz") . . .

As ever,
Malcolm

Sherman, Connecticut
November 1, 1950
[NL]

Dear Kenneth:

So I'm not going to Minnesota. When they first invited me a month ago I wrote them a long letter saying that I had done this and this in the 1930s and also had had some trouble at Seattle and didn't want to come to Minneapolis under any misapprehensions on their part. They consulted about the letter and told me to come anyway—but then at the last moment the dean showed the letter to the president and the president, who is a liberal and has done some good things, refused to confirm the appointment. There's apparently quite a lot of anger and humiliation on the English faculty, but nothing to be done about it. My little prophecy in September wasn't so far wrong after all.

Would rather stay home anyhow and can get along without beautiful Minnesota salary, so it's not such a harsh blow to me personally—but it's certainly one more instance of the way things are going. I wrote to one of the profs, Sam Monk, who had sent me a letter of sympathy: "We can call it 'the advance of reaction' or 'the erosion of our liberties' if we don't mind using old phrases. But the liberties are not being eroded; they are being atrophied by failure to exercise them; and reaction is not advancing except into territories that have already been abandoned by their defenders and ceded to reaction."

Love to all.

As ever,
Malcolm

Andover, New Jersey
November 3, 1950
[PS]

Dear Malcolm,

Helndamnaysh. Looking at it hindsight, maybe you shouldn't bring up all the untoward possibilities when such matters are under consideraysh. There are even circumstances wherein the very man who knew of all such refinements would gladly ignore them unless you made it impossible for him to do so. When thus gleaming in the light of the imagination alone, they can come to have much greater semblance of importance than if they were merely treated as insignificant, and damn the guy who says they ain't. (Particularly inasmuch as you already had the University of Washington experience to bring forward as justification for your judgment. I.e., you had this for presenting *afterward,* in case any stir *did* develop.)

As for your diagnosis (anent atrophied liberties): I'd say that the U.S. cult of "all modern conveniences" (equals "higher standard of living"— equals "culture") is gradually coming to take its toll. It fits in beautifully with the general abnegation you speak of. (And alas! though I treat as a sellout each acquisition which the club-offer gazettes teach us to treat as a triumph, I must admit that the ideal of living in a hotel-equals-hospital gradually gains with me, in proportion as my ailments gain. If I last through my fifties, flatter me, flatter me. If I last through my sixties, lave me. But if the future is as my heart-consciousness leads me to think it will be, then I'll be laved never.)

Meanwhile, since you are staying home (as of November 3rd!): what do you think of corresponding via one of the new mediums? I.e., a secondhand tape recorder. If only I hadn't had so damned much trouble with mine, I could be more emphatic. But my difficulties result from a stupid error. I was put on to a good machine, for $125, but got the address wrong, and came away with a decrepit structure that has given me much sorrow, and frustrations more vexing than any that a Freudian could ever conceive of. Yet, there were some ecstatic hours when it did work—and I got so excited I even wept into it; and it wept back, and tolerably.

. . .

Too bad! All is property! How see the world beyond it! How be honest (i.e., how have a property in exposing property). And that reminds me: Someone . . . filched my Viking *Hawthorne.* It was full of marks (that I could use so much better than anyone else). I discovered the loss when, one student in my present class at Bennington having chosen to theorize on the nature of a dance built around the processes of catharsis in *The Scarlet Letter,* I reviewed my notes on that, and then started to expand—whereat I found I had been robbed, doubly, since as I recall, 'twas a book from you. Or was it? Bah! Damn the human race! Damn the trivial TRIVIAL human race. No good competent thief took that book. Nobody who could use it better than I could. That book was stolen in *lassitude.*

But my drink runs low, and I am called to dinner. So I desist.

Sincerely,
K. B.

Sherman, Connecticut
November 10, 1950
[NL]

Dear Kenneth:

. . . Things begin to look still worse than they did when I got news from Minnesota. This election is more ominous than that of 1946, when all the Northern Democrats were licked. This time there was a selection among Democrats. The radicals had been crossed off four years ago and the liberals went this time, the liberals being roughly equivalent to the Protestants and Jews in the Democratic Party. The rest of the party in the North is composed of various Catholic racial elements, notably Irish, Italians, Poles, and, in New England, French Canadians. The Democrats elected belonged to these racial groups, which could not be assailed for communism. Meanwhile the McCarthy wing of the Republicans was victorious, so that we'll see a great unearthing of past records now. And behind this the folly of war with China, leading to war with Russia. And the liberals so effectually divided—more than that, fragmented, isolated one from another—that they are making no resistance and are quitting the battlefield even before being attacked. They don't even have a press any longer and have to communicate by letters. The talkative ones, living by words, have been forced into silence and they don't know how to live underground.

As ever,
Malcolm

Andover, New Jersey
November 16, 1950
[NL]

Dear Malcolm,

. . . [S]till avoiding doctors, I'm beginning to wonder whether my fantastic gulpo-gaggo-gaspo session of recent weeks may be not heart at all, but asthmatic. The difference between throwing words out and letting them mull around inside (between lecturing and writing) seems to be becoming an abrupt change of quality with me; and almost within a few moments after I go to work on the internal kind, I find myself just about stifled. I fight for a breath like a man sinking in a mud hole. Also, I find that, at such times, I have been holding my breath. Oh, this living and dying by the Word. A certain kind of interference with breathing is natural when speaking, so maybe I can fool the jinx by that subterfuge.

. . . Nosologically, as regards my great Migratory Symptom, the project seems to have developed thus: For the *Grammar,* high blood pressure; for the Devices portions of *Rhetoric* (still unpublished) a stinging, ringing burning left ear; for the aspects of the *Rhetoric* that lead toward "pure persuasion," a laggard heart, and when I got to the middle paragraph on "suspended animation," p. 294, I just about melted away; and now, for the Symbolic (or at least, the Poetics section of the Symbolic), a really sustained battle with the gaspo-gaggo-gulpo symptom, which I have had on and off, but which now seems to want to move in permanently, for a spell at least. On the whole, bodily symptoms have at least the consolatory fact about them, that they replace mental symptoms, fears of going off one's trolley; and I suppose that, if I got rid of all the physical symptoms, things would but have been cleared away for a new worry about mental ones?

Which reminds me, incidentally: I do hope I have not lost the notes I took during one period, near the end of the section on the Philosophic Schools, in the *Grammar.* I fear I may have, for by my computations one fairly large batch of notes on the Symbolic has disparooed. But I still remember the essence of the incident. Though I could not recover the tiny succession of details. 'Twas to do with a series of fantasies that gave me a choice between feeling that I was all bound with ropes and feeling that I was like a tablet dissolving in water. (The fantasies of being bound went with one plan for continuing the chapter; the fantasies of dissolving went with an alternative plan. Then came a series of dreams that seemed so on-the-verge of something, I got up in the night and wrote down each one. Then finally came the discovery: that the five terms[1] were ceasing to be their abstract selves, and were trying to become my five children. Hence, the intolerable alternatives. In proportion as this motive came through, if I planned to keep the terms abstract, then I felt bound; but if I planned to so finish the chapter that their logical functions yielded to their personal implications, then, understandably, I felt like a tablet fizzing away into nothing. Once I spotted the confusion, I went on a two-day bat and talking jag, laid off the book for a week, then finished the section sans the fantasies. But I can still show vestiges of the "personalities" lurking behind the terms.) . . .

Sincerely,
K. B.

1. Act, scene, agent, agency, purpose. They are discussed at length in the first section of *A Grammar of Motives*.

Andover, New Jersey
February 22, 1952
[NL]

Dear Malcolm,

. . . Structurally, and as regards the way one's heart performs when on parade in the doctor's office, I came through in good shape. But the fancy things continue. The local doctor (a New York surgeon who lives in the next valley, and is trying to retire from the big stuff by picking up a practice hereabouts) gives what amounts to a psychosomatic explanation. "Coronary spasms," resulting from tension (his slogan is: Each of us should be sure to have a Lester Jeeter [sic][1] in him. Guess I need more Jeeter and less jitters. But, alas! how does one write sans jitters?). Incidentally, his remark gave me a notion of this sort: Might all that fantastic deterioration of the car in the novel be a kind of roundabout symbolization for bodily deterioration under mental strain? That is: the mental strain is "denied" in one sense, and in another sense it is making its mark all the while. It's possible. I'll have to go back and look over the book sometime, along those lines.

Meanwhile, all sorts of ideas, even apparently innocuous ones, will of a sudden produce in me a kind of stoppage so that, literally, I forget to breathe. The engrossment that goes with the pursuit of an idea, at such times, seems to produce a "state of arrest." Same thing sometimes happens when I am going to sleep. Can sometimes mitigate the symptom by a bit of alky. But you can't win—for the alky goes racing through the body and, in a very short time, awakens me, demanding an exit . . .

. . . Butch, by the way, is becoming set in the technology direction (perfect son of an anti-technology pap!). Telephone conversations with his boyfriends concern grids, condensors, spark coils, and many other such material things that to me always seem so cryingly symbolic. Sometimes, for amusement, he sits down and draws designs for "hookups" (all the old man's concern with "communication" thus being paralleled, you might say, antithetically). Problem: what should I do about it? Raise a fuss, so that he will, by opposition, get further *intensity* into his efforts? Or give him the backing of extreme approval? Etc. You can imagine the many possible variants—plus the one I carry out; namely: pretty much nothing . . .

Sincerely,

K. B.

1. Jeeter Lester is a character in Erskine Caldwell's novel *Tobacco Road*. Burke had written about the novel in *The Philosophy of Literary Form* (pages 350–360).

Sherman, Connecticut

February 28, 1952

[NL]

Dear Kenneth:

Funny, the doc's report on your condition tends to confirm my hypothesis (yours too, I note) that your health is in some measure an effect of your work—when you're taking things easy your health is good, when you're trying to invent new theories, when you're riding your demon until your demon takes to riding you, then heart and mind start acting up. It happened for the first time when you were finishing *Towards a Better Life*. Think you had better take a vacation right now, two weeks or even a month . . .

I think the piece on "Ethan Brand" is a little obsessional.[1] At least it doesn't quite fit into my own picture of Hawthorne and what I know about his life. It doesn't show a sufficient attention to dates and probabilities. Thus,

1. Hawthorne's "reflexive"—i.e., masturbating—period lasted from some undisclosed beginning until some time in the years 1839—42. He was married in '42 and was a most passionate husband—though the sense of guilt remained and was reflected in stories written during the next few years—then it disappeared for the time. After his third child was born, in '53 I think, Hawthorne and Mrs. H became very careful about sex and may even have stopped it, in the lack of birth-control measures (funny how much we know about such a reticent man), with the result that he *may* have yielded to the vice again in his later years. Incidentally he and Sophia may have been lovers for three years before they were married.

2. He made a trip to North Adams in the summer of '38, which is recorded at length in his American notebook, Randall Stewart edition. One of the things he recorded was the characters, including the dog, who appeared in "Ethan Brand." He didn't write the story so much as he put it together out of his notebook—and until one has read the notebook one can't talk with authority about the story.

• • •

5. If you want the "reflexive" element in Hawthorne, look for it in "Young Goodman Brown," "The Minister's Black Veil," "The Bosom Serpent," "The Birthmark," where it's clear and manifest and where the story itself is what Hawthorne wanted it to be, not what he managed to make it in a period of fatigue . . .

. . . Meanwhile, like all of us, I follow the course of the great Irish American job hunt. Somebody from the staff of "Counter Attack"[2] has compiled a great list of Red or ex-Red intellectuals, which he is proposing to sell for $500 a copy, as part of a Service. Free copies, I take it, to the Catholic War Veterans of each town. On the other hand, the opposition to this or these shenanigans is also beginning to take shape. We'll survive if the country does. For my own part I'm waiting with some curiosity to see whether Whittaker Chambers mentions me in his memoirs of my dead life—of *his* dead life, I mean. Fortunately I didn't meet the creature until 1940. When I heard about him in earlier years, from Bob Cantwell, I thought he was a figure of comedy and I still think so, but everybody has forgotten how to laugh. Why doesn't he call his book, "I Was a Red Rover Boy"?

No more. I must get to work. Remember that when you're overfatigued with the sort of work you're doing, alcohol is the worst thing in the world for you. Loses its narcotic qualities and becomes a stimulant. Sets up a spiral action. Let us keep away from spirals.

As ever,
Malcolm

1. Burke had just published "Ethan Brand: A Preparatory Investigation," in *The Hopkins Review* (Winter 1952).

2. "Counter Attack" was an anticommunist newsletter published by John B. Keenan, director of public safety in Newark, New Jersey.

Andover, New Jersey
August 8, 1952
[NL]

Dear Malcolm,

Q: Was I hot?

A: Jeez, I was HOT.[1]

At first I even feared I couldn't take it. But at those times, one usually survives, if only through sheer meanness. Sometimes, all day and late into the night, I sat in my room in my shorts, batting at my typewriter, drinking large glasses of sugarless lemonade with a slight edging of gin, and oozing my drinks almost as fast as I swallowed them. Every few hours I'd take a shower, and start over. I did a lot of my own cooking (out of a can); and with the help of an a-telephonic personality (I had the phone disconnected) I worked up a kind of mild Creative Morbidity that was just what I wanted. All told, I'd say that the season went well, though not excessively so (we must be moderate in all things). Bloomington is a pretty town; the campus is varied and picturesque (you can discern traces of its origins in a woodland); and the people were pleasant (with only the amt. of tension among the faculty that is normal to a batch of prima donnas). Was given the standard invitation to return next year; but have nay-said, account I am due to resume at benny Bonnington that autumn—and I can't teach thus consecutively.

You ask about U. of Washington.[2] In reply, would say: have passed all the faculty committees, but am still being processed as regards the administraysh. Things further complicated by arrival of a new president, not the official with whom I had been negotiating up to this time. I told them every peculation I could think of, patiently, respectfully, *but not apologetically*. The last I heard was that Regents meet circa August 16, and I should get a definitive answer then. Inasmuch as I taught at a state university this summer, and gave talks at both Illinois and Ohio State universities (talks that were very amiably received), while an official in another state university has offered to arrange a tour of several other state universities, I'm wondering how in the hell anybody could make out a case proving that a turndown at the U. of Wash. would be in the interests of Academic Freedom (which is, perforce, the slogan of the unhappy and hard-pressed Administraysh). But we'll see. Meanwhile, have been offered more money for less work elsewhere during that period (not teaching, however); but, as I wrote the Administraysh, I'd rather await their decision. Heilman[3] has been working for me. But I learned recently that he hadn't even seen the letters I sent, telling of my sinister days as a left-wing cultural democrat on the council of the lig of Am. night-writers.[4] Meanwhile, happy to learn that Ted[5] got his drag from the Ford Fund, though regrettably that may mean he won't be there next wint, in case the Affair Burpius is decided favorably . . .

.   .   .

How goes it with your ailment? I hope that by now you have seen your way clear to avoid the knife-men. (Someday, when their skill becomes expert enough, they will be persuading all blue-eyed people to be operated on for brown eyes, and v.v.) . . .

Sincerely,
K. B.

1. Burke had spent part of the summer lecturing at Indiana University in Bloomington.

2. In a letter that has not survived, Cowley asked Burke about his pending appointment as a visiting professor at the University of Washington in Seattle. He had been invited by the English department, but the appointment was beginning to encounter opposition at the administrative level.

3. Robert Heilman, a member of the English department at Washington.

4. The League of American Writers.

5. Theodore Roethke.

Sherman, Connecticut
September 4, 1952
[PS]

Dear Kenneth:

Whoosh. Settled in bed with the heating pad under me, big thin volume of Hieronymus Bosch on my knees, first written words since Sunday. When your letter came on Tuesday I was lying here as helpless as a paraplegic. Lumbago, sacroiliac, whatever the doctors want to call it, my aching back . . . The letter was bad news, bad for you, bad for me, bad for the University of Washed-White-as-lamb's wool. It shows how much worse things have grown in the three years since they hired me in 1949. I'd have little trouble if I hadn't testified for Hiss . . .

These are bad times, and the liberals run without fighting, as I found in the Minnesota business in 1950. But the times are worse for the universities than for you and me. We've managed to survive and will survive, even financially. (For example I'll have earned as much money this year as any year in the past and it's not lack of work but my own incapacity to work that has kept me from earning more. True, some of that incapacity is due to my feeling the need to keep silent on some matters—the silence infects me and keeps me from speaking easily about anything.) I wonder if others have the same trouble . . .

. . . When are we going to see each other? I'd like to hear the Washington story as a whole. You'd better call it a lost battle now and not waste any more time and adrenaline. Our troubles are an issue in the present election—I doubt that Stevenson can do much for us, but so far he's fighting on our side and Eisenhower chose a vice-presidential candidate for the sole purpose of working against us . . .

As ever,
Malcolm

Andover, New Jersey
September 6, 1952
[NL]

Dear Malcolm,

Heckaroo! I'm sorry to learn that you have been ailing. I keep telling myself: We mustn't ail; if only out of sheer spite, we must have health enough. A beautiful sentiment—if only I didn't, while saying it, gasp and gag and gulp.

Faugh!

I can't imagine what they think they have on me. So I begin to suspect that their main document may be the stuff I wrote about myself, in answer to their inquiries! (I always said, proudly, that I could do myself so much more damage than my pissant enemies could do.)

. . .

Don't write me off too soon, as regards my pedagogical racket. Heilman has written the administration some pretty good letters. I also have been non-bellicose (or rather, have made frank peace offerings after brief bellicose flare-ups); and I'll swear I don't see how they can justify their stand, unless they have some professional perjurers who will swear by the rood that they saw me in bed with Uncle Joe [Stalin]. There are a few minor squibs written in my salad days that can embarrass me a little, but that don't justify a decision of this sort. So I keep puzzling as to what they think they have on me, to justify their claim that I would be a subversive influence in the classroom. If things came to a showdown, I would in all conscience suggest that my former students be polled . . .

How about proposing this as the test: A brief note to my former students asking them, "In your opinion, was Mr. Burke's course in accordance with the political institutions of our country, or was it 'subversive,' state briefly in what respect or respects." My idea is to force these guys, not with challenges, but with many proposals of this sort, in this spirit. For instance, I have written Schmitz[1] asking that I be permitted to appear before him and the Board of Regents, to explain exactly what I will deal with in my course (on the theory of language); and Heilman has seconded this proposal. Meanwhile, Heilman has also written a very forceful letter, asking for a bill of particulars, to justify the Administration's stand.

. . . Teaching has become an integral part of my work. It provides me with the equivalent of an experimental laboratory. And the sight of the new Hopefuls is, to me . . . one more visible reason to hang on if one can, to try once more, cardiacally, to take heart. I must watch, at every stage, that I do not get shoved into a role not my own. In many ways I'm a bum, as you know if anybody knows. But I nonetheless feel confident that I can squeak through. And, having through-gesqueaked, I dare feel that my most poisonous of all resources can stand me in good stead. I mean: my frankness, my possibly even morbid frankness, my poor battered virginity.

. . . If these men insist upon engaging me, then so it must be. We live but once; and this in itself is a dingy issue; but I will work at it as though God and/or the Nature of Things had appointed me for a truly serious task. I will do what I can do. And as a man who feels death in his bones, however long he may prolong the sentence, I assure you, Malcolm, I am not any longer just trying to "get along" or "get ahead." I must not embarrass my two wonderful boys (my girls have already proved their Burke-Batterham competence). I am leaving them a piece of property, enough for more of our breeding. The girls too have acres enough, if ever they want to look at the stars from a grounding registered as theirs at the county seat. (I tell you these things at this moment because I tell myself things like that, day after day. Or ask myself. Our place is parklike now. Several acres have been recovered from the threatening jungle, by one who prays to the jungle, at night, in the throbbings of Sept-Oct. The grass each year grows richer.)

We'll take a chawnst, Malcolm. I'm a guilt-ridden man; but I do dare feel that I am pious as those reactionary, unregal among the Regents are not . . . I love my country with a fury that farts cannot deny me. And I thank God, there is amply much of democracy left for me still to be able to prove it.

Sincerely,

K. B.

1. Henry Schmitz was the new president of the Board of Regents of the University of Washington.

Sherman, Connecticut
September 11, 1952
[NL]

Dear Kenneth:

Let me tell you about the actual alignment of forces at the University of Washington, or as much as I know about it.

Your great enemy: the Church, or a faction in the Church. Purpose of this enemy: to get control of U.S. policy by creating the notion that loyalty and Americanism are Catholic virtues ("We must prove that we are more loyal than anybody else," said a Catholic bishop at a recent communion breakfast). Incidentally to get non-Catholics fired from government, TV, movie, radio, and university jobs and replaced by Catholics. If public education is weakened in the process, there is no objection.

. . .

Your trouble: simply that your name is listed somewhere, I don't know exactly where: Hartnett's list,[1] "Counter Attack" (the Red Channels weekly newsletter), the Legion's list, certainly by the Un-American Committee in Washington. The trouble was brewing before you wrote a single letter about your own activities (that I know from Jack Matthews).[2] More of your trouble: the new president of the University has evidently backed out of the question. The liberals on the board have evidently decided to drop you so as to avoid a row. The only thing that would change them is the promise of a still bigger row on the other side.

. . .

I hope you fight the thing through and you will receive good support from the faculty. If I were in your case I don't know that I *would* fight it through, because I'm not combative, and am even fearful of the results on me of combat, the psychological results. That isn't an accurate statement. I actually am wildly combative when angry, usually end by making a fool of myself, and therefore am afraid of letting myself get angry. But if we applied Kant's principle to the situation my conduct would be judged immoral—if everyone does the same, the situation won't get any better. So fight it through, if you feel that's the thing you need and want to do, and you'll be fighting for all of us and throwing a scare into the Board of Regents. But make sure that you point out how your theories are—as indeed they are in fact—diametrically opposed to Communism . . . anti-totalitarian, individualistic, realistic, whereas your opposition at Washington has been subscribing to totalitarian principles. Give them a moving statement of belief, tell them you are fighting not for yourself but for American principles . . .

As ever,
Malcolm

1. Vincent Hartnett, who was affiliated with "Counter Attack," started his own anticommunist organization, AWARE Inc. It published lists of those it deemed communist sympathizers.

2. Jackson Matthews, the scholar-critic, had been a member of the faculty at the University of Washington.

Andover, New Jersey
September 23, 1952
[NL]

Dear Malcolm,

Many thanks indeed for yours of inst., with relevant info anent the sichaysh thereabouts.

Would say:

Things took a surprising shift, as Schmitz, recognizing that he had nothing on me, veered to an attack upon the English department at the University of Washington. His argument was: the department is too leftist; Burke calls himself a "left liberal"; hence, in appointing him, the administration would be but intensifying the present leftness of the department, which is not representative of the community.

I have not yet heard from Heilman how the department wants to proceed from there. Meanwhile, I wrote Schmitz again, explaining at greater length what I meant by my entitlement. Basically, my point was: I have been on the fringes of many movements, at the center of none. I have developed not by recantation, but by "principle of the chambered nautilus." I consider such "cultural imperialism" essentially "liberal." I call it "leftist" because it also contains a Marxist coordinate. And "there are two ways in which one can cheat oneself with regard to Marxism: by trying to make of it everything, and by trying to make of it nothing."

. . . I'm a poor excuse for a champion. I'm just a guy who built up a course in the analysis of language, and who is out to peddle it honorably. But, begad, he *will* peddle it honorably, that he will . . .

Sincerely,
K. B.

Sherman, Connecticut
September 27, 1952
[PS]

Dear Kenneth:

Written mostly to say that I received your letter of 23rd inst. and approve of sentiments therein expressed. Once you can start talking or writing to the bastards you can back them into a corner. It was a tactical error to describe yourself as a left liberal. You are in many ways a conservative, a liberal conservative or vice versa. Why not cop onto that terminology in these times? What you didn't realize is that "left liberal" (or "extreme liberal" or New Dealer) has become one of their cusswords, practically equivalent to the Bad Word itself.

. . .

Just back from a week at Yaddo, where everything was pretty serene. Except for trouble early last summer from members of a sect (one got arrested and had to bribe his way out, another took an overdose of sleeping pills). Back in the thirties the majority sect among the guests at Yaddo was the leftists. Defeat of the leftists. What other large political group will take over? At first the group promised to be the organized anti-communists, but they aren't numerous enough. No, the present large integrated group in the literary-political world is the homosexuals, who are taking over to fill the vacuum. What a depressing way to fill a vacuum.

> Zever,
> Malcolm

> Andover, New Jersey
> October 3, 1952
> [NL]

Dear Malcolm,

Recent letter from Heilman would indicate that the uncleansed U. of Washington is sacrificing a chance to be talked-at by a leading literary figure of Byram Township.[1] Heilman went before the Regency to plead my case, but he informs me that all was nothing. The matter of either my political purity or my pedagogic competence did not come up. The squeezing was apparently done, for the most part, via the fact that there are three ex-CPUSAns in the department.

Meanwhile, am leaving for NYC today, to catch plane for California tomorrow. (To see about possibilities of all the Burkes' spending some months there soon.)

. . .

(Am not at all regretful that I called myself a "left liberal," though God only knows just what I am! Since I had to read over again, for proofs, my chapter, "Program," in *Counter-Statement*, I was struck by the fact that the muddle I discussed then is still quite with us, including the inability to know whether one is progressive or reactionary. The main reason I am glad that I called myself a "left liberal" is because it would not be ingratiating. My plan was to be wholly cooperative; to give them any information they asked for, and more; neither to challenge, nor to apologize;—but, more later. Must prepare for the trip.)

> Sincerely,
> K. B.

1. Burke's township in New Jersey.

Sherman, Connecticut
October 8, 1952
[PS]

Dear Kenneth:

So you lost the battle of Puget Sound without even a chance to engage the enemy. Exactly that happened to me at Minnesota—except that in the Minnesota case I didn't even try to fight . . . Your own loss is chiefly of time. Think of the others: poor Harry Slochower caught over a barrel and his purse stolen legally—what's he going to do now? And moving into a more political realm, think of Earl Browder[1] and his wife, cast out by the communists, then arrested with that sort of personal vindictiveness of which the department of Justice has offered so many examples . . . And for another example reported in the same paper, the brave university of Tennessee has canceled a series of old Chaplin films at the demand of the American Legion.

Bad times here. Worse times coming. The political campaign has turned sour since McCarthy won his three-to-one nomination in Wisconsin. Eisenhower is sailing to victory on his resemblance to Daddy Warbucks, and like Daddy Warbucks he's taken to machine-gunning the Reds, except that there are no Reds around to machine-gun . . . These are times to salt a little cash away, if one can get hold of it—but of course there *is* no individual salvation, not even subsistence farming.

Nevertheless we'll survive, for twenty years or so, and hope for better luck for our children. Let me hear what happens on your trip to the Coast.

Zever,
Malcolm

1. Earl Browder (1891–1973), a member of the American Communist Party, and its secretary general 1930–1944. He was imprisoned for passport fraud in 1940, but freed by President Roosevelt in 1942. In 1946 he was removed from the Communist Party for having urged closer cooperation between the Soviet Union and the West during World War II.

Hermes Publications
Los Altos, California
January 16, 1953
[NL]

Dear Malcolm,

How.

Egregious boast: my gaspo-gaggo-gulpo has greatly abated. And often even I have slepp. What more could one ask, as he modestly perches on his peak (alas! quite often cloud-capped, with doubtless fertilizing moisture).

Mainly I am, as it were, getting my papers in order.[1] The typesetting of *Counter-Statement* is now finished, and the plating has begun. I am next to prepare for a new edition of *Permanence and Change*. (Hope to get started on that next week. Have decided to make only a few stylistic changes, and to leave the ideationally problematical statements as they were, but give them a semanticist twist by footnotes.)

Enclosed herewith is the offprint of an article you already saw.[2] (Incidentally, you also figure passim in an item by me in the last *Accent*.)[3]

Further, I enclose page proofs of an epilogue I have added to *Counter-Statement*.[4] Knowing how much items like this by me usually burn you up, I am sending this one in the hopes that you'll be able to say that this one didn't burn you up. Try real hard. (Incidentally, it will give you a cue as to what I mean when I speak of "semanticizing" *Permanence and Change*.)

. . .

Typical day: Rest of family gets up at six. Shorty drives the young gents three miles down the road, in the rain or mist, to meet the schoolbus. Papa gets started around eight, closing the shop about one. (Last hour begins with some unexpected bright spots and ends with a couple of swiftly moving pages which, nearly always, must be thrown away. Pappy has been drinking.) Lunch, snooze. In afternoon, mild woodgathering, or walks about the breasty knolls hereabouts. Punish piano. Cocktail hour. Dinner. Read, or sit by fire talking in evening. To bed, and quite frequently, to sleep.

. . .

Hope later to visit missions, wineries, etc. So far, have been north to San Francisco and south [to] Monterey (where I was entranced with the Fishermen's Wharves). Sea between Monterey and Carmel is a rock-torn turmoil, with seal island close enough for us to watch, through our poor glasses, the tough lesson in private property supplied by the Big Shots who would mark off wide areas of nookie for themselves alone, at a terrific cost in vigilance.

But I talk too much. And besides, I have a lot more talking to do.

Sincerely,
and love to all,
K. B.

1. Hermes was undertaking to publish new editions, with some new and revised material, of three of Burke's books.

2. "Thanatopsis for Critics: A Brief Thesaurus of Deaths and Dying," which appeared in October 1952 in *Essays in Criticism*.

3. "A 'Dramatistic' View of Imitation," published in the Autumn 1952 issue of *Accent*.

4. Burke's "epilogue" was entitled "Curriculum Criticum."

Sherman, Connecticut
January 25, 1953
[PS]

Dear Kenneth:

. . . I envy you up on your mountain and away from this Eastern winter, which so far has been a dreary one, snow, fog, rain, snow, fog. And just as well, for you, not to be at the U of Washington, but not so well for the U. Peter [Blume] and I were mildly arguing last night about whether you had been right to invest so much energy into a vain fight to teach there. Peter is somber about the general situation (as I am too) and thinks that the only course for writers and artists is not to fight but to find interstices in the system where they can still work effectively, at least for the time being—painting pictures, writing books, writing plays for Broadway, and leaving Hollywood, TV, radio, and state universities to the bastards to do what they like with. That way, he said, the artist saves all his energy for his work. I said that human energy wasn't like a fixed quantity of electric current that could be used either for one purpose or for another—it was sometimes generated in a fight and lost by not fighting, so that the man who surrendered too easily in the face of a hopeless situation might find that he also surrendered in the face of his work. It was an old argument and we got nowhere, but in the end I don't think you lost objectively by doing your utmost with the dumb president of Washington and his board of regents.

The situation is bad. At present I don't see anything to stop the bastards. One trouble is that the American educated classes are so other-directed—to use David Riesman's term—that is, they are so trained to adapt themselves to other people's attitudes, so lacking in inner conviction, so convinced that when somebody says anything loudly enough "there must be something in it," that the acts and opinions of the bastards cut through our society as through cheese; there's no real resistance . . .

·   ·   ·

I won't make long comments on the two documents you enclosed. Remember that I saw the "Thanatopsis" in manuscript. I wonder if you shouldn't do the same sort of job on Love (only that would be much more difficult). The "Curriculum Criticum" is a useful job for anyone who wants to follow your career. I think it is more self-deprecatory than it needs to be and if you're going to make any more proof changes (cutting the first sentence was an admirable change) they ought to be in the direction of dropping the apologies. It is wonderful that your works are being revised and republished. What about some x-references as a guide to students (I mean notes in *Counter-Statement* and *Permanence and Change* and *Attitudes Toward History* informing the reader that such and such a topic had been developed at greater length in Chapter N of a later volume)? I still think that a book from you that would sell widely is a handbook of literary criticism, principles with examples, made up from your already published work. Why not think about that? . . .

Zever,
Malcolm

Hermes Publications,
Los Altos, California
February 6, 1953
[NL]

Dear Malcolm,

Greetings, mong songblabble.[1] Which is to say that I had three teeth ripped out yesterday, thereby having a sound moralistic reason for getting mildly plastered. Today I don't know whether my considerable wooziness is due to the novocain or the alky. But I must say: so far, I have experienced practically no pain at all. Here's hoping that yours was equally delightful, including the fantastic record of more than seven hours of motionless slumber, sitting with my clothes on, in a chair by the fire.

Woke up gradually, full of plans. (Might it even be possible that the occasional ringing and stinging of my left ear was due to those teeth? We'll see.)

If the plans have since gone up the spout, what's the diff?

•   •   •

When do we re-trek East? If all goes as planned, we so do sometime in Avril (which is French for April). And as for your fears: Forget them. Jeez, we grew up during Republicanism. And we learned how to behave. Why forget what we learned? (We got so in the habit of wincing every time Truman did a botcho, as though we had done that one, too, that each day's news was like another nail in our coffin. But now the Ins got what they were asking for. Let them have it. That's not too hard, is it? When Dulles does what Acheson did, the difference is this: Under Acheson, *I* did it; under Dulles, *he* does it. And even if we're hell-bent for heaven, Dulles can't make me hold my breath as Acheson did.)

Jeez, how little they know! The stupidity of putting businessmen in those key jobs! Those jobs should be held by politicos who do the dirty business that the businessmen want done, *and who take the blame for it* whenever blame is being passed around. With a politico, even a Democratic politico, as cabinet member, General Motors could easily have doubled their drag on war contracts, without a flurry. But with Wilson in the cabinet,[2] even a ten-cent increase will be scrutinized as carefully as though one were getting a bead on something in season.

Yes? No? We'll see. (Unquestionably, in any case, these "foretellings" will need revision of some sort. Everything always does, as the fellow says. Natheless . . .)[3]

Flourish. (May we *all* flourish.)

Sincerely,
K. B.

1. "Mong songblabble" plays, of course, on the famous lines from Baudelaire's *Fleurs du Mal*, "—Hypocrite lecteur, —mon semblable, —mon frère!"

2. Charles E. Wilson, secretary of defense from January of 1953 to October of 1957. Before his appointment, Wilson was president and chief executive officer of General Motors.

3. Burke's ellipses.

Sherman, Connecticut
February 13, 1953
[NL]

Dear Kenneth:

. . . A plate in the mouth, with a sheet of pink plastic for the tongue to rest against instead of one's own palate, is an indignity offered to the human body. But there's no doubt that the disappearance of eight teeth, plus the appearance in the house of hundreds of black capsules designed to create a calcium deficiency in the system, has made me feel less perpetually weary and even able to finish some of the little jobs that have been oppressing me all fall.

One of those jobs was an article on the New Fiction that will lose me many friends among the New Fictionists and the New Critics. The real point of the article (outside of some funny stuff) was that the New Fictionists are trying to create a sort of pure or ontological fiction, which they call Moral Realism as opposed to Social Realism and which presents characters as existing independently of any human institutions and confronted only with "permanent" dilemmas of a moral nature. But our principal moral problems, today—as always—are in a context of institutions and in fact consist of resistance or adjustment to institutions—so that Moral Realism is morally unrealistic. Result: novels that are like tidy rooms in Bedlam.

This morning heard on the radio that the Pope is advising clemency for the Rosenbergs. What a situation, when the great anti-communist himself is more merciful than our crusaders for human dignity. If he had spoken two weeks ago, Iron-Hewer[1] might have gathered up courage to make a sensible gesture. You are certainly right in your observations about the danger to the corporationists in accepting responsibility along with power. Meanwhile let us stay in our woodchuck holes and meditate until the winter is over.

As ever,
Malcolm

1. President Eisenhower.

Sherman, Connecticut
August 29, 1953
[PS]

Dear Kenneth,

I write to say Hi! and because I have just finished reading your prologue to *Permanence and Change*, and because I have so much other work to do that writing letters becomes a wicked folly, and how I love folly. I was much interested in the prologue, but not at all certain that it will perform the function for which it was designed, of taking readers by the hand and setting them on the path through the maze. All your prologues are epilogues, all your first chapters are last chapters, all your introductions wander into new territory and require a knowledge of Burkeranto that transform them into afterwords . . . Was very much interested in the discussion of the primacy of poetics—that's part of your general position and I don't know whether you have stated it so clearly in any other connection. It has something to do with the cultural configurations of the anthropologists—one society will have a cooperative configuration, another a configuration of selfishness and distrust—the configuration is a sort of central idea of the society and is of course expressed *in words* before it is expressed in institutions. Did you ever read Margaret Mead's "Sex and Temperament in Three Primitive Societies"?

I wrote for the *New Republic* a very unsatisfactory note on *Counter-Statement*. It's too negative in its distribution of comments—but later I may combine it with the review of the *Rhetoric* into an essay for publication in a book, and thus do you more justice. In the hot summer I had a hell of a job writing that piece; the thinking organism didn't want to operate; hence the unsatisfactory result.

•   •   •

I'm trying to put together a book on The Literary Situation for publication in spring 1954. The old head creaks rustily, but I have some things to say.

As ever,
Malcolm

Bennington College
Bennington, Vermont
September 17, 1953
[NL]

Dear Malcolm,

Saw your review last night, reading it under hit-and-run conditions. So these are very hasty first impressions:

Thanks, most of all, for the references to the Hermes angle,[1] and thanks for many kind and gentle lines.

I think you're tragically wrong about the Hitler piece,[2] though as a student of effects I can certainly see the effect you get by that statement. I'd say, for instance, that my pieces on *Julius Caesar*, *Othello*, and *Faust* are all better, decidedly—for, when one is equal to it, the method does better by a better book. (Since you have never seen my analysis of the *Oresteia*, I can't kick about your ignoring of that. But when it is published, it will be answer enough.)

I had often thought of making my public answer to you, Tate, and Blackmur on that point when Blackmur's work on Adams appears. (If it ever does!) I thought I'd analyze the amount of stuff that was said, sans reference to literary quality.

To give you an idea of what I mean: Suppose I were to use a similar effect when writing of your *Exile's Return*. I could say: "The trouble with the book is that it gives such a big play to fourth- and fifth-rate literary personalities. And the basic error of his methods is revealed by the fact that the book *attains its very culmination* in the analysis of a journal by an inferior writer."

Or, suppose I wanted to mention the Hitler piece so as [to] produce an effect other than the kind you wanted. Then I could say: "There is a sense in which even a poor writer is remarkable. And Burke's method is based on this principle. There are occasions when a bad book can be more *worthwhile reading about* than it would be *worth reading*. And under such conditions, a critical analysis can be like a translation that is better than the original." Animus is all! Vive the getting of effects!

I also think you should have replaced that hodgepodge paragraph by one showing *how I developed my definition of form in the book itself*. That is, you should have showed how the concept was subdivided (syllogistic, qualitative, repetitive, minor—and how applied, as per the various subdivisions of the *Lexicon*). By omitting this, you get the effect that I was but late in discovering something Poe had already discovered.

For purely sales reasons, I also wish you had mentioned the fact that the *Curriculum Criticum* had been added. (Incidentally, as against your report of what I am supposed to have said to you about literary criticism and myself, in the "Curriculum Criticum," at the end, there is a quite accurate statement on this point.)[3]

See you soon—and shall hope by then to have got a more considered look at the review. Meanwhile, again, thanks for the several things there are there to thank you for. And as for the "effects" masking under the guise of criticism, I've been in the business long enough now to know that it's "normal" to us all, as literary politicos.

Haste, for breakfast—

> See you soon,
> Best luck,
> Sincerely,
> K. B.

1. Cowley's review of the new edition of *Counter-Statement*, published in the *New Republic* on September 14, began by stating that Hermes publications had undertaken to republish Burke's early books.

2. In his review, Cowley writes that Burke's essay on Hitler's *Mein Kampf* is "possibly" the "most brilliant of all the examples" of how his critical "art" helps "explain strategies of persuasion." Burke had been especially sensitive to accusations that his method ignores, or fails to be concerned with, critical judgments or standards of value. Cowley raises this criticism in his review.

3. Near the end of "Curriculum Criticum," Burke emphasizes the relationship between his works of fiction and his criticism, writing that "whatever one may think of their intrinsic merit," they "have been of great value to him, because he can now remember them as from without, whereas once he experienced them drastically from within—and he has found this double vision useful for his analysis of motive."

> Sherman, Connecticut
> July 28, 1954
> [PS]

Dear Kenneth:

. . . I haven't written you or anyone else because I've been working on . . . *The Literary Situation* . . .[1]

. . . Page proofs ought to be back next week, and the book is to appear in the last week of October. By being slow with it I missed a lot of magazine sales—so far only an article to *Harper's* and one to *Saturday Review*, outside of what I had sold already. I can't look forward to much financial profit, though the book is written on a more popular level than *Exile's Return*, I hope without weakening whatever structure of ideas it possesses; writing more popularly means chiefly not taking any knowledge for granted on the part of one's readers, but explaining eveything. Anyway I can begin to live a human life again, see more people, hoe the garden, hunt woodchucks . . .

I'm beginning to think about my next book. What I'd like to do is brood about the 1930s and carry out that old project, feeling myself back into the past (it's the age to do that now, *our* age to turn ourselves into literature) and at the same time looking for more adventures in the present . . .

As evermore,
Malcolm

1. The following paragraph quotes from the first paragraph of the foreword, where Cowley describes the book as "a social history of literature in our times." "I like and admire criticism 'in depth,'" he writes, "but there are occasions when one should stand back to survey the situation in breadth, from a perspective in space or time."

Sherman, Connecticut,
July 29, 1954
[PS]

Dear Kenneth:

Not having written you for six months or thereabouts, here I am writing two days in succession. There are sequels to what I said, or started to say.

Everything has been baking and drying out on our gravel bank. The lawn, so-called, looks like the top of a crew-cut head, except for green weeds among the dead grass. I could see the pine trees suffering, making little more than half their normal growth and their last year's needles falling in June instead of October. There would have been no garden if I hadn't watered it—thank God, we have a deep well. Yesterday evening at six exactly we had a heavy thunder shower, then at ten another heavy shower without thunder. During the second shower I was in bed going through your letters to me from 1928–1945.

It was the beginning of an exercise in self-rediscovery. I forget so much and so easily. At the age of 56 (on August 24) I propose to ask once more who and what I am. Your letters told me a good deal, but not enough. I could find out what we were arguing about in a given year. I was reminded how often I have been ill (broken arms, appendicitis, lots of grippe) and I was scolded, Lord, how I was scolded for writing this or that, for promising and not fulfilling, for being a bureaucrat—and there was too, too much truth in this last reproach. For the last five years on the NR (1935–40), I was leading a public and institutional life that I didn't any longer believe in and that drained my private life of any meaning. I escaped into gardening, which is a silent occupation. But there was only the shadow of this in your letters, since both of us have developed the bad habit of writing about ourselves, not about the other. Your letters are a marvelous record of your own adventures, especially the writing of TABL, which you related declamation by declamation.

I'm suggesting now that we trade letters, as we did once before—this time exchanging everything up to 1945. You'll be getting more than you give, because you wrote more letters in those years and had more to say. But I'll need my own letters, briefer and more superficial as I fear they are, to discover what I was in those years. I hope I can write the book now that I planned to write in 1940. Or not that book, because what I do will be more subjective, but at least a book dealing with the same years.

· · ·

. . . *Exile's Return* was in part, but only in part, a death-and-rebirth ritual, especially in its earlier form, though much less in the revised edition. I know that the book on the 1930s won't be that at all, because I don't want to disavow what I did. I also know that the method will be selection and synecdoche, an attempt to find the little incidents and situations that stand for a bigger situation. But what's going to come out of it, beyond that point, I still don't know, and I'm not going to start by decreeing a conclusion . . .

As ever,
Malcolm

Andover, New Jersey
August 11, 1954
[NL]

Dear Malcolm,
. . . Quite a batch of your letters are already collected in one pile. Some months ago, Shorty[1] began going through all the letters here, as Bill Williams wanted his. So at the same time, she sorted out the various names. However, there are several packets that she has not yet gone through. Are you in much of a hurry? . . .

· · ·

Have perforce got into your area, since the article I have been doing is on Walt Whitman,[2] and the correlations between the cult of "manly attachment" and the cult of the All-Mother are everywhere. In my first section, I deal with the Vistas, pretty much in merely summarizing fashion. In my second section, on the Leaves, I show in general how the policies of Vistas look, when poetically personalized. Then in section three I narrow down to the Lilacs poem (building on the fact, not previously noted to my knowledge, that the trinity of star, bird, and bush involves sight, sound, and scent respectively—and also, I think, makes a trinity of paternal, filial, and maternal respectively, though my main investment is in the sight-sound-scent alignment) . . .

As for your paragraph about the relation between particulars and generalizations: I think I understand your point quite thoroughly. May you have better luck than I have had, on this score, at the hands of critics like Blackmur, Tate, and Cowley.

But what a hell of a place on which to end a letter. Perhaps I should add, for the record, that your second letter arrived before your first; that one could drown in our pond if he stood on his head; that when I stood by the pond at midnight, our friendly skunk came up and started picking up crumbs left by the children, and neither of us stank the other . . .

> Sincerely—and to
> Muriel,
> K. B.

1. Shorty is Burke's wife, Libbie.

2. Burke's article on Whitman, "Policy Made Personal: Whitman's Verse and Prose—Salient Traits," was published in 1955 in *Leaves of Grass One Hundred Years Later*, a book edited by Milton Hindus.

> Sherman, Connecticut
> January 16, 1955
> [NL]

Dear Kenneth:

. . . I spent ten weeks in Chicago last winter. No hint there now of the sort of life that was lived in old houses on Rush Street. No literary life at all, except among the young but not too damned talented friends of Nelson Algren, and a collection of bowties around *Poetry*, which is reeling and ready to fall . . .

Do you ever see Nathan Asch, who lives in Mill Valley?

Life is too short for me to read [William] Burrough's manuscript. Kerouac told me about him. Kerouac is a natural writer like a natural spitball pitcher, but no sense and no control. Burroughs has every manifestation of genius except the genius.

> As ever,
> Malcolm

Andover, New Jersey
March 16, 1955
[NL]

Dear Malcolm,

. . . Mysteriously . . . my ailments have eased. (Jeez, but they do keep me bepuzzed. Trouble is: there are always *combinations* of things preceding a change; and it's the very devil to figure out what particular thing within that combination, or what smaller combination of things within the larger combination, may have been the Deciding Factor. But, anyhow, I'm always lurking, in the hopes of finding out. And if one great critic, though young yet, said that my major specialty is Burkology, it is even much more likely that my major ailment is Burkitis.)

.   .   .

Well, bejeez, I was granted a scare-shiver. Lightning hit the wires close nearby in a trick way, at a time when we didn't even know that a storm was brewing. And it smacked around the room, jumping between telephone and light wires with frenzy, and putting a big mark on the wall, and startling me into a spontaneous fury of fright, rage, and sheer automatic outcry . . . Anyhow, it all added up to a state of affairs whereby, through merely recalling the incident, I could *make* myself shiver. For several hours I was completely free of my difficulty (though I nearly choked when the damned thing happened). But later, when the Old Dispensation started filtering back, I bethought me of this possible subterfuge—and it worked.

.   .   .

As for the *Book of Moments: Poems 1915–1954*, I think the printer starts work on it tomorrow. (I mailed final corrected page proofs via airmail Monday.) Tis a tiny turd, considering that it is the digest of 40 years . . . I have not the least idea whether it will help me, hinder me, or (what is most likely) be unnoticed and leave everything just as was. Have thought of sending copies to Wilson and Mumford—and if you think it's worth a flyer, I wonder if you could give me addresses for them. Because the book really leads up to and away from the things I did in the Thirties, I found myself essentially Thirty-minded when thinking of possible persons to whom I might send copies . . .

Meanwhile, while I have sat here mainly budgeless, some of the younger educators and educatrices have been somewhat cottoning to me. (More and more, I begin to realize that I left school because I wanted to be a teacher, and could never be if I went all the way through that mill. Some can, but I couldn't.) And they are an evangelical brood, bejeez. So, as I sicken and sag, I begin at least to get the satisfaction (that people only get usually in rare dreams) of being an observer at my own funeral . . .

K. B.

Sherman, Connecticut
March 24, 1955
[NL]

Dear Kenneth,

You have always been one of those persons about whom people say, on hearing of their complaints, "It's only psychosomatic," as if psychosomatic ailments weren't as real as any others. This last year for the first time I have been getting truly disturbed about you. But I can't do anything except hover at a distance and offer the name of my internist (wonderful word), who has literary interests and is the best diagnostician I ever met. He is Dr. William H. Resnik, of the Yale Medical School . . .

As ever,
Malcolm

Andover, New Jersey
January 21, 1956
[NL]

Dear Malcolm,

Holla! I just learn by the papers that you are our new President.[1] Felicitations, indeed. May you, with God's guidance, pilot our Sturm-und-Drang-tossed ship of statement safely into portliness. I trust also that you are voffing 'em at Hooverville.[2] (Give my regards to that horse's ass, Yvor Winters.)

Would I had but a trace of your great ministerial prowess. Meanwhile, I sink ever deeper into the morass of my monomania (man as symbol-using animal, goaded by hierarchal psychosis) and my psychosomatic ailments (tipping inexorably toward the somatic slope that will be the end of me).

I worked far too hard at school last term (slogan: full-time job at part-time salary). For the month since school ended, I have been somewhat aimlessly digging out from under (mainly by trying to put my papers in order). However, I wrote one article, "The Seven Offices," reducing mankind to seven basic jobs (aside from the shithouse, and of course the basic job of trying to figure out at what gazettorial door I should knock with this article, 25 pages along the lines of a post-behaviorist, Dramatistico-semantic, neo-Ciceronian *De Officiis*) . . .

Sincerely,
K. B.

1. Cowley had just been elected president of the National Institute of Arts and Letters.
2. Cowley was a visiting professor at Stanford University.

2120 Santa Cruz Avenue,
Menlo Park, California
January 23, 1956
[NL]

Dear Kenneth,

Thangsfryourletter. Do I deserve congratulences or condoleations? The president of our institution has seldom been one of its most distinguished members. Usually he's a member who can't run fast and the nominating committee catches up with him. I didn't even have a chance to run, since I was at Stanford when the election took place—had I been in New York I would have ducked out of the honor or onus by suggesting another victim. My name was substituted at the last moment for that of Isabel Bishop, who has taken side in art controversies and therefore has enemies; when she heard that she would be opposed, she withdrew her name. The dodos accepted me because they liked the way I had conducted the last dinner meeting, which you didn't attend. That's the job of an institutional president: to attend and conduct meetings and neglect his own work. I'm not exactly proud of having displayed that talent.

But now the question strikes me: Can we do anything with the Institute? Direct it along any new lines or into any new undertakings? Or simply keep it as before and try to make it a little better? With your hierarchical mind, what would you suggest?

•   •   •

We haven't been (secret) terribly happy out here. No complaints about the university or about the students, who are a pleasant lot. But the weather has been frightful—the sun has shone exactly two of the twenty-three days since our arrival . . . The people are nice but not so amusing as those in Seattle—they don't drink or talk so much and keep an eye on academic advancement, whereas the Seattle people had almost abandoned hope or fear . . .

As ever,
Malcolm

Andover, New Jersey
February 6, 1956
[NL]

Dear Malcolm,

'Twould seem that I have pulled out of my slump, at least the worst of it. Now have a quite regular schedule, each morning writing up my lecture notes on "The Ancient Mariner" (at last!), chores and a walk each afternoon, and "indexing" at least ten pages of *Mrs. Dalloway* each evening (in preparation for next term's work at Bennington) . . .

But I'm the last guy in the world to consult, for advice. I am so unassertive these days, I'd even hesitate to tell somebody to go and blow his brains out. My assumption is that, except for very minor matters, the Institute is about as pliant as a whited sepulcher.

.   .   .

I can well understand your beefing about Menlo Park in rainy weather. In fact, I doubt whether you'd like the climate much even in the dry season. Many a time we'd leave the mountain, where it was sunny, and find the valley choking with smog, mostly industrial fumes. Industry in California valleys is almost lethal—and every year apparently there is to be more of it . . . Flaubert saw it coming, and it made him sullen—but jeez, it's damned little he had to kick about. The one that burns me up most now, every time I think of it, is the atomic-powered submarines. For here's betting a thousand to one that they keep dribbling their murderous waste matter into the sea. . . .

Sincerely,
K. B.

[Postscript] Among my tinkerings, I have finally reduced my definition of man to a Flowerish:[1]

man is

the symbol-using animal,
inventor of the negative,
separated from his natural condition
by instruments of his own making,
and goaded by the spirit of hierarchy

---

1. A "flowerish" is a peculiarly Burkean poetic form in which "prose epigrams" are printed in designs that approximate the ornamentation of a flourish and the shape of a flower (the Latin root of flourish—*florere*—means "to blossom"). They appear in his *Collected Poems*.

Sherman, Connecticut
September 12, 1956
[NL]

Dear Kenneth,

. . . Time's winged chariot drawing near. There's a great hiatus in expe-
riential literature, the hiatus of age. When people begin to feel it, they
haven't enough energy to write about it. Yet there are all these interesting
little changes—first the purely physical ones that we know all about, the
heart that pounds when we do a little physical work, the joints that feel
stiff, the crick in the back . . . And sight too—not that my sight is failing,
but just that it's not such a pleasure to look at things closely, it's easier to
look through the inner eye. And sex, which is no longer so imperious. And
memory—The first sign there of change is the difficulty in remembering
names, then it becomes hard to remember nouns, then one notes that the
distant past is becoming much more vivid than last week.

And all the time the feeling that I have done so little I wanted to do,
that I must hurry to put things into shape. And that other feeling that I
should make some complete change while there is still time for changes,
if there is still time. I'd like to get out two more books in prose, and I'd
like to put my poems into shape, with new ones.

I sound much more doleful than I feel. For that's the analgesic side of
age—the sorrows are there but you don't feel them any longer. 58 now.
Two years to sixty. And what about you? Seems to me you're right spry,
from what I last heard and saw . . .

As ever,
Malcolm

Andover, New Jersey
September 17, 1956
[NL]

Dear Malcolm,

. . . I hope to get my Symbolic definitively revised before the first of the
year. Then I'll take with us my notes for the fourth book (the damned
trilogy having become a godam tetralogy)—and we're going to improvise
as to where we stay, in the lands of the soft-spoken, cross-burning South-
erner.

Yes, I know what you mean, as regards a disinclination to write about
one's symptoms. We get beyond the point where we can take our ailments
as accomplishments. I'm just plain bored with my ailments, so bored that
I don't even bore other people with them as much as I should. To disbelieve

in success is no great burden; the real terror comes when one even disbelieves in failure, and that's where I am. But what bad observer or corrupt reporter ever gave you the notion that I am "quite spry"? I am dying on my feet—and if I may paraphrase the poet, the only way I can live long enough is by taking long enough to die. Meanwhile, know that I could match you, symptom for symptom, any time . . .

Sincerely,
K. B.

Sherman, Connecticut
October 5, 1956
[NL]

Dear Kenneth,

. . . No more matching symptoms. You win.—But for God's sake be moderate in your triumph. Now that the laurel crown is on your brow, don't have any more symptoms just to prove that you're a genius at having them. Take care of yourself, rest, and prolong your stay in this vale of aches.

How did you get a bilateral inguinal hernia? Or discover that you had it? Might it have something to do with your shortness of breath? Will the repair job clean up some of your other ills? . . .

I'm working on Thomas Wolfe.[1] You'd be fascinated by his letters. He had a single-minded ambition to eat the world and digest it into words; everything he touched had to be written down in words; and he saved the words in a big packing box that was like a miser's hoard. Much as he wanted to be famous, it gave him a trauma to lose the words, to have them printed in a book. After each book, he had a prolonged fit of depression that almost amounted to dementia. He died of overwriting, a good death, like one from overfucking, but I'd rather die of extreme old age, a hell of a long time from now.

Therefore no more symptoms.

As ever,
Malcolm

1. At the time, Cowley was working on an essay on Wolfe, "The Miserly Millionaire of Words," which appeared in the *Reporter* on February 7, 1957.

American Academy in Rome,
Via Angelo Masina, 5
February 9, 1958
[NL]

Dear Kenneth,

The European venture is drawing to a close. In two weeks more we'll be leaving the Academy and Rome, then on March 2 we'll be sailing from either Genoa or Cannes on the *Constitution*—we haven't decided which port to use, and we can wait till the last minute to do so. In many ways the trip has been a disappointment—I waited too long and lost some of my power of adaptation, as well as too damned much of my sense of hearing. I won't forget arriving in Genoa at dusk in a rainstorm without a word of Italian and finding that for almost the first time in my life I was effectively lost. After a while I managed to buy a map, una pianta (I'd been asking for una carta, which is a sheet of paper), and couldn't locate our position on it. Then I crossed a busy highway and had the rear fender banged into by a streetcar. A crowd gathered, and fortunately someone in the crowd spoke English, so that I obtained directions from him, at the cost of twenty thousand lire to straighten the fender. That was the worst moment, but there was another bad one leaving Paris in the mist, when, with the tiny car loaded to the roof, other cars began flashing lights at us (they're not allowed to blow horns), and we found that one of the rear doors was gaping open. Later, in Tours, we discovered that Muriel's dress coat was missing, and also all the papers that certified our ownership of the car—without them we couldn't cross the border . . . But all the same it has been wonderful to see things I had only read about, and to live here in the bright air (no better than Stanford, but wonderful all the same), and to sink chin deep in Roman antiquities.

Thursday we drove to Naples . . . Friday we hired a guide to Pompeii and Herculaneum, Saturday morning we visited the Pompeian relics at the Naples Museum. That was the high point of the trip for me, walking through those Roman streets, peering into Roman houses, and later seeing the collection of art objects and appurtenances of daily living that were found in the houses. It was seeing a civilization stopped and carbonized in full flight: this is exactly how it was on August 24, 79; here are the election scrawls on the walls, here is the phallus incised in the pavement to point the way to the whorehouse, and here is the whorehouse, with sixty-nine positions painted on the walls and comments by the guests scratched into the plaster. The painted frescoes, now in Naples, aren't very moving— rather dull colors, except for the reds and deep blacks, and a curious lack of depth that one associates, by way of Spengler, with the picture of a culture that lived entirely in the foreground—but the mosaics are incredible;

perhaps the added difficulty of that form made the artists more venturesome. Certainly if our own civilization was turned to stone, it could show nothing in the nature of art that seemed to be so intimately connected with every moment of life . . .

> As ever,
> Malcolm

> Center for Advanced Study
> in the Behavioral Sciences
> 202 Junipero Serra Boulevard,
> Stanford, California
> April 22, 1958
> [NL]

Dear Malcolm,

The only interesting *usable* story of Hart I think of firsthand (as you know, Matty and Bill Brown have some good ones), is this:[1]

I remember a party one night at Bill and Sue's when they were still married. Party had got to humming, and Hart had got to the stage where he felt it was time for him to become angry. I happened to be near the door, when I saw him stamping across the room, all ready to leave in a huff. I said, "What's the matter, Hart?" He began muttering about how awful "all these people" were. Whereat I, being in a good-naturedly impish stage, decided to spoil his rhythm. I pointed out that he had no reason to be indignant. Everybody here was his friend, we all thought him a great poet, nobody's fighting—so what more did he want? He decided to stay, and went back, getting lost in the general turmoil. A little later, the same pattern. Hart storming toward the door in a mighty rage. So I went through my part of the routine again. I said I simply could not understand why he felt so resentful, when everybody thought so highly of him, etc. Why "these awful people"? So, Hart went back a second time. A bit later, of course, came the third time: Hart storming out, and my plaintive, mollifying interruption, "Now wait a minute, Hart; what's the matter now?" Hart turned and pointed: "I can't stand that damned dog!" he shouted. Since I didn't see how I could discuss the dog's high opinion of his talents, I gave up, and Hart stormed out. (I vaguely remember Munson once telling me that Hart got angry at parties because, since the mood was generally heterosexual, he felt subtly excluded.)

· · ·

You seem to be developing from analyst to annalist. My memory is so bad, I must keep moving on. The past is still too skimpy for me to live with, though every once in a while a new bit of it pops up. What I'd like to do is be able to recall with accuracy exactly what it was like to begin learning language (the state of emergence into articulacy out of infancy). But it would be a somewhat risky stage to be good at. I am becoming more and more engrossed with this puzzle: When one says something, just what in the name of God or the Devil is doing the talking? To a large extent, I am sure, we are simply like a telephone exchange run by an automatic dialing system. Things go in and out of us much as though we were the coordinating center that didn't even know what was being said. Experimentally, I often turn the usual perspective around, and think not of us as using language but of language as using us to get itself said . . .

Sincerely,
K. B.

1. In an earlier letter, apparently lost, Cowley asked Burke if he had any stories about Hart Crane that would be appropriate for an article he was writing. "Matty" is Matthew Josephson, and Bill Brown is William Slater Brown.

Sherman, Connecticut
July 19, 1958
[NL]

Dear Kenneth,

The Hart Crane piece was finished a couple of weeks ago.[1] It uses your story, which is a double character study, of Hart and KB as well. I'd be grateful if you read it and made notes in the margin, as Allen[2] has already made them. One of his notes will mean a lot of rewriting—that it wasn't "The Wine Menagerie" but "Passage" that Hart wrote the first draft of on Sunday, July 5, 1925. God, how fallible our memories are! Allen's memory is also fallible, for Hart *did* come out with a draft of the poem, which all of us read. I sent the piece to him first because Oscar Cargill is now accusing him wrongly of having betrayed Hart.[3] (About two-thirds of the piece will appear in *Esquire* for $850, but I want the whole piece for a book.) . . .

As ever,
Malcolm

1. "The Leopard in Hart Crane's Brow," which appeared in *Esquire* in August of 1958.

2. Allen Tate.

3. In an article in *The Nation* entitled "Hart Crane and His Friends" (February 15, 1958), Oscar Cargill had accused Tate of misunderstanding the symbolism of *The Bridge* and of being mistaken about its theme.

Andover, New Jersey
July 29, 1958
[NL]

Dear Malcolm,

Oof! Back home, and semi-doubly crazy with scrambled papers, etc., to be if possible unscrambled.

So as not to hold you up, however, I hasten to return your Ms. Toward the end, I think, it gets quite good. It finally gets things established. (First part is oke, but latter part is better.)

I showed it to [John Crowe] Ransom, who happened to say that he was next taking up Hart Crane in his class. He seemed to think highly of it. However, I happened to have told him about the anecdote of the dog. I had told him of it some days before. But when he read the article, afterward he said he thought the anecdote was better with the last point which you omitted. Since he offered this advice without my in any way asking for it or even having expected it, I think it's worth considering.

Incidentally, the party was *not in the Village, but at the Browns' place in the country.*

A major reason I am taking a full-time job next year has to do with the financial problems involved in this matter.[1] My godam insomnia is dirty mean lowdown in adding to my troubles. Yes, I do at times take sleepoes. But I distrust them greatly. I know that they are tearing down some part or other of one's body: as an old Christian Scientist, I devoutly believe that there is a payoff for every dope. Every godam one of 'em wears you down somewhere. So I dodge between wearings-down via sleepoes and wearings-down via total abstinence from same. (My main trouble is in trying to sleep on somebody else's schedule.)

• • •

Here's hoping that, when I get this place shoveled out, I can be a bit more contemplative, and write accordingly. Meanwhile, know that we live at a time when our country is caught in the sheer pragmatics of living. Surely there was never a time in the world's history when more worthless gestures were absolutely necessary. The world is being Amurricanized, and we are being worldized. We sell our birthright for a pot of message.

Holla! Give thanks, for the New Era is near at hand! To him who will promise me the most, I will sell my vote. We must have promises, promises, promises. Promises, to keep the heart going. Promises, to make people incur debts. Promises, to get done all sorts of things not worth the doing. Promises, whereby there may be a future, whereby in turn there may be a present. Promises, great big turdlike promises, such as our neighbor's dog leaves around our house. A lover of protocol, he is. A believer in the way things ought to be. With his nose to the ground, seeing the cypress trees shine through the stars.

Holla!

Sincerely,
K. B.

1. Burke was helping to care for his father, who was ill.

Sherman, Connecticut
August 4, 1958
[NL]

Dear Kenneth,

Hastily. What *was* the last point which I omitted in your anecdote about Hart and the dog? You quoted Munson's explanation of Hart's conduct and I used it before the anecdote, instead of after, on the ground that "I can't stand that damn dog" was the snapper of the story, and comments fall limp after a snapper.

In your letter the anecdote started with the sentence, "I remember one party at the Browns' when they were living in the Village." Are you sure now that the party was in or on Tory Hill? Could it have been the 4th of July bust in 1925?—when Hart did his cannibal dance?

I *didn't* remember that line, "People will love Hart when he's dead." Matty remembered it and repeated it three times, so I wouldn't forget to use it. The piece on Hart is damn near an anthology of ancecdotes, in which others supplied the gaps in my memories. I thought I'd covered you in the phrase, "Kenneth Burke, usually tolerant"—which God knows you usually are. Except when you feel infringed . . .

As ever,
Malcolm

Andover, New Jersey
August 9, 1958
[NL]

Dear Malcolm,

Maybe you're right about the omitted line. Anyhow, it ran thus: "Since I didn't see how I could discuss the dog's high opinion of his talents, I gave up, and Hart stormed out."

In my records, the first line of my anecdote was: "I remember a party one night at Bill and Sue's, when they were still married." (Cf. letter of April 22.) Perhaps you interpreted this line differently, and copied down your interpretation. The incident occurred in the country, in Bill's place at Paterson. As I recall, he had just piped water to the house.

If Matty wants that alleged remark of mine left in so badly that he told it to you three times, then he must want it in, so let's keep it. But I'm certainly entitled to ask that he fill out the context for you (what the occasion was on which the remark was made). And if he can't do that, could I not at least ask that you give him credit for it?

My ironic quandaries are of this sort: I did not see much of Hart during his later, more rambunctious stages. So I had no firsthand reason for complaining about him. Thus, the remark must have been either an alcoholic wisecrack of a sort that could have been made even in Hart's presence, or it was made on some occasion when Hart's friends were telling me of *their* troubles with him . . .

Sincerely,
K. B.

Andover, New Jersey
June 23, 1960
[NL]

Dear Malcolm,

Ailments, ailments, ailments. But what to do, when one considers literature, even at its best, an ailment, surpassed only by that much severer ailment, the lack of literature?

•   •   •

Today, in a way, I guess I finished a book,[1] though I'm not sure that I'll use this last section in the book. It's a dialogue between The Lord and Satan, in which both of them talk suspiciously alike, because both of them talk suspiciously like one K. Burke, in a mood of weighty academic levity.

I have always liked the Greek idea of rounding out three solemn tragedies with a satyr-play that says the same sort of thing in terms of caricature. I use the device somewhat as an ending for my first long essay in *Philosophy of Literary Form*. Here, after three straightaway pieces on my theories of language (as revealed mostly by analysis of theological texts), I try disporting myself in a burdensomely playful "Prologue in Heaven," with The Lord (a Blakean patriarch) telling Satan (a young hothead who is a great admirer of The Lord but finds the human race "revolting") just what is to "transpire" if he goes through with his plan to create a symbol-using animal.

The device is remarkably handy, and got me to going quite airily. But there still remains the fact that I am trying to recapitulate the various points I made in earnest. And I fear that, for most readers, the subject is categorically not funny, and that's that.

Well, ennihow, it's done—so I can plague myself in other ways, such as reverting to my Poetics, into which this Logology stuff intruded, or out of which it protruded, though in a way that required separate treatment.

Jeez, when I think of all the things I used to be so godam sure about! Now I couldn't even say for sure that it all goes down the drain. I guess that I'm sure now only when I think of myself as in an argument about theories of language . . .

Sincerely,
K. B.

1. *The Rhetoric of Religion: Studies in Logology*, published in 1961.

Sherman, Connecticut
June 25, 1960
[NL]

Dear Kenneth,

Ailments, ailments, I'm sick to death of them. And at this time when they're all around us and I quail to open letters . . . Van Wyck Brooks (cancer of the colon, very successful operation, but he's beginning to look frail). Peggy ex-Cowley thinks she has cancer of the breast, but her real trouble is that she broke some bones . . . Dorothy Hicks, cancer of the cervix; successful operation . . .

· · ·

So, having finished this litany, I turn about to praise and exult in your having finished a book. Have you a carbon or anything of your "Prologue in Heaven" that I could read? What is the title of the book going to be? Why don't you now take a rest, lie in the sun, and vow not to think a thought till you leave for Bennington?—By the way, I ran across a most flattering reference to you in the *New Statesman*—should have clipped it out and mailed it to you, but I was reading an office copy. Have they been publishing your books in England, and if not, why not? . . .

As ever,
Malcolm

Andover, New Jersey
July 20, 1960
[NL]

Dear Malcolm,

. . . The book is an extension of three talks I gave at Drew [University] about three years ago. Tentatively, I think of calling it by the title of the first, "On Words and The Word," possibly with the winsome, best-seller subtitle, "Studies in Logology." It begins by showing how several theological positions can be applied analogically to a secular analysis of language (as vs. the various reductionist schemes usually considered "scientific"). The second is a revision of my long piece "On Verbal Action in St. Augustine's *Confessions*." He fits especially well because of his turn from pagan word-merchant (*venditor verborum*) to preacher of The Word. Primarily, the essay is a "close analysis" of his language, along with a gimmick designed to show that, being a Trinitarian, he had to go through three stages of conversion (the first two involving Father and Son, mostly prior to the big moment in the garden when he broke into tears, etc., the occasion that, with the final click of the Holy Spirit, rounded out the lot). The third section is the revision of my stuff on Genesis (a small portion of which appeared in an issue of *Daedalus* some time back). Then comes my summing up, in the dialogue, that would disport itself with some heavy academic witticisms (with the probable Endresultat that the dialogue will alienate those who liked the first three sections, whereas those who like the dialogue will not like the first three sections). I'll try to send you a copy of it, when one is available.

A friend showed me one quote from *New Statesman*: "and coming to full flood in Kenneth Burke's magnificent theory of symbolic action," a glorious observation, to be sure, but too soon over! . . .

· · ·

I'm trying to figure out a way whereby I can make the students at Bennington do more work than I. So far, they have always managed to outwit me, so that I nearly murder myself, since every attempt to keep them busy is multiplied for me by the number in the class. One trick, for instance, was a requirement that each student send me in a brief report each week, without the guaranty on my part that I read all of the reports (the notion being that, like the income-tax investigators, I should pick only a certain percentage for close inspection). But they all began asking for special appointments in which they could discuss with me the various papers they had submitted. They had to know whether they were on the right track, etc.! So, I ended by not only reading all the papers, but by adding a whole set of special conferences besides . . . Who knows? Maybe I'll learn yet! (I gotta, if I'm to survive next year. I simply gotta.)

And so it goes.

Sincerely,
K. B.

490 Oregon Avenue,
Palo Alto, California
February 9, 1961
[NL]

Dear Kenneth,

. . . I've finished three-quarters of my Stanford assignment. This quarter has been good as far as the courses are concerned—only a four-hour writing class and a four-hour seminar on Emerson and Whitman, all on Mondays and Wednesdays, leaving me a four-day weekend . . . I've never gotten the answer, the real answer, to the Emerson problem, except that what he was preaching in his vigorous period was neo-platonism, almost unadulterated save for a Wordsworthian glorification, literally deification, of the sense of duty. I tried to apply your notion of the Unholy Trinity,[1] but so far haven't been able to do so. A lot of breath images, however; that might be a clue to something. And I could write an essay on the fact that Emerson's ethical system, totally unrealistic as it seems to be, is a very practical system for a writer with not much vigor except at moments. He learned to anthologize his moments, so that when he's going good he reads like one long orgasm. He also learned to trust in Providence, or the unconscious, something every writer has to do, and learned not to worry about his own popular success and not to be jealous of anyone else's—those worries and jealousies exhaust about nine-tenths of many writers' energies internally, leaving one-tenth of the energies for their work. Anyhow, Emerson is neglected today, and worth working on—but here I haven't time.

•   •   •

How're you and Libbie surviving the snows? Apparently they haven't been as deep in Vermont as in the New York area and southwestern Connecticut. And whadda you think about the taking over of Washington by the intellectuals and the Irish ward bosses, in alliance? Have you noted the to-date resemblance between Kennedy and Roosevelt—I don't mean FDR, but the other Roosevelt, the one who recited pomes at his Cabinet meetings? They won't be your pomes, or mine, but still, some of our friends will have jobs, and we can visit Washington without feeling, as I have felt for the past 12 years, that I was skulking into enemy territory disguised as a businessman.

As ever,
Malcolm

1. In *The Rhetoric of Religion*, Burke notes a "likeness" between the "design of the trinity" and the relation between words and things in language. He elaborates a theory of the "unholy trinity" in the sense that he sees something like a "trinatarian principle" operating on a secular level. This is particularly the case for St. Augustine who, Burke writes, "saw manifestations of this supernatural principle in all sorts of sheerly natural phenomena. Every triad, however secular, was for him another sign of the Trinity."

B.C. 2/16/61 A.D.
[Bennington, Vermont]
[NL]

Dear Malcolm,

. . . School resumes here after the first week of March. The main question is: will I, or will I not, kill myself before school ends in mid-June? In any case, I have decided that I am too old for the pace here, at least for my way of running. So I have resigned, under the friendliest of conditions. Though there is no tenure at Bennington, we have a kind of five-year arrangement that is habitually renewed (barring catastrophes) until the incumbent (tossing in his bed) reaches the age of 65. Then he goes back to a one-year arrangement, since (naturally) he is thereafter under the strong suspicion of slipping. But though I accept the sheer logic of this development, and though I cannot blame the dear school for the ravages of fate, the fact remains that I bristle at the idea of becoming a second-class citizen (psst: sag'es niemandem!). And I feel that I'd do better in cutting loose while all is well than in waiting until I got ast out. Even if things turn out handsomely, I know that I'll often regret this move; for my attachment to this place is quite poignant, no matter how many ways I have contrived of being elsewhere for long stretches. And since things doubtless won't turn out handsomely, I'll prombly have even more regrets. Yet even an ole drooperoo of 65 must have spirit—and who can have spirit if he hangs on until he is ast out? My better half reminds me that in May I'll be 64.

. . . I have the (fertile) idea of buying a place by either a quite turbulent stream or a big lake—and I dare to feel that such a place can still be bought for a modest price down east. Ennihow, whatever the differences (and I need not tell you how great they are!) I feel somewhat as I did about this time circa forty years ago, when I was living in a semi-basement in the Village; and each evening when I brought up the ashes to the street, the squeak of the handle of the ash-can sounded like the vaguely promissory note I had heard several times, when standing on the platform of a Pullman car. I knew then that I had to get out, and I got out. True, it's greatly different this time. But again I gotta get going. Then I just hungered. Now of a sudden I sometimes cry. But so it goes.

Holla!

Sincerely,
K. B.

490 Oregon Avenue,
Palo Alto, California
February 22, 1961
[NL]

Dear Kenneth,

Your letter: Intimations of Mortality from Recollections of Early Second Childhood.

. . . . Were you right to resign from Bennington? Maybe so. I'm beginning to dwell in that Emersonian faith that we're always right to obey our deeper instincts, then everything will come out right in the end.

I'll tell you about lecturing if you'll listen. I'll tell you how to do it and not rack yourself into an early grave. The principle to remember is this: Lecturing is one of the performing arts, not one of the creative arts. When you perform, do so from a script. Prepare a lecture for yourself, or three or five or a dozen lectures. When invited by a university, give them a choice of *your* topics, then read from your ms. with attention to delivery, not substance. Don't let them print your lecture until you're sure you don't want to use it again—and don't let them print it even then; sell it for a better price. Don't let them broadcast it except to the immediate area, i.e., if you're lecturing in Idaho State they can use it in Idaho but not in Utah. If delivering the same lecture five or six times, you can revise and perfect it, as my friend Emerson did, noting the portions of it that did or didn't get across. The creative or inspirational side of lecturing can be reserved for informal sessions in the classroom; usually the academics will want them too. But never let them kill you, as apparently they tried to do at Penn State.

• • •

Forty-two years. Jesus Christ, I think of them and of the years still to come. I never forget that you and I were pretty obscure persons until we were fifty years old. I had an instinct or impulse or urge or drive, all the words are unsatisfactory, *not* to become a celebrity, but that was partly a conscious decision too. I'd seen too many talents ruined by an early success: what a price they pay for it in this country! I know you had that same instinct, and suspect that you made the same conscious decision, or series of little choices. Jesus X, ability isn't so widely distributed in our field that we both couldn't have been successful early by doing something only a little different from what we did. I feel now that the decisions were sound, though we were running the risk of bucket-kicking prematurely. Having survived into our sixties, things are a little easier and I'm no longer afraid of being well known or earning money—the big problem now is that with somewhat declining vigor (I'm speaking of mine not yours)—with, for me, somewhat increasing deafness, and sleepiness in the afternoons, and a less sharp eye for other people's conduct—I still have to create or put together a body of work while there is still time . . . And the great advantage—this time for you as well as me—is precisely that we *were* obscure, that the vast fickle public didn't get tired of us, that now we have the experience and part of the freshness too . . .

> As ever,
> Malcolm

> Sherman, Connecticut
> September 29, 1961
> [NL]

Dear Kenneth,

It's been ninety years since I wrote you or had a letter from you. I forget who owed a letter to whom when the correspondence lapsed. All I know is that I don't get time to write anything but business letters, and am damned slow about writing even them . . .

·   ·   ·

Tonight I reread "The Psychology of Literary Form" [sic] for quite practical reasons. On October 11 I have to give a lecture on Art and Ethics at a Connecticut state teachers' college. Not only that, I have to write the lecture and give them the manuscript to publish (for a good honorarium of $525). Well, I have a reasonable number of things to say on the topic, and especially about the special ethic developed by writers. Very often the choice between two words is a moral choice, so that a work of literature becomes an aggregate of small moral decisions. Also, in one sense every story is a fable. A story is a situation that leads to an act, as a result of which *something is changed*. The nature of the change provides the moral of the fable. I have a good deal to say on both those topics, as well as on the function of art, the social function, I mean, which lies very largely in the domain of morals, since one of the functions is to provide archetypes of character and conduct. There will always be a conflict between artists and institutions, in so far as institutions quite rightly try to preserve themselves, and artists, speaking for the unconscious minds of a new generation, are a threat to established institutions. That's easy to say, but what does it lead to in terms of social policies? I think it justifies censorship, and also justifies the resistance to censorship—the only answer I can find is that the conflict is dialectical, unending, and often fruitful. But how to make a lecture out of this material I don't yet know, and I'm reading to find hints or, better yet, something that makes me so mad I'll be impelled to answer it. Most of my writing—and yours? and almost everybody's—is also dialectical, and an angry reply to somebody.

Anyhow, in your writing I find lots of hints, more than anywhere else, but nothing, or almost nothing, to make me rush to the typewriter with an angry retort. Obviously if a poem is a symbolic action and a strategy to encompass a situation, it falls at least partly into the field of morals; the action is "good" or "bad," as is its effect on the reader. But I don't think you have ever stated your notions of what a social policy toward literature might be. One trouble with censorship is that the state is a poor judge of what is "good" or "bad" for people.

It's too late at night for me to be verbalizing . . .

As ever,
Malcolm

Andover, New Jersey
October 4, 1961
[NL]

Dear Malcolm,

As for stuffo on relations between artist and society, I guess I said more about that subject in *Counter-Statement* than anywhere else. In fact, I think that every article in that book ends on that theme. And though I'd now temper it with age (which has its own peculiar kinds of ill temper), I guess that, by and large, I'd still subscribe to the same position. Perhaps the last few pages of the "Lexicon Rhetoricae" (sections 38 and 39) sum it up best. Section 37, alas! (beefing about "perfection") would need revision, not because I disagree with what I say there, but because I now have another use for the term "perfection," in a quite different sense. (I also rather like section 21 of the "Lexicon R.")

•   •   •

Recently I published another book.[1] I asked the publishers to send you a copy, though I doubt whether you'll find much of it interesting. So far, it has met with total silence, though I do expect that it will eventually get some treatment in the academic quarterlies 'n sech.

.   .   .

I resigned from Bennington, having decided that it would be safer for me to try living on lectures, pedagogic quickies, and crumbs from my books, than to go on teaching steadily under conditions where I have to take dope constantly . . . I turned down (or rather, vaguely postponed) the offer of a ten-week stint at another school for five megatons next spring; but I may risk this later, if it's still available . . . Five and one-quarter megatons for one local visitation, however, soars so far above my powers of imagination the idea does not even cause me to salivate. I respond normally to a signal of about two megatons per visitation (and, psst! have been known to settle for less).

I agree with you, that the battle of censorship simply has to waver back and forth. But it's astounding how many *standard* authors, poets, etc. were "sinners" in their day. I refer to people like St. Thomas Aquinas and Palestrina (that is, people who had to fight even to become pillars of society, as contrasted with the Rimbaud type of reputation, which will probably never be of that sort). At the time when I wrote *Counter-Statement*, I thought of the artist simply as a permanently "break-away" type. But there are also those who must fight like fiends even to uphold the orthodoxy in a decent way. Of course, the point loses its force insofar as the innovation itself becomes standard (as per Wordsworth). So maybe this distinction dissolves . . .

Sincerely,
K. B.

1. *The Rhetoric of Religion.*

(As of) Sherman,
Connecticut
April 13, 1962
[NL]

Dear Kenneth,

We're sweating out the last two days at our Republican house in Berkeley. A Republican house is conservative, prosperous middle class, with wall-to-wall carpeting, a washing machine, a dish washer, and no book shelves. I do my typing at a rather shaky bridge table. In the garage is a Republican car, a conservative, prosperous 1956 Oldsmobile with automatic shift and power brakes. Those last are something I don't want to have again—if you see an obstruction close at hand and put your foot down hard on the pedal, the car bucks like a bronco and dies. Mostly we use the car for going out to dinner, and there's a hell of a lot of that in Berkeley, at least five nights a week. Muriel returned some obligations with a cocktail party for 40 facultarians, followed by a dinner for 14. I wake every morning with a mild hangover.

The best feature of the trip was that I managed to write four lectures on the 1930s. I'm thinking of expanding them into a book this summer, the only difficulty being that it would conflict with the book that Matty is now researching. But I'm inclined to go ahead notwithstanding, for the simple reason that I didn't like Matty's book on the 1920s, which was mean and superior to almost everyone except Matty, and I suspect that his work on the 1930s will be no more admirable.[1] If only the damned thing had been well written, I could forgive everything; it wasn't. Then he gave an interview to *Herald Tribune Books* in which he claimed the credit for inspiring *Exile's Return* . . . Matty wants to present himself as always the prime mover. I got a private earful of him that evening we had dinner together—he insulted me for not declaring that I was ready to testify against Edmund Wilson (that was while you and Libbie were in the front room) and I was, Jesus, on the point of walking out of the house. Anyhow I propose to write a book in which I'm not mean to anybody, not even Sidney Hook, the bastard. I've been thinking about it since 1940, as you know, and it's time to get the stuff on paper . . .

As ever,
Malcolm

1. Matthew Josephson's book on the '20s is *Life Among the Surrealists*, published in 1962. His book on the '30s, published in 1967, is *Infidel in the Temple: A Memoir of the 1930's.*

And/or
4/18/62
[NL]

Dear Malcolm,
Welkim East.

As for who owns the Thirties: I incline to think that they're still in the public domain. I'll admit, however: I was under the impression that the idea of our all writing a book together was Matty's, though I don't see that that makes a godam bit of difference thereafter, inasmuch as we didn't write the book together.

•　　•　　•

The godam Poetics is NOT finished. A whole, as they say, spate (or do I mean cowflop?) of invitations for me to peddle my wares turned up—and I didn't have the character to turn them down. For they are exactly the sorta thing I'm looking for; namely: quickies here and there, with intervals in which I can tell Father Nembutal to f——q himself . . .

. . . At the moment, I'm jagging the old nag to finish a paper that has to be submitted now for a conference in June. I also must whip up the old nag to prepare for the Commencement address at benny Bonnington (a talk I am giving for a song, but I couldn't turn it down when learning that the darling Studententum had made the choice of speaker) . . .

Sincerely,
K. B.

Sherman, Connecticut
April 23, 1962
[NL]

Dear Kenneth,

. . . I'll take your word that a book of joint memoirs was his idea, but I'd been planning for a long time to write the story of that altercation at the Rotonde—that's why I could write while others were drinking. The thing that bugs me is Matty's attempt to take credit for everything, as well as his patronizing attitude toward everyone who enters his story—everyone, that is, except Aragon. It was really a terrible scene when Matty burst out at me for not being willing to testify against Edmund Wilson. He wanted to prove that Wilson was a drunkard and was losing his mind; in fact, he wanted to destroy him like a stinging insect that had buzzed into his hearing. I came away shaken.

As ever,
Malcolm

Sherman, Connecticut
February 7, 1963
[NL]

Dear Kenneth,

. . . I'm trying to prepare to get ready to go to Calif.[1] I feel spurred, whipped, and harried all the time, out of my old habit of taking on too many things. Wish I had your good sense in getting away from things and telephone calls and shooting off somewhere to hear the sea slapping at the sand. I've seen Mary Hemingway a couple of times. Apparently Mr. Papa had been writing steadily for all those years when he didn't publish anything. Possibly some of what he wrote is quite good—nobody has seen anything except a short volume of Paris memoirs[2]—but he didn't get anything in final shape for publication; he just went on writing, like Mark Twain in his last ten years. We know why Mark Twain didn't publish; he thought that what he was writing would alienate his public; but what made Ernest start things, nearly finish them, then start something else? It's an absolute puzzle to me. Meanwhile Mary H. really doesn't *want* to know what is there until she has made a settlement with the inheritance-tax people, who would like to set such a high appraisal on the mss. that she would be left penniless (then income-tax her again for everything she got out of them) . . .

My address from Feb. 16 to March 9: c/o Dept. of English, University of California, Davis, Calif. Muriel will stay here and see that the furnace doesn't go out . . .

As ever,
Malcolm

1. Cowley had accepted an invitation to visit the University of California at Davis, later in the month.

2. *A Moveable Feast*, published posthumously in 1964.

Route 1—Box 327 AA,
Englewood, Florida
February 22, 1963
[NL]

Dear Malcolm,

. . . When you get this, I'll be expatiating at Gainesville, where we are to occupy the Governor's Quarters (a situation much to be envied because otherwise I'd have to pay for lodgings). Three seminars (in literature, theater, and terminese), and one public address (where I'll trot out my one sure-fire exhibit, the Burpian "Definition of Man" . . .). As for the Hemingway problem, I'd tentatively line it up thus: He worked up a love-and-war act (one that I considerably resent, as you perhaps do not). There was a lotta shit implicit in the war side of that setup; and late on in life these implications began to make themselves more urgently felt. But being first of all a bully (as indicated by his love of bullfights), he kept being puzzled by the intuitive accuracy which brought him abreast of bullshit. So, when shit started coming out, he went back and tried starting over again. And if he did start over again and shit didn't transpire, he knew that that kind of development was somehow a lie, too. So, either way, he was caught. For his next phase required kinds of humility and/or humiliation for which his superb technique of bullying did not make allowance. This is my huncho, this is my song; I will praise Jesus all the day long . . .

Sincerely,
K. B.

Sherman, Connecticut
September 4, 1963
[NL]

Dear Kenneth,

It was good to see you and Libbie and even to receive your lecture on not writing you . . . This time the sin was worse, because I wanted to say that the poem to Cummings was marvelous.[1] It's strange what you have done starting with book reviews (starting with reviews of your own book, *Towards a Better Life*, you once said) till inexorably you are led into grammar, rhetoric, poetics, psychology, and metaphysics. But not only to those ends: by God, you're the first writer in history, the first I can think of, who transformed a book review into poetry, real, inventive, out-on-the-limb poetry that remains at the same time a book review. It would be strange if we all became defunct—*when* we all became defunct—if you were remembered primarily as a poet.

. . . . .

I've been trying to get my uncollected works into hard covers. There are maybe two hundred thousand words that are worth reprinting—I think of them as a volume of essays about writers of the 1920s, another volume about American writers of earlier times, and a volume of general essays . . . Then a week ago I woke in the middle of the night cold-sweating about my delay in finishing the book on the 1930s, of which I have now written sixty thousand words without getting beyond the spring of '33. So I decided to piece together the essays on writers of the twenties, and I produced a book-length manuscript in six days of fast pasting, not fast writing. But it will take me another month to make it publishable, all subtracted from the thirties book. (I used the Hart Crane piece, but subtracted your name from the statement that people would love Hart when he was dead.)

For the thirties book, I'm still hoping to get something from you about the first writers' congress and your argument for "the people," not "the masses," and how you got sat on, and how the party line immediately changed to "the people"—after Dimitrov's speech in Moscow on August 2.[2] It's a funny and typical story; I should have asked you about it when you were here. For Christ's sake we'll have to not let years go by before another meeting. Where will you be this winter?

As ever,
Malcolm

1. "To The Memory of e. e. cummings," which was published in the April issue of *Poetry*.

2. George Dimitrov, general secretary of the Soviet Comintern, spoke on August 2, 1935, at the Seventh Congress of the Communist International. In his speech he called for alliances with Social Democrats, trade unions, and other organizations in the West, and the creation of a "people's anti-fascist front." He also announced his willingness to support any anti-fascist government, not just a communist one, and chided American communists for berating the New Deal.

Sherman, Connecticut
February 5, 1964
[NL]

Dear Kenneth,

It seems to me you were a little goddamned self-righteous the other, I mean, last night. Injuries inflicted on KB, letters not written to KB, the sacrificial lamb, the scapegoat that is really a saint. And the logologist misled by logology into a narrative interpretation of a circular situation.

—But not purely circular, alas. The narrative element, the "something changed" that is the essence of true narrative, is that we are both, we are all, getting not older but just old. You've held out much better than I, damn you and congratulations. I'd be incapable of the energy and vehemence you displayed last night . . . Your system must manufacture pep pills—it takes one of the damn things to bring me nearly up to you, and give me your insomnia. Otherwise I'm slowing down, walk slow, talk slow, think slow, write slow, sleep a lot . . .

· · ·

So the voices say to each of us, "Hurry up please, it's time." I want to get *some* of my work into books before the bar is closed. I can see that you're also struck with that impulse to round things off, by the references in the *Logology* to your former works. A good thing, too, those references. For a long time you were so busy with always new ideas that the structure seemed to sprout in all sorts of wings, gables, and bow windows. Now you're clearing away the scaffold and letting us see the outlines of the edifice.

About the application of logology to the mystical experience, I don't deny it, but neither do I see it. You'll have to do the work on that. The experience itself seems to leave the *experiendi*—is there any Latin justification for that word on the analogy of "analysand"?—with a feeling that what they have felt cannot be put into words; that through union with something, God, the universe, the oversoul, all humanity—the "something" can't even be defined—they have achieved a direct knowledge of universal relations and have been liberated from Time. Would that be passing from the narrative into the circular? But they have also lost their feeling of hierarchy; everything has dissolved into Unity and other capital letters. There's a hell of an interesting book by Heinrich Zimmer, *The Philosophies of India*; I mention it in the Whitman introduction.

Back to your complaints. They were wholly justified and left me with a good heavy sense of guilt—"Another failure of mine," the inner voice said several times—but then too they were wrong. Because now we've all got to do an awful lot of forgiving and taking for granted of good intentions. I can't tell you everything my inner voice has said to you, but it has said a lot, day by day.

As ever,
Malcolm

R.D. 2, Andover,
New Jersey
February 6, 1964
[NL]

Dear Malcolm,

Truce! Truce! (I don't say "Peace! Peace!" For to me "Peace" means *requiescat in pace*.)

"Godam self-righteous," perhaps—but in any case, godam drunk. I had spent a week in Iowa sitting on the lid. I enjoyed myself, since I like to get paid for peddling my wares. But all week it was "Watch yourself, Burke; watch yourself, Burke"—and a greater number of talks, conferences, lunches, teas, dinners, and sleepless nights (except when murderously logged with Nembutals) I have never so far encountered in one week. Things went well, so my heart behaved. If things had gone wrong, I believe the godam thing would simply have slowed down and stopped. Or fluttered away like a birdie.

But the more valiant are my attempts to contain tangles of that sort, the stupider and blunter are my over-simflications (I'm trying to say over-simplifications) when I get stewed and let loose. Then *one* thing seems perfectly, totally, unquestionably clear, and the *only* thing in all the world that should be talked about. And almost always it's something unreasonable.

•   •   •

In any case, I will get that book by Heinrich Zimmer you mention. I *should* be able to translate it into logologese. But there's one point about "mystic oneness" that I'll give on, even before I start; to whit to whoo: In one sense, every one of us merges into the universal context of which he is a part. The contrasted *physical* grounding of *individuality* seems to me (as per Bergson) to reside in the centrality of the nervous system (whereby *my* bellyache is my private property and not *yours*). Personal name and capitalist laws of ownership can accentuate such a sense of the separate individual (the "self"), despite the obviously *collective* nature of the language and traditions in which we are defined by the accidents of our "Geworfen-heit" (to swipe one of Heidegger's best terms). Us logologers claim that the mystic's sense of a tie-in with Universal Oneness involves essentially a *terministic* duplication. That is, "natural" to language there are processes whereby things get duplicated. Simplest example: The *thing* tree and the *word* "tree." Subtler example: the *enacting* of a process, and the *principle* of such enactment. Most wondrous relations of all along those lines are the shifts back and forth between *logical* priority and *temporal* priority. And, for a heroic one with comic possibilities: If I so build a set of terms that I am restated in terms of the Absolute, and if I have but the amount of "reflex-iveness" that is normal to the experience of masturbation, lo! I shall experience immediately the intuition of my oneness as a microcosm with the macrocosm. It's all set up, like an artificial Japanese flower, to be dropped into the water, and allowed to exfoliate according to the "natural" pro-pensities built into its maker . . .

Sincerely,
K. B.

Sherman, Connecticut
December 2, 1964
[NL]

Dear Kenneth,

I sorta like the idea of having ourselves a symposium on the First Amer-ican Writers' Congress. Something like that is worth taking pains with. Who would transcribe the tape or tapes? Miss Libbie? She'd do the job superb, but it sounds like an awful chore for her. On the other hand, if *we* did the talking and arranged for the transcribing, correcting, and retyping, the whole business would belong to us and no others. We could arrange other financing—for example, *The American Scholar* would probably be glad to undertake the whole job for magazine rights, as it did long ago with the New Criticism, in this case we reserving the book rights. I'm just popping off with ideas at this point, not making recommendations (and always with the idea in the back of my mind that the simpler we keep it, the more likely we are to do it).

· · ·

Under your hat for ten days, I got elected to the Academy. The other three immortalized this year are Sandy Calder, Allen Tate, and Glenway Wescott. Candidly I don't know that I'd have voted for me if I had been entitled to vote, though I may have as much claim to the honor as Allen or Glenway. But there are others with better claims, including yourself, and I'll try to see that the oversight is rectified. You're not going to get the Gold Medal, as you predicted. Too many members of the Institute are simply general public as far as medalists are concerned, and general public is more familiar with Walter Lippmann (and for the painting medal, with Andrew Wyeth). But you're going to get more votes than you expected. At the dinner to discuss the medals, one person after another spoke for you . . . Ralph Ellison ascribed his birth as a writer to you . . . [1]

As ever,
Malcolm

1. Burke and Ellison have been friends since the 1930s.

And/or
4/13/65
[NL]

Dear Malcolm,
. . . .From three different guys who have written treatises on my sick Selph, I get letters telling of a convention in Chicago, where they went to worry over me. I guess you know what I mean when I say I wish somebody had thought of at least letting me listen in. Apparently [Northrop] Frye is king. (At one stage in my journeys, they told me of a slogan, "Frye Burke." I promptly proposed the obvious emendation, "Burke Frye.")

· · ·

In the meantime, would say: I'm sure we can do a good job on that Writers' Congress Bizz. I tried it with one of the social science classes at

Bennington—and they loved it. (Actually, three classes had been compounded.)

There's no future but death, quick death, or a disgraceful drifting toward death. But at the moment, maybe for just a spell, I think that I'm profiting by a kind of Ultimate Accuracy. I mean: When I go over various notes that I had written years ago, I have the feeling that I can slash through them, to the essence. What I was fumbling around with, now seems statable as obviously as a slogan on a billboard (if billboards have slogans). I have that thought (right or wrong) to console me, and the thought of my family—and all of them, I believe, are beginning to sense how these many acres can pay off; property and thought and family are (at least for the time being) all working together. It's my variant of Pascal's wager. "Let's live as though this were our last summer." And if it turns out that there are other summers, what have we lost?

K. B.

Sherman, Connecticut
September 5, 1965
[NL]

Dear Kenneth,

. . . We left home Tuesday morning, stopping at the post office to pick up our mail, which included a letter from Libbie. Now we're spending two days on the Cape. We had dinner yesterday with the Aikens, and in half an hour we're going there for lunch; the other guests will be Francis Biddle[1] and his wife. Conrad is becoming grumpier in his convictions; at present he's supporting Johnson in the Vietnam business, and we have to keep away from that topic of conversation. Historical parallel: the argument in literary circles about the Philippines in 1900. Vietnam is worse than the Philippines, in its probable consequences, but for some reason I haven't been able to get excited. I must be losing my capacity for social indignation. Being utterly convinced that the human race is going to extinguish itself by poisoning the soil, the water, the air, possibly even before it blows the world up. I believe in Henry Adams's law of acceleration. Things are moving faster and faster—toward what, if not extinction? . . .

As ever,
Malcolm

1. Francis Biddle, a lawyer, was chairman of the National Labor Board 1934–1935, and U.S. attorney general from 1941 to 1945.

Sherman, Connecticut
April 23, 1966
[NL]

Dear Kenneth,

Proof received from *The American Scholar*.[1] I got bored reading it; maybe that was because I had read it too often. Anyhow the moderate elation of that evening had disappeared for me, and I wonder whether readers will catch any of it . . . You were fine on the whole episode of your speech. Let 'er ride, I say.

.   .   .

I have to say a few, maybe 1,200 words, well chosen words at the UPenn library at the formal acceptance of the Waldo Frank papers. Waldo will be there, subdued, broken, timid, almost childlike. He hasn't been able to find a publisher for his last two novels. He has had a couple of heart attacks. What'll I say? I spent a day reading his work. The style of the novels is preposterous, as I felt when I first read some of them. I read a thesis on the novels written by Robert Bittner and published by the UPenn Press in 1958. It has been at the Yale Library for eight years, and I was the fourth borrower. From it I learned one thing, that Frank had a series of mystical experiences in 1920. Apparently those were the source of his messianism and his fuzzy-wuzzy style . . . On the other hand, what enormous talent and dreams and ambition, what consecutive growth over the years, have gone into the construction of a huge monument that nobody visits: "My name is Ozymandias, king of kings." "Round the decay / Of that colossal wreck, boundless and bare, / The lone and level sands stretch far away." . . .

As ever,
Malcolm

1. The proof Cowley refers to was the transcription of his discussion about the First American Writers' Conference with Burke and others, published in the Summer 1966 issue of *The American Scholar*. It was moderated by Daniel Aaron.

R.D. 2, Andover,
New Jersey
April 28, 1966
[NL]

Dear Malcolm,

Many thanks for thine of the 23rd. Your description of Waldo comes pretty close to a description of me today, as I feel after a sudden swat of flu (that caused me to cancel a trip to Indiana this week and a trip to Wisconsin in early May). Blee me, I'M BOPPED . . .

The one thing I feel O.K. about, in re the *American Scholar* item, is that I could tell my story without tying it in any way to the Kumrad,[1] whom I wanted to use functionally for the story but wanted in no way to involve personally. On the other hand, here's ardently hoping that my quatrain anent the Phartisan survives . . . My memory of myself does not fill me with great admiration, except as regards my pigheaded attachment to some of my ideas; and I suspect that, if I knew then what I know now, I'd not have had the guts or whatever to do more than make a faint bleat in the direction I eventually took . . .

Holla!

K. B.

1. The poet and critic Joseph Freeman. He had helped found *The New Masses*, and was a member of the John Reed Club. Freeman had reacted angrily to Burke's speech at the First American Writers' Conference.

University Village,
Apt. 22,
E. Illinois Street,
Ellensburg, Washington
November 8, 1966
[NL]

Dear Malcolm,

. . . As for your notion that, had I made a big sale of *Towards a Better Life* when it first dropped into this vale of tears, I'd have simply abandoned it and moved on: You may be right, who knows? But I have my doubts. For I doubt whether you would have abandoned your poems, had they sold like Robert Frost or Edgar Lee Masters. My hunch is that you'd still be working over them, just as you are now. And in my case, there is a special problem (not typical of our trade but certainly not a *special* case in the sense of its applying to me alone). The inability of critics to see what was going on there was a godsend to me *as a critic*. I'm not arguing here as to whether the book is good or bad. All I'm saying is that the godam stupid baystards couldn't even see what is going on there, regardless of whether they like it or not. Jeezoos Keerist, they can't even see what is being dealt with! There's a lotta stupid people in this business of ours, fellah, and I ain't telling you anything you don't know.

As I sees it: That item was my analogue of Nietzsche's *Also Sprach Zarathustra*. That is, it was my fictive way of summing up the implications of my critical way. And just as you have had reasons for hanging on regardless of sales, so I have had reasons for hanging on. We're just that kind of guy.

. . .

Heck, Malcolm. At any minute, it's over. And may it be over fast! But damn the luck, until then, there's a job to be done. I had a job here,[1] introducing a new kind of course. Necessarily, I improvised. And, necessarily, at any minute things may 'gin gang agley. But so far, the old dog's attempt to use his old tricks in a new situation has worked out well enough. Indeed, some of his improvisings (as regards conferences with students) have worked out exceptionally well. Because I deliberately cut my salary in half, in order to do my work well, I have been able to give my students a kind of attention that they cannot ordinarily get. And bejeez, I think they are beginning to realize this, after their fashion . . .

Holla!
K. B.

1. Burke was a visiting professor at Central Washington University.

PART FOUR

1967-1981

I n February of 1980, Cowley wrote to Burke that

> *For both of us a mild consolation is that we're not just stumbling into
> the shadows. Both of us are better known in our eighties than we were
> in our sixties. It's funny what different sorts of fame for two who started
> from the same place, in the same business. Your light is more intense, as
> it deserves to be, while mine is more diffuse and dimmer. But it's pleasant
> for both of us to have some recognition.*

For both men, that recognition was the fruit of a long lifetime's work. But
it was also the result of hard work late in life. The 1970s turned out to be
Cowley's most prolific decade (measured by books rather than reviews and
essays), and for Burke they were years in which he crisscrossed the country
teaching and lecturing with astonishing energy for a man in his eighth
decade. In these years, Cowley began to do less teaching and lecturing than
Burke, choosing to remain closer to home. He supervised the publication
of two volumes of essays he had written earlier: *Think Back On Us . . . A
Contemporary Chronicle of the 1930's* was published in 1967, and *A Many-
Windowed House: Collected Essays on American Writers and Writing* was pub-
lished in 1970 (both were edited by Henry Dan Piper). He also published
his *Blue Juniata: Collected Poems* in 1969, and wrote four books: *A Second
Flowering: Works and Days of the Lost Generation* (1973), *—And I Worked
at the Writer's Trade: Chapters of Literary History, 1918–1978* (1978), *The
Dream of the Golden Mountains: Remembering the 1930's* (1980), and *The
View from 80* (1980). Burke, on the other hand, lectured and taught at
Harvard, Washington University, Wesleyan University, the University of
Pittsburgh, Princeton, the University of Washington, the University of Reno,
and Emory University. While on the road (he referred to himself during
this period as a "wandering scholar"), and at home at Andover, Burke
published his *Collected Poems: 1915–1967* (1968), and *Dramatism and Development* (1972). In addition, he wrote a number of "summarizing" essays

on Dramatism, symbolism, technology, the body, and satire. Burke's light began to burn more intensely for scholars and critics in the fields of literature, psychology, speech and communication, and philosophy, while Cowley's more "diffuse" light illuminated the history of modern American literature for an increasingly wide audience.

These letters, like the previous group from the '50s and '60s, represent an intimate record of aging, the struggle with the body in the midst of the mind's continued—even accelerated—activity. They range in subject matter from hearing aids to structuralism, the moon landing to psychoanalytic criticism. Burke takes his first trip abroad in 1969, visiting Italy and France in the wake of his wife's death in May. A good part of the next few years are spent coming to terms with this loss ("since Libbie cleared out, I have quit putting out my books. For two reasons: The second is that she helped so much by having been a secretary; the first is that she helped so much by my being so crazy about her, I was driven to prove, prove, prove, only roundabout to the shitten world, because so directly every day and night to *her* I was appealing . . . If I could but believe that she lives on, and is looking down on me, I could still be driven . . . "). It is perhaps for this reason that his "Symbolic of Motives" has never been published.

In these late letters the past is always palpably present to both men. For Cowley, as he writes his three retrospective books and helps to collect earlier essays, that past becomes the focus of his work, but for Burke, who avoids autobiography (he calls it "Proust's disease"), the past haunts the present, and the two often eerily converge. "I'm mine own tradition," he writes Cowley in the winter of 1977. "There's no place I go, not just here [Andover], but anywhere, that doesn't remind me of some other time . . . Every day is so real . . . Yet somehow not even one single day happens for the first time. And there's not a single spot hereabouts that is not to me just a place, but a little shred of history." The present, too, is often confusing. Cowley writes during these years with an air of amused bafflement about contemporary fiction ("I try to puzzle out what the voices are saying, and it seems to be 'Geez, Ma, ain't it all useless, ain't we all absurd' "), about an SDS demonstration at Harvard, and contemporary literary theory ("why, I don't know the difference between Structuralism and Post-Structuralism, never read a damned one of those new Continental authors. Who is Paul de Man? Is Harold Bloom allied with the Structuralists?").

What comes through most clearly in these letters, however, is not a sense of confusion or belatedness, but a sense of satisfaction, a recognition that the pace of their careers has been just about right. This is perhaps best summed up by Cowley in a letter to Burke in the spring of 1981, congratulating him on winning the National Medal for Literature (Cowley himself was about to receive the Gold Medal from the American Academy and Institute of Arts and Letters):

> *By Jesus, the whole thing is working out the way you wanted it to work out. I mean careerwise, without respect to the intimate disasters. You didn't want to make an early success. You pissed on success and everything that would lead to it. At the same time you wanted to be honored by the community and to have the world beat a path to your door. That took a long time . . . but the intrepid admirers . . . arrived at your kitchen door bearing incense and myrrh and checks for fifteen grand. And toward the end, too, so that there wouldn't be much time for anticlimax. That's the way we ought to structure our lives, with the best coming last, in a graded series.*

Box 231,
Tecate, California
February 2, 1967
[NL]

Dear Malcolm,

Have been doing my homework, shopping around in thy latest.[1] I think the various items hold up impressively well, particularly when one considers the vast amount of doctrinaire excesses one had to pick one's way among during that decade. Again and again, you make just, or even shrewd, appraisals. What I get constantly is a sense of good judgment and good placement, with remarkable expertness in characterizing for the reader the book you are discussing. And the pieces serve exceptionally well to recover the nature of the times.

To be sure, the Iron Laws of Dialectics sometimes lead you to an overstress upon the society side of the relations between the author and his tribe (sociality being stressed antithetically to the earlier days of aesthetic individualism)—but it's obvious enough, and easy to discount. And of course I'll never give on my claim that my theory of the "grotesque" is needed, to place TBL properly between attempts to read it as comedy and attempts to read it as out-and-out tragedy[2] (though I agree that yours, the latter, is much closer than the angle that Donoghue and Adams[3] inclined to stress).

And I always keep feeling that you would outlaw many of my pet concerns if you could, a conviction of mine that is tempered by the realization that I would, too, if I could! Your way makes for much pleasanter reading than my terministic entanglements whereby even comparatively easeful items like my essay on Emerson's *Nature* or my "Prologue in Heaven" (in *Rhetoric of Religion*) give the impression of trying to shift weights around . . . Ennihow, it's a recovery job well worth the doing—and please hand on my compliments to Dan the Piper, though it's my hunch that, on p. xiv, he piped up with a quickie judgment about a book which he has never read.[4]

For today a Big Blow was scheduled. But already, before noon, things seem to be tempering off.

Holla!

K. B.

1. Burke is referring to Cowley's *Think Back On Us . . . A Contemporary Chronicle of the 1930's*, edited by Henry Dan Piper. It contains selected articles written by Cowley in the 1930s, most of them taken from the *New Republic*.

2. Burke suggests in his preface to the second edition of *Towards a Better Life* that what is "grotesque" about the novel is its tactical intermixing of the tragic and the comic.

3. Denis Donoghue and Robert Adams, critics who had reviewed Burke's novel when it was reprinted in 1966 by the University of California Press.

4. Evidently Burke is referring to Piper's reference to Burke's novel, *Towards a Better Life*, in his introduction to *Think Back On Us*. Piper writes that the novel is a "lesser work by an important writer."

Sherman, Connecticut,
February 8, 1967
[NL]

Dear Kenneth,

. . . I humbly accept your comments on *Think Back On Us*. The book has given me some pleasure—first from the thought that those pieces on which I had worked so hard weren't all of them buried in the back files of the *New Republic*, and then, when I read the manuscript, a certain gratification from the fact that it read well and held *my* interest, at least. I was accurate, but not profound. I had hold of one truth, which I overstressed, that we are all parts of one another; also that a good deal of one's energy is social energy, based on the consciousness of speaking for "us" and not only for "me." As you note in your letter, I understressed the other term of the dialectic, the "I." And I did not make the exagminations into meaning that I should have made. But now it's all part of the historical record. —Did you read my note at the end of the book? It sets forth my emphasis on construction, form, writing that led to (or was it compensation for?) a lesser interest in ideas.

. . . Robbers broke into the Josephson house and stole TV, radio, record player, etc., and Muriel wonders whether we too will be robbed in our absence. Nevertheless we'll take that risk . . .

Write me a poem!

As ever,
Malcolm

Box 231, Tecate,
California
2/12/67
[NL]

Dear Malcolm,

Your maieutic utterance, "Write me a poem," coupled with recent references,[1] plus some odds and ends I had from away back, brought forth this attitudinizing aggregate, with reminiscence as a sentimental ending:

AMBULANDO SOLVITUR
An Exercise in Free Translation

> It is solved
> by walking
>
> It is solved
> by walking very very fast
>
> It is solved
> by walking out
>
> It is solved
> by the ambulance
>
> It is solved
> by the perambulator
>
> It is solved
> by a walk in space,
> query
>
> It is solved
> by talking back and forth
> while going for a walk
> together

Yep, I read the first chapter. In fact, since you obviously wrote it last, I assumed that it was the introduction, so I read it first. Me and Aristotle would rate it rhetorically high, under the heading of "ethos" (character-buildup). The author is presented persuasively as the conscientious and competent craftsman that he really is. And your use of narrative was a good contribution toward appeal by identification (c.f. Ignatius Burpius, *Rhetorica Motivorum*).

. . .

I was sorry to hear about the Josephson robbery. So far, our pathetically humble hearth has been spared such depredations—but youthful vandalism can be so arbitrary, we always are uneasy . . . And that reminds me, I forgot to tell you: The indications are that the Burke clan's privies[2] have been invaded by a local lost soul who, every once in a while, gets stoned, and nothing can quiet him but descent into the ultimate recesses of a shithouse, a psychic accommodation which is becoming harder and harder for him to find. Honest to Gawd! Butchie and I obligingly restored the seat of our kahn in such a way that it can easily be removed without the need to tear the place apart. But it's just possible that that's no help. For maybe part of the cure is the need to *rape* the lowly place, before total immersion in, or identification avec, its Essence.

Love, love, love,
K. B.

1. See the end of paragraph two of Cowley's letter of February 5, 1964.
2. The Burkes still used an outside privy.

Sherman, Connecticut
July 3, 1968
[NL]

Dear Kenneth,

The eve of the Fourth. With the old man's habit I think about the eves of long-ago Fourths when I set off one firecracker just to prepare me for the dozens I'd set off when I woke at sunrise—then in the afternoon I'd go fishing with Doss Paul. Tomorrow I'll stay home and try to think of something to say about the fiction of the 1960s, which I really don't much like, or not much of it. John Cheever is really good because he has retained a sense of wonder and a taste for the preposterous (as in his story of the old woman dying in a town where death was contrary to the zoning laws: "The Death of Justina"). Norman Mailer is good in a fashion, as well as awful in a fashion; he's good because he tries hard to be great. Saul Bellow and Bernard Malamud write with authority, and there are many of what used to be regarded as unusual talent; today it can be acquired at the State

University of Iowa along with an M.A. in Creative Writing. But reading a lot of the fiction in sequence, as I have just been doing in an enormous new anthology, leaves me with a feeling of depression and with self-pitying voices ringing in my ears. I try to puzzle out what the voices are saying, and it seems to be "Geez, Ma, ain't it all useless, ain't we all absurd." . . .

As ever,
Malcolm

Sunday,
9/29/68
[NL]

Dear Malcolm,

Shorty is in the hospital, with a stroke. Things are just about over. There's one thing to console us: The fates at least have spared her the respiratory horrors that were in store for her otherwise.

Please do not phone me, for I make a fool of myself.

A man is a fool ever to be so close to a woman for so long. The emptiness is beyond belief. And the meanest trick of all is that one is in a position where one wants one's dearest thing to die.

Best love to my friends,
K. B.

Standish Harbor View
Hotel, Rm. 60,
169 Columbia Heights,
Brooklyn Heights,
New York
10/6/68
[NL]

Dear Malcolm,

Back from a quick one-night trip to Bennington, where I drank to the inaugurating of a new dormitory, traveling at mine own expense, and all for love of my Alma Soror.

Besten Dank for kind words to cheer me up. I suppose that, in my alcoholic shrewdness, I knew I could get a few enouraging words by weeping. And I'm most grateful that you dint just walk away and let me weep all to my lil ole morbid selph.

But now you must console me all over again. As the Great Inventor of the Flowerish would put it, "He praises me in private, while setting things up so that I must praise him in public."

I admit, that's o'ersimplifying things for epigrammatic purposes. But the pernt is that that bastard *New York Times*, which has blacklisted me for years, has finally lifted the ban. And how? Yes, you guessed it. They asked me to review The Juniata Blues.[1]

Needless to say, I have accepted, and am steamed up to be as winsome as I can, in praise of *thy* winsomeness. They asked for somethinks twixt eight hunnert and a thousand winged words. I'll give them a thousand and one, and refuse to let them cut.

Meanwhile, best luck.

Sincerely,
K. B.

1. Burke is referring to Cowley's book *Blue Juniata: Collected Poems*.

Sherman, Connecticut
March 10, 1969
[NL]

Dear Kenneth,

I just finished a 1,500-word piece on Valéry after spending ten days on it. I read and read before starting it—partly because Valéry makes fascinating reading; chiefly because I have to overcome all sorts of resistances before sitting down to type. The two worst resistances are bodily fatigue and simple sluggishness of mind. Now I ought to go on to do a long piece about Valéry, for which I have more than enough material; there simply isn't time.

· · ·

Thanks for thinking about me in connection with the trip to France. It sounds grand for you; for me at the present time it would be suicidal. Incidentally the subject is one that would have sent Valéry into a polite rage. He was against the psi factor. He achieved obscurity by dint of being or trying to be completely lucid. He wrote: "Shamelessly the spirit whispers a million absurdities for every great idea it abandons to our grasp; and the value of that lucky chance depends, even so, on our ability to shape it to our ends." This implies that inspiration is necessary but constant—"a million absurdities"—whereas the *variable*, and hence the important factor, is the conscious reworking of inspiration into an intellectual construction.

I don't at all agree with his anti-inspirationism, but he is a marvelous man to read. Full of ideas. Muriel said when she looked at my piece on him, "Isn't he a lot like Kenneth."

Love to Libbie. The next time I spend a night in NYC, I'll let you know so that we can get together.

As ever,
Malcolm

Stan Dish
[Standish Harbor View Hotel]
4/21/69
[NL]

Dear Malcolm,

. . . Just now, I should be packing. (Tomorrow I get up early, catch a plane to Madison, do a two-hour stint that same afternoon, then a show that eve, then another two hours the next morning, then drive to Chicago, definitely doing jobs on Thursday and Friday, and possibly, one on Wednesday eve, plus a dinner party. Needless to say, my mind just now is a total blank.)

Only one more tough deal on the Academic Circuit this season: several days at Dartmouth, the week of May fifth . . .

Shorty's illness has had a revolutionary effect upon me. For the first time in my life, I have an excuse to be greedy. Hence, paradoxically, just when I should be easing off, I am overdoing. But I shall stop soon, willy-nilly. After the week at Dartmouth, we revert to Andover—and I shall do some Creative Rotting . . .

Coupla days ago, I received an unsewed, unbound copy of an epoch-making tome, *Critical Responses to Kenneth Burke.* "Unsewed, unbound" suggests to me "Bloody, but unbowed." I'll be bloody, for sure; but will I be unbowed? When Bill Rueckert first mentioned this project to me in honor of my inseptuagenescence, I vetoed the idea of niceties. I said, said I: "Why not, rather, go back over the things that were said pro and con, o'er the years, and make a document out of them?" Lo! he did same. So the book contains several stinkos. (I myself, for instance, had begged to have the [Sidney] Hook ones included. And there they are, although for a long time Bill couldn't even get an answer to inquiries.) Maybe mine enemies will settle on the stinkos . . .

Avec Liebe,
K. B.

May 25, 1969
[NL]

Dear Malcolm,

Poor Shorty is gone. She left in her sleep last night. At least, she escaped the year or two of hell-on-earth that was in store for her, had the disease run its "normal" course.

A good deal of my reason for existence has gone with her. And, I fear, also a sizable portion of my reason. For her companionship worked constantly to redeem me from my nature as a born loner.

It is so good to be surrounded by one's family at such a time. It does help.

There will be no funeral. This is our understanding; this is our deal; and it goes for all of us. We will deal with our grief in our own way.

In a tangle,
K. B.

Sherman, Connecticut
June 4, 1969

Dear Kenneth,

We think about you. Among other things we think about your trip to Europe and wish we were taking it with you. See if you can charm somebody at Venice into driving you to Paris—the various countrysides are marvelous—and if you don't get a free ride, take the train, infinitely superior to American trains and once again passing through marvelous countrysides—probably it would be dawn as you passed through Burgundy. You'll be abashed by the prices in Paris; they're as bad as New York prices except for taxis and subways. Still, you really ought to blow yourself to one superb meal in a French restaurant, one of those with three stars and a lot of crossed knives and forks in the *Guide Michelin*. What about picking out one thing to see in Paris—the Louvre, for example—and going there every day of your visit?—I know very little about London, but if you spend a day there you ought to pay a visit to your English publisher, just out of curiosity. Everybody says that Cambridge is superb; and I envy you the walks in Ireland.

·   ·   ·

I tried to ride a bike yesterday. Found I could just propel it on the level, with a good deal of wobbling. Today I went into New York, and now at ten in the evening I feel as if someone had beaten me a long time with a soft whip. On Monday Muriel and I drive up to the 50th reunion of the class of '19. Never thought I'd make it. We think about you every day.

As ever,
Malcolm

7 roo Jarry, [Paris]
25 Juin [1969]
[NL]

Dear Malcolm,

Official announcement: I'm gettin outa this godam dump as fast as I know how. (And I'm not yet sure that I do know how.) Last night (by what I now realize was dumb luck[)], I got a place on the boulevard Montmartre for 71 francs. It was only for the one night. Today, though I got down on my knees and was willing to pay 90, all I could get was a hole in the wall for 51. The chambermaid seems friendly, but the proprietor is a bear. And when I dropped in around the corner for a beer, the owner's dog bit my hand as I was passing him without even noticing his anti-American presence. "Il n'aime pas les Américans," I said in my most winsome frangsay. But the bastard was right; he had ESP—I had already decided to get the hell outa here as fast as I know how (if I do know how!). The clairvoyant bastard even broke the skin a bit—so I have that to add to my worries.

Let them keep this fuckn place to theirselves.

The trip from Milan to Paris was a flop. I shoulda kept my original plan of going to Zurich. The part of the Alps we passed through was pleasant enough, but not spectacular. And for the most part it was raining. The one good break was that I passed up Amsterdam, which is apparently due for troubles in a big way, owing to the latest move in the pollution bizz. Otherwise, it would have been good to compare Amsterdam and Venice. (Venice is a place to love. I'm awfully glad I went to Venice, though doubtless the company of Jerre and Pat Mangione[1] added a lot to that experience. "Dear Venezia, / it is as though there were no tomorrow— / as though all were always to be today's sunlight, / even while, / from the waves of the Vaporetto, / the threats of sure destruction / lap about your feet." I had in mind the way in which the waves have already gnawed away the lower part of so many doors.) . . .

[Sincerely,]
[K. B.]

1. Jerre Mangione is a Sicilian-born writer who has lived and taught in America.

Sherman, Connecticut
July 11, 1969
[NL]

Dear Kenneth,

So you got back safe to &over [Andover]. We were cheered by your card from Venice, depressed by your letter from Paris (I should have warned you to reserve a room). Now I wonder what sort of time you had in England and Ireland . . . Muriel and I went to the 50th reunion of the class of '19 and it was a better occasion than I had expected it to be . . . The students looked different from those of my time: lots of long hair, sideburns, beards, even bare feet; lots of radical sentiments (as expressed by two commencement orators). An expelled member of SDS was given ten minutes that infuriated the alumni and didn't much please the graduating seniors. It turned out that perhaps a third of the graduating class had planned to walk out of the commencement exercises. SDS insisted that its members were going to shout and create a disturbance, whereupon everyone else refrained from the planned walkout. The SDS speaker wouldn't stop when his ten minutes were up; I wondered whether the cops would be called in and whether there would be a riot. But no; the class officers surrounded him in their long black robes and swept him off the platform as if they were pallbearers at a very efficient funeral. Thereupon about fifty seniors walked out, quietly, and later many of them returned.

•   •   •

That's our news. I too am reviewing Unterecker's book,[1] and I don't know what to say about it—or rather, I *do* know what to say, but can't get started on the review. Unterecker impresses me by his fairness and exhaustiveness. No, I didn't cry about Hart; I only felt moist-eyed at the moments when he proclaimed what a grand, reasoned career he was going to have. His vigor was stupendous. He burned himself up. Sometimes I think of him as one of those self-destroying mechanisms of Tinguely's[2]— by the age of sixteen, his future was a drama written in advance and inevitably leading to death by sea. The immediate causes of his suicide were more or less accidental. The distant causes were necessary and included most of all his notion that he must be a great poet, that great poetry depended on vision (or ecstasy, or frenzy), and that vision could best be produced by alcohol.

All our love, as ever,
Malcolm

---

1. John E. Unterecker had recently published a biography of Hart Crane, *Voyager: A Life of Hart Crane*.

2. Jean Tinguely, a Swiss sculptor born in 1925, is known for his meta-mechanical moving constructions. In 1960 he became interested in the idea of destruction, and built his first "auto-destructive" work, *Homage to New York*. It was demonstrated at the Museum of Modern Art in New York, but it failed to destroy itself as planned, and caused a fire.

> And/or
> 7/17/69
> [NL]

Dear Malcolm,

. . . To my traumatic loss of Libbie (doubly traumatic, because, like her, we also wished her death, along with our desire to keep her with us), add my cwazy trip to Europe, which was supposed to be a help. And then, in the course of going through this biography of Hart, I found so many memories stirred up that aren't on those pages at all (and I'm not saying there's any reason why they should be).

I'm digging into the roots of me, even while carrying on Business as Usual.

Then I went into the bank vault yet--and it all adds up to surprisingly much, in view of what a cheapskate I was and what I gave away, to get Libbie and me legalized. But all along, I've known the stupidity of having most of one's funds in bonds. I jes dint have the time to think otherwise.

Now I know where the best investment would be. Namely: stock in Paris taxis. When they start confiding to you about la circulation, or les voitures, or le trafeek, you can be sure they're getting ready to take you up a side street where you stagnate for hours, while the meter becomes a perfect model of Progress.

·   ·   ·

Thank God, I have enough enemies to keep me living. Otherwise the self-kill would be all about me. One must watch everywhere one turns. For instance, a publisher writes, saying that a certain thing of one's is "gorgeous." And one wakes up just in time to catch the mail, with one's answer to him *on a postcard*.

Two things: (1) I want to make sure that my keets [sic] get the best deal possible out of what I can leave them; (2) those bastard shits, the Phartisan Crowd and sech, I wanna hold out as long as I can, against those poops.
(3) ?

> Avec Liebe,
> K. B.

Sherman, Connecticut
July 22, 1969
[NL]

Dear Kenneth,

I stayed up to see the moon walkers, or jumpers on their trampoline, and they looked to me like nothing but two misty white figures like ghosts in the comic strips, in this case groping over a white surface. Was this trip necessary? All it does for us on earth is to shoot away some of our irreplaceable hydrogen and hydrocarbons out of the atmosphere, and the atmosphere growing poorer month by month, now moment by moment, so that we can now definitely picture the time when the earth will be as lifeless as the moon. Henry Adams wasn't so crazy after all with his law of acceleration leading to the big smash.

• • •

I too just finished a review of Unterecker. I too worked on it too long and took too many notes—bet I worked on it longer than you did on yours, because the old bean refused to function in the heat. I was less moved than you, having worked on the material before, but still a lot of things were dredged up from the past. Did you know that Hart was responsible for my putting together and publishing *Blue Juniata*? He worked hard at that project in the summer of 1928, and out of pure friendship. I told the whole story for the book of Hart's letters to the Browns and to me that Sue has done for Wesleyan University Press. Also I put the story into my review (for *Sewanee*), but Andrew Lytle[1] may ask me to take it out, unless he can find room for the review in his fall issue (on account of the publication date of Sue's book, November 13). Having done her first book at 73, Sue is cackling and joyous as an old hen that has laid her first egg . . .

As ever,
Malcolm

1. Andrew Lytle was the editor at *Sewanee Review*.

Busyville
8/2/69
[NL]

Dear Malcolm,

One good turn deserves another. I enclose my effort anent the Crane biography.

It's a very good job you did there. But, though the second half is intrinsically good, I tend to agree with Lytle that it strains at the edges of reviewdom. I once heard Yvor Winters make a highly laudatory speech,

introducing Marianne Moore. It was all about her sympathy and percep-
tiveness as a critic of other people's work. And as evidence, he confined
himself to explaining how soon and how accurately she had appreciated his
poems.

Your second half is not just that. For your story serves to bring out the
Hart Crane aspect of the thing you're talking about. And I can see how it
would fit perfectly in the book of Sue's. But the proportions seem wrong
for a review.

Howe'er, in the first of my seven pages, note that I too got into the act.

Jeez, how different our approaches are! And yours wins by a walkaway
on the humanity angle. In a couple of places I might even be accused of
being a bit of a stinker. The greatest virtue and greatest danger of a review
is to build around some one generating principle, which may o'ersimplify
things. The importance of *The Bridge*, plus the accident of a relevant question from the floor, got me to doing as I did. Your further communing with
Unterecker helps a lot toward getting the quality you aimed at . . . You
keep getting more humane; I keep hankering, as usual, after La Dialec-
tique . . .

· · ·

As for my trip to Europe, the trouble is: I wrote down quite a number
of impressions (Venice e'en moved me to verse); but as usual, things are
lost among my papers. Too much of my time was expended on the mere
pragmatics of getting from one place to another, making connections, ver-
ifying reservations, and kindred godam nuisances. I have decided that, if
ever I go to Europe again, I'll pick one place, and stay until I'm ready to
come home . . .

The place near Nice would have been a dream, except that walking was
impossible. The charming narrow winding road, obviously made for oxcarts,
was plagued with a constant succession of racing fools in cars. It was the
only place where walking was possible, and one constantly had to flatten
himself against the stone walls of the terraces. To walk on the road at all
was to play chicken, with all the risks on your side. And there really was
no other place to walk . . .

Holla!

K. B.

Sherman, Connecticut
August 13, 1969
[NL]

Dear Kenneth,

I see that your piece on Hart is out in the *New Republic* this week—but I was glad to get the ms. well in advance of its appearing in print. It's a dandy piece and it develops one of the central themes, perhaps *the* central theme, in Hart's life and work. If I were to talk about his work again, I'd take those words "dialectic" and "transcendence" and play around with them, using different examples from yours. That's how his mind worked: thesis, antithesis, and not mere synthesis, but transcendence. That's how his poems are constructed: "Faustus and Helen," "Voyages"—and *The Bridge* is not merely dialectical as a whole, with "Atlantis" as a final transcendence (written first, incidentally), but dialectical in one of the constituent poems after another. Life-Death: Resurrection; Past-Present: Future; Europe-Asia: America; Land-Sea: Voyage, Bridge; Past-Present: Eternity (not Future). Whitman had that same form or category of thought, and Hart is rewriting "Passage to India"—sometimes he's even using the dreadful language that Whitman falls into in "Passage"; it's a wonder he didn't write "eclaircise the myths Asiatic" or "trains carrying freight and passengers"—Whitman's grand structural talent impressed him so that he accepted (in "Cape Hatteras") a lot of the Barnum with the Bard.

Anyhow, you were striking through the mask, right at the heart of the problem. In some ways, though, we were saying the same things in our different fashions, except that I only hinted at the bridging in such phrases as "dialectic" (used once) and "conflicts that had been internalized." For the rest, we hit on many of the same points, one after another: vitality, the danger of the alcoholic approach to poetry, the fact that much of Hart's problem was literary, professional. Etc. You say my piece is more human. Yours is more central.

But I insist that even though I was getting into the act, in those last 5pp of my piece, still they are part of the review, in so far as it reviews biography in terms of my own memoir. And the memoir reveals a side of Hart that people don't know about. Why shouldn't the reviewer say, "I know the guy and here's how he was"? I still hope to persuade Andrew to print it all.

As ever,
Malcolm

Sherman, Connecticut
October 17, 1970
[NL]

Dear Kenneth,

An addendum to yesterday's letter. The letter from Dan Piper arrived. He wants me to make a two-day stand, on a Monday and a Tuesday.[1] He didn't say whether he had two jobs in mind for you—he specified a Monday evening joint talk, preferably on "The Future of Criticism: What Now Needs to Be Done." If that should be your only chore, I'd sort of background myself and feed you—considering in any case that you have more to say on that subject than I have. He wanted each of us to speak for 30 minutes, then feed us thirty minutes of questions. I asked him whether a round-table setup wouldn't be better, with Dan feeding us the questions, and letting us answer them at length, after somewhat briefer opening statements. That would give you an opportunity to talk more, and me somewhat less . . .

As ever,
Malcolm

1. Cowley had been invited to speak at Southern Illinois University, in Carbondale.

8166 Whitburn Drive,
Apt. 13,
Clayton, Missouri
10/20/70
[NL]

Dear Malcolm,

. . . At the moment, I write you in haste. When my boss[1] heard that you were to be in Carbondale, he immediately wondered about your doing a stint here at the same time. Dan Piper sent me a letter about the events in Carbondale, but I can't find it. I wrote him yesterday, crying out, and giving him my apartment phone number, in case things call for speed. But in the meantime, think of the possibility of somethinks here (particularly since, if youenz are coming by plane, you'll doubtless be in St. Louis anyhow). My boss is Dick Ruland. He and his wife, Mary Ann, met you at some doings in New Haven, where everybody but you was all set to be a solemn bore . . .

Rejerce,
K. B.

1. Burke was visiting as a lecturer at St. Louis University.

Sherman, Connecticut
November 14, 1970
[NL]

Dear Kenneth,

A letter from Dan Piper making all arrangements for Carbondale. They're okay with me; I hope they are with you. My chief worry is about our Table Round on Tuesday evening. My God, I haven't any ideas about the Future of Criticism. I have always avoided thinking about Criticism in my effort to think about the work being criticized and in trying to approach it without preconceptions. Criticism flourished during the 1950s; now it's less flourishing or even in a state of decay. That is because the methods developed in the 1950s or earlier were fruitful when applied to a work for the first or second or third time—on the fourth round they began to seem tired. One work after another was exhausted as a field for study—first *Moby Dick*, then *The Waste Land*, then *Absalom, Absalom!*, *The Great Gatsby*, even *Ulysses* and *Finnegans Wake*—it was an exhaustion of resources like that of opened and receding frontiers. Either new subjects or new methods are required. Hence the wild divagations into Mythical Criticism, the Norman O. [Browns], the efforts of the critic to become an all-knowing psychologist and transform the work into a patient or even a corpse for dissection.

Could we go back to Aristotle and work the general forms of narrative: exposition, development, counterpoint, confrontation, restatement, coda (or as you early called it, tangent)? T[homas] Mann did that superbly with his own work. But that too requires continually new subject matter; the critic is dependent on the artist. Unless he becomes like you a philosopher of symbolic action or of communication as the specifically human activity . . .

As ever,
with the sun shining
for once in November,
Malcolm

1927 East River Terrace,
Minneapolis, Minnesota
January 20, 1971
[NL]

Dear Kenneth,

I spoke this afternoon in Murphy Auditorium, a little hall the size, and the temperature too, of a baked potato. You would have thought they were trying to keep my first public lecture a deepdark secret . . . [T]he lecture was scheduled in conflict with the first of a series by John Berryman. Nevertheless I had a capacity audience, for Murphy, and they promise a bigger hall and more publicity for the second lecture. Now I'm feeling weary, with a class lecture to give tomorrow.

. . .

The University of Minnesota Press gave me its three Burke items. Two of them by William Rueckert; I haven't read *Kenneth Burke and the Drama of Human Relations*, but I paged through *Critical Responses to Kenneth Burke*, and it seemed a well-balanced collection, with the balance resting firmly on the plus side. Then to my horror I read *Kenneth Burke*, the Minnesota pamphlet by Merle E. Brown, and found it a masterpiece of misreading. Sometimes of deliberate misstatement, or something close to that. Brown has the fantastic notion that philosophers don't think in words—ah, they're too good for words. But in general his technique is that of Anthony addressing the Roman mob: "And Burkus is an honorable man," he seems to be repeating. He ought to be subjected to strategic analysis.

I hadn't realized what a subject of contention you were in critical circles. Or how many whitehats there were among the blackhats trying to rob your corpse while still alive. Looks to me as if the whitehats were winning out . . .

'Zever,
Malcolm

c/o Stanford Resort,
1765 Gulf Blvd.,
Englewood, Florida
December 15, 1971
[NL]

Dear Malcolm,

Your book is a job you are entitled to be considerably proud of.[1] I read it admiringly throughout. The chapters on Hawthorne and Whitman seemed to me just right. And I thought you were quite reasonable and convincing in your reservations about Pound and Frost. I remembered the O'Neill piece, which has a good base in narrative. Your various figures along the way help a lot. They are never strained, and they effectively reinforce your point. (Here's an amusing accident: In your piece on "Sherwood Anderson's Book of Moments," you refer to his seeing all sorts of faces when going to sleep. This used to be an engrossing experience of a guy who wrote a book by that title; and his father was familiar with the same phenomenon. It is marvelous the way they kept twisting from one into another. And I always felt that if I had been able to draw, I'd have made a life's work out of doing sketches for such a gallery.) . . .

But to return: I was astonished and happy to realize how, though we had each gone his different way, in these pages I never resisted a godam thing you wrote. The probable fact is that, implicit in all our work, there somehow survives the common experience of our walkie-talkie days back and forth on Ellsworth Avenue. Things work out somewhat as on that deal at Carbondale. At first it looked as though we were miles apart. And though people usually love a fight, some who were friendly to us were wretched because they thought things would turn into a fight. Yet, though we had our different routes, our roots were not essentially different at all—and we pretty much allowed for the same things.

To be sure, as regards the text: My stress upon "Dramatism" (patent applied for) is a bit out of line with your biographical stress. But decidedly *not* to the extent that I rule out such considerations. And though we come out of the woods from different directions, we end up by finding ourselves in pretty much the same clearing. True, there are places where I wish you had let me in explicitly. I have particularly in mind my way of undercutting the "intentional fallacy." But the likelihood is that you haven't run across it (or at least hadn't when you wrote on that sumjick). My one bleat would be that, when resisting a trend, you bear down on guys like Fiedler[2] (or Stanley[3] at a weak moment), rather than presenting the whole problem. Yet that's not correct either, as regards Pound or Frost. I guess it's only as regards the whole problem of criticizing criticism. Whenever you are talking about the primary texts and their authors, what you say is quite convincing . . .

> Great daze,
> K. B.

1. Cowley had recently published a book of essays, *A Many-Windowed House: Collected Essays on American Writers and American Writing*, edited by Henry Dan Piper.

2. The literary critic Leslie Fiedler.

3. Stanley Edgar Hyman, literary critic and a good friend of both Burke and Cowley.

> Sherman, Connecticut
> December 20, 1971
> [NL]

Dear Kenneth,

. . . I'm pleased, nach, (natch), that you like the multifenestrated house. You pick out the pieces that interested me most (though, as I should have but didn't say in a footnote to the Whitman piece, the attention to his homosexuality that I felt to be necessary in 1947 seems disproportionate in 1971). I too like the effort to be just that I was making in the Frost and Pound pieces, and I too was a little apologetic, in my mind, about the generalities on criticism in the final essay. At Southern Illinois I didn't have fears about a Confrontation, for I knew we would end up on the same side, even if we came into the clearing by very different paths.

Just now, as I think I told you, I'm working on another collection of essays, this one about the mostly fiction writers of the Lost Generation. The stuff is almost all written, but there are gaps to be filled and a lot of inner adjustments to be made. It will be a happy project to occupy my time in Florida—though I could wish that we were nearer to a university library. There will have to be a lotta books in my baggage . . .

> Be thankful,
> Malcolm

R.D. 2,
Andover, New Jersey
May 4, 1972
[NL]

Dear Malcolm,

. . . Just now I'm getting vaguely, flutteringly, hypertensively ready for next week at Penn State. (I believe I let myself in for a rough time. It looks to me as though things are so set up that I'll do the most work for the least money in all my nearly 75 years—[by] then it'll be 75.)

· · ·

Since one of the classes in which I am to talk has been tinkering with the criticisms of James Dickey, I started to bone up—and I found that he had done a short piece on my *Book of Moments*. Sometimes pleasant, but on the whole exasperating. But my poems, when assembled in a book, do raise one problem that I don't know how to solve. Whereas most poets tend to do a lot of their poems in the same groove, I hop from one mood to another.[1] Hence it's hard to set up a single shingle, even for one book. This goes particularly badly with a guy like Dickey, who was trained in writing advertising copy, with its demands for banging away at one slogan until the public is beaten into accepting it. Of course, if I do decide to discuss the guy's review in said classroom, this lil trick of a comment won't not get tried . . .

I miss our walks greatly. And tell dear Muriel how greatly I miss those sun-going-down hours. But such sentiments are no surprise to me, for I knew, every minute of the time, how happy I was to be with youenz.[2] We move on—yes, we move on. But there was a kind of lovely poignancy in our aging friendship there. It's not the sort of thing that could be reclaimed. If we tried it again, it would probably be as Marx says about the difference between tragedy and farce. It's gone beyond recovery (except that, in my memory, I recover it again and again).

I am so grateful, not just to youenz, but to the nature of things, that I can carry away with me the sense of our truly humane relationship in that interim. To you, and to dear Muriel,

Thanks,
K. B.

1. Burke acknowledges this tendency in the epigraph to his *Collected Poems*: "Our moods do not believe in each other." The line is from Emerson.

2. Burke had recently vacationed in Florida with Cowley and his wife, Muriel.

Sherman, Connecticut
May 10, 1972
[NL]

Dear Kenneth,

. . . I too deeply appreciated the Florida trip. Even Muriel has come to enjoy it in memory, especially the sunset drinks and the dinners. But why does it have to be the last and the signing off? God damn it, I refuse to be resigned, to do things for the last time. I fight every infirmity. I'll hold out as long as I can. I'll make plans to spend the winter of '74 with you, if we can still totter and talk.

Be stubborn,
Malcolm

R.D. 2,
Andover, New Jersey
June 1, 1972
[NL]

Dear Malcolm,

Having checked off the date (since I'm not getting the daily edition of the *New York Times*, I have trouble remembering the day, month, year, and century we're in), I wish to make an official announcement (which I make not without trepidation, for this is the sort of utterance that invites bad luck): . . . I think I pretty well know how I want to proceed. The damnable BLANK is no more.

Mainly, the job involves an explicit squaring with the various kinds of corks that bob on the nearby waters (if one can square with corks). Such as . . . Dickey (built around his review of *Book of Moments*, an item I saw only recently), [B. F.] Skinner . . . and there's a momentous job to tackle, Lévi-Strauss, who is really somethinks, whose approach is often quite in the same groove as mine (although, so far as I have read, he strikes me as but *aiming at* the same target that I have hit in the middle, with my distinctions between mythology and logology). I haven't yet read enough of him to see how his use of analogies from music squares with my stuffo on "chord" and "arpeggio," aired as early as *Philosophy of Literary Form*. But there seems to be a basic overlap there, too. Also, of course, there's the brutal fact that his familiarity with fieldwork texts in anthropology makes him rhetorically as unanswerable as Niagara Falls. The reader expends such terrific effort in just trying to hang on, by the time he gets through a text he is exhausted . . . His general lineup compares and differs strategically with mine (as per *Language as Symbolic Action*, p. 374, originally published in *Anthropological Linguistics*, 1962).[1] His four are: (1) physical and political geography; (2) economic; (3) social and family organization; (4) mythological. My third and fourth would closely correspond with his third and fourth. My first would include both his first and second (though a bit that he includes under "political" in his first would fit better as a part of my third). The most notable difference is that he has no equivalent for my second, though he necessarily deals with it from start to finish. *Tentatively*, the methodological issue seems to center in this difference, though he deals [at] considerable length with verbal resources as such.

Well, we'll see . . .

Universal love,
K. B.

1. In "What Are the Signs of What," an essay in *Language as Symbolic Action*, Burke distinguishes among four different classes of words: words for "the sheerly natural," words for the verbal realm itself (the terms of rhetoric, poetics, etc.), words for the sociopolitical realm, and words for the supernatural.

Sherman, Connecticut
June 12, 1972
[NL]

Dear Kenneth, Doctorissimus,

Muriel came upstairs to announce that Edmund Wilson had died at 77. I won't piss on his grave. He was a good man and a character, if arrogant.

Since 1940 he hasn't done much that I wanted to read, except for tributes to distressed or dying old friends: Dawn Powell,[1] Newton Arvin,[2] Van Wyck Brooks. *Patriotic Gore*, his last big book, had some fascinating accounts of Civil War worthies, but the introduction to it was out of touch with reality. The time when he played a key part in literary life was during the twenties and thirties, especially the twenties. Nobody has equaled him since in the function he performed then, of introducing a new literature to the public while influencing the new writers themselves. Requiescat. We're in the front-line trenches now.

I've been reading a not-too-good book with some fascinating stuff in it: *Feasting with Panthers, a New Consideration of Some Late Victorian Writers*, by Rupert Croft-Cooke (Holt, 1967). Croft-Cooke . . . is persuaded that almost everyone . . . in the literary world was homosexual—except Swinburne, who was a masochist, Dowson, who was a drunk, and the Reverend C. L. Dodgson, who had a letch for little girls and photographed them naked. When they first menstruated, he kicked them out and found other little girls. The mother of Alice Liddell, the original of Alice in Wonderland, burned all of Dodgson's letters to her. The beach at Eastbourne was where he used to pick up little girls. He wrote to a friend, "I still make friends with children on the beach, and sometimes even (being now an old man who can venture on things that 'Mrs. Grundy' would never permit to a younger man) have some little friend stay with me as a guest." . . .

Love, love, loaf,
Malcolm

1. Dawn Powell was a writer who died in 1965.
2. Newton Arvin died in 1963. He was a literary critic and teacher affiliated with Yaddo.

Puzzleville
6/18/72
[NL]

Dear Malcolm,
. . . Wilson is a lucky guy. I envy anybody who no longer has to worry about this damnable choice between hanging on and clearing out. Yes, he was competent. But I think that a part of his reputation was due to his being a journalist. His great trick, lots of the time, was not in being a critic, but in giving you the news about books—and people could read the news without reading the books. I believe *Axel's Castle* came out the same year as *Counter-Statement*. An ironic fact is that, after the article I did on him for the *New Republic* and showed to him but never published (owing to our

battles about my refusal to cut it in half), he did his thing on *The Turn of the Screw*.[1] Without knowing of his, I did one, too, using of course the method of "indexing" which I had been developing for the analysis of a text. I couldn't do a damned thing about mine. For it was enough like his for people to say that I owed mine to his. And the piece was so much my own, the thought was intolerable. So, it still rots in manuscript. Since I never saw him again, I don't know how he interpreted the fact that my Wilson essay (which he liked) never appeared. The article on him by Roger Strauss (in today's *New York Times*) makes me realize all over again what an incompetent mess I . . . ah, shit . . .[2]

Love, love, love,
K. B.

1. Wilson published one of the first psychoanalytic readings of *The Turn of the Screw*, "The Ambiguity of Henry James," in the April-May, 1934, issue of *Hound & Horn*.

2. Ellipses Burke's.

Sherman, Connecticut
July 3, 1972
[NL]

Dear Kenneth,

On the matter of purloined books, I empathize.[1] Though mine—only the books I need, curiously never the others—mostly disappear through borrowings, and I always forget who borrowed them. Or they simply get misplaced, and in this houseful of books I can't find them. I have been working on guess who—on KB—and the disappeared books were *The Philosophy of Literary Form* and *The Rhetoric of Religion*. Yes, I had them both. Where are they now?

I have extra copies of some, through your generosity and forgetfulness. *Permanence and Change*, Hermes edition, 2 copies. Could you make use of one?

I enclose a draft of the pages I did on you. They go into the last chapter of the book, which is now five or six pages from the very end.[2] The last chapter tries to make a book out of the ten essays that have preceded it . . .

Happy (sigh), happy,
Malcolm

1. Burke had written in a previous letter about visitors stealing books from his home.

2. *A Second Flowering: Works and Days of the Lost Generation*, which was published in 1973. The final chapter contains a brief overview of Burke's work, prefaced by the observation that "I should have written about Burke and could have done so more easily if he were not my oldest friend."

Placidity Meadows
7/8/72
[NL]

Dear Malcolm,

. . . Besten Dank for paragraphs anent my (at present quite alien) agitated Selph. But I feel as incompetent to comment on them as you felt to comment on me, and for the same reason . . .

Necessarily, for a windup you are generalizing (as vs. your tying more closely to particular quotes of the author in your long chapters). I don't see that there is any way to get around that. Yet, no—I think that within the limits you had at your disposal, you did pick central quotes. But you have violated Burke's Law. As I understand Burke's Law, no discussion of boik-woiks can possibly satisfy Burke unless it views his novel as a literary marvel which no filthy bastard son-of-a-bitch (and there are no other kinds of writers) could possibly duplicate (and above all, I include here Burke himself). The second implication of Burke's Law is that no one is competent to write on boikwoiks in general unless he has read the dialogue between Satan and The Lord in *The Rhetoric of Religion*. Though it would be too unwieldy for you to deal with them, I think that De Burp's concepts, the "paradox of substance"[1] and the "temporizing of essence,"[2] are basic to his bleats—and ditto, for grand finale, his new twists on the Aristotelian concept of the entelechy (as viewed in terms of Dramatism). I see no reason why you should bestir yourself to deal with these concepts. For they would require a lot more space. And in any case, for a quite relevant summarizing specification, I'm glad that you brought in the pernt about behaviorism, my attitude toward which involves all three of those concepts.

•   •   •

Give t'other copy of *Permanence and Change* to some Cause or other. Incidentally, if you want replacements of *The Philosophy of Literary Form* and *The Rhetoric of Religion*, I'll be glad to send 'em. The only condition is that you'll promise someday, not necessarily during your present pressures, to read the "Prologue in Heaven," the epilogue of *The Rhetoric of Religion*.

Buddhistically
calmistically,
K. B.

1. "The paradox of substance" is the subject of pages 21–23 of *A Grammar of Motives* The "paradox" Burke discusses has to do with the fact that "the word 'substance,' used to designate what a thing *is*, derives from a word designating something that a thing is *not*."

2. Burke explains the "temporizing of essence" in *A Grammar of Motives*, pages 430–440. The term is meant to denote the process whereby logical principles are sometimes translated into a *narrative* of origins. The term becomes important in his discussion of the book of Genesis in *The Rhetoric of Religion*.

Sherman, Connecticut
July 19, 1972

Dear Kenneth,

. . . I finished my book. No, I didn't finish it, but I managed to get the last page written, and the rest of my job will be minor revisions. In the paragraphs anent your Selph I found it hard to make changes. I couldn't bring in the Negative, the Entelechy, or that really valuable to me concept of the Temporizing of Essence. There's not much I can do about *Towards a Better Life* except slip in a phrase to indicate admiration. I also will have a footnote giving Stanley H[yman] credit for "Burkology." But what I had to do in those paragraphs was not to expound—I was beyond the point for exposition—but merely to suggest. I'm weary and feeble at present—something, I don't know what, is physically wrong and it affects my capacity to work or bleat. The last section of the book, a sort of epitaph and restrained judgment, was ferociously hard to do—eight pages took me three weeks or more.

I should be eternally grateful for a copy of *The Philosophy of Literary Form*—who in Christ's name walked off with mine?—and for *The Rhetoric of Religion*. Yes, I have read them both, and in RR I was particularly impressed by what you derived from the first chapters of Genesis, as well as by the dialogue between Satan and The Lord . . .

'Zever,
Malcolm

Beardswards
7/19/72
[NL]

Dear Malcolm,

. . . [L]et's talk about you for a while. What do you say about my book [*Towards a Better Life*]? (Won't you grant, it's one of the fundamentalest jokes in the langwitch?) Frankilee, my pernt is this: If my novel is as good as I say it is, and lots of the books which you are farting around with are pissant (feeble-minded) books in comparison, and you quote them respectfully, *the job is for me* to prove it. And I dare tell myself that things are going my way. Modestly: My TBL is to my critical books as Nietzsche's *Zarathustra* is to his others. (That is, it's the ritualized essence out of which comes the existence of my detailed analysis. And those NYC shits can't stop me. For reports are coming in now from France, Germany, Japan. Give me a few more years, and the things will get done. Honest to God, Malcolm, those Phartisan Review CIA shits have shot their wad. Give me but two more years, and I'll prove my point. The world is catching on. And my novel is the ritual initiation. And I'll prove it.)

You're right, I'm drunk. And lemme tellyuh, felluh, when I drag myself off to bed tonight, I'll hardly be able to climb the stairs. So, don't try to out-weary me. But a funny thing happened, as you may see in the enclosed pages. Malcolm, I am growing a beard. And each night I am impatient to see how it did while I slept. Malcolm, if you don't believe in heaven, or if, even if you do believe in heaven, you doubt whether you're going to get there—and I hope you won't, Malcolm, because I'd think it heaven if you were down there haggling with me in hell—caetera desunt (whatever that means) . . .

> Be,
> K. B.

> R.D. 2,
> Andover, New Jersey
> August 3, 1972
> [NL]

Dear Malcolm,

Jeez, maybe I know more than you, how it is to get wankly on one's pins. Last night, walking in the darkness on our last piece of unpaved road (and loves it), I slipped on the pebbles, ripping a chunk out of my knee. So, atop all else, I must worry about tetanus. And tonight, right by the porch, things all went wrong, ending with a punched-in screen. Though neither of these jobs was totally sans alcohol, so little was involved it would bring tears to your eyes.

. . . .

I was quite gloomy tonight, walking solo while Butchie was hereabouts but not along with. But I know I'm wrong at such times. The acreage is lousy with generations and kinds and friends of generations of kinds. And after all, that's what I wanted. Hence, beginning solo, I should take solo-itude for granted.

Meanwhile, along with my petty careerist ambitions, I have reestablished a purely biological mode of futurism. For, having got too lazy to either bathe or shave, I solved the bathing problem by going to the pond; and by ceasing to shave entirely, I find that I can hardly wait to see tomorrow. The thing has not yet reached the stage where I have to decide how I should make it behave. But I'm as delighted with it as a woman with a baby, and it doesn't need to be nearly so pampered . . .

Love to theenthine,
K. B.

80 High St.,
Kenilworth, Warwickshire,
[England]
16 February, 1973
[NL]

Dear Kenneth,

. . . We have had a somewhat lonely time in Kenilworth. I have made two friends here, and one of them, Claude (C. A.) Rawson, is just as nice as a man can be—his wife Judy, too—and Muriel is going across the street tonight to read to their delightful children. Otherwise we lead a rather secluded life in a big, comfortable bungalow on a street of low seventeenth-century cottages, some of them covered with genuine thatch. The ruins of Kenilworth Castle are at the foot of a gentle hill. The university is spic-and-span new, attended by bright lower-middle-class boys and girls with such broad Midlands accents that I often don't understand what they are saying. Clean white-tile buildings (with some of the tiles falling off); raw red Warwickshire clay where the bulldozers have dug into it; cranes looming over the sixth story—in some ways it reminds me of Davis or Riverside.[1] The U.K. in construction.

But the poor U.K., the United Kingdom of Great Britain and Northern Island (and of nowhere else, not even Malta or the Fiji Islands) is degringolating into Europe while uttering American cries. From the newspapers, which are pretty good, one gets the impression that America is where the action is, where the styles are being set, where the headquarters are of the companies that are opening branch offices all over the U.K. The English are suffering from consumeritis, and every time they make a brave effort to produce for themselves, the labor unions go on strike. Right now it's a gas strike that has closed down factories all over the Midlands and put another crimp in British exports. This bungalow is heated by natural gas and so far hasn't been affected, but they say our time is coming, as it has come already for houses heated with "town gas."

You sound, my God, you sound so busy that you haven't time for anything but insomnia, your only avocation . . . It also sounds as if going to Princeton has turned out to be a most convenient arrangement. Lemme hear more when you can find time for a letter.

> Peace, piece, peas,
> Malcolm

1. There are University of California campuses in both Davis and Riverside.

> 204 Graduate College,
> Princeton, New Jersey
> 3/16/73
> [NL]

Dear Malcolm,

'Twas good to hear from thee, as always. You know: Sometimes I'm up, sometimes I'm down—and I wish the same to you. At the moment, for reasons best known to Our Maker, I'm up. I'm ptikly up because, whenever a note occurs to me, I know which one of my sub-personalities (or book projects) to file it under. And after all, what was Dante's point in assigning all them guys to various circles along the way? Paradise, me lad, is knowing exactly where to file something. And Hell is a place where you don't know to file anything you hit upon, on your way up, through Purgatory.

· · ·

Yes, for the moment, I have attained my much-vaunted ideal (namely: to be as mellow as an overripe canteloupe). And though I write with a bit of alky, I promise you that the mood does not all come out of a bottle. Dis is de way I have been feeln, aside from a fan letter I got from a sweet young thing (I know she is a sweet young thing, and only recently a mother, for I know her, she has talked with me, we palled together, in my kitchen) and the darling said to the ole rundown baystard that, on the platform, he looked "ravishing." You top that one, you baystard. Maybe you can still ravish. But can you *look* ravishing? . . .

So, as you can figger out for yourself, everything worked out pretty perfick. But alas, maybe by the time this reaches you, I'll be downer than down.

> Love to theenthine,
> K. B.

80 High St.,
Kenilworth, Warwickshire,
England
29 March 1973
[NL]

Dear Kenneth,

. . . Without a car we live an incredibly quiet life at Kenilworth. Just now it's vacation time and I try to write, but something in me fights away from the typewriter. Read *The Times*, which is dull but carries a lot of news. Look at telly, which is immeasurably better sometimes, usually on Sunday evening, than it is in the States—at other times it's simply amateurish. We took a trip to Birmingham to see 19th-century English pictures, you know, Burne-Jones, Rosetti, Frith, Holman Hunt, Ford Madox Brown, all the painters we learned to sneer at. They're amusing and are sometimes no worse than Italian baroque and Thackeray. Tobacco here costs $1 per ounce; it's like smoking shredded banknotes. The English keep abreast of the latest developments in far-out American literature. Kerouac is in Penguin; Sherwood Anderson isn't. John Barth is solemnly discussed and Norman Mailer dismissed as a sexist reactionary. Black fiction is all the rage and one of my colleagues teaches his class Negro novelists I haven't even heard of.

England does some things a hell of a lot better than Usonia: frinstance, a city is a city here, a village is a village, and country is still country though within walking distance of the town center. None of that crazy business of eating up good farmland for detached houses each on an acre of unused land. They build motor roads like the Usonians, but there's a hell of a row when the road comes too close to a village. England is deliquescent but nice—I think I gave you a disquisition on how the working class fights for a bigger slice of the pie, works on rules, goes on strike, and makes the pie smaller for everybody. When I was here forty years ago, English goods were the best in the world; now they're getting to be the shoddiest. Everything good is imported.

Be good to yrself in
&over,
Malcolm

Hanging-On
XI/26/74
[NL]

Dear Malcolm,

Here's hoping that the family's ailments have let up. So far my time here in Solitary hasn't been nearly so unpeopled as I had anticipated . . .

Meanwhile, I have received an invite from Corbett[1] . . . who proposes to squander all of six hunnert bayries on me if we perform togidda.

Naturally, I will not say that you blabbed, thereby making me realize that I am being asked to be the second-class citizen that I unquestionably am. But I do feel that, with your permish, I might propose somethinks along this line:

Corbett says (and rightly!), "There are a lot of people from our Speech department too who would love to hear you talk." Would you object if I blandly suggest that, for Efficiency's Sake, in addition to something that you and I might figger out for the English Department, I add a special talk for the Speech Department, plus a smaller drag from them? I can give them a tock especially pitched for their occupational psychosis . . .

If they say yes, I'd suggest we try to work somethinks out along the line of a discussion involving comparisons and contrasts and overlaps anent where you go from the text to background and where I go from the text to background. I am almost certain that we could do this not as a debate but as a discussion. And I believe that our hearers would be quite engrossed by it. Also, unless we got surprised by the turning up of the unexpected, there'd be nothing invidious in it. I have great respect for your kind of competence, and I dare hope that you have something ditto anent mine. And I think that it could be a good civilized show. Basically, I think it would all berl down to a distinction between what you mean by "literary situation" as background, and what I would sloganize as "logological" context of our poetizings. (They're not mutually exclusive by a damsight, but they do emphasize differently. And yours has the advantage that mine is attached to that cursed Mesopotamian word, "logology," which has against it all that our frenn Allen T[ate] would associate with "methodology.")

'Twould be fun. But I will not answerve (sic) Corbett until I have heard from thee. If it looks too entangled, jes say so—and I'll write saying that time does not permit.

Avec Universal Liebe,
K. B.

1. Corbett was a professor at Ohio State, where Cowley had already received an invitation to speak.

Sherman, Connecticut
1 December 1974
[NL]

Dear Kenneth,

Ohio State. The offer to me of $1,000, no expenses, was one of those amalgamated offers: speech, graduate class, a couple of undergraduate classes, in other words, work hell out of the visiting bastard . . . So you're not being second-rowed in the offer of $600 for just a speech . . .

I like the prospect of doing a show with you. The subject you suggest would give you most of the advantages because, as you know, I've always been weak in theory, with my strength, if any, lying in history and biography and "the situation." Of course language itself is a mirror of the situation— note the appearance of words like "chutzpah," "cool," "uptight" as moral judgments. Your glossary of words for "the divine" is in some respects a history of human aspirations.

· · ·

I note that the three candidates for the Gold Medal in belles lettres this year are you, Trilling, and Meyer Schapiro.[1] Why Schapiro, who hasn't published a book? According to Bill Meredith, who was on the nominating committee, he tried to put my name in, but was voted down by the New York mob. Maybe Trilling and Schapiro will split the vote of the New York mob, and Burke will come sailing in, as he deserves to sail. Wish you could come to the Academy meeting December 6—there will be the brief but important discussion of whether the Academy should amalgamate with the Institute (that discussion taking place at 11 A.M.) . . .

Bugger all,
Malcolm

1. The Gold Medal is awarded by the American Academy and Institute of Arts and Letters.

Hanging-On
December 8, 1974
[NL]

Dear Malcolm,

Jeezoos, I was astonished by the info in your letter, anent your being counteracted by the "New York mob." I had always taken it for granted that you were pretty well-favored by the jernt, as you deserve to be, since you contribute greatly to its organizational welfare. And I wondered what the hell happened in this case. Had we both been on, we'd probably have canceled each other considerably. But even with you not on, an examination of how the statement of my case got botched convinces me that I'm out beyond all hope.

When Aitch N.[1] wrote me, saying that he was minded to propose me, I answered along these lines: "I always do something stupid at every one of those May-meetings. So I had decided that I'd stay away next year. Now they'll think I'm staying away because I'm pouting about my being spurned." But I think I will stay away from all the meetings for a while now. For it's a skientifick fack that I always muss myself up somehow. So, if you know roughly what date the May-meeting will be, please tell me, so that I can actually have (if viable) an obligation to be holding forth elsewhere. . . .

· · ·

Harry Chapin, a grandson, whose income now is in the hunnerts of thousands, was here yestiddy, trying to help cut down his income tax by doing a kind of documentary on his two grampaps, the other being the painter James—Harry was here yestiddy with Tommy[2] (who sings some Harry-songs on "Make a Wish," every Sunday morning, TV 11:30 A.M., station 7). And they let this ole geezer expatiate about this and that and the other. So the rules are that you say too much, and then out of it you say things that they can pick and put together their own way. I cooked for them, and Harry did the dishes. Some further such pleasant ordeals are to be arranged for . . .

. . . Is it a rule always, or a rule for different situations, that when one is competing with two academic guys like Trilling and Schapiro, one should not mention my six honorary degrees (Bennington, Rutgers, Fairfield, Dartmouth, Rochester, Northwestern)? What the hell are the damnthings worth if not for just situations like that? And why couldn't they at least list all my books, even to the extent of throwing out *Counter-Statement*, which was a pretty basic step along the way in our time? It would almost be as though, when referring to your list, they had left out *Exile's Return* . . . Don't worry, me frenn, the job has been effectively done. So we can go on feeling sorry for each other—and that's one heck of a lot more important than whether Trilling or Schapiro outdoes me. My notion is that Trilling and I may cancel each other off (after all, we have a lot in common with my *Permanence and Change*, though I'm not sure that space permitted him to say so)—and though space didn't even permit my basic books to be listed, the impression is given that several *articles* by Schapiro are *books*. Frankilee, I hope that *Schapiro* wins. I love the thought that Trilling and I may cancel off each other, to that end. Until the very end, dear frenn, as long as can be, I am still from comedy as vs. tragedy (on the theory that tragedy is asking for it, but comedy knows how to enjoy it).

Avec Universal Liebe,
K. B.

1. The poet Howard Nemerov, a longtime friend of Burke's.
2. Tom Chapin, Harry Chapin's brother.

Sherman, Connecticut
24 December 1974
[NL]

Dear Kenneth,

It was happy news that you were going to get the Gold Medal. How did Bernard Malamud learn about it? No whisper of the outcome had reached this quarter . . . The New York mob had insisted on putting up two of their own as candidates, and Meyer Schapiro had eaten into Trilling's vote—that's the electoral process—but you would have won the medal anyway, if by a smaller margin. Still, I felt relieved and exultant . . .

'Zver,
Malcolm

Sherman, Connecticut
22 January 1975
[NL]

Dear Kenneth,

Ohio State. The last dates Bob Canzoneri suggested to me were Febuary 24 and 25, Monday and Tuesday. We were to speak together on Tuesday afternoon the 25th. Does that fit in with your Indiana plans? If not, you had better write pronto to get your jointificating pontification shifted to Monday.

I think maybe the easiest for this time would be "Two Approaches to Criticism," as you suggested in one of your letters, logology and response to a situation (personal and social). With a lot of overlap, viz., I find logology extremely useful to interpretation of an author. Today I read somebody's (whose?) distinction between *vision* and *opinion*—oh, it was Saul Bellow who said that—an author's conscious opinion is something quite different from the vision he conveys. But the vision is partly conveyed by linguistic forms of whose meaning he is probably unconscious until a Burkean gets to work on his prose. If you wrote out a talk and left me to comment on it, as in your satire piece—well, that would be possible, though it would give you all the advantages, but I'd be poifeckly glad to give it to you, so long as I saw the piece in advance . . .

All our cheers,
Malcolm

Princeton University
Program in Comparative Literature
326 East Pyne
Princeton, New Jersey
March 4, 1975
[NL]

Dear Malcolm,

Here's hoping that you enjoyed our interchange, and attendant moments. I certainly did. But the godam train didn't leave until 6:30 A.M. Fortunately, the boom compenyons who contracted to stay up with me got wound up enough to stay the whole time, except one who had to be abandoned to his profuse puking. I drank too much, but not like that. At one stage, two of our band 'gan responding to their adrenaline, and I had one hell of a time persuading them to lay off. But my mixture of pleas and rebukes eventually prevailed, and from then on all was calm, except for the one would-be fistic champion who had o'ertrained.

The dawlink girl who runs the show at Indiana writes me, feeding the ever-sickly ego thus: "You made this weekend a moment for all of us to cherish. One of my students said, 'I was so afraid to meet him—and I love him, I really do.' Everyone else agreed with her." She ends by warning me against the wiles of the East.

• • •

The Harold Bloom book has suggested to me a trick way of reviewing it.[1] His notions about what he calls the "anxiety of influence"[2] are a ball of yarn more tangled than the Gordian knot, if you read him his way; if you read him my way, he'd want to shoot me. And given my way of cutting the Gordian knot, I believe I can successfully review this ingeniously tangled book of literary criticism within the thousand-word length commissioned. Fortunately he has, for his prime exhibit, an analysis of "Childe Roland to the Dark Tower Came"—and in proposing to pit my analysis of the poem against his, I got a whole new slant on his whole job. But he's got another trick, which has to be dealt with a bit differently. He has found a sixteenth-century Kabbalistic "master of theosophical speculation" whom he would use after the fashion of my piece, "The First Three Chapters of Genesis"— but I think that that plays into my hands, too. And though I'm always in favor of just dropping dead, I'm now afraid lest I drop dead before I do the final draft of this review. The guy is exceptionally competent, but with a new, ingenious pretentiousness that would be ideal except that any pretentiousness is a sitting duck for a bit of comedy. So, I hope both to give him credit for his unquestionable ability and yet get in a few paragraphs of good clean (query) fun.

But jeez, of all the things I should be doing the while I gabble! I desist.

Avec Universal
Liebe . . .
K. B.

1. Burke's review of *A Map of Misreading* appeared in the April 17th issue of *The New Republic*.

2. Bloom's ideas about literary influence were presented in an earlier book, *The Anxiety of Influence*, published in 1973.

Sherman, Connecticut
27 April 1975
[NL]

Dear Kenneth,

. . . Things ended or ending: Yes, Allen had another deterioration—all of them are irreversible; he gets worse, but there is no chance of his getting better. It sounds now as if the end might be near, though the doctors say he may go on for some time before the next deterioration. His wife is getting impatient at being housebound all day; apparently there is no help to be found in Sewanee, up there on the mountaintop . . .

· · ·

I've been sitting in on committee meetings about amalgamating the Academy with the Institute. I'm not dreadfully enthusiastic about the idea, and yet, by anomaly, the plan for amalgamation is partly my handiwork. Apparently it is now going through: 29 academicians voted for amalgamation and only 8 voted against it (with 10 not voting at all, but that's to be expected in an organization with so many members bedridden). One of the great arguments was about the name for the former Academy in the new joint organization: Upper House? Council of Fellows? Board of Governors? Over my dead body the committee voted for what seems to me the worst name of all: "Council of Deans." I hope *that* can be changed . . .

With all my alls,
Malcolm

Same Day
(VI/9/75)
[NL]

Dear Malcolm,

. . . Wadda battle! Recently I have slept a remarkable number of nights in succession sans nembies—and I caint decide whether I should consult a medical doctor or a psychologist to find out what might be the aetiology of my condition. Obviously something's wrong. (Yet it may be simply that, not being on an institutional schedule, I can as it were live somewhat sans timeclocks.) In the early days, men stayed awake, waiting for the Savior. In my early traumatic days, I stayed awake, for all [the] time I feared to be robbed of a great treasure. And rightly so.

The thing is, Malcolm, since Libbie cleared out, I have quit putting out my books. For two reasons: the second is that she helped so much by having been a secretary; the first is that she helped so much by my being so crazy about her, I was driven to prove, prove, prove, only roundabout to the shitten world, because so directly every day and night to *her* I was appealing. Maybe she had to die before me because she knew she was magic to me; and though the rules weren't her rules, I was not just assiduous, but also after a fashion brilliant. Few women have been courted, through all kinds of developments, as she was by the same compulsive pleader. If I could but believe that she lives on, and is looking down on me, I could still be driven as I once was until 5/25/69 (the lilac time—and when I came back a week later this time, the lilac-bloom of death had died).

To be sure, I have overtrained. By now it's three o'clock, by clocktime. And I still haven't started to warm up what I had planned for lunch. Then of a sudden I remember how my boys liken me to the Jewish momma who urges to eat more and more—for one is proud of one's cooking, even if some of it comes out of a can.

But dooty calls. And, as always

Avec Universal Liebe,
K. B.

Sherman, Connecticut
14 September 1975
[NL]

Dear Kenneth,

In these crisp September days the mind becomes a little more active. I finished a pretty long essay on Literary Generations—I want to show it to you, but that can wait . . .

. . . .

The Academy: I've never been really hot for amalgamation with the Institute. I got my name attached to one proposal for amalgamation simply through a desire to reach a consensus and get the matter settled one way or another, at least for the next few years. Now I see that a consensus isn't going to be reached on those terms. There will be a directors' meeting on October 17 with our lawyer present and the discussion will move to a further stage . . . As things stand I should probably vote against my own proposal for amalgamation, and to hell with consistency.

I've been wondering whether I shouldn't get out another collected volume. There's a good deal of uncollected material, several thousands of words, several hundreds of thousands. The trouble is, I feel that a collected volume should have a theme. Instead of having a theme, my volume would divide into pieces about authors (Aiken, [S. Foster] Damon, Coates, etc.) and think pieces, like this recently written opus on literary generations. I don't know that there's enough in either one of these two categories to make a book. I'll think about it . . .

Yr buddy in affliction,
Malcolm

[Postscript] (I have a coupla good photographs of you, Libbie, and the very small boys. Would you like to have them, or would they be painful?—M)

Ad Interim
IX/28/75

Dear Malcolm,

Thanks, I would like to have the photos. I'm a specialist in the pleasure-pain dimension.

You described pretty much the *design* for the title of your reprinted pieces; namely: "Authors and Trends." One section, "Authors," the other "Trends," with some pages on how they overlap. Now all you gotta do is find exciting words for "Authors" and "Trends." Maybe "Trends" could be "Whithers," and "Authors" could be (in that most desolate of puns) "Witherers." I'm tinkering with the same sort of enterprise. Analogous design: Literature in particular; Language in general—with an intermediate statement about how both could fall under the head of Human Relations. I think fondly of trying to dig up a title out of Santayana's *Scepticism and Animal Faith*, adding some pages to what I say of him in my *Grammatica Motivorum*. He lends himself pretty well to my bleats anent Logology, and my flat "post-Cartesian" distinction between non-symbolic motion and symbolic action. If I can't find in Santayana the title I'm looking for, I can at least do a daunce telling why I looked there.

· · ·

Harold Bloom continues to blossom with his ingenious Revisionist mixture of Freud and Lurianic Kabbalism. I am fascinated with his elucubrations, which both parallel and counter mine. I keep trying simultaneously to understand him in his own terms and translate him into my brand of Logologese. (He prefers "logocentric" to "logological"; and versus my "Dramatism" he plumps for "Psychoesthetics.") Down with Chess and Banking— Up with the Neo-Patriarchalist Anxieties of Predecessors and ephebes. To give you some idea of the issues, I enclose a copy of my *New Republic* review and Bloom's letter acknowledging it . . .

> Avec Universal Liebe,
> K. B.

> [Andover]
> III/14/76
> [NL]

Dear Malcolm,

. . . That's a quite appealing article.[1] And I do envy you your so much wider range of *memories*.

I incline to remember only big jolts. You got things by applying for them. Little that I applied for did I ever get. The first big important step in my career came when (as I probably told you), I was asked to take a temporary job on *The Dial* because (as I learned by accident much later) they couldn't locate you. To this day I still tremble when I wonder what would have happened to me out here without that "lucky break." You were in there "contacting" all the time—I was always slinking away. Looking back, I sometimes think that the only "advances" I ever made were when, as an adolescent, I felt of girls in the subways and movie houses. Most closely "communicating" through the medium of *total anonymity*. But never "forcing" one's attentions. Always, by "signs," being "invited."

. . . It really is a good and effective presentation. Your role as an adoptive son of Murger appeals to me greatly, as it doubtless appeals to others. You really do have the "Neo-Bohemian" aptitudes that I enviously can't put across, as an essential part of my *persona*. And you can because, along with your literary ability, you were much closer to that way than I. Though Lily and I started by scrounging around, we never missed a meal through lack of funds . . .

Forgive me if I can't keep out of it. Any memories you write about stir me up in all sorts of unusable ways. For your clear memories of your beginnings make me dig into the murk of mine.

So I'm not a test. But my hunch is that, for whatever other reasons, all decently intelligent readers will go along with your attestations. And they should.

Yes!
K. B.

(next morn—at high noon)

. . . Whatever my failures of memory, I do remember an ecstatic snow-storm when you and I tramped for some hours in the night, down West Street and then around on South, stopping in at bars now and then along the way, and shouting with unholy glee while snow kept piling up. It doubt-less cost the city a lot, but for us it was pure poetry. I began losing that vision when I had to shovel the "three ways," to the spring, the outhouse, and the mailbox. (Only in the cause of Magic Three do I omit reference to the most vexing one of all; namely the undoing of what the snowplow deposits in the road to the garage. But for quite some time after coming to Andover, we didn't have a car.) . . .

1. " 'And Jesse Begat . . .' A Note on Literary Generations," published in *The Southern Review* in January of 1976. It later became the first chapter of —*And I Worked at the Writer's Trade*, which appeared in 1978.

Copesmithery
VII/1/76
[NL]

Dear Malcolm,

. . . The trouble with the whole godam English Department[1] (as with psychoanalysis at its feeble-minded moments) is that, when they get around to talking about formal matters, they explain myths in terms of myth (or images in terms of images). For instance, you say, "Doubling and Incest."[2] Incest is *one image* for the *form* of doubling. And revenge is *one variation* on the *theme* of repetition.

Unless you sold my copy of *Rhetorical Motivorum* to Schulte for one-fourth list price, you might, just out of sheer bravado, take a backward glance at pages 10–20. The "author-castrating complex" is mythic for what I dealt with in my *Rhetorica Religionis*, anent how, implicit in the idea of setting up an order, there are the conditions for getting bat down and/or batting down oneself . . .

Perforce I hurry on,
K. Copesmith B.

1. Burke is not referring here to a specific English department, but to academic literary criticism in general.

2. Cowley had written Burke about a book on Faulkner by John T. Irwin that he was currently reviewing. Its title is *Doubling & Incest/Repetition & Revenge: A Speculative Reading of Faulkner*. It was published in 1975.

Sherman, Connecticut
6 July 1976
[NL]

Dear Kenneth,

. . . Reread pages 10–20 of the *Rhetoric*, not always agreeing with my own notes in the margins. What you said about the Oedipusians talking about regression when they were looking for first causes was very much to the point. I've been whacking Irwin's book more on the ground of misreading Faulkner's text than on the ground of philosophy. Boy, can he twist everything into parricide and castration! . . .

When Freudian concepts are used by literary critics, their whole vocabulary becomes billingsgate. That statement applies less to clinical analysts, who are trying to cure their patients by naming their aberrations, but naming them only in case histories filed away in cabinets. The same names used by literary critics are pure abuse. "Regression" is an ugly word even without being "infantile." Uglier terms are "incest," "oral" and "anal fixation," "voyeurism" (for curiosity), "exhibitionism" (for bragging), "sado-masochism," and all the others. Leslie Fiedler likes to flaunt his several children in the faces of the great authors whose work he is discussing, as if to say, "I am a mature genitally-directed critic and here is my evidence. Whereas you poor bastards are only novelists and poets, orally regressed and fixated in secondary narcissism. You can't get it up." . . .

> Love and all that,
> Malcolm

> Sherman, Connecticut
> 30 July 1976
> [NL]

Dear Kenneth,

I've been meaning to write you for a week or more, but I got blocked on a book review. A man named Geoffrey Wolff, inspired by the Harry Crosby chapter in *Exile's Return*, has written a big book on Crosby; *Black Sun*, he calls it. He found some fascinating material. But then, moved by the parricidal impulse that afflicts all writers, he set out to quarrel with and demolish all the general statements I had made in the Crosby chapter. Crosby wasn't symbolic of anything, he said, putting me down. He was violently singular. There were no American exiles in Paris. There is no such thing as a literary generation. I had obvious answers to all this, but very little space for the answers in a book review. The scheme of it wouldn't come to my mind (I've always had trouble with structuring my pieces). But finally I solved the problem and last night I finished and mailed the review. Muriel and I drove to the P.O. She was feeling fine.

. . .

. . . I enclose a not-quite final draft of my long piece on John T. Irwin's "speculative reading" of Faulkner. I had some good hints from *The Rhetoric of Motives*—the passages you mentioned—but wasn't able to use the stuff from *Permanence and Change* because I decided to omit the page I had written on Freudian naming, a fascinating subject for which I had not sufficient space (or knowledge) to do it justice. It amuses me that in Freudian terms the "show-off" becomes an "exhibitionist," i.e., a man who shows his prick to little girls. "Paul Pry" becomes "Peeping Tom," guilty of a misdemeanor. A "putter-downer" becomes a "castrator"—and so through the list of mild social offenses, all of which are transformed by being smeared with semen. With this topic omitted, I think I did a pretty good job on Irwin. The piece will appear in the January number of *Southern Review* . . .

> As ever,
> Malcolm

The Copesmithery
VIII/4 (5?)/76
[NL]

Dear Malcolm,

In modern midnight (3 A.M.). Am on the gloomy side. Should I go downstairs and pour myself some chemical joy?

• • •

Felicitations on your review. It sounds convincing to me. But I think you miss the "curative" aspect of Freudian terminology. The "cure" is in the assurance that it's "normal" to be polymorphous-perverse. It's Froyd's equivalent of Luther's thesis that we can't keep the Commandments, so there's Christ to die for us. Memmer the story of Freud saying, "Yes, gentlemen, this cigar I'm mouthing is a phallic symbol. Also, it's a damn good cigar."

• • •

To my surprise and bepuzzlement, the editor of *Behaviorism* has been quite friendly about my (30-page) piece anent Skinner's autobiography. Or maybe it's just the flattery that editors always pay to authors who contribute to gazettes that don't pay. It's to appear in the same issue with an article by a Behaviorist who is to review Skinner's book in his way, and to have at me if he feels so inclined. He *has* to have at me—for my windup centers on the noisy assertion that the psychology of dumb animals is necessarily a bad fit as a psychology for homo loquax. I keep going back to that "War, Response, and Contradiction" article which, back in the dirty Thirties, didn't exactly cement our frennship. As versus the Behaviorist thesis that the difference between us and other animals is but a matter of *degree*, I shout it out that it's a difference in *kind*. Human motivation is complex in the sense of being *self-contradictory*. Also, no animal serves as a fit model until you find some species that "roars with laughter." Compared with man, a hungry pigeon is as rational as a machine.

9:30 A.M. Sleepy-sleepless. Itshay.

K. B.

Sherman, Connecticut
1 October 1976
[NL]

Dear Kenneth,

... Pretty soon I'll be facing up to a problem on which you could help me. It's the rewriting of a piece, never really finished, called "A Defense of Story Telling." First, the recent attack on story telling—the nonstories with nonplots, the effort to disregard time in fiction and abolish continuity, etc. I've got that part okay, though I should bring it up to date. But then I launch into the notion that story telling is a fundamental human activity, one of the oldest, and I use some of your stuff in *The Rhetoric of Religion* about the embodiment of timeless doctrines in sequential stories such as the creation of the world. Doctrine into story, story into doctrine, post hoc into propter hoc. I think I have that passage okay, but I'm sort of worried by a phrase in your letter: "what goes wrong 'logologically' when you try to make a *narrative* about Heaven (i.e., tell about the *timeless* in terms of *time*"). I hadn't thought of that qualification and I never read Empson's Milton[1] and I can't find *The Rhetoric of Religion* to see whether you mentioned it there. I had the book. Somebody must have walked off with it. Maybe Peter [Blume] has a copy.

In the essay I go on to define what a story is, my notion being that the essential element is "something is changed"—i.e., things at the end of the story are different from what they were at the beginning, and the change is as irreversible as time itself. Then I'm going to assert that every story is a fable, because the change is either for the better or worse. I think I have some moderately useful observations, but in thinking about them I self-acknowledge my ignorance in critical theory—why, I don't know the difference between Structuralism and Post-Structuralism, never read a damned one of those new Continental authors. Who is Paul de Man?[2] Is Harold Bloom allied with the Structuralists? Would you (request) lend me the Harold Bloom book that you reviewed so well? . . .

As ever,

Malcolm

1. Cowley is referring to William Empson's book, *Milton's God*, published in 1961. Burke reviewed it in the June 16, 1962, issue of *The Nation*.

2. Paul de Man was at the time Sterling Professor of comparative literature at Yale University. One of the most important critical theorists of his generation, de Man came to be closely associated with deconstruction. He died in December of 1983.

The Supercopesmithery
X/6/76
[NL]

Dear Malcolm,

As I write, the Harold Bloom book is on the way. Kindly make sure that it doan get purloined . . . (I am planning a fairly extensive discussion of our diversities and togethernesses.) But I join you in not trying to keep abreast of Structuralist mandarinisms.

My discussion of Empson's book is not in *The Rhetoric of Religion*. It's reprinted, with some errors of editing, in a "Yearbook" (1968), *Perspectives in Literary Symbolism*, edited by Joseph Strelka, that is doubtless already rarer as could be. My pernt is reducible to this: Empson says that Big Shot must have been a sadist for letting the battle go on so long betwixt the good and bad angels, when he could have stopped it in a flash—but where the heck would Milton's epic be if narrative worked that way? In fact, as I make tearfully clear in my essay on "The First Three Chapters of Genesis," the logological analysis of the theology turns things around—and whereas in theology our disorders start from the revolt in Heaven, in logology the revolt in Heaven is derived from our disorders. Or, viewed logologically, "Order" and "Disorder" are "polar" terms that "timelessly" imply each other. But *narratively* they can be "processed," going *from* "Order" *to* "Disorder" or vice versa, including twists whereby they're doing a bit of both . . .

·   ·   ·

[E]'en though The Philosopher tells us that at my age one turns mostly to the past, I find myself perforce still forward-looking, though not with hope. Nor wholly without hope. I'm still in there with both feet, but 'twere better that I hadn't gone on delaying getting my hearing aid. I miss just about everything except what one could surmise by being my age, in my situation, and anticipating what is most likely to be said.

And here's hoping that youenz all are feeling a vast lot more joyous than I am.

K. B.

Sherman, Connecticut
18 October 1976
[NL]

Dear Kenneth,

A Map of Misreading arrived promptly and safely. I will cherish it with all its underlinings and see that it gets back to you. Besten dank. But I'm going to have a hard time reading Bloom because I revolt instinctively against his notions. For him and others of his school poetry is a self-contained and self-generated structure, coming out of books, going back into books as a misreading (and parricide), and having no source in life or effect on life. Poetry becomes a sort of patrilinear family.

·   ·   ·

I continue to retype my essays. There's work to do on some of them, with the continual danger of getting stuck, blocked, as I am today on a new beginning of an essay on the 1930s (which is Chapter VII, the first six chapters or essays being in pretty good shape[)]. Matty is in terrible shape—

high blood pressure, worries about his heart. This afternoon Muriel has driven him to the nursing home; he was afraid to do the driving. Poor Hannah isn't recognizing people even when she's awake. Muriel says, "It's terrible to think that you want a dear friend to die," but I think even Matty has reached that point. It's been a hell of a year, so let's all sing Hallelujah.

Yours,
Malcolm

The Supercopesmithery
X/23/76
[NL]

Dear Malcolm,

References to de Man incline me to assume that he seems to be tinkering with attacks on the notion of the poem as representing some situation rather than as being something in its own right. If this is so, I take it that he'd not go along with my pages on "the Symbol" in my "Lexicon Rhetoricae" (in *Counter-Statement*). Howe'er, if that's how it stands, I could ask him to look closer. For my point there is to show how, though the Symbol, as an organized principle, may reflect a personal attitude of the poet's, *the development of it raises issues which must be resolved purely in response to conditions that the writing itself brings up*—and in this respect the work is not to be judged as the representation of a "prior condition." In my *Grammar of Motives*, on *"act" itself* as a locus of motives, I cite the French proverb, "l'appétit vient en mangeant."

My sniffer may be wrong—but that's how it sniffs to me, sans having on mine own gone through his "Rhetoric of Temporality" (the title of which, incidentally, makes me wonder whether it might cut across my "temporizing of essence" concept, as per "The First Three Chapters of Genesis," in ways likely to try my impatient patience).

Two issues are interwoven here (maybe three). The basic one involves narrative sequence as versus sheerly nontemporal implications among terms. Cf. *The Rhetoric of Religion*, my "Cycle of Terms Implicit in the Idea of 'Order' " (page 184). The terms there imply one another "timelessly," in the sense that their internal relationships are all there at once. You can start from any one of them, and pick your way to any of the others. But once you *narratively personalize* their functions, they are in one irreversible order. Thus, at one particular place in the sequence, Temptation enters in the role of the Serpent, etc., with corresponding modulations via imagery, etc. Then there's the point with regard to the relationship between the poem and the poet's "literary situation." And ultimately, I contend that all this line must center in ye "Dramatistic" definition of man as an "active" (symbolizing) animal grounded in the realm of totally nonsymbolic motion. (That's where the current nouveaux thinkeroos are, by my theory, ultimately involved. And they are bitter because we cannot live by the *word* for "bread" alone—so they cry out that The Word has let them down. No words can be as real as physiological sensation. And them mandarins who live somehow by peddling words resent the fact that our grounding in the realm of physiological sensation involves a kind of immediacy which the sheerly *symbolic* resources of verbalizing livelihood cannot duplicate.)

Meanwhile, Malcolm, jes think: I'm making Saul Bellow move over. The American Academy of Arts and Sciences is offering me a grant of One Grand, if I will consent to be the recipient of the "first American Academy Award for Humanistic Studies." The Council chose me in the light of my "important influence on both the humanities and the social sciences." My sickly ego loves it. But please do make sure that Saul Bellow doesn't hear of it. I'd hate to have him feel conscious of the need to share with me.

Towards . . .
K. B.

Sherman, Connecticut
16 November 1976
[NL]

Dear Kenneth,

Creeps on this petty pace. From day to day I work ahead, when not incessantly interrupted, and don't get anything done to my satisfaction. The book won't be a very good one, as book, though it will contain a few pretty good essays. I don't know how good I'll be able to make "A Defense of Story Telling," just rewriting it from what I did five or six years ago. Some of the theoretical part of it is simply adapted from your RR (with due credit)—but I emphasize more the human proclivity for presenting timeless doctrine in terms of temporal sequence. Then I define a complete story in these terms: A situation leads to a decision, which leads to events, as a result of which something is changed. Put that into terms of scene, agent, purpose. But for me the "something changed" is the essence of a story; it represents the irreversibility of time. I'll think more about that when I come to rewriting the essay. But first I ought to read de Man (that title, "The Rhetoric of Temporality," is intriguing in relation to your work). Obviously you ought to read him too—but I haven't been able to manage a trip to the Yale Library.

Harold Bloom is very hard for me to read. In fact I didn't grow up with that whole vocabulary of "hermeneutics," "anagogic," and all the other words that you know well and that Bloom peppers his prose with. Cheez, how you have underlined that book! I'll see that it gets back to you safely . . .

As ever and always,
Malcolm

Sherman, Connecticut
21 June 1977
[NL]

Dear Kenneth,

So there's nothing much to report from this end, but, like you, I'm trying to get to work on a little piece and that's a fine moment to bat out a letter . . . I read, I take notes, that's easy, but when the time comes to reduce the notes to order, that's when the old brain stops functioning.

Right now I'm thinking about saying something that will illuminate my own attitude to the unbelievable 1960s, when a new generation came forward as different from past generations as anything can be and yet obeying a sort of historical alternation between diastole and systole—the age group of the 1950s had been systolic, contractive, uptight, so here appeared a new age group, open, full of illusions, and crazy. And here I was, feeling sympathy for most of the causes that engaged the youngsters—revolt against American business, black liberation, war against the war in Vietnam, back to the land, ecology, women's lib (not so much sympathy for that)—but dismayed by what they said and how they acted and especially by their innocent faith in the Coming Revolution; here I was, outside the littery life, no longer going to openings or publishers' cocktail parties, deaf, living in the country, getting my news from the newspapers, unable to read the new fiction, waiting for all the kids to be disillusioned, as they shortly would be (in 1972). How can I say all that in 1,200 words, which are all the words I want to write?

So instead I write you a letter . . .

With all them best
wishes and love,
Malcolm

R.D. 2, Box 293
Andover, New Jersey
VIII/11/77
[NL]

Dear Malcolm,

Did I get taken? Four-fifty for a Widex. It seems to work well. One tiny battery, on my left ear, but a line to my right. The job done locally. The NY League for the Hard of Hearing audiologist advised against doing the bone-conduction stuff on the right. (Charge for examination, thirty. But a fitting in NY would have involved a total medical examination as well.) At the start, at least, the outfit seems to work quite well, and is not hard to adjust.

· · ·

Meanwhile, in general, I'm vexingly depressed. Partly because I see more troubles looming in re my problems as a social animal. To an extent I actually welcome loneliness, yet to an extent nothing of the sort. I suspect that I may be getting back into the time when, as the result of his neck-breaking accident, "little Kenney had fits," so I spent early years alone when all the other kids were at school. I dote on public occasions, then suddenly want to be as alone as Garbo, then feel as though in solitary. "Where turn?" And my work becomes alarmingly more inefficient, not because I don't have anything to say, but because I'm so godam garrulous I can't decide what not to say.

Then I try whiling my night hours away with music programs. But did you say "garrulous"! I had forgotten how fantastically many ways Beethoven had piled up for delaying that grand moment when the voice was finally let loose (and from then on, "naturally," the job was to hang on as long as possible). Unless you succumb to the benumbing, the repetitive principle in music is, by its very nature, the caricature of itself. But in any case in the last analysis music engloomifies me, since it always keeps reminding me of what all I wanted to do and didn't, and most of the few things I did feel good about got lost. (In any case, praise God, Harry [Chapin] is doing my feeble-minded "One Light in a Dark Valley"—and *Critical Inquiry* has taken kindly to my "Chorale Omega,"[1] which I had lost but recovered, and which I have saddled with a theory of "commonplaces" in my words, to match the commonplaces of the music . . .

Wow!
Did I say "garrulous"?
K. B.

1. "Chorale Omega" is an "unorthodox tune" Burke composed and analyzed in his essay "Post-Poesque Derivation of a Terministic Cluster." It appeared in the Winter 1977 issue of *Critical Inquiry*.

R.D. 2, Box 293
Andover, New Jersey
IX/5/77
[NL]

Dear Malcolm,

Shit, whom report to? Ennihow, I seem somehow to have survived (after having gone from bed, 7 A.M. September 2 hereabouts to same bed an hour past midnight of September 3, with but an interval of three hours in bed between 4 and 7 A.M. on the morn of the toyd).[1]

And when being processed by three speakers along the way, I forgot my grandest line; namely: "With regard to our subject, 'The Achievement of Kenneth Burke,' we can all know for sure that he achieved the art of living through 80 years of polluted food, polluted physical environment, and polluted climates of opinion." I must hurry up and say it somewhere, in the cause of ingratiating lightness.

Toward the end of the second day, one is a bit sluggish about such twistings.

But there was a Celebration at which, if I chose, I could of ordered a piece of meat up to 19 tears [dollars]. Being parsimonious at heart, I ordered lamb sheeshkabob for seven-fifty. It was as tender as a baby's cheek, though we'll never know how accurate the analogy is unless we've tried both.

· · ·

The third guy to process me was a Yaley Marxist[2] who had managed to tangle Marx's notion of "ideology" (as per the *German Ideology*, which he presumably never understood, if he ever read it) in ways that only the Hermeneutics is capable of. I was furious that, although I had brought all sorts of baggage with me, I didn't have p. 104 of *A Rhetoric of Motives*,[3] and thus couldn't dispatch the guy as quickly as I could of. Marx's meaning is as clear as a flash, yet the guy was in a fog due to a vague smear of the other meanings I list on that page, made new because he is entangled in the deconstructionist structuralist stuff he's trying to take on, the very thought of which would have led Marx to damn him as an idealogue.

Also, like all expert Marxists, he knew how to manipulate what I call the wiles of "administrative rhetoric" (as per pp. 158–166). In his case the trick was that he "had to leave" before I could confront him. Hence I had no chance to have it out with him. And though I had an ample opportunity to say my say, I couldn't press *him*.

But that may give the wrong impresh. All told, the setup was as kind to me as one could reasonably ask for. Though I didn't manage to get my position stated as well as I hoped to, I came away feeling that I had established fairly good rapport . . .

Summarizingly,
K. B.

1. Burke had been attending the annual meeting of the English Institute at Harvard. There was a special session devoted to his work, which was published in 1982 as a book edited by Hayden White and Margaret Brose, entitled *Representing Kenneth Burke*.

2. Fredric Jameson, who now teaches at Duke University. Jameson's paper on Burke, "The Symbolic Inference; or, Kenneth Burke and Ideological Analysis," was published in the Spring 1978 issue of *Critical Inquiry*. Burke's long reply to Jameson's paper, "Methodological Repression and/or Strategies of Containment," was published in the Winter 1978 issue of *Critical Inquiry*.

3. In his paper, Jameson criticized Burke for not dealing at length and explicitly enough in his work with the term "ideology." Burke's reply centers in part on his nine-page discussion of ideology (centered on Marx's *The German Ideology*) in *A Rhetoric of Motives*. It begins on page 104.

Sherman, Connecticut
22 September 1977
[NL]

Dear Kenneth,

I've been slaving over two long reviews; that's why I didn't write you. The enslavement was due to the simple fact that my sluggish mind wouldn't bestir itself; it took me days and days in each case to write a first sentence. The sluggishness was partly due to age, simply, and partly to the absence of libido or urge (except financial) to write those particular reviews, both of which were on subjects I've said my say about in the past: Conrad Aiken and Edmund Wilson . . .

Now I'm going to stop flogging my mind for a couple of weeks and clean up some little jobs around the house: putting books away, etc. . . .

I had a report of the English Institute from Claude Rawson, professor at the University of Warwick, who had a speaking part (expenses paid from England). He didn't have a chance to hear the three professors dissect you, but he heard your rebuttal and was impressed by it—said you had a lively mind. Was it still lively at midnight of September 3?

I wish you'd sit down and tell me what Structuralism is. I suspect from the examples I've read that it has something to do with finding Deep Structures in writing, but most of those DS's seem to have something to do with the Oedipussycat complex. In other cases the DS has something to do with jerking off and the fear of death that is said to follow the last jerk, as note a recent book on *Leaves of Grass*, or rather, on "Song of Myself." How that would mix with Marxism I can't understand (and neither, so you suggest, could the would-be mixer). I'll look up your references to *A Rhetoric of Motives* [pages] 104 and 158–166. But not on this dull, dull afternoon when my arthritic knees are wobbling and "the air has an autumn chill," as I remember dull people saying . . .

Yours, as permanently,
Malcolm

R.D. 2, Box 293
Andover, New Jersey
XI/22/77
[NL]

Dear Malcolm,

Helndamnaysh, here's a pathetic boast, of sorts.

I had been intending to write you, of my many bleats and bellyaches. Then last night I slept like an honest man. So I felt so set up, toward sundown I went for a walk. I took chawnces, e'en as the sun hurried on its way. Then I realized that I no longer knew my way around in that growing wilderness . . . So one hasty thing misled to another, until I finally got to places up to my knees in muck, though at least I still knew where I was, and could walk across the board on the spillway of the dam, sans quite to fall off. From then on, 'twas easy. I changed my clothes and dwank—and I'm ready for the next time, whatever.

I'm mine own tradition, Malcolm. There's no place I go, not just here, but anywhere, that doesn't remind me of some other time. (A couple of weeks ago, when at the University of Chicago, behind all the immediacies, and they were all to the good, I kept missing Libbie, for we had equally good times there.)

Every day is so real (so real that I never dare leave unwashed dishes in the kitchen sink). Yet somehow not even one single day happens for the first time. And there's not a single spot hereabouts that is not to me just a place, but a little shred of history. Many of the related people to whom I might write are dead (some even by their own hand); others are I know not where.

.   .   .

If I can be disposed of in a hurry, that's all to the good. I fear the risks of an accident whereby I am left hanging on, a curse to myself and my family, and a blessing only to the medical racket that might perpetuate me after its fashion . . .

Love to all,
K. B.

[Andover, New Jersey]
III/7/78
[NL]

Dear Malcolm,

All obligations o'er until late April, when I fare forth to yipe in Southern California and Northern Washington. Then some bits in midwest May.

One minor error in your yellow pages anent me.[1] By that time I did have a car. And I think that you wrong yourself (or maybe me) in saying that we fought because my work "went back for revision." The biggest fight we ever had of that sort was when I was working at *The Dial* and you were having an operation in Pittsburgh. Marianne Moore, without my knowing a thing about it, suggested some changes in a review. You saw my vicious hand and wrote me, challenging me to a fist-fight when you had recovered. I don't recall your ever tinkering with my style, etc., though you did cut things down. Though I tried to get in as much as I could, I took it for granted that I was tugging at the leash. The only time I remember being furious was when you told me that Bliven wanted to cut my article on Wilson in half. And though I was damned sore, I didn't expect you to resign. I did the resigning by saying to hell with youenz . . .

·   ·   ·

'Tis true, I write you too much. And if what had happened to my letters-upon-letters had happened to yours,[2] you'd have been considerably inconvenienced in writing your classic of the Twenties. And it *is* a classic. My collectings helped you locate dates, etc. (Jeez, I caint remember anything in its place.)

·   ·   ·

But Jeezoos Keerist, Malcolm, when I look back over my published stuff of the Thirties, I also get a twist of this sort: "Jeez, Burke, when you were so godam crazy, with your lovelife, etc., how could so much of *Permanence and Change*, *Attitudes Toward History*, and *The Philosophy of Literary Form* be so shrewdly reasonable? Already you had worked out the three principles of form you still hold to, Burke: 'progressive, repetitive, conventional.' And you have gone on, spinning it all from there."

I but eskyuh, don't jes *mood*ify me out of my steps along the way, theory-wise. At least give me a page or two, showing how I was working toward what the indications are that I have sewed up, as per my "(Nonsymbolic) Motion/(Symbolic) Action"[3] routine (which will bust loose this spring). In my MLA session, I noted the steps along the way from the three principles of form in *Counter-Statement* ("Lexicon Rhetoricae"). I'll be glad to sum up that summary, if that would be along your line at all, though I can see how your narrative (biographic) emphasis might invite you to turn the eyes elsewhere . . .

That's it!
K. B.

1. Pages 275–279 of Cowley's book *The Dream of the Golden Mountains: Remembering the 1930's.* They describe the hostile reaction Burke's paper, "Revolutionary Symbolism in America," received when he delivered it at the First American Writers' Congress in New York in the spring of 1935.

2. At this time Burke thought he had lost the box containing his letters to Cowley for the years 1915–1929. They were subsequently found.

3. Burke's essay was published in the Summer 1978 issue of *Critical Inquiry.*

Sherman, Connecticut
13 March 1978
[NL]

Dear Kenneth,

Matty died today suddenly, of a heart attack. He had spent the winter in Santa Cruz [California], as you know, and was coming back east tomorrow. Santa Cruz has a dreadful climate for Matty's chest condition; he had been ill for a time but had apparently recovered. Matty was 79 on February 15, not quite a year younger than I and two years younger than you. I wish I had been closer to him during these last years. But I had quarreled with him during Hannah's last illness; I think he was jealous because so many people came to see her; he was certainly distraught. So he attacked me, I mean shouted at me, on Bank Street in New Milford [Connecticut], and I shouted back. After that our relations were correct. Matty was a son of a bitch in some ways; he was stingy and cantankerous . . .

It hurts me that our friendship cooled over the years, when we were so close in the twenties and early thirties. And yes, you and Matty and I were at one time a triumvirate. Matty had an imagination that I respected and an enormous capacity for getting things done. He also had a bad habit of claiming credit for other people's achievements. He didn't really respect the language. He was a mild disaster on the *New Republic* when he took my place for two months. "But it wasn't so bad," Mary Updike told me— she was the book department secretary; "I didn't let him send out many books for review." I suppose that was when we began to be mildly estranged. Last summer he never came to see us; I went to see him once . . .

Matty young was large-gestured, picturesque, admirable. I wonder how many of us take a slow nosedive after thirty or forty? Then feel somewhat embittered at lack of recognition? As Matty certainly did, though we have known many others.

I feel sad as I make these rough notes for an obit that will never be written.

About that little piece on KB at the writers' congress . . . I *tried* to suggest the complexity of motives in your paper at the congress. But I was writing about the congress and tried to keep everything relevant to that one theme, so I couldn't mention the three species of form . . . They will have to be saved for a piece about *you*, not about the writers' congress . . .

> Yours, sadly,
> Malcolm

> Abiturus, FIU
> (III/21/78)
> [NL]

Dear Malcolm,

Ah, heck. Please tell me, on the enclosed postcard, to whom I should best write, and where. Every day all days and all nights, I think death-death-death, except when I'm in the middle of writing something up. And if you clear out ahead of me, by Gawd I'll haunt you. You'd better hang on.

I have a story as real about Matty as that *gospodin* story (about the Thirties deal) you rejected. It goes like this: When I started at Columbia, feeling lonesomer as hell (to recall Jake's fun with the langwitch), I saw news of a poetry club. I went to a meeting, and got trampled on. When leaving, after fighting back and in desolation, I heard a flute-voiced voice say, "Don't go out the door, go out the window." We did so—and one thing led to another from then on.

Over the years, beginning with some problems in Maine, when we were both improvising in the problems of being married, we haggled a lot. But I have always thought of Matty as my second oldest friend. Yet he always let our correspondence languish (as you can well understand!).

· · ·

When I left there that night, thinking I was destroyed, I will never forget, nor be ungrateful for, the difference in my life that I owe to Matty's decision, an intuition of almost "fateful" implications, so far as I am concerned. Those of us who have known Matty closely know that somehow this quality was always intrinsic with him. My hunch is that shrewd as he was, Matty himself didn't suspect the depths of his sheer spontaneous responsiveness. Maybe Matty would scheme, and maybe even think of himself as doing so. But if he did, he didn't quite know the depths of himself, which we sensed somehow, even when being vexed. The irony is: I often thought of a showdown with him, in which I said things like this to him; but things moved on and developed elsewhere.

So that's that. If the fuzzy suggestion helps your obit, please use it as you care to, or not . . .

Avec universal Liebe,
K. B.

Route 1, Box 184,
Sherman, Connecticut
25 May 1978
[NL]

Dear Kenneth,

. . . I was surprised, as I told you, by the many long and rather glowing reviews of —And I Worked at the Writer's Trade. Why didn't they talk that way about earlier and better books? Maybe the reviewers are just atoning for earlier oversights. I've been kept busy answering letters and being interviewed—so damned busy that I haven't done any writing for a month. When'll I get back to it, I wonder. Perhaps I'm wasting too much time on the garden, as I have done every spring (except last spring) for forty years . . .

• • •

You've heard about the Allen Weinstein book on the Hiss case. The Sunday Times reviewer of The Writer's Trade, Benjamin DeMott, brought it up at the end of an otherwise favorable piece in order to cast some question on my complete candor. I've only dipped into Weinstein's book, but I read enough to find that it was anything but a judicious review of the case. He was trying to prove something, that Whittaker Chambers was essentially telling the truth—that there was in this country a huge Soviet apparatus of subversion during the 1930s—and hence that the Cold-War liberals were right to encourage and participate in the anti-communist purge of the 1950s; Chambers was their guru. I might serve as an example of his impartiality. Weinstein made a trip to the Newberry Library in Chicago to go through my papers, obviously in an effort to impugn my testimony at the Hiss trials. He didn't find anything except two letters from Maus V. Darling, who was working for Time in 1942 and hated Chambers. But he must have read and read, for, in an article for The New Republic, he quoted another letter in my files, from an Englishwoman named Brenda Willert, whom I never met (though I knew her husband). With all this reading, Weinstein never once tried to get in touch with me. I could have shown him other things, including two newspaper interviews in which Chambers lied about me when he knew that I knew he was lying. He was a scrupulous liar, that much I know and can prove. But if I talk about Weinstein and Chambers, I won't be able to stop.

Time for bed . . .

As ever,
Malcolm

The Copesmithery
Lingerlag Lane
Clutchers Gulch
II/6/79
[NL]

Dear Malcolm,

In the light of your long silence, here's expressing the hope that your doings on your Eightieth have not been as much of a blow to you as mine were to me. (I'm still taking the pills, though the amount is less.)

But at least, as you will see by the enclosed,[1] I can shift my morbidities a bit. The battle to which I refer was outrageous. And whereas the ice has gone from the rest of the area, there is still one hell of a lot just right down through our garden, to the road. And for two days I was so beaten down, I thought I had a slipped disk. Every once in a while an electric twinge went through me, and suddenly bent me double.

Today, hearing that more snow is on the way, I burned the burnables and smashed the smashables, having also hurried forth to buy stuff and get some xeroxing done. Come the thirteenth, I'm scheduled to try about a week in California—then no scheduled forays until May, though a pleasant couple of days roughly in your direction seems shaping up.

There has been one benign development. Harry (my millionaire grandson Chapin) had put my "One Light in a Dark Valley" jingle into one of his albums. And lo! my drag was $1,899.02—so I can heat with electricity, thereby dodging my battles with kerosene, which turns me dizzy. My life is so *factual*, with a space heater to take the edge off the biting cold when I crawl naked out of bed to pee, and much interesting music on the radio all night . . .

Holla!
K. B.

1. Burke enclosed the following poem, entitled "Clima(c)tic Situation."

If you would feel sorry for yourself
imagine you're eighty-one, it's January, and
your backyard is a glacier,

accumulated from several crusts of sleet and freezing rain
rolling down the hillside
up there behind the house,

embracing all in a slithery surface on a slope,
so seeping into the garage that the tires of the car
got sunk into the flooded floor as if set in concrete.

Using a pitchfork for a walking stick, to help keep from sliding
you put down things that themselves slide—
Geology tells us you can't buck a glacier.

Right down to the mailbox
one single horizontal icicle
flattened out as by a rolling pin

the course of the centuries in miniature
here bearing down upon us
time moving in from the slope behind the house.

What a tautology, a pleonasm: Age in the grip of Ice,
worse than piling Ossa upon Pelion, it's piling
Pollution atop Ossification—so what do?

Taking pen in hand you bear witness
which is to say, Etymology tells us, you are Chosen Martyr
to the inexorably surrounding Cause.

Age in the Grip of Ice
pronounce his name "Kennéth"—
the word thus altered nice
quite neatly rhymes with ***** . . .

Route 1, Box 184
Sherman, Connecticut
9 February 1979
[NL]

Dear Kenneth,
   Allen Tate died this morning at 5:30, in his sleep. The vice president of
Vanderbilt University phoned me. I phoned Helen, who was a little more

distraught than I had expected; she had been hoping for a year or more that Allen would die. His last months were pretty gruesome. Helen had taken away the telephone from his bedside, so that he had no communication with the world. He couldn't read. When he got up for some reason, he trailed behind him a long plastic tube attached to an oxygen tank. Helen says that he was "confused" during the last weeks—didn't always know where he was—had hallucinations. Ten days ago she had him moved to the Vanderbilt University nursing home. There his mind was clearer and they took him off the oxygen tank, but he could eat hardly any food . . .

· · ·

God damn, God damn it to hell, there's no good news to report. Except that the country is going to hell, like many of our friends. We have lived through the career of the United States as a world empire, the great Victorian era of our country; now we're going the way of England, and in a messier fashion. The event that marked the sharp beginning of our decline was the assassination of Jack Kennedy. Some day historians may speak of the years from 1933 to 1963 as the Age of the Four Good Presidents, just as Roman historians speak of the Five Good Emperors. The presidents weren't so good (neither were Antoninus Pius or Nerva), but they presided over a hopeful country. After them came Caracalla . . .

Fly the flag high,
Malcolm

Route 1, Box 184,
Sherman, Connecticut
13 January 1980

Dear Kenneth,

Sunday. Gray day. Cold. I'm still shivering in my pajamas at four in the afternoon. Not much to report, except that on Friday I made a trip to New York to see a two-hour film that John Lowenthal has assembled on the Hiss case. Hiss was at the showing; so were his black employees, the Catletts; so was Nathan Witt,[1] so was Edmund Chubb,[2] so were two members of Hiss juries, now persuaded of his innocence. I had a speaking part in the film. It's going to be released about the same time as *The Dream of the Golden Mountains* and it's going to bring some Trotskyite critics down on the book, as if I had stepped on a nest of yellowjackets. 1979 was my lucky year. Several incidents persuade me that 1980 isn't going to be lucky . . .

As everly,
Malcolm

1. Nathan Witt was an attorney and secretery of the National Labor Relations Board. He was accused by Whittaker Chambers of being a communist sympathizer.

2. Oliver Edmund Clubb, U.S. consular official in China before the revolution. His loyalty was called into question in 1950 by the state department's loyalty board. He was cleared, but left the department.

R.D. 2, Box 293
Andover, New Jersey
January 17, 1980
[NL]

Dear Malcolm,

The reason I use letterhead stationery for correspondence among friends is that I asked Butchie to get me some more for business purposes, and he ordered two reams instead of one. Being penurious, I hate the thought of leaving too many sheets unused. So I'm hurrying things, in the cause of economy.

. . .

My o'erall view of the Hiss case has always been purelyandsimply this: The lawyers should have been *educators*. They should have built the case by making it clear exactly how the standard leaking of evidence goes on always. And along with that, they should have pointed out just what leftist sympathies meant at the time when the leaking that Hiss was accused of took place. (There was a stage when the Party was hardly other than the far left wing of the Democrats.) Instead they valiantly tried to prove that Hiss didn't "leak" the things which, at those times, it would have been quite "reasonable" to leak. As I recall those days, I can imagine his leaking such data because "Why not?" Also, atop their being mutts as regards the educational aspects of the case, there was the bad magic of Hiss's name. Cf. in Milton's Pandemonium "the hiss of rustling wings." In a problem of his sort, it's tough to have a name so essentially, poetically associated with the snake in our langwitch as his. This haint a mere afterthought. I was disgusted with the way they handled that case from the start. A vast effort was expended in "proving" that Hiss *didn't* do what, at the time when it was said to have been done, it would have not at all been the kind of act it could be made to look like when the situation had changed. But the last thing in the world those high-priced barristers who mismanaged that case would ever have done was to present the issue in terms of what yoursonlytootruly would call the "scene-act" ratio (as per his artikkel on "Dramatism" in *The International Encyclopedia of the Social Sciences*, a piece of poor-paying wisdom for what, at least, he got the whole set of volumes as his drag) . . .

K. B.

Route 1, Box 184,
Sherman, Connecticut
10 February 1980
[NL]

Dear Kenneth,

So I dug out your last letter and found it was dated 17 January. I don't even know where you are or how you got there. Can't blame you for not answering what I didn't write . . .

This evening I feel no joy about being 81-plus. All the damned little ills such as Prostatitis, Poor Circulation, Deafness, Cataracts, Dizziness, Short Breath (emphysema?), and various etceteras are starting to combine into a Grand Inanition. Then, rereading your letter, I picture you in that chill house where the glaciers have started to flow downstairs, and reflect that I'm comparatively fortunate.

For both of us a mild consolation is that we're not just stumbling into the shadows. Both of us are better known in our eighties than we were in our sixties. It's funny what different sorts of fame for two who started from the same place, in the same business. Your light is more intense, as it deserves to be, while mine is more diffuse and dimmer. But it's pleasant for both of us to have some recognition. (The moment has come to boast of what I heard last week on a trip to the office, that the first printing of *The Dream of the Golden Mountains* has been doubled from 7,500 to 15,000 because of promising advance orders. I never had anything like that before.)

Ego massage. We both can use it. Everybody can use it . . .

Yours,
Malcolm

R.D. 2, Box 293
Andover, New Jersey
February 15, 1980
[NL]

Dear Malcolm,

Good luck, young one. (A difference of one year betwixt us at this time of life is more than two decades' difference as we look back at earlier years.) My envious felicitations indeed anent the good auguries in re the forthcoming First Printing.

But I had my good luck, too. Butchie decreed that we should reshingle a piece of the roof. The guy who did the job slink-slank-slunk away leaving on the porch all the papers in which the shingles had been packed. So I fared forth to burn them. Something happened. Of a sudden some kind of blast burst forth, sizzling my forehead. Had it struck one and a half inch lower, I'd have got it straight in the eyes. If mine eyesight survived at all, my eyelids would have been caked up for at least as long as my forehead was (o'er a week before chunks began falling off) . . . [I]f mine eyes had been even temporarily blinded I couldn't have handled that sichaysh, or even have known how to get out of there, and it's e'en possible that the whole hillside would have gone . . .

. . .

As for ailments, I've got this one tentatively in the oven: A D L D, addled with thoughts of Age, Disease, Lonesomeness, and Death.

> Love to all,
> K. B.

Emory University,
Graduate Institute of the Liberal Arts
Atlanta, Georgia
February 6, 1981
[NL]

Dear Malcolm,

Two copies of our Superette just received.[1] By heck, that was a gracious job you done. You can have no idea how grateful I am. And I liked the whole way of how it comes about, sandwiched in among bits of the Organization business. It seems to me an ideal presentation of my cause. It's possible, though, that the "voice" angle may be in error.[2] As I told you recently (regarding my last time at the Academy, when I had forgot my hearing aid), I heard every word of *yours* perfectly. And I think it was because I had heard that voice from away back. And you may be hearing my voice in those *printed* items from just as far back. With us oldsters, just what does go on? !!!

. . .

About our other similar vexations, more anon. I am gradually trying to risk walking hereabouts for a short time before dinner (if you call it a dinner when I take a bit of that out of the refrigerator and serve it on some dishes all of which I keep in the refrigerator; for though the clones of Kafka are peace-loving creatures,[3] I doan like em crawling on my kitchenware). But during my tiny walks, I am in continual fear of finding, on the way back, that I had passed thepointofnoreturn.

Meanwhile, know of me as abjectly grateful to you for your kindness anent my attitudinizings (which is the only way I know how to call them).

See over. Ah, shit!
K. B.

1. *Poetry Pilot*, published by the Academy of American Poets. The January issue contained a selection of Burke's poetry with a brief appreciative commentary by Cowley.

2. Cowley had written that Burke's poems are "always spoken in a voice to be recognized as Burke's and nobody else's."

3. Cockroaches. The reference is to Kafka's *The Metamorphosis*.

Route 1, Box 184
Sherman, Connecticut
28 February 1981
[NL]

Dear Kenneth,

I was moved by your "Epistolation," almost to the point of having wet eyes.[1] I thought about the Carnegie Library and those walks home along Ellsworth Avenue. Also the poem brought to mind our present situation. Thank God you can hear me. I did buy a new hearing aid, small, expensive, and now I can hear a lot of people, if there's not too much noise in the background.

Damn near lost the new kid in an accident on Wednesday the 18th. Jim Munch was finishing up the job of cutting the red pines. There was a dead white pine, the top blown off, and I asked him to cut it too. Jim told me to stand back and I did, but not far enough. The snag, in revenge for being cut, aimed straight at the top of my head and tried to scalp me. It nearly succeeded. I said, "I must have a concussion," and lay down on the pine needles bleeding centiliters. The volunteer ambulance crew arrived in less than 15 minutes and rolled me over on a stretcher. In the emergency room I lay on the table for two and a half hours while Jeff Ferris shaved and sponged and stitched away. Two nights in hospital, two black eyes, and a dreadfully stiff neck. Still I'm undertaking to go to Brockport in two days and do a lecture, plus a seminar, plus two taped interviews. Hope to survive . . .

As ever,
Malcolm

1. "An Epistolation" is the poem Burke wrote about listening to Cowley speak about him at the American Academy and Institute of Arts and Letters. In part, it reads:

. . . Whereat I of a sud. recalled not long ago
at a meeeting of our Acad.-Inst. cultural enterprise
me having forgot my hearing aid

hence missing an awful lot of the verbatims
put forth by the various thinkeroos
as the official meeting doodled on

I natheless understood sans effort every word
that you as Ipse Dixit judgmentally pronounced
during our severely solemn deliberations.

You sat much farther from me
than many of the others—and not turned in my direction
and spoke with much less volume than many,

yet I missed nary a word. And here's the why:
It has to do with how things keep with time,
as time folds back for us verbalizing-wise.

To each of us, you me, our ways of saying back and forth
with each of us the longest way, I think,
hence as though backer at home than each of us with others,

you from all that time back, you and I have gone on
having heard me from then asseverating at you
and both of us hearing you doing ditto me-wards.

Beethoven, grown deaf, could hear his music
if spread out on the page to look at—
yet not at all the thunderous applause his symphony was getting.

You, looking at my pages (alas! to which the world is deaf)
(you, unlike Cousin Allen who rebuked me for not writing in one
groove)
in all of them you hear our same East Liberty and no place else's . . .

> Route 1, Box 184,
> Sherman, Connecticut
> 13 March 1981
> [NL]

Dear Kenneth,

So I'm getting the Gold Medal. I phoned Maggie[1] this week and asked her whether the votes had been counted. She swore me to secrecy. The award must absolutely not be divulged until the Ceremonial. Nevertheless, if I wouldn't tell Nobody, I had gotten twice the votes of either of the other two candidates. You had certainly designed a nice ticket for me, though Howard Nemerov's plea for Cleanth Brooks was so eloquent that I was tempted to vote for him. I wish him well, but I'm delighted to have the medal, even if it's not solid gold any longer, like the one that you received. I'll cherish it.

* * *

An advance copy of David Shi's life of Matty[2] arrived this week. It looks impressive, especially the photographs of you, me, Allen, Tzara, and others, and a marvelous close-up of Matty in his last year, with all the wrinkles. The back of the jacket is devoted to statements by MC and KB. I'll be fascinated by the reviews—wait till [Sidney] Hook gets to work on it. He now has an organ for venom, *The American Scholar*, which, under a guy named Epstein,[3] has become the quarterly issue of *Commentary* (just as the *New Republic* is becoming its weekly issue) . . .

Ebulliently,
Malcolm

1. Margaret M. Mills, director of the Academy and Institute.

2. *Matthew Josephson: Bourgeois Bohemian.*

3. Joseph Epstein, editor of *The American Scholar*.

R.D. 2, Box 293
Andover, New Jersey
April 15, 1981
[NL]

Dear Malcolm,

Our Mageen has notified me that the relevant Authorities have asked whether I would sing in connection with the Presentation to thee. Wow! would I!

But when Haitch Immerauf[1] engaged himself to present me, he asked me if I had any notions—and we performed accordingly. Hence, ever the believer in tradition, I write now to ask if you have some angle or trend that you'd "privelege" (to use word-of-words these days). Jeez, we might e'en work that one in.

The mail that carried off my vibrant YES also brought hither the official notification of much-needed honorification, though sans mention of the filthy youknow.[2] But in the meantime, I'll go on trying to persuade myself that life might be worth still living even if . . .[3]

* * *

My mail is now in a different dimension. That thing in the *New York Times* was sheer magic.[4] I have neither more nor less respect for myself than I ever had—but by heck, for the last few days, weeks, or months still in the cards, I almost feel like playing deuces wild. I had never dared look up, though still trying to crawl up. I now dare tell myself (and MEAN IT) what I have been telling myself like whistling [in] the dark; namely, to wit, to woo: Maybe I really can clinch the whole deal before I move on . . .

But I talk too much,
K. B.

1. Howard Nemerov.

2. Burke was awarded the National Medal for Literature, which carried with it $15,000.

3. Ellipses Burke's.

4. The March 15 issue of the *New York Times* carried an article in praise of Burke and his career by Richard Kostelanetz.

Route 1, Box 184
Sherman, Connecticut
17 April 1981
[NL]

Dear Kenneth,

By Jesus, the whole thing is working out the way you wanted it to work out. I mean careerwise, without respect to the intimate disasters. You didn't want to make an early success. You pissed on success and everything that would lead to it. At the same time you *wanted* to be honored by the community and to have the world beat a path to your door. That took a long time, owing to down-timber and deadfalls you set up in the path— but the intrepid admirers cut through the logs, went around the deadfalls, and arrived at your kitchen door bearing incense and myrrh and checks for fifteen grand. And toward the end, too, so that there wouldn't be much time for anticlimax. That's the way we ought to structure our lives, with the best coming last, in a graded series. I share your pleasure.

And if you present me with the Gold (now plated) Medal, I will bow my head and say, "That's how it ought to be. Peabody High School Redivivus." And I won't, by Jesus, offer a suggestion as to what you should say. You'll know what to say. Keep it short . . .

As ever,
Malcolm

Route 1, Box 184,
Sherman, Connecticut
22 May 1981
[NL]

Dear Kenneth,

On the whole, in the large, it was a grand occasion. I appreciated your speech[1] and, if you have an extra copy of the retyped version, I'd love to have it and keep it with other valued papers. I'm enclosing the retyped version of mine, regretting that I let myself be bullied by Maggie into omitting the six lines from your poem,[2] to save a minute (but they'll go into the Proceedings). That last sentence of yours rang out loud and clear.[3] The standing ovation at the end of my speech was for both of us. Friends for more than 60 years? Why, it's unheard of in our dissolving society. Did you note that they handclapped the sentence, "We were classmates in the eighth grade and at Peabody High School in Pittsburgh"? A statement of simple fact that seemed an incredible affirmation . . .

Yours,
Malcolm

1. Burke's short speech praised Cowley's work as a critic and literary historian, especially his ability to blend the historical and the personal. "In his dual capacity as both spectator and sympathetic participant," Burke said, "the many windows of his criticism are looking both out and in, the details of his coverage being biographical, psychological, sociological, historical (particularly in terms of 'generations' and trends), and in their very essence *personalistic.*"

2. In his acceptance speech for the Gold Medal, Cowley reminisced about his friendship with Burke at Peabody High School. In the speech he quoted lines 25–30 of Burke's "An Epistolation."

3. In his last sentence Burke referred to how Cowley's choice of words is often "representative of the informing spirit that makes him so 'generation-conscious,' " and he closed with the example of Cowley's reference to a time when "the countryside began at the end of a five-cent street car ride."

Index